CHANGING YOUR ADDRESS?

OLD ADDRESS (Please Print)

Name _____

Address _____

City, State & Zip _____

NEW ADDRESS

Name _____

Address _____

City, State & Zip _____

Date New Address Effective: _____

19 ▪ P.

CHANGING YOUR ADDRESS?

OLD ADDRESS (Please Print)

Name _____

Address _____

City, State & Zip _____

NEW ADDRESS

Name _____

Address _____

City, State & Zip _____

Date New Address Effective: _____

19 ▪ P.

BUSINESS REPLY MAIL

FIRST CLASS PERMIT NO. 31 HAGERSTOWN. MD.

Postage will be paid by:

HARPER & ROW, Publishers, Inc

Medical Department
2350 Virginia Avenue
Hagerstown, Maryland 21740

NO POSTAGE
NECESSARY
IF MAILED
IN THE
UNITED STATES

BUSINESS REPLY MAIL

FIRST CLASS PERMIT NO. 31 HAGERSTOWN. MD.

Postage will be paid by:

HARPER & ROW, Publishers, Inc

Medical Department
2350 Virginia Avenue
Hagerstown, Maryland 21740

Psychiatry

Index

PSYCHIATRY

CHAIRMAN, EDITORIAL BOARD	**Robert Michels**
EDITOR	**Jesse O. Cavenar, Jr.**
EDITORIAL BOARD MEMBERS	**H. Keith H. Brodie**
	Arnold M. Cooper
	Samuel B. Guze
	Lewis L. Judd
	Gerald L. Klerman
	Albert J. Solnit

J. B. LIPPINCOTT COMPANY
Philadelphia
London   New York   Mexico City   St. Louis   São Paulo   Sydney

BASIC BOOKS, INC., PUBLISHERS
New York

Acquisitions Editor: William Burgower
Sponsoring Editor: Rachel Bedard
Manuscript Editor: Shirley Kuhn
Indexer: Tony Greenberg, MD
Production Supervisor: June Eberharter
Production Coordinator: Shirley Kuhn
Compositor: Bi-Comp, Incorporated
Printer and Binder: The Murray Printing Company

PUBLISHER'S NOTE

The reviewing process is a constant one in which new chapters, and those in need of revision, are identified by the editors and their authors. The material in these volumes is revised annually, providing you with a continually updated product. No effort is spared by the publisher and editors to keep the information in these volumes current with the needs of the resident and practitioner.

DRUG DOSAGE

The authors and publisher have exerted every effort to ensure that drug selection and dosage set forth in this text are in accord with current recommendations and practice at the time of publication. However, in view of ongoing research, changes in government regulations, and the constant flow of information relating to drug therapy and drug reactions, the reader is urged to check the package insert for each drug for any change in indications and dosage and for added warnings and precautions. This is particularly important when the recommended agent is a new or infrequently employed drug.

Library of Congress Cataloging-in-Publication Data
Main entry under title:

Psychiatry.

Includes bibliographies and index.
1. Psychiatry. [DNLM: 1. Mental Disorders. WM 100 P974]
RC454.P7824 1985   616.89   84-52584
ISBN 0-397-50686-4 (set)

I. Michels, Robert, Chairman, Editorial Board. II. Cavenar, Jesse O., Editor. Editorial Board Members: III. Brodie, H. Keith H. (Harlow Keith Hammond). IV. Cooper, Arnold M. V. Guze, Samuel B. VI. Judd, Lewis L. VII. Klerman, Gerald L. VIII. Solnit, Albert J.

Section Editors

Paul S. Appelbaum, MD

(Legal Psychiatry)
A. F. Zeleznik Professor of Psychiatry
University of Massachusetts Medical School
Worcester, Massachusetts

Donald J. Cohen, MD

(Child Psychiatry)
Director of Yale Child Study Center
Professor of Pediatrics, Psychiatry, and Psychology
Yale University School of Medicine
New Haven, Connecticut

Allen J. Frances, MD

(The Personality Disorders and Neuroses)
Associate Professor of Psychiatry
Director, Outpatient Department
Payne Whitney Clinic
Cornell University Medical College
New York, New York

Philip M. Groves, PhD

(Psychobiological Foundations of Clinical Psychiatry)
Professor of Psychiatry
University of California, San Diego
La Jolla, California

John E. Helzer, MD

(Schizophrenia, Affective Disorders, and Dementias)
Professor of Psychiatry
Washington University School of Medicine
St. Louis, Missouri

Jeffrey L. Houpt, MD

(Consultation–Liaison Psychiatry and Behavioral Medicine)
Professor and Chairman
Department of Psychiatry
Emory University School of Medicine
Atlanta, Georgia

Loren H. Roth, MD

(Legal Psychiatry)
Professor of Psychiatry
Chief, Adult Clinical Services
Director, Law and Psychiatry Program
Western Psychiatric Institute and Clinic
Pittsburgh, Pennsylvania

Michael H. Sacks, MD

(The Personality Disorders and Neuroses)
Associate Professor of Psychiatry
Payne Whitney Clinic
Cornell University Medical College
New York, New York

John E. Schowalter, MD

(Child Psychiatry)
Professor of Pediatrics and Psychiatry
Chief of Child Psychiatry
Yale University School of Medicine
New Haven, Connecticut

Myrna M. Weissman, PhD

(Epidemiologic Psychiatry)
Professor of Psychiatry and Epidemiology
Director, Depression Research Unit
Yale University School of Medicine
New Haven, Connecticut

Preface

The field of psychiatry and mental health continues to be one of the most rapidly expanding disciplines in medicine. An enormous number of new contributions related to the etiology, epidemiology, diagnosis, and treatment of psychiatric conditions have been made in the past decade. Such a rapid evolution of information makes it impossible to maintain up-to-date information in hard-bound volumes, even if new editions are forthcoming every few years. For this reason *Psychiatry* is designed in a loose-leaf format, so that the material can be kept current by the addition of new information as it occurs.

A task of this magnitude is more than one individual or one small group could hope to complete. As a result, the *Psychiatry* volumes have been formulated, planned, guided, and published with the assistance of an editorial board, consisting of the general editor, the chairman, and six board members. Each editorial board member chose one or more section editors with whom to share the responsibility for selection of contributors, development of content, and overall completion of the material.

The editorial board members and section editors listed in the front matter of this volume represent several major university departments of psychiatry. These individuals have assumed responsibility for the sections of the volume covering their areas of expertise. Thus, the six sections of the volume are divided in the following manner:

Cornell University	Personality Disorders and Neuroses
Duke University	Consultation–Liaison Psychiatry and Behavioral Medicine
Harvard University	Social, Epidemiologic, and Legal Psychiatry
University of California—San Diego	Psychobiological Foundations of Clinical Psychiatry
Washington University	Schizophrenia, Affective Disorders, and Dementias
Yale University	Child Psychiatry

Contributors, however, were not drawn only from these departments. Instead, the most qualified individuals—who are nationally and internationally known—were invited to contribute to *Psychiatry*.

The focus of these volumes is both to assist the trainee in learning and to enable the trained practitioner to remain current in the field. Today, the competent and well versed practitioner not only must have clinical skills but must also understand theoretical models, basic behavioral sciences, neurochemistry, sociological issues, the epidemiology of illnesses or syndromes, and many other issues. An attempt has therefore been made to address these and other topics, and to provide the most recent developments in each area.

Because the field of psychiatry has grown to such dimensions that no individual can properly address each of the areas covered in *Psychiatry*, we have invited experts in each area to contribute and to express their views. The judgment of the individual authors in the selection and accuracy of the material has been accepted and no attempt has been made to influence the views expressed. Rather, we have attempted to include all points of view about controversial subjects.

Multiauthorship may at times result in the duplication of material, as well as in variations and inconsistencies in writing style from chapter to chapter. However, careful editorial attention has reduced such problems, and it is the editor's belief that any duplication is more than compensated for by having contributions from the leaders of modern psychiatry. We hope that the differing opinions found in this text will stimulate creative thinking and scientific discourse.

An eclectic orientation is found throughout these volumes. A comprehensive clinical study should include biological, psychological, and psychodynamic thinking; it should use different theoretical models and schools of thought; and it should present material from relevant related disciplines. In the part of the volumes that deals with basic sciences, various theoretical models are presented together, again highlighting the eclectic approach.

Psychiatry follows *Diagnostic and Statistical Manual of Mental Disorders, 3rd ed (DSM-III)* nosology

only to the extent that the contributors agree with the diagnostic classifications found there. As the reader will find, several contributors disagree with that classification scheme and use terms such as "neurosis," "neurotic," or "psychoneurosis." The editor feels that a major text of this magnitude must provide a forum for discussing differing opinions and therefore has encouraged free expression of disagreement.

Because the list of references could be endless for many contributions, a policy decision was made to ask the contributors to limit the references to those that were necessary to provide thorough coverage of the topic. The reader will find that the number of references varies depending on the subject and the length of the contribution, and that in many cases a supplementary suggested reading list follows the references. Contributors have attempted to cite the classic, most quoted, major references; the supplementary lists name other important references that help the interested reader to pursue the subject in greater detail.

The production of these volumes required the assistance of many individuals over a 3-year period. The editorial board has done an outstanding job in organizing the essential task of completing the volumes and in selecting section chiefs for each component of this loose-leaf set. The section chiefs have performed admirably in their choice of contributors and their adherence to required time tables.

The assistance of Virginia Clegg of the Department of Psychiatry, Duke University Medical Center, who served as editorial assistant, is gratefully acknowledged. We are particularly indebted to Shirley Kuhn, the manuscript editor at J. B. Lippincott Company, who provided invaluable assistance and to Rachel Bedard of J. B. Lippincott Company, who provided much needed guidance in the early planning and all stages of production until the publication of this project. The completion of *Psychiatry* would have been impossible without the assistance of these individuals.

As editor, I would like to acknowledge my appreciation to all of the contributors who took time from their academic pursuits, patients, and families to join in the writing of these volumes. Their willingness to participate is a measure of their dedication to our profession.

Jesse O. Cavenar, Jr, MD

Introduction

Psychiatry is complex, rapidly evolving, and above all, intellectually exciting. We have tried to capture each of these characteristics in this new *Psychiatry* loose-leaf set. The complexity is reflected by the multiple contrasting, and at times by competing paradigms of contemporary psychiatric thought. Biologic, psychodynamic, sociocultural, developmental, behavioral, and phenomenologic perspectives have all been fruitful, and all have devoted advocates. One common textbook strategy strives for an eclectic resolution of the tensions and contradictions among these paradigms, but carries the danger of losing the intellectual vigor and excitement of the core concepts. An alternative approach selects a single perspective and views all of psychiatry from this vantage, assuring consistency, but now at the risk of relevance rather than of excitement. At this point in the evolution of the field of psychiatry, there is no single approach that is uniformly superior. We have chosen to preserve the vigor, excitement, and relevance of the field, and to trust our readers to tolerate the unavoidable inconsistencies of a burgeoning science. Each of the major areas of modern psychiatry is discussed by a group that has a specific perspective, one which has demonstrated its power and value in that area. We make no attempt to be consistent across areas, to present a uniform point of view, or to include every perspective on every subject. We do strive to present coherent and comprehensive perspectives on each of the major issues in psychiatry, those that have been interesting and fruitful, and that we believe have promise for the future.

This loose-leaf reference discusses much of modern psychiatry. In doing so, it not only presents what is known, it also creates a form for the discipline by its selection and organization of the subject matter; by its choice of perspectives, schools, and individual authors for each section; and perhaps most of all by its decisions regarding omissions and redundancies. For example, in selecting our six major sections we considered, but decided against, substance abuse, geriatric psychiatry, and brain disease, choosing rather to include each of these as they relate to the six areas we did select. We have described some schools of psychotherapy, while others are not mentioned. Psychodiagnostic evaluation is presented under several headings, the epidemiology of psychoses is discussed twice, of anxiety disorders once, and of personality disorders not at all. These decisions were based on our view of what is known, what is promising, and what best reflects the frontiers of new investigation in the field.

The rapidly evolving aspect of psychiatry is reflected by the loose-leaf format of the book, and particularly by the fact that one third of our chapter headings are "open," and will be added in future editions. If we have been successful in our presentation, the reader will join us in looking forward to the new findings in our field and to the forthcoming chapters in our book.

Finally, contemporary psychiatry is exciting. That excitement is reflected in the almost daily discovery of new solutions, new problems, and the incompleteness of our knowledge. We believe that *Psychiatry* also has problems and is also incomplete, but we are trying our best to make it as exciting as the discipline. We will try to make it better, but it may well be the best psychiatry book that can be written now.

Robert Michels, MD

Contents

SECTION 1. THE PERSONALITY DISORDERS AND NEUROSES

ARNOLD M. COOPER, ALLEN J. FRANCES, MICHAEL H. SACKS, *Editors*

Conceptual Models

1   **The Psychoanalytic Model**

Arnold M. Cooper, Allen J. Frances, and Michael Sacks

2   **Social Learning Models**

Theodore Millon

3   **A Biological Model for Selected Personality Disorders**

Richard I. Shader, Edward L. Scharfman, and Daniel A. Dreyfuss

4–5   **(Open)**

Treatment Issues

6   **Clinical Evaluation: A Multidimensional, Hypothesis Testing, Negotiated Approach**

Aaron Lazare, Sherman Eisenthal, and Anne Alonso

7   **Psychological Assessment**

John F. Clarkin and John A. Sweeney

8   **Psychoanalysis and Psychoanalytic Psychotherapy**

Anton O. Kris

9   **The Psychosocial Treatments**

John F. Clarkin, Allen J. Frances, and Samuel W. Perry

10   **Drug Treatment of Personality Disorders and Neuroses**

James H. Kocsis and J. John Mann

24   **The Avoidant Personality**
     Theodore Millon

25   **The Impulse Disorders**
     William A. Frosch, James P. Frosch, and John Frosch

26   **Dependent and Passive-Aggressive Personality Disorders**
     Aaron H. Esman

27   **The Masochistic Personality**
     Stuart S. Asch

28   **Changes in Personality Associated With Neurologic Disease**
     David Bear, Roy Freeman, and Mark Greenberg

29–30 **(Open)**

Neurosis

31   **Introduction to the Neuroses**
     Michael H. Sacks

32   **Panic and Anxiety Disorders**
     Jack M. Gorman and Michael R. Liebowitz

33   **Agoraphobia, Social Phobia, and Simple Phobia**
     Abby J. Fyer and Donald F. Klein

34   **Obsessive-Compulsive Disorder**
     M. Katherine Shear and William A. Frosch

35   **Somatoform and Factitious Disorders**
     Milton Viederman

36–38 **(Open)**

39   **Dissociative Disorders**

Margaret M. Gilmore and Charles Kaufman

Other Disorders

40   **Depressive Neurosis**

Michael H. Sacks

41   **Stress-Response Syndromes: Post-traumatic and Adjustment Disorders**

Mardi J. Horowitz

42–44 **(Open)**

Sexual Disorders

45   **Normal Sexuality and Introduction to Sexual Disorders**

Richard C. Friedman

46   **Paraphilias and Gender Identity Disorders**

Ethel S. Person

47   **Psychosexual Dysfunctions**

Helen S. Kaplan

48–50 **(Open)**

SECTION 2. SCHIZOPHRENIA, AFFECTIVE DISORDERS, AND DEMENTIAS

SAMUEL B. GUZE, JOHN E. HELZER, *Editors*

51   **The Medical Model and Psychiatric Disorders**

Samuel B. Guze and John E. Helzer

Volume 2

SECTION 1. CHILD PSYCHIATRY

ALBERT J. SOLNIT, DONALD J. COHEN, JOHN E. SCHOWALTER, *Editors*

Background

5   **Family Development**
     Alan Gurwitt and Roy C. Muir

6–8 **(Open)**

General Perspectives

9   **Neuroendocrinology**
     Åke Mattsson, Wayne H. Green, and Raphael David

10   **Strategies for the Genetic Study of Child Psychiatric Disorders**
     David L. Pauls

11   **Epidemiology and Child Psychiatry**
     Madelyn S. Gould and David Shaffer

12   **Clinical Neurochemical Strategies in Child Psychiatry**
     J. Gerald Young, Leonard I. Leven, and Donald J. Cohen

13   **Neurobiology of Memory and Learning in Childhood**
     J. Gerald Young

14–16   **(Open)**

17   **A Social Cognitive Perspective**
     David Elkind

18   **Psychodynamic Factors in Child Psychiatry**
     Albert J. Solnit and Peter B. Neubauer

Classification and Assessment

19   **Classification**
     Dennis P. Cantwell

20   **General Psychiatric Assessment of Children and Adolescents**
Melvin Lewis

21   **Psychological Assessment of Children**
Sara S. Sparrow, Jack M. Fletcher, and Domenic V. Cicchetti

22   **(Open)**

23   **Clinical Data Systems: Rating Scales and Interviews**
Thomas M. Achenbach

24–26   **(Open)**

Disorders

27   **Pervasive Developmental Disorders**
Fred R. Volkmar and Donald J. Cohen

28   **Mental Retardation**
Edward Zigler and Robert M. Hodapp

29   **Schizophrenia in Children**
Peter E. Tanguay and Robert Asarnow

30   **Affective Disorders**
Elva O. Poznanski

31–33   **(Open)**

34   **Organic Mental Disorders**
Edwin J. Mikkelsen

Treatment Approaches

89   **Substance Abuse: Alcohol**
John A. Ewing

90   **Treatment for Drug Abuse**
Everett H. Ellinwood, Jr, George Woody, and Ranga Rama Krishnan

91   **Medication-Induced Psychiatric Symptoms and Disorders**
Frederick G. Guggenheim and Milton K. Erman

92–94   **(Open)**

Psychiatric Emergencies

95   **Emergency Psychiatry**
William R. Dubin and Kenneth J. Weiss

Disorders of Joint Interest to Medicine and Psychiatry

96–98   **(Open)**

99   **Depression in the Medically Ill**
Alan Stoudemire

100   **The Somatoform Disorders**
Charles V. Ford

101   **The False Patient: Chronic Factitious Disease, Munchausen Syndrome, and Malingering**
Theodore Nadelson

102   **Anorexia Nervosa and Bulimia**
W. Stewart Agras and John A. Bachman

Therapeutic Approaches

Biopsychosocial Applications

115 Consultation Psychiatry: A Practical Guide

Steven A. Cohen-Cole

116 Psychiatry in Primary Care Medicine

Troy L. Thompson II

117 Consultation—Liaison Psychiatry in Subspecialty Medicine

F. Patrick McKegney and Rollin M. Gallagher III

118 Psychiatric Aspects of Cardiovascular Disease

Arthur M. Freeman III and David G. Folks

119 Geriatric Psychiatry

Burton V. Reifler and Soo Borson

120 The Psychiatric Aspects of Obstetrics and Gynecology

Carol C. Nadelson and Malkah T. Notman

121 The Surgical Patient

James J. Strain

122–125 (Open)

Biobehavioral Frontiers

126 Biobehavioral Factors in Cardiovascular Disease

Redford B. Williams, Jr

127 (Open)

128   **Brain, Behavior, and Immune Processes**

Marvin Stein, Steven J. Schleifer, and Steven E. Keller

129   **Health Promotion**

Lawrence W. Green and Alfred L. McAlister

Volume 3

SECTION 1. SOCIAL, EPIDEMIOLOGIC, AND LEGAL PSYCHIATRY

GERALD L. KLERMAN, MYRNA WEISSMAN, PAUL S. APPELBAUM, LOREN H. ROTH, *Editors*

Social and Community Psychiatry

1   **(Open)**

2   **Cross-Cultural Psychiatry**

Jane M. Murphy

3   **Economics of Mental Health**

Thomas G. McGuire

4   **Federal and State Roles in Mental Health**

Herbert Pardes, Paul Sirovatka, and Harold Alan Pincus

5   **Community Mental Health Services**

Harriet L. Wolfe and Boris M. Astrachan

6   **Chronic Mental Patients**

Jonathan F. Borus

7   **Family Psychiatry**

Henry Grunebaum

8–10 **(Open)**

Epidemiologic Psychiatry

11   **Epidemiology: Purpose and Historical Overview**

Myrna M. Weissman and Gerald L. Klerman

Legal Psychiatry

SECTION 2. PSYCHOBIOLOGICAL FOUNDATIONS OF CLINICAL PSYCHIATRY

LEWIS L. JUDD, PHILIP M. GROVES, *Editors*

43 **Chemical Communication in the Brain**

Floyd E. Bloom

44 **Anatomy and Physiology of Brain Monoamine Systems**

Stephen L. Foote

45 **Psychopharmacology**

Mark A. Geyer and David S. Segal

46 **Animal Models of Psychopathology**

David S. Segal and Mark A. Geyer

47–49 **(Open)**

50 **Receptors, Radioligand Binding, and Psychiatric Disorders**

Ian Creese

51 **Human Brain-Imaging: Basic Principles and Applications in Psychiatry**

Terry L. Jernigan

52 **Neuropsychometry as an Indirect Measure of Brain Function**

Igor Grant and Ronald Ruff

53 **Trait (and State) Markers of a Predisposition to Psychopathology**

Marc A. Schuckit

54 **Limbic-Hypothalmic-Pituitary-Adrenal Axis Dysregulation in Melancholia**

S. Craig Risch and David S. Janowsky

55 **Strategies for Studying Neurotransmitter Hypothesis of Affective Disorders**

David S. Janowsky, S. Craig Risch, and Robert Neborsky

56–58 **(Open)**

Contributors

Robert Abramovitz, MD
Chief Psychiatrist, Outpatient and Community Services, Division Jewish Board of Family and Children's Services, Inc, New York, New York; Lecturer, Yale Child Study Center, New Haven, Connecticut (*Vol 2, Chap 69*)

Thomas H. Achenbach, PhD
Professor of Psychiatry and Director, Center for Children, Youth, and Families, Department of Psychiatry, University of Vermont, Burlington, Vermont (*Vol 2, Chap 23*)

Ralph N. Adams, PhD
Professor of Chemistry, University of Kansas, Lawrence, Kansas (*Vol 1, Chap 64*)

W. Stewart Agras, MD
Professor of Psychiatry and Director, Behavioral Medicine Program, Stanford University School of Medicine, Stanford, California (*Vol 2, Chap 102*)

Hagop Souren Akiskal, MD
Professor of Psychiatry, Associate Professor of Pharmacology, and Director of Affective Disorders Program, University of Tennessee Center for the Health Sciences; Director of Mood Clinic, Northeast Mental Health Center; Associate Director of Baptist Memorial Hospital Sleep Disorders Center, Memphis, Tennessee (*Vol 1, Chap 61*)

Anne Alonso, PhD
Director of the Treatment Center, Boston Institute for Psychotherapy, Boston, Massachusetts (*Vol 1, Chap 6*)

Thomas F. Anders, MD
Professor of Psychiatry and Human Behavior, Brown University, Providence, Rhode Island (*Vol 2, Chap 52*)

Paul S. Appelbaum, MD
A. F. Zeleznik Professor of Psychiatry, University of Massachusetts Medical School, Worcester, Massachusetts (*Vol 3, Chap 32*)

Robert Asarnow, PhD
Associate Professor of Psychiatry, University of California; affiliated with Neuropsychiatric Institute, Center for the Health Sciences, Los Angeles, California (*Vol 2, Chap 29*)

Stuart S. Asch, MD
Professor of Clinical Psychiatry, Department of Psychiatry, New York Hospital, Cornell Medical Center; Faculty, Columbia University, Psychoanalytic Treatment Center, New York, New York (*Vol 1, Chap 27*)

Boris M. Astrachan, MD
Professor of Psychiatry and Deputy Chairman, Yale University School of Medicine, Department of Psychiatry; Director, Connecticut Mental Health Center, New Haven, Connecticut (*Vol 3, Chap 5*)

Joanne Buhl Auth, MHEd
Associate in Psychiatry, College of Medicine, University of Florida, Gainesville, Florida (*Vol 3, Chap 18*)

John A. Bachman, PhD
Clinical Director, Behavioral Medicine Program, Stanford University School of Medicine, Stanford, California (*Vol 2, Chap 102*)

David Bear, MD
Assistant Professor of Psychiatry, Harvard Medical School, New England Deaconess Hospital; affiliated with Massachusetts General Hospital and Beth Israel Hospital, Boston, Massachusetts (*Vol 1, Chap 28*)

Paul E. Bebbington, MA, MPhil, MRCP, MRCPsych
Honorary Senior Lecturer and Consultant Psychiatrist, Clinical Scientific Staff, MRC Social Psychiatry Unit, Institute of Psychiatry, DeCrespigny Park, London, England (*Vol 1, Chap 63*)

Elissa P. Benedek, MD
Clinical Professor of Psychiatry, University of Michigan Medical Center; affiliated with Center for Forensic Psychiatry, Ann Arbor, Michigan (*Vol 3, Chap 27*)

Thomas P. Beresford, MD
Chief, Psychiatry Service, Veterans Administration Medical Center; Associate Professor of Psychiatry, University of Tennessee Center for the Health Sciences, Memphis, Tennessee (*Vol 2, Chap 88*)

Jerrold G. Bernstein, MD
Assistant Clinical Professor of Psychiatry, Harvard Medical School; Assistant Psychiatrist, Massachusetts General Hospital, Boston; Director, Boston Psychopharmacologic Institute, Chestnut Hill, Massachusetts (*Vol 2, Chap 111*)

Benita A. Blachman, PhD
Assistant Professor and Director, Learning Disabilities Program, Division of Special Education and Rehabilitation, Syracuse University, Syracuse, New York (*Vol 2, Chap 48*)

Dan G. Blazer, MD, PhD
Associate Professor of Psychiatry, and Head, Division of Social and Community Psychiatry, Department of Psychiatry, Duke University Medical Center, Durham, North Carolina (*Vol 3, Chap 21*)

Floyd E. Bloom, MD
Director, Division of Preclinical Neuroscience and Endocrinology, Research Institute of Scripps Clinic, La Jolla, California (*Vol 3, Chap 43*)

James A. Blumenthal, PhD
Assistant Professor, Department of Psychiatry; Associate, Department of Medicine; Director, Behavioral Physiology Laboratory, Duke University Medical Center, Durham, North Carolina (*Vol 2, Chap 109*)

Soo Borson, MD
Assistant Professor, Department of Psychiatry and Behavioral Sciences, University of Washington, School of Medicine; Director, Psychogeriatric Inpatient Service, Seattle Veterans Administration Medical Center, Seattle, Washington (*Vol 2, Chap 119*)

Jonathan F. Borus, MD
Associate Professor of Psychiatry, Harvard Medical School; Director of Residency and Fellowship Training, Department of Psychiatry, Massachusetts General Hospital, Boston, Massachusetts (*Vol 3, Chap 6*)

Jeffrey H. Boyd, MD, MPH
Assistant Chief of the Center for Epidemiologic Studies, National Institute of Mental Health, Rockville, Maryland (*Vol 1, Chap 60, Vol 3, Chap 13*)

David L. Braff, MD
Associate Professor of Psychiatry, University of California, San Diego; Director, Psychiatric Inpatient Services, UCSD Medical Center, San Diego, California (*Vol 3, Chap 65*)

Dennis P. Cantwell, MD
Joseph-Campbell Professor of Child Psychiatry, Department of Psychiatry, University of California, Los Angeles, School of Medicine; affiliated with Neuropsychiatric Institute, University of California, Los Angeles, Los Angeles, California (*Vol 2, Chap 19*)

James L. Cavanaugh, MD
Associate Professor, Department of Psychiatry, Rush Medical College; affiliated with Rush Presbyterian–Saint Luke's Medical Center, Chicago, Illinois (*Vol 3, Chap 28*)

Domenic V. Cicchetti, PhD
Senior Research Associate, Department of Psychiatry, Yale University School of Medicine; affiliated with the Psychology Service, Veterans Administration Medical Center, West Haven, Connecticut (*Vol 2, Chap 21*)

John F. Clarkin, PhD
Associate Professor of Clinical Psychology in Psychiatry, Cornell University Medical College; Director of Psychology, The New York Hospital–Westchester Division, White Plains, New York (*Vol 1, Chaps 7, 9*)

Thomas J. Coates, PhD
Assistant Professor of Medicine, Division of General Internal Medicine, and Director of Behavioral Medicine Unit, University of California School of Medicine; Associate Staff, University of California, San Francisco Hospitals and Clinics, San Francisco, California (*Vol 2, Chap 77*)

Donald J. Cohen, MD
Professor of Pediatrics, Psychiatry, and Psychology, Yale Child Study Center, New Haven, Connecticut (*Vol 2, Chaps 12, 27, 38*)

Steven A. Cohen-Cole, MD, MA
Associate Professor of Psychiatry, and Head, Division of Consultation–Liaison Psychiatry and Behavioral Medicine, Emory University School of Medicine, Atlanta, Georgia (*Vol 2, Chap 115*)

James P. Comer, MD, MPH
Maurice Falk Professor of Child Psychiatry, Child Study Center, Yale Medical School; affiliated with Yale-New Haven Hospital, New Haven, Connecticut (*Vol 2, Chap 70*)

Hope R. Conte, PhD
Associate Professor, Department of Psychiatry, Albert Einstein College of Medicine/Montefiore Medical Center; Associate Director, Department of Psychiatry, Bronx Municipal Hospital Center, Bronx, New York (*Vol 1, Chap 15*)

Arnold M. Cooper, MD
Director of Education, Payne Whitney Clinic, Cornell University Medical College, New York, New York (*Vol 1, Chap 1*)

Ian Creese, PhD
Associate Professor of Neurosciences, University of California, San Diego, La Jolla, California (*Vol 3, Chap 50*)

Christine K. Cross, MA
Research Assistant, Group Operations, Incorporated, Rockville, Maryland (*Vol 3, Chap 20*)

Raphael David, MD
Professor of Pediatrics, New York University Medical Center–Bellevue Hospital Center; affiliated with New York University Hospital and Bellevue Hospital Center, New York, New York (*Vol 2, Chap 9*)

Kenneth Davison, FRCP, FRCPEd, FRCPsych, DPM
Lecturer, Department of Psychiatry, University of Newcastle Upon Tyne; Consultant Psychiatrist, Department of Psychological Medicine, Newcastle General Hospital, Newcastle Upon Tyne, United Kingdom (*Vol 1, Chap 69*)

Raymond S. Dean, PhD
Department of Psychology, Ball State University; Department of Psychiatry, Indiana University School of Medicine, Muncie, Indiana (*Vol 1, Chap 72*)

Daniel A. Dreyfess, MD
Assistant Clinical Professor of Psychiatry, Department of Psychiatry, Tufts University School of Medicine; Director, Psychopharmacology Clinic, Mental Health Unit, New England Medical Center Hospitals, Boston, Massachusetts (*Vol 1, Chap 3*)

William R. Dubin, MD
Associate Professor of Psychiatry, Temple University School of Medicine; Clinical Director, Philadelphia Psychiatric Center, Philadelphia, Pennsylvania (*Vol 2, Chap 95*)

David L. Dunner, MD
Professor, Department of Psychiatry and Behavioral Sciences, University of Washington; Chief of Psychiatry, Harborview Medical Center, Seattle, Washington (*Vol 1, Chap 59*)

Felton Earls, MD
Blanche F. Ittleson Professor of Child Psychiatry, and Director, Division of Child Psychiatry, Washington University School of Medicine, St. Louis, Missouri (*Vol 3, Chap 12*)

Sherman Eisenthal, PhD
Associate Professor of Psychology, Department of Psychiatry, Massachusetts General Hospital, Harvard Medical School, Boston, Massachusetts (*Vol 1, Chap 6*)

David Elkind, PhD
Professor of Child Study and Visiting Scholar, Lincoln Filene Center for Citizenship and Public Affairs, Tufts University, Medford, Massachusetts (*Vol 2, Chap 17*)

Everett H. Ellinwood, Jr, MD
Professor of Psychiatry, and Director, Behavioral Neuropharmacology Section, Duke University Medical Center, Durham, North Carolina (*Vol 2, Chap 90*)

Milton K. Erman, MD
Assistant Professor of Psychiatry, University of Texas Health Science Center; affiliated with Presbyterian Hospital, Dallas, Texas (*Vol 2, Chap 91*)

Aaron H. Esman, MD
Professor Clinical Psychiatry, Department of Psychiatry, Cornell University Medical College and Payne Whitney Clinic, The New York Hospital, New York, New York (*Vol 1, Chap 26*)

John A. Ewing, MD
Professor Emeritus of Psychiatry, and Founding Director of the Center for Alcohol Studies, University of North Carolina, School of Medicine, Chapel Hill, North Carolina (*Vol 2, Chap 89*)

F. David Fisher, MD, MPH, MDiv
Assistant Professor of Psychiatry, Yale University School of Medicine; Assistant Director, Psychiatric Consultation–Liaison and Ambulatory Services, Yale-New Haven Hospital, New Haven, Connecticut (*Vol 2, Chap 81*)

Jack M. Fletcher, PhD
Chief, Developmental Neuropsychiatry Research Section, Texas Research Institute of Mental Sciences, Houston, Texas (*Vol 2, Chap 21*)

David G. Folks, MD
Assistant Professor of Psychiatry, Consultation–Liaison Service, University of Alabama School of Medicine; affiliated with University of Alabama in Birmingham Hospitals and Veterans Administration Hospital, Birmingham, Alabama (*Vol 2, Chap 118*)

Marshall F. Folstein, MD
Eugene Meyer Professor of Psychiatry and Medicine, The Johns Hopkins University School of Medicine; Director, Division of General Hospital Psychiatry, The Johns Hopkins Hospital, Baltimore, Maryland (*Vol 1, Chap 73*)

Stephen L. Foote, PhD
Assistant Adjunct Professor, Department of Psychiatry, University of California, San Diego; Associate Adjunct Member, Research Institute of Scripps Clinic, La Jolla, California (*Vol 3, Chap 44*)

Charles V. Ford, MD
Professor of Psychiatry, and Director, Consultation/Liaison Service, Department of Psychiatry, Vanderbilt University School of Medicine, Nashville, Tennessee (*Vol 2, Chap 100*)

Randal D. France, MD
Assistant Professor, and Medical Director of Clinical Specialty Unit, Department of Psychiatry, Duke University Medical Center, Durham, North Carolina (*Vol 2, Chap 104*)

Allen J. Frances, MD
Associate Professor of Psychiatry, Cornell University Medical College; Director Outpatient Department, Payne Whitney Clinic, The New York Hospital, New York, New York (*Vol 1, Chaps 1, 9, 14*)

Arthur M. Freeman III, MD
Professor and Vice-Chairman, Department of Psychiatry, University of Alabama School of Medicine, Birmingham, Alabama (*Vol 2, Chap 118*)

Roy Freeman, MB, ChB
Instructor in Neurology, Harvard Medical School; affiliated with Beth Israel Hospital and New England Deaconess Hospital, Boston, Massachusetts (*Vol 1, Chap 28*)

Richard C. Friedman, MD
Clinical Associate Professor of Psychiatry, Cornell University Medical College; New York Collaborating Psychoanalytic Studies, Columbia University, New York, New York (*Vol 1, Chap 45*)

James P. Frosch, MD
Clinical Instructor in Psychiatry, Harvard Medical School, Boston; affiliated with McLean Hospital, Cambridge, Massachusetts (*Vol 1, Chap 25*)

John Frosch, MD
Professor of Psychiatry, Department of Psychiatry, New York University School of Medicine; Attending Psychiatrist, University Hospital; Director Emeritus of Psychiatry, Brookdale Hospital Medical Center; Attending Psychiatrist, Bellevue Medical Center, New York, New York (*Vol 1, Chap 25*)

William A. Frosch, MD
Professor and Vice-Chairman, Department of Psychiatry, Cornell University Medical College; Medical Director, Payne Whitney Clinic, The New York Hospital, New York, New York (*Vol 1, Chaps 22, 25, 34*)

Edward H. Futterman, MD
Clinical Professor of Psychiatry and of Pediatrics, Child Study Center, Yale School of Medicine, New Haven Connecticut (*Vol 2, Chap 47*)

Abby J. Fyer, MD
Assistant Professor of Clinical Psychiatry, Columbia University College of Physicians and Surgeons; Co-Director, Anxiety Disorders Clinic, New York State Psychiatric Institute, New York, New York (*Vol 1, Chap 33*)

Rollin M. Gallagher III, MD
Associate Professor of Psychiatry and Family Practice, University of Vermont; affiliated with Medical Center Hospital of Vermont and Central Vermont Hospital, Burlington, Vermont (*Vol 2, Chap 117*)

Ronald Geraty, MD
Chief of Psychiatry, New England Memorial Hospital, Stoneham, Massachusetts; Clinical Instructor in Psychiatry, Harvard Medical School, Boston, Massachusetts (*Vol 2, Chap 64*)

Mark A. Geyer, PhD
Associate Professor of Psychiatry, Department of Psychiatry, School of Medicine, University of California, San Diego, La Jolla, California (*Vol 3, Chaps 45, 46*)

J. Christian Gillin, MD
Professor, Department of Psychiatry, University of California, San Diego; affiliated with San Diego Veterans Administration Medical Center, San Diego, California (*Vol 3, Chaps 60, 61*)

Margaret M. Gilmore, MD
Clinical Assistant Professor, Department of Psychiatry, Cornell University Medical College, New York, New York (*Vol 1, Chap 39*)

Jack M. Gorman, MD
Director, Biological Studies Unit, New York State Psychiatric Institute; Assistant Professor of Clinical Psychiatry, College of Physicians and Surgeons, Columbia University; Assistant Attending Psychiatrist, Presbyterian Hospital, New York, New York (*Vol 1, Chap 32*)

Madelyn S. Gould, PhD, MPH
Assistant Professor of Clinical Psychiatry, Columbia University, College of Physicians and Surgeons, New York, New York (*Vol 2, Chap 11*)

Igor Grant, MD, FRCP
Professor of Psychiatry, University of California, San Diego; Assistant Chief, Psychiatry, San Diego Veterans Administration Medical Center, La Jolla, California (*Vol 3, Chap 52*)

Lawrence W. Green, DrPH
Professor, Department of Family Practice and Community Medicine, University of Texas Medical School, Houston, Texas (*Vol 2, Chap 129*)

Wayne H. Green, MD
Assistant Professor of Psychiatry, Department of Psychiatry, New York University School of Medicine; affiliated with University Hospital and Bellevue Hospital, New York, New York (*Vol 2, Chap 9*)

Mark Greenberg, PhD
Instructor in Psychology in Psychiatry, Harvard Medical School; Fellow in Clinical Neuropsychology, New England Deaconess Hospital, Boston, Massachusetts (*Vol 1, Chap 28*)

Maurice Grossman, MD
Emeritus Clinical Professor of Psychiatry, Stanford University School of Medicine, Stanford, California (*Vol 3, Chap 31*)

Philip M. Groves, PhD
Professor of Psychiatry, University of California, San Diego School of Medicine, La Jolla, California (*Vol 3, Chap 42*)

Henry Grunebaum, MD
Clinical Professor of Psychiatry, Harvard Medical School, Boston; Director of Family Psychotherapy Training, Cambridge Hospital, Cambridge, Massachusetts (*Vol 3, Chap 7*)

Frederick G. Guggenheim, MD
Associate Professor, Department of Psychiatry, Southwestern Medical School; Chief, Psychiatric Consultation–Liaison Service, Parkland Memorial Hospital, Dallas, Texas (*Vol 2, Chap 91*)

Alan Gurwitt, MD
Associate Clinical Professor, Yale Child Study Center and Department of Psychiatry, Section of Child Psychiatry, University of Connecticut Health Center, New Haven and Farmington, Connecticut; Faculty Member, Hartford Child Psychiatry Training Consortium and Western New England Institute for Psychoanalysis, Hartford and New Haven, Connecticut (*Vol 2, Chap 5*)

Thomas G. Gutheil, MD
Associate Professor of Psychiatry and Director of the Program in Psychiatry and the Law, Massachusetts Mental Health Center, Harvard Medical School; Visiting Lecturer, Harvard Law School; President, Law and Psychiatry Resource Center, Boston, Massachusetts (*Vol 3, Chap 36*)

Samuel B. Guze, MD
Spencer T. Olin Professor and Head, Department of Psychiatry, Washington University School of Medicine; Psychiatrist-in-Chief, Barnes and Renard Hospitals, St. Louis, Missouri (*Vol 1, Chap 51*)

Richard C. W. Hall, MD
Director of Research, Monarch Health Corporation, Medical Director, Psychiatric Programs, The Florida Hospital, Orlando, Florida (*Vol 2, Chap 88*)

Beatrix A. Hamburg, MD
Professor of Psychiatry and Pediatrics, The Mount Sinai School of Medicine; Director of Pediatric Consultation/Liaison, Mount Sinai School of Medicine, New York, New York (*Vol 2, Chap 4*)

Gordon Harper, MD
Associate in Psychiatry and Medicine, Children's Hospital; Assistant Professor of Psychiatry, Harvard Medical School, Boston, Massachusetts (*Vol 2, Chap 64*)

Gary Hawk, PhD
Affiliated with Center for Forensic Psychiatry, Ann Arbor, Michigan (*Vol 3, Chap 27*)

John E. Helzer, MD
Professor of Psychiatry, Washington University School of Medicine; Psychiatrist, Barnes and Renard Hospitals, St. Louis, Missouri (*Vol 1, Chaps 51, 54; Vol 3, Chap 15*)

Robert L. Hendren, DO
Assistant Professor of Psychiatry, Behavioral Sciences, and Child Health and Development, George Washington University School of Medicine and Health Sciences; Attending Psychiatrist, George Washington University Hospital and Children's Hospital National Medical Center, Washington, DC (*Vol 2, Chap 60*)

Stephen P. Herman, MD
Assistant Clinical Professor of Psychiatry, Cornell University Medical Center, The New York Hospital, New York, New York (*Vol 2, Chap 51*)

Eleanor W. Herzog
PhD Candidate, Department of Psychology, Tufts University, Medford, Massachusetts (*Vol 2, Chap 41*)

James M. Herzog, MD
Assistant Professor of Psychiatry, Harvard Medical School; Director of Training in Child Psychiatry, Childrens Hospital Medical Center; Coordinator, Human Development Curriculum, Boston Psychoanalytic Society and Institute, Boston, Massachusetts (*Vol 2, Chap 41*)

Steven A. Hillyard, PhD
Professor of Neurosciences, Department of Neurosciences, University of California, San Diego, La Jolla, California (*Vol 3, Chap 62*)

Robert M. A. Hirschfeld, MD
Chief, Center for Studies of Affective Disorders, Clinical Research Branch, National Institute of Mental Health, Rockville, Maryland (*Vol 3, Chap 20*)

Robert M. Hodapp
Research Associate, Psychology Department, Yale University, New Haven, Connecticut (*Vol 2, Chap 28*)

Mardi J. Horowitz, MD
Professor, Department of Psychiatry, University of California, San Francisco; Director, Center for the Study of Neuroses, Langley Porter Psychiatric Institute, San Francisco, California (*Vol 1, Chap 41*)

Thomas B. Horvath, MD, FRACP
Vice-Chairman, Department of Psychiatry, Mount Sinai School of Medicine; Clinical Director of Psychiatry, Bronx Veterans Administration Medical Center, New York, New York (*Vol 2, Chap 87*)

Jeffrey L. Houpt, MD
Professor and Chairman, Department of Psychiatry, Emory University School of Medicine, Atlanta, Georgia (*Vol 2, Chap 76*)

Leighton Y. Huey, MD
Associate Professor, Department of Psychiatry, University of California, School of Medicine, San Diego; affiliated with San Diego Veterans Administration Hospital, La Jolla, California (*Vol 3, Chap 66*)

Carroll W. Hughes, PhD
Associate Professor of Psychiatry, University of Kansas, School of Medicine, Kansas City, Kansas (*Vol 1, Chap 64*)

Joseph J. Jankowski, MD
Associate Clinical Professor of Psychiatry, Tufts University School of Medicine; Director of Ambulatory Services and Community Child Psychiatry, Division of Child Psychiatry, New England Medical Center Hospital, Boston, Massachusetts (*Vol 2, Chap 56*)

David S. Janowsky, MD
Professor of Psychiatry and Director, UCSD Mental Health Clinical Research Center, University of California, San Diego, La Jolla, California (*Vol 3, Chaps 54, 55*)

Terry L. Jernigan, PhD
Assistant Professor of Psychiatry, University of California, San Diego, School of Medicine; Staff Psychologist, Veterans Administration Medical Center, San Diego, California (*Vol 3, Chap 51*)

Kathleen Jordan, MA
Research Associate, Department of Psychiatry, Division of Social and Community Psychiatry, Duke University, Durham, North Carolina (*Vol 3, Chap 21*)

Helen S. Kaplan, MD, PhD
Clinical Professor of Psychiatry, New York Hospital–Cornell Medical Center; Clinical Attending Psychiatrist, The New York Hospital, New York, New York (*Vol 1, Chap 47*)

Charles Kaufman, MD
Senior Staff Fellow, Adult Psychiatry Branch, National Institute of Mental Health, Bethesda, Maryland (*Vol 1, Chap 39*)

Alan E. Kazdin, PhD
Professor of Child Psychiatry and Psychology, and Research Director, Child Psychiatric Treatment Service, Department of Psychiatry, University of Pittsburgh School of Medicine, Western Psychiatric Institute and Clinic, Pittsburgh, Pennsylvania (*Vol 2, Chap 61*)

Francis J. Keefe, PhD
Associate Professor, and Director, Pain Management Program, Department of Psychiatry, Duke University Medical School, Durham, North Carolina (*Vol 2, Chap 104*)

Marcia A. Keener, PhD
Research Associate, Division of Child Psychiatry and Child Development, Stanford University School of Medicine, Stanford, California (*Vol 2, Chap 52*)

Steven E. Keller, PhD
Research Associate Professor of Psychiatry, Mount Sinai School of Medicine, New York, New York (*Vol 2, Chap 128*)

Robert E. Kendell, MD, FRCP FRCPsych
Professor of Psychiatry, Edinburgh University; Royal Edinburgh Hospital, Edinburgh, Scotland (*Vol 1, Chap 53*)

Kenneth S. Kendler, MD
Assistant Professor, Department of Psychiatry, Mount Sinai School of Medicine; affiliated with Veterans Administration Medical Center, Bronx, New York (*Vol 1, Chap 16*)

Thomas A. Kent, MD
Assistant Professor of Psychiatry, University of Kansas, School of Medicine, Kansas City, Kansas (*Vol 1, Chap 64*)

Otto F. Kernberg, MD
Professor of Psychiatry, Cornell University Medical College, New York; Medical Director, The New York Hospital–Cornell Medical Center, Westchester Division, White Plains; Training and Supervising Analyst, Columbia University Center for Psychoanalytic Training and Research, New York, New York (*Vol 1, Chaps 18, 19*)

Chase Patterson Kimball, MD
Professor of Psychiatry and Medicine, and Professor in the College, The University of Chicago, Chicago, Illinois (*Vol 2, Chap 78*)

Donald F. Klein, MD
Professor of Psychiatry, Columbia University College of Physicians and Surgeons; Director of Research, New York State Psychiatric Institute, New York, New York (*Vol 1, Chap 33*)

Gerald L. Klerman, MD
Director of Research, Department of Psychiatry, Massachusetts General Hospital, Boston, Massachusetts (*Vol 1, Chap 52; Vol 3, Chap 11*)

James H. Kocsis, MD
Associate Professor of Psychiatry, Cornell University Medical College, New York, New York (*Vol 1, Chap 10*)

Daniel F. Kripke, MD
Professor of Psychiatry, University of California, San Diego; Director, Sleep Disorders Clinic, San Diego Veterans Administration Medical Center, San Diego, California (*Vol 3, Chaps 59, 61*)

Anton O. Kris, MD
Training and Supervising Analyst, The Boston Psychoanalytic Institute, Boston, Massachusetts (*Vol 1, Chap 8*)

Ranga Rama Krishnan, MD
Assistant Director of Psychiatry, Duke University Medical Center, Durham, North Carolina (*Vol 2, Chap 90*)

Marta Kutas, PhD
Assistant Research Neuroscientist, Department of Neurosciences, University of California, San Diego, La Jolla, California (*Vol 3, Chap 62*)

Aaron Lazare, MD
Professor and Chairman, Department of Psychiatry, University of Massachusetts Medical School, Worcester, Massachusetts (*Vol 1, Chap 6*)

James F. Leckman, MD
Associate Professor, Departments of Psychiatry and Pediatrics, Yale University School of Medicine; affiliated with Yale-New Haven Hospital, New Haven, Connecticut (*Vol 2, Chap 38*)

Hoyle Leigh, MD
Professor of Psychiatry, Yale University School of Medicine; Assistant Chief of Psychiatry, and Director, Psychiatric Consultation–Liaison and Ambulatory Services, Yale–New Haven Hospital, New Haven, Connecticut (*Vol 2, Chap 81*)

Leonard I. Leven, MD
Research Fellow in Child and Adolescent Psychiatry, Division of Child and Adolescent Psychiatry, Mount Sinai School of Medicine of the City University of New York, New York, New York (*Vol 2, Chap 12*)

Dorothy Otnow Lewis, MD, FACP
Professor of Psychiatry, New York University School of Medicine; Associate Attending Physician, NYU–Bellevue Medical Center, New York, New York; Attending Physician, Yale–New Haven Hospital, New Haven, Connecticut (*Vol 2, Chap 37*)

Melvin Lewis, MB, BS, FRCPsych, DCH
Professor of Pediatrics and of Psychiatry, Yale Child Study Center, and Director of Medical Studies, Yale Child Study Center; Attending Psychiatrist, Yale–New Haven Hospital, New Haven, Connecticut (*Vol 2, Chaps 20, 42*)

Ronald Liebman, MD
Clinical Associate Professor, Departments of Psychiatry and of Pediatrics, University of Pennsylvania School of Medicine, Philadelphia, Pennsylvania (*Vol 2, Chap 62*)

Michael R. Liebowitz, MD
Director, Anxiety Disorders Clinic, New York State Psychiatric Institute; Assistant Professor of Clinical Psychiatry, College of Physicians and Surgeons, Columbia University; Assistant Attending Psychiatrist, Presbyterian Hospital, New York, New York (*Vol 1, Chap 32*)

Thomas L. Lowe, MD
Associate Professor of Psychiatry, University of California School of Medicine, Langley Porter Psychiatric Institute, San Francisco, California (*Vol 2, Chap 43*)

Doyne W. Loyd, MD
Clinical Instructor, Department of Psychiatry and Human Behavior, Brown University; Staff Psychiatrist, Psychiatric Epidemiology Research Unit, Butler Hospital, Providence, Rhode Island (*Vol 1, Chap 70*)

Richard A. Lucas, PhD
Staff Psychologist, Durham Veterans Administration Medical Center; Clinical Assistant Professor, Department of Psychiatry, Division of Medical Psychology, Duke University Medical Center, Durham; Adjunct Associate Professor, Department of Psychology, University of North Carolina, Chapel Hill, North Carolina (*Vol 2, Chap 112*)

Alfred L. McAlister, PhD
Associate Professor of Psychiatry, University of Texas, Houston, Texas (*Vol 2, Chap 129*)

John F. McDermott, Jr, MD
Professor and Chairman, Department of Psychiatry, University of Hawaii School of Medicine; affiliated with Queen's Medical Center and Saint Francis Hospital, Honolulu, Hawaii (*Vol 2, Chap 39*)

Peter McGuffin, MB, MRCP, MRCPsych
Senior Lecturer and Consultant in Psychiatry, Institute of Psychiatry, Kings College Hospital Medical School; affiliated with Mandsley Hospital and Kings College Hospital, London, England (*Vol 1, Chap 62*)

Thomas G. McGuire, PhD
Associate Professor of Economics, Boston University, Boston, Massachusetts (*Vol 3, Chap 3*)

Paul R. McHugh, MD
Henry Phipps Professor of Psychiatry, The Johns Hopkins University School of Medicine; Psychiatrist-in-Chief, The Johns Hopkins Hospital, Baltimore, Maryland (*Vol 1, Chap 73*)

F. Patrick McKegney, MD
Professor of Psychiatry and of Medicine, University of Vermont; affiliated with Medical Center Hospital of Vermont, Burlington, Vermont (*Vol 2, Chap 117*)

Arnold J. Mandell, MD
Professor of Psychiatry, and Head, Laboratory of Biological Dynamics and Theoretical Medicine, University of California, San Diego, La Jolla, California (*Vol 3, Chap 72*)

J. John Mann, MD
Associate Professor of Psychiatry, Cornell University Medical College, New York, New York (*Vol 1, Chap 10*)

Åke Mattsson, MD
Professor of Psychiatry and Pediatrics, New York University Medical Center; affiliated with New York University Hospital and Bellevue Hospital, New York, New York (*Vol 2, Chap 9*)

Frederick Towne Melges, MD
Professor of Psychiatry, Duke University Medical Center; Director of Psychiatry, Durham County General Hospital, Durham, North Carolina (*Vol 2, Chap 110*)

Kathleen R. Merikangas, PhD
Assistant Professor of Psychiatry, Yale University School of Medicine, New Haven, Connecticut (*Vol 1, Chap 60; Vol 3, Chap 14*)

Edwin J. Mikkelsen, MD
Director, Division of Child Psychiatry, Massachusetts Mental Health Center, Harvard Medical School, Boston, Massachusetts (*Vol 2, Chaps 34, 35*)

Theodore Millon, PhD
Professor of Psychology, Director of Doctoral Program in Clinical Psychology, and Co-Director of Doctoral Program in Health Psychology, Graduate School, University of Miami, Coral Gables, Florida (*Vol 1, Chaps 2, 24*)

Roy C. Muir, MB, FRANZCP
Associate Professor, Department of Psychological Medicine, Otago University Medical School; Chief, Child and Family Psychiatry, University of Otago Medical School, Otago, New Zealand (*Vol 2, Chap 5*)

Emily Mumford, PhD
Professor of Clinical Sociomedical Sciences in Psychiatry and Public Health, Columbia Presbyterian College of Physicians and Surgeons; Chief, Division of Health Services and Policy Research, New York State Psychiatric Institute, New York, New York (*Vol 2, Chap 79*)

George E. Murphy, MD
Professor of Psychiatry and Director, Psychiatric Outpatient Service, Washington University School of Medicine, St. Louis, Missouri (*Vol 1, Chap 71*)

Jane M. Murphy, PhD
Lecturer, Department of Psychiatry, Harvard Medical School, Boston, Massachusetts (*Vol 3, Chaps 2, 15*)

David F. Musto, MA, MD
Professor of Psychiatry and History of Medicine, Child Study Center, Yale University School of Medicine, New Haven, Connecticut (*Vol 2, Chap 1*)

Arthur Mutter, MD
Professor of Psychiatry, Tufts University School of Medicine; Vice-Chairman, Department of Psychiatry, and Chief, Division of Child Psychiatry, New England Medical Center Hospital (*Vol 2, Chap 56*)

Carol C. Nadelson, MD
Professor and Vice-Chairman, Department of Psychiatry, Tufts University School of Medicine; affiliated with Tufts–New England Medical Center Hospital, Boston, Massachusetts (*Vol 2, Chap 120*)

Theodore Nadelson, MD, MA
Clinical Professor of Psychiatry, Tufts University School of Medicine; Chief, Psychiatry Service, Boston Veterans Administration Medical Center, Boston, Massachusetts (*Vol 2, Chap 101*)

John M. Nardo, MD
Assistant Professor of Psychiatry, and Director of Medical Student Education in Psychiatry, Emory University School of Medicine, Atlanta, Georgia (*Vol 2, Chap 82*)

Robert Neborsky, MD
Associate Clinical Professor, University of California, San Diego; affiliated with University Hospital, Tri City Hospital and Scripps Clinic and Research Foundation (*Vol 3, Chap 55*)

Peter B. Neubauer, MD
Clinical Professor of Psychiatry, The Psychoanalytic Institute, Bellevue Hospital; Training Analyst, Psycholanalytic Center for Training and Research, Columbia University, New York, New York (*Vol 2, Chap 18*)

Malkah T. Notman, MD
Clinical Professor of Psychiatry, Department of Psychiatry, Tufts University School of Medicine; affiliated with Tufts–New England Medical Center Hospital, Boston, Massachusetts (*Vol 2, Chap 120*)

John M. Oldham, MD
Associate Professor of Clinical Psychiatry, Columbia University College of Physicians and Surgeons; Deputy Director, New York State Psychiatric Institute, New York, New York (*Vol 1, Chap 22*)

Herbert Pardes, MD
Lawrence Kolb Professor and Chairman, Department of Psychiatry, Columbia University; Director, New York State Psychiatric Institute; Director, Columbia-Presbyterian Psychiatric Service, New York, New York (*Vol 3, Chap 4*)

Morris B. Parloff, PhD
Clinical Professor of Psychiatry, Georgetown University Medical School; Lecturer, Department of Psychology, American University; Faculty, Washington School of Psychiatry, Washington, DC (*Vol 1, Chap 11*)

Rhea Paul, PhD
Associate Research Scientist, Child Study Center, Yale University, New Haven, Connecticut (*Vol 2, Chap 49*)

David L. Pauls, PhD
Assistant Professor, Child Study Center and Department of Human Genetics, Yale University School of Medicine, New Haven, Connecticut (*Vol 2, Chap 10*)

Michael L. Perlin, JD
Training Consultant, Forensic Psychiatry Clinic, Hospital of University of Pennsylvania; Instructor, Faculty for Continuing Education Program in Psychiatry, The Institute of the Pennsylvania Hospital, Philadelphia, Pennsylvania (*Vol 3, Chap 35*)

Samuel W. Perry, MD
Associate Professor of Clinical Psychiatry, Cornell University Medical College; Associate Director of Consultation–Liaison Psychiatry, The New York Hospital, New York, New York (*Vol 1, Chap 9*)

Ethel S. Person, MD
Clinical Professor of Psychiatry, Columbia University; Director and Training and Supervising Analyst, Columbia Psychoanalytic Center for Training and Research, New York, New York (*Vol 1, Chap 46*)

Irving Philips, MD
Professor, Department of Psychiatry, and Director, Child and Adolescent Psychiatry, University of California School of Medicine, San Francisco, California (*Vol 2, Chap 58*)

Harold Alan Pincus, MD
Special Assistant to the Director, National Institute of Mental Health, Rockville, Maryland; Assistant Professor of Psychiatry, George Washington University School of Medicine, Washington, DC (*Vol 3, Chap 4*)

Robert Plutchik, PhD
Professor of Psychiatry, Albert Einstein College of Medicine/Montefiore Medical Center; Associate Director, Department of Psychiatry, Bronx Municipal Hospital Center, Bronx, New York (*Vol 1, Chap 15*)

William H. Polonsky, MS
Psychology Intern, Division of General Internal Medicine and Behavioral Medicine Unit, University of California School of Medicine, San Francisco, California (*Vol 2, Chap 77*)

Charles W. Popper, MD
Clinical Instructor in Psychiatry, Harvard Medical School, Boston; Director, Child and Adolescent Psychopharmacology, Hall-Mercer Children's Center, McLean Hospital, Belmont, Massachusetts (*Vol 2, Chap 59*)

Elva O. Poznanski, MD
Professor of Psychiatry, University of Illinois; affiliated with the University of Illinois Medical Center, Chicago, Illinois (*Vol 2, Chap 30*)

Sheldon H. Preskorn, MD
Associate Professor, Departments of Psychiatry and Pharmacology, University of Kansas School of Medicine, Kansas City, Kansas (*Vol 1, Chap 64*)

Sally Provence, MD
Professor of Pediatrics, Yale Child Study Center; Attending Pediatrician, Yale–New Haven Medical Center, New Haven, Connecticut (*Vol 2, Chap 2*)

Kyle D. Pruett, MD
Associate Clinical Professor of Child Psychiatry, Yale Child Study Center, New Haven, Connecticut (*Vol 2, Chap 50*)

William H. Reid, MD, MPH
Professor of Psychiatry, and Director of Education and Training, Nebraska Psychiatric Institute, University of Nebraska Medical Center, Omaha, Nebraska (*Vol 1, Chap 23*)

Burton V. Reifler, MD, MPH
Associate Professor, Department of Psychiatry and Behavioral Sciences, Director, Geriatric and Family Services Clinic, and Head, Division of Aging, University of Washington, School of Medicine, Seattle, Washington (*Vol 2, Chap 119*)

Nils Retterstøl, MD
Professor of Psychiatry, University of Oslo; Medical Director, Gaustad Hospital, Oslo, Norway (*Vol 1, Chap 68*)

Charles F. Reynolds III, MD
Associate Professor of Psychiatry and of Neurology, and Director, Sleep Evaluation Center, Western Psychiatric Institute and Clinic, Pittsburgh, Pennsylvania (*Vol 2, Chap 105*)

John P. Rice, PhD
Associate Professor, Department of Psychiatry, Washington University, St. Louis, Missouri (*Vol 1, Chap 62*)

Charles L. Rich, MD
Assistant Professor of Psychiatry, University of California, San Diego; Chief, Inpatient Psychiatry, San Diego Veterans Administration Medical Center, San Diego, California (*Vol 3, Chap 68*)

Elliott Richelson, MD
Professor of Psychiatry and Pharmacology, Mayo Medical School; affiliated with St. Mary's Hospital and Rochester Methodist Hospital, Rochester, Minnesota (*Vol 1, Chap 55*)

Mark A. Riddle, MD
Assistant Professor of Psychiatry and Pediatrics, Yale Child Study Center, New Haven, Connecticut (*Vol 2, Chap 63*)

S. Craig Risch, MD
Associate Professor of Psychiatry, University of California, San Diego; affiliated with University of California Medical Center, San Diego Veterans Administration Hospital, San Diego, California (*Vol 3, Chaps 54, 55*)

Samuel Ritvo, MD
Clinical Professor of Psychiatry, Yale Child Study Center, Yale University School of Medicine, New Haven, Connecticut (*Vol 2, Chap 57*)

Lee N. Robins, PhD
Professor of Psychiatry, Washington University School of Medicine, St. Louis, Missouri (*Vol 3, Chap 19*)

Richard Rogers, PhD
Assistant Professor of Psychiatry and Psychology, Rush Medical School; affiliated with Rush Presbyterian–Saint Luke's Medical Center, Chicago, Illinois (*Vol 3, Chap 28*)

Loren H. Roth, MD
Professor of Psychiatry, University of Pittsburgh School of Medicine; Chief, Adult Clinical Services, and Director, Law and Psychiatry Program, Western Psychiatric Institute and Clinic, Pittsburgh, Pennsylvania (*Vol 3, Chap 30*)

Bruce J. Rounsaville, MD
Associate Professor of Psychiatry, Yale University School of Medicine, New Haven, Connecticut (*Vol 3, Chap 17*)

Ronald Ruff, PhD
Assistant Professor of Psychiatry and Neurosurgery, University of California, School of Medicine; Chief, Neuropsychology Unit UCSD Medical Center, San Diego, California (*Vol 3, Chap 52*)

Michael H. Sacks, MD
Associate Professor of Psychiatry, Cornell University Medical College; Unit Chief, Inpatient Service, Payne Whitney Clinic, The New York Hospital, New York, New York (*Vol 1, Chaps 1, 31, 40*)

Edward L. Scharfman, MD
Assistant Professor of Psychiatry, Department of Psychiatry, Tufts University School of Medicine; Director, Center 3, Inpatient Psychiatry Service, New England Medical Center Hospitals, Boston, Massachusetts (*Vol 1, Chap 3*)

Steven J. Schleifer, MD
Assistant Professor of Psychiatry, Mount Sinai School of Medicine; Assistant Attending Psychiatrist, Mount Sinai Hospital, New York, New York (*Vol 2, Chap 128*)

John E. Schowalter, MD
Professor of Pediatrics and Psychiatry, and Chief of Child Psychiatry, Yale University School of Medicine, New Haven, Connecticut (*Vol 2, Chap 72*)

Marc A. Schuckit, MD
Professor of Psychiatry, University of California, San Diego; affiliated with San Diego Veterans Administration Medical Center, San Diego, California (*Vol 3, Chap 53*)

S. Charles Schulz, MD
Associate Professor of Psychiatry, and Medical Director, Schizophrenia Module, Western Psychiatric Institute and Clinic, Pittsburgh, Pennsylvania (*Vol 2, Chap 105*)

David S. Segal, PhD
Professor of Psychiatry, Department of Psychiatry, School of Medicine, University of California, San Diego, La Jolla, California (*Vol 3, Chaps 45, 46*)

Richard I. Shader, MD
Chairman and Professor of Psychiatry, Department of Psychiatry, Tufts University School of Medicine; Psychiatrist-in-Chief, New England Medical Center Hospitals, Boston, Massachusetts (*Vol 1, Chap 3*)

David Shaffer, MB, BS, MRCP, FRC, PSYCH
Professor of Clinical Psychiatry and Pediatrics, Columbia University College of Physicians and Surgeons; Director, Department of Child Psychiatry, New York State Psychiatric Institute; Director, Division of Pediatric Psychiatry, Babies Hospital, Columbia–Presbyterian Medical Center, New York, New York (*Vol 2, Chap 11*)

Theodore Shapiro, MD
Professor of Psychiatry, Professor of Psychiatry in Pediatrics, and Director, Child and Adolescent Psychiatry, Cornell University Medical College, New York, New York (*Vol 2, Chap 3*)

Bennett A. Shaywitz, MD
Director of Pediatric Neurology, and Associate Professor of Pediatrics and Neurology, Yale Child Study Center, New Haven, Connecticut (*Vol 2, Chap 36*)

Sally E. Shaywitz, MD
Director of the Learning Disorders Unit, Department of Pediatrics, Yale-New Haven Hospital, New Haven, Connecticut (*Vol 2, Chap 36*)

M. Katherine Shear, MD
Assistant Professor of Psychiatry, Cornell University Medical College; Director of Anxiety Disorders Clinic, Payne Whitney Clinic, New York, New York (*Vol 1, Chap 34*)

Arthur P. Shimamura, PhD
Research Fellow, Department of Psychiatry, University of California, San Diego, La Jolla, California (*Vol 3, Chap 71*)

Larry J. Siever, MD
Associate Professor of Psychiatry, Mount Sinai School of Medicine, New York; Director, Outpatient Psychiatry Clinic, Bronx Veterans Administration Medical Center, Bronx, New York (*Vol 1, Chap 16*)

Michael Silver, MD
Clinical Assistant Professor of Psychiatry, University of Pennsylvania School of Medicine; Medical Director, Child and Family Inpatient Service, and Director of Child Psychiatry Training, Philadelphia Child Guidance Clinic, Philadelphia, Pennsylvania (*Vol 2, Chap 62*)

Paul Sirovatka, MS
Public Information Officer, Division of Communications and Education, National Institute of Mental Health, Rockville, Maryland (*Vol 3, Chap 4*)

Ralph Slovenko, LLB, PhD
Professor of Law and Psychiatry, Wayne State University School of Law, Detroit, Michigan (*Vol 3, Chap 31*)

Albert J. Solnit, MD
Sterling Professor of Pediatrics and Psychiatry, Yale University School of Medicine, New Haven, Connecticut (*Vol 2, Chaps 18, 71*)

Sara S. Sparrow, PhD
Associate Professor and Chief Psychologist, Yale Child Study Center, Yale University, New Haven, Connecticut (*Vol 2, Chaps 21, 48*)

Larry R. Squire, PhD
Professor of Psychiatry, Department of Psychiatry, University of California School of Medicine, La Jolla; Research Career Scientist, Veterans Administration Medical Center, San Diego, California (*Vol 3, Chap 71*)

Marvin Stein, MD
Esther and Joseph Klingenstein Professor and Chairman, Department of Psychiatry, Mount Sinai School of Medicine; Psychiatrist-in-Chief and Director, Department of Psychiatry, Mount Sinai Hospital, New York, New York (*Vol 2, Chap 128*)

Michael H. Stone, MD
Clinical Professor of Psychiatry, Beth Israel Medical Center, Mount Sinai School of Medicine; Visiting Lecturer, New York State Psychiatric Institute, New York, New York (*Vol 1, Chap 17*)

Alan Stoudemire, MD
Assistant Professor of Psychiatry, Emory University School of Medicine, Atlanta, Georgia (*Vol 2, Chap 99*)

James J. Strain, MD
Professor of Clinical Psychiatry, Department of Psychiatry, Mount Sinai School of Medicine; affiliated with Mount Sinai Medical Center, New York, New York (*Vol 2, Chap 121*)

Albert J. Stunkard, MD
Professor of Psychiatry, University of Pennsylvania; affiliated with Hospital of the University of Pennsylvania, Philadelphia, Pennsylvania (*Vol 2, Chap 103*)

John A. Sweeney, PhD
Instructor of Psychology in Psychiatry, Cornell University Medical College; Professional Associate, The New York Hospital, Westchester Division, White Plains, New York (*Vol 1, Chap 7*)

Paula Tallal, PhD
Associate Professor, Department of Psychiatry, University of California, San Diego, La Jolla (*Vol 3, Chap 67*)

Laurence R. Tancredi, MD, JD
Kraft Eidman Professor, Medicine and The Law, The University of Texas, Health Science Center at Houston, Houston, Texas (*Vol 3, Chap 29*)

Peter E. Tanguay, MD
Professor of Psychiatry, Director, Child Psychiatry, Clinical Research Center, Associate Director, Division of Child Psychiatry and Mental Retardation, University of California, Los Angeles, California (*Vol 2, Chap 29*)

Troy L. Thompson II, MD
Associate Professor of Psychiatry and Medicine, Consultation–Liaison Psychiatry, University Hospitals, University of Colorado School of Medicine, Denver, Colorado (*Vol 2, Chap 116*)

Gary L. Tischler, MD
Professor of Psychiatry and the Institution of Social and Policy Studies, Yale University; Director, Yale Psychiatric Institute, New Haven, Connecticut (*Vol 3, Chap 22*)

Ming T. Tsuang, MD, PhD, DSc
Professor and Vice-Chairman, Department of Psychiatry and Human Behavior, Brown University; Director, Psychiatric Epidemiology Research Unit, Butler Hospital, Providence, Rhode Island (*Vol 1, Chap 70*)

Milton Viederman, MD
Professor of Clinical Psychiatry, Cornell University Medical College; Director, Consultation–Liaison Service, and Training and Supervising Analyst, Columbia Psychanalytic Center for Training and Research, New York, New York (*Vol 1, Chap 35; Vol 2, Chap 108*)

Lawrence A. Vitulano, PhD
Assistant Clinical Professor of Psychology in The Child Study Center and The School of Nursing, Yale University School of Medicine, New Haven; Clinical Director, Greater Bridgeport Children's Services Center, Bridgeport, Connecticut (*Vol 2, Chap 63*)

Fred R. Volkmar, MD
Assistant Professor of Psychiatry and Pediatrics, Yale Child Study Center; affiliated with Yale–New Haven Hospital, New Haven, Connecticut (*Vol 2, Chap 27*)

George J. Warheit, PhD
Professor of Sociology in Psychiatry, College of Medicine, University of Florida, Gainesville, Florida (*Vol 3, Chap 18*)

Orest E. Wasyliw, PhD
Assistant Professor, Departments of Psychology and Psychiatry, Rush Medical College; affiliated with Presbyterian–Saint Luke's Medical Center, Chicago, Illinois (*Vol 3, Chap 28*)

Kenneth J. Weiss, MD
Associate Professor of Clinical Psychiatry, University of Medicine and Dentistry of New Jersey, Rutgers Medical School at Camden; Cooper Hospital/University Medical Center, Camden, New Jersey (*Vol 2, Chap 95*)

Myrna M. Weissman, PhD
Professor of Psychiatry and Epidemiology, and Director, Depression Research Unit, Yale University School of Medicine, Departments of Psychiatry and Epidemiology, New Haven, Connecticut (*Vol 1, Chap 60; Vol 3, Chaps 11, 13, 14*)

Redford B. Williams, Jr, MD
Professor of Psychiatry, Associate Professor of Medicine, Lecturer, in Psychology, Duke University Medical Center, Durham, North Carolina (*Vol 2, Chap 126*)

Harriet L. Wolfe, MD
Assistant Professor of Psychiatry, Yale School of Medicine; Director, Community Services Division, Connecticut Mental Health Center, New Haven, Connecticut (*Vol 3, Chap 5*)

George Woody, MD
Clinical Associate Professor of Psychiatry, University of Pennsylvania; Chief, Substance Abuse Treatment Center, Veterans Administration Medical Center, Philadelphia, Pennsylvania (*Vol 2, Chap 90*)

Joseph L. Woolston, MD
Associate Clinical Professor of Pediatrics and Psychiatry, Child Study Center, Yale University School of Medicine; affiliated with Yale-New Haven Hospital, New Haven, Connecticut (*Vol 2, Chap 40*)

Richard N. Wortman, MD
Assistant Professor, Department of Psychiatry, Mount Sinai School of Medicine, The City University of New York; Assistant Attending Psychiatrist, Mount Sinai Medical Center, New York, New York (*Vol 2, Chap 4*)

J. Gerald Young, MD
Professor of Psychiatry and Pediatrics, and Director of the Division of Child and Adolescent Psychiatry, Mount Sinai School of Medicine of the City University of New York, New York, New York (*Vol 2, Chaps 12, 13*)

Stephen J. Young, PhD
Specialist (Research), Department of Psychiatry, School of Medicine, University of California, San Diego, La Jolla, California (*Vol 3, Chap 42*)

Edward Zigler, PhD
Sterling Professor Psychology, Yale University; Director, Bush Center in Child Development and Social Policy; Head, Psychology Section, Yale Child Study Center, New Haven, Connecticut (*Vol 2, Chap 28*)

Subject Index

Numbers following an entry refer to volume, chapter, and page, respectively. For example, Academic achievement tests can be found in Volume 2, Chapter 21, page 10. Page numbers in **boldface** indicate a major discussion of a topic.

Abandonment, malpractice related to (3) 29: 7–8
Abraham, K., on compulsive personality disorder (1) 22: 3
Abreaction
  in psychotherapy (2) 108: 2
  in stress-response syndromes (1) 41: 12
Abstraction, test of (3) 52: 8–10
  nonverbal tasks (3) 52: 9–10
  verbal tasks (3) 52: 8–9
Abulia, in frontal lobe syndrome (1) 28: 10
Abuse
  of child. See Child abuse
  of elderly (2) 119: 9
  sexual. See Rape
Abuse liability (2) 90: 1
Academic achievement tests (2) 21: 10
Accident insurance, testimonial privilege applying in claims (3) 31: 3
Acetaldehyde, as marker in alcoholism (3) 53: 10
Acetylcholine. See also Cholinergic neurons
  in affective disorders (3) 55: 3–5
    increased sensitivity to (3) 53: 5
  in Alzheimer's disease (1) 73: 7–8; (2) 87: 8
  in electroconvulsive therapy (3) 68: 4
  in extrapyramidal toxicity of neuroleptics (1) 55: 21–22
  and limbic-hypothalamic-pituitary axis dysregulation in melancholia (3) 54: 6–7
  receptors
    and neuroleptic side effects (1) 55: 25
    neuroleptics interaction with (1) 55: 19
Acquired immune deficiency syndrome (AIDS), in drug abuse (2) 90: 3
Acromegaly, psychiatric manifestations (2) 88: 13–14
ACTH, in regulation of cortisol secretion (3) 54: 1–2
Acting out (1) 25: 1
Action potential
  initiation and propagation of (3) 42: 4–5
  integration of synaptic events in time and space related to (3) 42: 4
Activity levels
  in attention deficit disorder (3) 66: 7
  distinguishing age-appropriate overactivity from hyperactivity (3) 66: 14
Adaptation. See also Coping strategies
  in child development (2) 2: 3

DSM-III on (2) 19: 11, 13
in early childhood (2) 21: 6
evaluation in mental status examination in children (2) 20: 12
in infants (2) 21: 3
to medical illness (2) 78: 6
in middle childhood and adolescents (2) 21: 9–10
psychosocial (2) 58: 1, 2
to surgery (2) 121: 8
Vineland Adaptive Behavior Scales for (2) 21: 3
Addiction
  definition (2) 90: 1
  narcotic withdrawal (2) 90: 12
  sedative-anxiolytic withdrawal (2) 90: 10–11
  supportive intervention during hospitalization of angry and distrustful patient (2) 108: 10–11
  withdrawal symptoms (2) 90: 2
Addison's disease. See Adrenal insufficiency
Adenylate cyclase. See Cyclic AMP
Adjustment disorders (1) 41: 7
  in childhood and adolescence (2) **51: 1–6**
  classification (1) 41: 7
  clinical manifestations (2) 51: 4–5
    validity of concept (2) 51: 3
    variation in (2) 51: 2
  with depressed mood (1) 59: 5
  DSM-III definition (1) 41: 7
  post-traumatic stress disorder distinguished from (2) 51: 2, 3
  psychosocial pressures precipitating (1) 41: 7
  stressful life events in (2) 51: 1–3
  terminology (2) 51: 1–3
  treatment issues (2) 51: 5–6
Adjustment reaction of adolescence (2) 4: 10
Administration, in hospital and residential treatment of children (2) 64: 8–11, 15
Adolescence (2) **4: 1–15.** See also Adolescents
  adjustment reaction of (2) 4: 10
  body image concerns in (2) 4: 6, 8
    chronic illness impact on (2) 4: 14
  cognitive function in
    in early stage (2) 4: 7
    Piaget's stages of development (2) 4: 2
    social perspective on (2) **17: 1–8**
  definition (2) 4: 1
  development (2) **4: 1–15**

Adolescence *(continued)*
  early (2) 4: 5–7
  Erikson's stages (2) 4: 2
  and family development (2) 5: 8
  historical perspectives on (2) 4: 2
  impact of early versus late maturation (2) 4: 6
  late (2) 4: 8
  latency transition to (2) 3: 5
  major physical events at (2) 9: 5
  middle (2) 4: 8
  onset of puberty in (2) 9: 4–5
  peer group alienation in (1) 24: 7
  psychoanalytic concepts of (2) 4: 3, 5
  psychosocial tasks of (2) 4: 6–8
  secular trend for lowered age of menarche (2) 4: 1
  stages (2) 4: 3–8
    biological (2) 4: 3, 4
    early (2) 4: 5–7
    late (2) 4: 8
    middle (2) 4: 8
    psychoanalytic (2) 4: 3, 5
  termination (2) 4: 1
Adolescents. *See also* Adolescence; Children
  adjustment disorders in (2) **51: 1–6.** *See also* Adjustment disorders
    clinical manifestations (2) 51: 4–5
    life events causing (2) 51: 2–3
    treatment issues (2) 51: 5–6
    validity of concept (2) 51: 3
    variation of clinical features (2) 51: 2
  affective disorders in, epidemiology (3) 12: 18
  alcohol abuse in (2) 35: 2–3
    prevalence (2) 35: 1–2
  amphetamine and sympathomimetic agents abuse in (2) 35: 4–5
  anorexia nervosa in (2) 40: 7–8; **102: 1–9.** *See also* Anorexia nervosa
    epidemiology (3) 12: 19
  antisocial personality in (1) 23: 2; (3) 19: 10–11
  arylcyclohexylamine derivatives abuse in (2) 35: 5
  attention deficit disorder in (3) **66: 1–22.** *See also* Attention deficit disorder
    prognosis (3) 66: 9
  barbiturate abuse in (2) 35: 3–4
  borderline personality disorder in (2) **42: 4–7**
    behavior therapy (2) 42: 6
    drugs (2) 42: 7
    parent involvement (2) 42: 7
    psychotherapy (2) 42: 5–6
    treatment (2) 42: 5–7
  bulimia in (2) 40: 6–7
  chronic illness impact on (2) 4: 14–15
  cocaine abuse in (2) 35: 4
  community mental health programs targeted to (2) 69: 5
  compliance in medical regimen by (2) 4: 14
  cortisol levels related to delinquency in (2) 9: 9
  delinquency in. *See* Conduct disorders; Juvenile delinquency

depression in (1) 59: 11–12
  dexamethasone suppression test in (2) 30: 6–7
  diagnosis (2) 30: 4
  differential diagnosis (1) 59: 11–12
  epidemiologic studies (3) 12: 16–17
  mood fluctuations and misery distinguished from (2) 4: 11–12
  prevalence (2) 4: 9–10
  sleep disorders in (2) 30: 7; 52: 10
  treatment (2) 30: 7–8
    lithium (2) 30: 7
    psychotherapy (2) 30: 7
    tricyclic antidepressants (2) 30: 7
developmental psychopathology in (2) 4: 11–15
  chronic illness impact (2) 4: 14–15
  drug abuse (2) 4: 13–14
  mood fluctuations and misery (2) 4: 11–12
  sexuality and pregnancy (2) 4: 12–13
drug abuse in. *See under* substance abuse in *below*
eating disorders in (2) **40: 1–8.** *See also* Eating disorders, in children and adolescents
epidemic hysteria in, epidemiologic studies (3) 12: 17
epidemiologic studies of psychiatric disorders in (3) 12: 16–19. *See also* Child psychiatry,
family therapy of (2) **62: 1–11.** *See also* Family therapy, of children and adolescents
firesetters (1) 25: 5
group psychotherapy for (2) **63: 1–7.** *See also* Group therapy, for children and adolescents
  developmental considerations (2) 63: 6
hallucinogen abuse in (2) 35: 5
histrionic personality disorder in (1) 19: 6
hospital and residential treatment for (2) **64: 1–9.** *See also* Hospitalization; Residential treatment
  in psychiatric emergencies (2) 62: 11
hypothalamic-pituitary-gonadal axis in (2) 9: 3–4
hysterical personality disorder in (1) 19: 6
increasing mortality rate of (2) 4: 2
insomnia in (2) 52: 10–11
interviewing in psychiatric assessment (2) 20: 2–4
leading causes of death in (2) 4: 2
learning disabilities impact on (2) 48: 7–8
manic-depressive illness in (2) 30: 5
marijuana in (2) 35: 5
mental health services for (3) 12: 26
as mentally disordered offenders (3) 28: 24–25
mood fluctuations and misery in (2) 4: 11–12
narcissistic personality disorder in (1) 18: 5
neuroleptics in, embarrassing side effects (2) 59: 13
opioid abuse in (2) 35: 4
parents relationship with (2) 4: 10–11
pharmacology of psychotropic medications in (2) **59: 1–22.** *See also* Psychopharmacology, in children and adolescents
phencyclidine abuse in (2) 35: 5

pregnancy in, biological and psychosocial risks (2) 4: 13
psychiatric assessment in (2) **20: 1–15.** *See also* Children, psychiatric assessment in
psychiatric emergencies in (2) 62: 9–11
psychological tests in (2) 21: 6–10
  academic achievement (2) 21: 10
  adaptive assessment (2) 21: 9–10
  cognitive assessment (2) 21: 6–7
  neuropsychological assessment (2) 21: 7–9
  personality (2) 21: 10
psychoses in, epidemiology (3) 12: 18
rebelliousness in (2) 4: 10–11
schizophrenia in, epidemiology (3) 12: 18
sedative-hypnotic abuse in (2) 35: 3–4
self behavioral assessment by (2) 11: 9
self-consciousness of (2) 17: 4
sexual behavior in
  conflicting values and (2) 4: 12
  trend toward younger age of inititation (2) 4: 12–13
sexuality of (2) 4: 12–13
sleep disorders in (2) 52: 8–11
  insomnia (2) 52: 10–11
  narcolepsy (2) 52: 8–9
  sleep apnea-hypersomnia syndrome (2) 52: 9–10; 105: 11
societal impact in U.S. (2) 4: 1–2
somatoform disorders in (2) **47: 1–7.** *See also* Conversion disorders, in children and adolescents
stuttering in (2) 49: 2–3
substance abuse in (2) 4: 13–14; **35: 1–6.** *See also* Substance abuse
  alcohol (2) 35: 2–3
  amphetamine and sympathomimetic agents (2) 35: 4–5
  antisocial personality disorder related to (2) 35: 2
  arylcyclohexylamine derivatives (2) 35: 5
  barbiturates and sedative-hypnotics (2) 35: 3–4
  cocaine (2) 35: 4
  contributing factors (2) 35: 2
  epidemiologic studies (3) 12: 17–18
  hallucinogens (2) 35: 5
  high school statistics on (3) 17: 9
  marijuana (2) 35: 5
  opioids (2) 35: 4
  peer group related to (2) 35: 2
  personality factors in (2) 35: 2
  phencyclidine (2) 35: 5
  psychodynamics (2) 35: 2
suicidal behavior in (1) 71: 5–6
  cognitive development and (2) 11: 14
  developmental aspects (2) 11: 13–14
  epidemiology (2) 11: 13–14; (3) 12: 18, 19
    attempts (3) 12: 18
    prevalence (2) 4: 12
superego in (2) 4: 12

thinking development in (2) 17: 3–4
  imaginary audience (2) 17: 4
  personal fable (2) 17: 4
turmoil and unrest in (2) 4: 8–10
violent deaths in, epidemiology (3) 12: 19
Adoption studies
  in affective disorders (1) 62: 15–16; (3) 53: 4–5
  of alcoholism (3) 53: 10
  application in psychiatric research (2) 10: 2
  in schizophrenia (1) 54: 7–8; 62: 8–10; (3) 15: 7; 53: 12
    schizophrenia spectrum disorder (1) 62: 9
Adrenal disorders
  hyperplasia (2) 88: 10
    gender identity in virilized female with (2) 9: 6–7
    gender-role behavior in (2) 9: 7
    and intelligence (2) 9: 8
    male characteristics in female patients (1) 45: 4
    and sexual orientation (2) 9: 7–8
  psychiatric manifestations (2) 88: 8–10
    Addison's disease (2) 88: 9–10
    Cushing's syndrome (2) 88: 8–9
    hyperadrenocorticism (2) 88: 8–9
    hypoadrenocorticism (2) 88: 9–10
    steroid psychosis (2) 88: 9
Adrenal insufficiency
  organic mental disorders in children due to (2) 34: 7
  psychiatric manifestations (2) 88: 9–10
Adrenarche (2) 9: 3
Adrenergic blockers, beta. *See* Beta-adrenergic blockers; Propranolol
Adrenergic-cholinergic balance hypothesis (3) 55: 3–5
Adrenogenital syndrome, psychiatric manifestations (2) 88: 10. *See also* Adrenal disorders, hyperplasia
Adrenoleukodystrophy, organic mental disorders in children due to (2) 34: 8
Adversity. *See also* Stressful life events
  in depression (1) 63: 5–9
  distant events role in psychiatric disorders (1) 63: 11
  methodologic problems in quantifying (1) 63: 3
  mode of action in psychiatric disorders (1) 63: 11–12
  predictive power and specificity in psychiatric disorders (1) 63: 10–11
  in psychiatric disorders (1) 63: 3–12
  in schizophrenia (1) 63: 9–10
  social correlates (1) 63: 8–9
  and vulnerability to depression (1) 63: 6–8
Advertising, smoking and alcohol abuse related to (2) 129: 5
Advocacy
  legislation on (3) 35: 14
  for mental patients (3) 35: 13–15
  in treatment planning (2) 56: 9

Affect
  comparison between pathologic and normal de-
      pression (1) 40: 3
  depressive, definition (1) 40: 2–3
  evaluation in mental status examination in chil-
      dren (2) 20: 11
  in major psychiatric syndromes (2) 95: 2
  in psychodynamic mental status examination (1)
      6: 10–11
  in schizophrenia (1) 53: 9
  shallowness of (1) 28: 10
Affective disorders (1) **59: 1–12; 61: 1–26.** *See also*
      Bipolar disorder; Depression
  atypical (1) 59: 4–5
  in avoidant personality (1) 24: 9
  biological heterogeneity in (1) 61: 4–5
  biological model for (1) 3: 2–5
  borderline personality disorder related to (1) 3: 6
  brain metabolism in (1) 64: 13
  in bulimia (2) 102: 5
  in children and adolescents (2) **30: 1–8.** *See also*
      Depression, in children
    diagnosis (2) 30: 1–4
    differential diagnosis (2) 30: 5
    epidemiology (2) 30: 5; (3) 12: 18
    etiology (2) 30: 6–7
    historical background (2) 30:
    juvenile manic-depressive illness (2) 30: 4–5
    treatment (2) 30: 7–8
  classification (1) 59: 1–2; 60: 2; 64: 7; (3) 13: 1
    before DSM-III (1) 59: 5–7
    genetic considerations (1) 62: 18–19
    relevant to treatment (1) 61: 2–5
  clinical course (1) 60: 11
  in cyclothymia (1) 3: 4
  definition (1) 60: 2; (3) 13: 1
  in dependent personality disorder (1) 26: 3
  depression (1) **59: 8–12.** *See also* Depression
  depression in physical illness distinguished from
      (1) 61: 2
  depressive neurosis relation to (1) 40: 1
  differential diagnosis (1) 59: 4–6
    in children (2) 30: 5
  DSM-III criteria for (1) 59: 1–4
  in elderly (2) 119: 4–5
  endocrine causes and correlates (1) 61: 2; (2) 9:
      10
  epidemiology (1) **60: 1–12;** (3) **13: 1–13**
    bipolar disorder (1) 60: 7–11; (3) 13: 8–12
    in children (2) 30: 5
    depression (1) 60: 2–7; (3) 13: 1–8
    nonbipolar major depression (1) 60: 2–7; (3)
        13: 1–8
    unsolved problems (3) 13: 12–13
  etiology
    in children (2) 30: 6–7
    neurotransmitter hypothesis (3) 55: 1–2
  as final common pathway (1) 61: 2

  in frontal lobe syndrome (1) 28: 10
  genetics (1) 3: 3; **62: 12–19;** (3) 53: 4–9
    adoption studies (1) 62: 15–16; (3) 53: 4–5
    biological markers and linkage study (1) 62: 17–
        18
    heterogeneity (1) 62: 18–19
    mode of inheritance (1) 62: 16–17
    population and family studies (1) 62: 12–14
    schizophrenia and (1) 62: 19–20
    twin studies (1) 62: 14–15; (3) 53: 4
  hallucinogens causing (2) 35: 5
  historical background (1) 52: 18–20
    classification (1) 52: 18–19
    psychoanalysis impact (1) 52: 19–20
  HLA antigens as marker in (1) 62: 17–18
  Huntington's disease related to (3) 12: 20–21
  hypothalamic-pituitary-adrenal axis in (1) 64: 10–
      12; (3) 55: 5
  insulin insensitivity in (1) 64: 12
  major depression (1) **59: 8–12.** *See also* Depression
  markers in (3) **53: 4–9**
    antigens in blood (3) 53: 7
    behavioral excitation with amphetamine chal-
        lenge (3) 53: 6–7
    catechol-O-methyl transferase levels (3) 53: 8
    cholinergic hypersensitivity (3) 53: 5
    cholinergic rapid eye movement test (3) 53: 7
    dexamethasone suppression test (3) 53: 5
    event-related potentials (3) 53: 8
    lithium intracellular accumulation in red cells
        (3) 53: 6
    methadone and metoclopramide challenge (3)
        53: 6
    monoamine oxidase levels in platelets (3) 53: 7–
        8
    monoamines (3) 53: 6
    muscarinic cholinergic receptors (3) 53: 8
    neurologic and cognitive deficits (3) 53: 9
    REM sleep (3) 53: 5
    skin conductance-electrodermal activity (3) 53:
        8
    TSH response to TRH challenge (3) 53: 6
    tyramine levels in urine (3) 53: 9
  medical illness causing (1) 61: 3
  mood-congruent and incongruent symptoms in (1)
      59: 2–3
  morbid risk (1) 62: 12–14
  neurobiological model for (1) **64: 1–2, 7–15**
    altered receptor function (1) 64: 9–10
    metabolic function in brain (1) 64: 12–13
    monoamine hypothesis (1) 64: 8–9
    neurotransmitters and neuropeptides in (1) 64:
        10–12
    research advances in (1) 64: 7–8
  neurochemistry of (1) 3: 3
  neuropsychological assessment (1) 72: 14
  neurotransmitters in (1) 61: 4; (3) **55: 1–8.** *See
      also* Neurotransmitters

adrenergic-cholinergic balance hypothesis for (3) 55: 3–5

catecholamine hypothesis (3) 55: 2–3

etiologic hypotheses (3) 55: 1

final common pathway hypothesis (3) 55: 7–8

models between psychological and biological explanations (3) 55: 7–8

opioid hypothesis (3) 55: 6

receptor down-regulation hypothesis (3) 55: 6

research strategies in (3) 55: 1–8

serotonin hypothesis (3) 55: 5–6

serotonin-norepinephrine dichotomy hypothesis (3) 55: 6

norepinephrine in (1) 64: 8–9

organic (1) 59: 5; (2) 87: 12–13

  in children (2) 34: 2

  definition (2) 87: 1

overlap with neurotic and personality disorders (1) 61: 1

personality characteristics predisposing to (1) 61: 5

personality disorders associated with (1) 3: 2–5; 14: 3

prevention (1) 61: 24–26; (3) 13: 13

primary versus secondary (1) 59: 6

prognosis (1) 60: 11

psychobiological final common pathway hypothesis (3) 55: 7–8

REM sleep latency in (3) 55: 4

right hemispheric deficit in (1) 72: 14

schizoaffective disorder as form of (1) 70: 2–3. See also Schizoaffective disorder

schizoaffective disorder distinguished from (1) 70: 6

and schizophrenia (1) 62: 19–20; 70: 2. See also Schizoaffective disorder

schizophrenia boundary with (1) 53: 18–19

seasonal variation in (1) 61: 3–4

secondary (1) 61: 2–3

serotonin in (1) 64: 8–9; (3) 55: 5–6

suicide in (3) 20: 12–14

treatment (1) **61: 1–26**

  bipolar disorder (1) 61: 18–24

  in children (2) 30: 7–8

  classification relevant to (1) 61: 2–5

  depression (1) 61: 5–18. See also under Depression

  personality type related to (1) 61: 5

  underdiagnosis in adolescents (1) 61: 24–25

  vasopressin in (1) 64: 12

Affective personality disorders, biological model for (1) 3: 2–5

Aftercare, patients' rights to (3) 35: 10–13

Age. See also Adolescents; Children; Elderly

antisocial personality disorder related to (3) 19: 5

  at onset (3) 19: 10–11

  and remission (3) 19: 12–13

biological (2) 4: 3

as bipolar disorder risk factor (1) 60: 10; (3) 13: 10

and childhood psychiatric disorders (2) 11: 10

as depression risk factor, nonbipolar disorder (1) 60: 6; (3) 13: 5–6

and drug-related behavioral effects (3) 45: 6–7

and neuropsychological assessment (1) 72: 8

and psychological test performance (3) 52: 21–22

as schizophrenia risk factor (1) 54: 13; (3) 15: 8

and sleep timing, duration and character (3) 60: 9

social (2) 4: 3

suicide rates by (3) 20: 4, 5, 10–11

Agency

  definition (3) 36: 5

  in forensic psychiatry (3) 36: 1–5

  informed consent in resolution of conflict in (3) 36: 4

  management of conflicts in (3) 36: 4

  for mentally disordered offender (3) 28: 10–11, 18

  mixed (3) 36: 2–3

  psychiatrist serving various masters (3) 36: 2

  in forensic matters (3) 27: 2

Aggression. See also Passive-aggressive personality

brain role in (1) 45: 3–4

depressive neurosis and (1) 40: 9

endocrine correlates (2) 9: 10–11

in hypochondriasis (1) 35: 12

Aging. See also Elderly

dementia distinguished from (1) 72: 11

and family development (2) 5: 9

neuropsychological function and (1) 72: 11

normal process (2) 119: 1

sexuality in (1) 45: 3

Agitation, in organic brain syndromes (2) 87: 16

Agnosia (2) 87: 11

  finger (3) 52: 10

Agoraphobia. See also Anxiety disorders

age of onset (1) 33: 5

clinical presentation (1) 33: 4–5

definition (1) 33: 2

dependent personality disorder distinguished from (1) 26: 3

depression distinguished from (1) 33: 6

differential diagnosis (1) 33: 6

drug and alcohol abuse in (1) 33: 5

DSM-III criteria for (1) 33: 2

family studies (3) 14: 10

fears in (1) 33: 4

genetics of (1) 33: 9

natural course (1) 33: 5

without panic attacks (1) 32: 3–4

  behavior modification in (1) 10: 6–7

  clinical presentation (1) 33: 4

  definition (1) 33: 2

  drug therapy (1) 10: 6, 7

  DSM-III on (3) 14: 5

  etiology (1) 33: 9

  genetic factors in (1) 33: 9

  treatment (1) 33: 11–13

Agoraphobia, without panic attacks, treatment
      (continued)
      combined use of anti-panic medication and
            psychotherapy (1) 33: 11–12
      efficacy (1) 33: 12
      psychotherapy (1) 33: 11–12
   panic attacks causing (1) 33: 4
   prevalence (1) 33: 3
   psychosis distinguished from (1) 33: 6
   social phobia distinguished from (1) 33: 7
   stressful life events in (1) 41: 8
   treatment (1) 33: 11–13
      behavioral programs (1) 33: 12–13
      efficacy (1) 33: 12
   trusted companion effect in (1) 33: 4
   twin studies (3) 14: 10
Agranulocytosis, neuroleptics causing (1) 55: 25–26
Agraphia (3) 52: 6–7
AIDS. *See* Acquired immune deficiency syndrome
Airway obstruction, in sleep apnea (3) 61: 8
Akathisia
   neuroleptics causing (2) 91: 3; 95: 7
   treatment (1) 55: 23, 24
Al-Anon (2) 89: 10
Alateens (2) 89: 10
Alatots (2) 89: 10
Alcohol
   advertising influence on use (2) 129: 5
   cellular effects (2) 89: 2
   cognitive dysfunction related to (3) 21: 7–8
   costs of disease related to (2) 79: 1–2
   hallucinations related to (2) 87: 13
   health problems related to (3) 18: 2–3. *See also*
            Alcohol abuse; Alcoholism
   health promotion in prevention of abuse (2) 129:
            5–6
   historical aspects of use (2) 89: 1
   jealousy related to (2) 87: 14
   maternal ingestion, and attention deficit disorder
            (2) 36: 3
   per capita consumption in U.S. (3) 18: 5–6
   psychotropic drugs used with (2) 59: 20
   sanctions influence on control of abuse (2) 129: 5–
            6
   smoking related to use (2) 129: 5
   statistics on use (3) 18: 2
   teratogenic effects (3) 12: 23
Alcohol abuse (2) **89: 1–23**; (3) **18: 1–16**. *See also*
            Alcoholism; Substance abuse
   in adolescents (2) 35: 2–3
      prevalence (2) 35: 1–2
   in adulthood (3) **18: 1–16**
   aggressive acts related to (2) 37: 6
   in agoraphobia (1) 33: 5
   anxiety related to (3) 18: 14–15
   clinical description (2) 89: 4–5
   cognitive function in (1) 72: 12
   costs to society (3) 3: 3–5
   definition (2) 89: 2–3

   depression associated with (1) 59: 9–10; (3) 18:
            11–14
   differential diagnosis (2) 89: 7
   DSM-III on (2) 89: 2–3
   epidemiology (2) 89: 3–4; (3) **18: 1–16**
   etiology (2) 89: 5
   family impact of (3) 18: 2–3
   insomnia related to (3) 61: 6–7
   liver cirrhosis deaths related to prevalence (3) 18:
            3–5
   mental illness related to (3) 18: 9–16
   neuropsychological assessment in (1) 72: 11–12
   in panic disorder (1) 32: 11
   prevalence (3) 18: 3–9
      in adolescents (2) 35: 1–2
   problems in definition and measurement (3) 18: 1
   psychosocial dysfunction related to (3) 18: 15–16
   scope of problem (3) 18: 2–3
   in social phobia (1) 33: 6
   treatment (2) 89: 7–12
      controlled drinking (2) 89: 4
Alcohol amnestic disorder, amnesia distinguished
            from (1) 39: 6
Alcohol dehydrogenase, as marker in alcoholism (3)
            53: 10
Alcohol dependence. *See also* Alcoholism
   controlled drinking in (2) 89: 4
   definition (2) 89: 2
Alcohol hallucinosis (2) 35: 3
Alcoholics Anonymous (2) 89: 9–10
Alcohol intoxication
   in adolescents (2) 35: 2–3
   alcohol levels related to (2) 35: 2–3
   DSM-III criteria for (2) 35: 3
   idiosyncratic (2) 35: 3
Alcoholism. *See also* Alcohol abuse; Substance abuse
   antisocial personality related to (3) 19: 6
   attention deficit disorder related to (2) 89: 6
   biomedical factors in (2) 89: 5
   blackouts in (2) 89: 3
   clinical description (2) 89: 4–5
   cognitive recovery in (3) 52: 19–20
   communication of suicidal intent in (1) 71: 7
   concept of cure in (2) 89: 10
   counselors with previous history (2) 89: 4–5
      relapse (2) 89: 5
   dementia due to (2) 87: 8–9
   depression complicating (1) 59: 10
   diagnosis (2) 89: 5–7
   differential diagnosis (2) 89: 7
   disease concept (2) 89: 1
   etiology (2) 89: 5
   genetics (2) 89: 2–3; (3) 53: 9–10
      adoption studies on (3) 53: 10
      family studies on (3) 53: 9
      twin studies on (3) 53: 9
   history-taking in (2) 89: 5–6
   Korsakoff's syndrome in. *See also* Korsakoff's syn-
            drome

markers in (3) 53: 9–12
  acute reaction to ethanol (3) 53: 11
  2-butanediol (3) 53: 11
  dopamine beta-hydroxylase (3) 53: 11
  ethanol-metabolizing enzymes and acetaldehyde
    (3) 53: 10
  linkage studies (3) 53: 11–12
  monoamine oxidase (3) 53: 10–11
nervous system role in etiology (2) 89: 6–7
neuropsychological assessment in (1) 72: 11–12
neuropsychological deficits in (3) 52: 17–18
other substances abused in (2) 89: 3
personality disorders predisposing to (2) 89: 3, 5
predisposing factors (2) 89: 5
prevention (2) 89: 12; (3) 12: 24
primary form (2) 89: 6–7
protecting factors (2) 89: 3, 5
psychiatrist role in (2) 89: 2
psychological manifestations (2) 89: 3
psychotherapy benefit in (1) 11: 5
in remission (2) 89: 3
secondary (2) 89: 7
suicide in (1) 71: 3, 4; (3) 20: 12
  recent loss related to (1) 71: 4
  risk (1) 71: 10
treatment (2) 89: 7–12
  controlled drinking (2) 89: 4
  disulfiram (2) 89: 10–12
  family services (2) 89: 9–10
    for patient not ready to be seen (2) 89: 7–8
  hospitalization (2) 89: 9
  initial detoxification (2) 89: 8
  psychotherapy (2) 89: 8
  self-help groups (2) 89: 9
underdiagnosis (1) 71: 9
withdrawal syndrome, treatment (2) 89: 8
Alcohol withdrawal delirium (2) 35: 3
Alcohol withdrawal syndrome (2) 35: 3
Aldomet. See Methyldopa
Alexander, Franz, contributions to psychosomatic
    medicine (2) 76: 3; 78: 2–4
Alexia (3) 52: 6
Alexithymia (1) 35: 1–2
  in masked depression (2) 100: 4
  in medical illness (2) 99: 3
  in psychogenic pain disorder (1) 35: 9
  in psychosomatic disorders (2) 78: 5
Alienation
  in avoidant personality (1) 24: 4–5. See also
    Avoidant personality
  peer group (1) 24: 7
Alkalosis
  metabolic, and panic attack (1) 32: 8
  respiratory, and panic attack (1) 32: 7–8
Allegiance
  conflict for psychiatrist in forensic psychiatry (3)
    36: 3
  definition (3) 36: 5
Allele (1) 62: 3

Alliance
  existential (3) 36: 6
  in forensic psychiatry (3) 36: 4–8
  in involuntary commitment (3) 36: 12
  irrational (3) 36: 7
  medical (3) 36: 5–6
  rational (3) 36: 6–7
  situational (3) 36: 8
Alpha-adrenergic receptors
  neuroleptic interaction with (1) 55: 20
  and neuroleptic side effects (1) 55: 25
Alpha-delta sleep disorder (2) 105: 8–9
Alprazolam. See also Benzodiazepines
  in agoraphobia with panic attacks (1) 33: 11
  in depression with anxiety (1) 61: 11
  in panic disorder (1) 32: 11–12
  psychiatric side effects (2) 91: 3
Alveolar hypoventilation syndrome (2) 105: 9–12.
    See also Sleep apnea
Alzheimer's disease (1) 73: 5–8
  acetylcholine role in (1) 73: 7–8
  aphasia in (1) 73: 6–7
  brain pathology in (1) 73: 5–6
  clinical manifestations (1) 73: 6–7
  coexisting illnesses (2) 119: 2–3
  computed tomography in (3) 51: 6
  delusions and hallucinations in (1) 73: 7
  depression in (1) 59: 12
  diagnosis (2) 119: 1–2
  drug therapy in (2) 119: 3–4
  genetic factors (1) 73: 8; (3) 21: 7
  incidence (2) 119: 1
  locus ceruleus neurons in (3) 44: 6
  neurochemistry of (1) 52: 15–16; 73: 7–8; (2) 87:
    8
  neurologic signs in (1) 73: 7
  neurotransmitters in (1) 52: 15–16
  pathophysiology (2) 87: 8
  personality change in (1) 28: 4, 8
  Pick's disease distinguished from (1) 28: 4
  prognosis (2) 87: 7
  supportive treatment (2) 119: 4
Amantadine
  in extrapyramidal side effects of neuroleptics (1)
    55: 23, 24
  psychiatric side effects (2) 91: 7
Ambition, sex differences in (2) 17: 5
Ambivalence
  in dependent personality disorder (1) 26: 3
  in passive-aggressive personality disorder (1) 26: 5
Ambulatory care
  of chronic mental patients (3) 6: 7–9
  comprehensive health centers (2) 69: 5
  medical setting for treating psychiatric patient (3)
    22: 6–8
  for mentally disordered offenders (3) 28: 16–18
  neighborhood service center (2) 69: 4–5
  office-based private psychiatric practice (3) 22: 5–
    6

Ambulatory care *(continued)*
  psychiatric patient characteristics (3) 22: 5
  treatment planning for (2) 56: 7
Amenorrhea, in anorexia nervosa (2) 102: 3
American Academy of Child Psychiatry (2) 1: 5
American Association of Psychiatric Clinics for Children (2) 1: 5
American Orthopsychiatric Association, history (2) 1: 3–4
American Psychiatric Association, Model State Law on Civil Commitment of the Mentally Ill (3) 32: 8–9
Amines, biogenic. *See* Catecholamines; Dopamine; Neurotransmitters; Serotonin
Amino acids, as neurotransmitters (3) 43: 2
Amitriptyline. *See* Antidepressants
Amnesia (1) **39: 2–6**; (3) 71: 6–10. *See also* Dissociative disorders
  in alcoholism (2) 89: 3
  anterograde (1) 73: 18; (3) 71: 6–7
  bitemporal versus diencephalic (2) 13: 4
  brain in (2) 13: 4; (3) 71: 7–8
  case studies (1) 39: 3–4
  classification (1) 39: 3
  and competency to stand trial (3) 27: 6
  continuous (1) 39: 3
  definition (1) 39: 2–3
  in dementia (1) 72: 11
  diagnosis (1) 39: 5–6
    difficulties in (1) 39: 3
  diencephalon in (3) 71: 7
  differential diagnosis (1) 39: 5–6
  after electroconvulsive therapy (2) 87: 10–11
  epidemiology (1) 39: 5
  etiology (1) 39: 5
  fugue state distinguished from (1) 39: 3
  functional versus organic (3) 71: 14
  generalized (1) 39: 3
  after head injury (1) 72: 10; (3) 71: 7
  incidence (1) 39: 5
  localized (1) 39: 3
  multiple personality distinguished from (1) 39: 9
  new learning related to (3) 71: 7–10
    declarative (3) 71: 9–10
    procedural (3) 71: 8–10
  physiologic model (1) 39: 5
  protein synthesis inhibitors producing (2) 13: 6
  psychogenic, brief reactive psychosis distinguished from (1) 70: 13
  regression role in (1) 39: 5
  retrograde (3) 71: 6–7
    functional (3) 71: 14
    test of (3) 71: 12–13
  selective (1) 39: 3
  social model (1) 39: 5
  stages of (1) 39: 3
  symptoms at onset (1) 39: 4–5
  in temporal lobe lesions (3) 71: 7
  treatment (1) 39: 6

Amnesic syndrome (2) 87: 10–11. *See also* Organic mental disorders
  in children (2) 34: 2
  definition (2) 87: 1, 10
  etiology (2) 87: 10–11
  treatment (2) 87: 11
    memory disturbance in (2) 87: 16
    psychotherapy (2) 87: 17
  Wernicke's encephalopathy causing (2) 87: 10
Amok (1) 68: 12
Amoxapine, psychiatric side effects (2) 91: 2
Amphetamines. *See also* Stimulants
  abuse (2) 35: 4–5; (3) 17: 13–14
  in attention deficit disorder (2) 59: 6; (3) 66: 15
    methylphenidate compared with (3) 66: 17–18
    pemoline compared with (3) 66: 18
    side effects (3) 66: 18–19
  catecholamine effects of (3) 55: 2
  challenge test in depression (3) 53: 6–7
  growth effects (3) 66: 19
  legal restrictions on (3) 17: 13
  in narcolepsy (2) 105: 13–14; (3) 61: 13
  organic mental disorders precipitated by (2) 34: 5–6
  pharmacokinetics in children (2) 59: 4
  psychiatric side effects (2) 91: 4
  psychosis due to (1) 64: 4; (2) 90: 8–9
    animal model for (3) 46: 6–12
  stereotypies due to (3) 46: 10–11
  structure (2) 59: 6
  tolerance to (2) 35: 4
Amputation, phantom pain after (2) 104: 5
Amygdaloid. *See* Limbic system
Amytal interview. *See* Sodium amytal
Anaphylaxis, brain modulation of (2) 128: 8
Anatomy. *See* Neuroanatomy
Androgens (2) 9: 2. *See also* Sex hormones; Testosterone
  adrenal secretion at adrenarche (2) 9: 3
  antiandrogens for sexually dangerous offender (3) 28: 23–25
  homosexuality related to deficiency at critical period (1) 45: 7
  prenatal use
    and gender identity (2) 9: 7
    and gender-role behavior (2) 9: 7
    and sexuality (1) 45: 3–4
    and sexual orientation (2) 9: 8
  psychiatric manifestations of (2) 88: 15
  and sexual differentiation in fetus (2) 9: 2
  sexual disorders related to (2) 88: 15
  in sexuality (1) 45: 2, 3
  and spatial ability (2) 9: 8–9
Anemia, factitious (2) 101: 4
Anesthesia
  in electroconvulsive therapy (3) 68: 1
  interaction with monoamine oxidase inhibitors (2) 111: 8–9
  lithium interaction with agents (2) 111: 10

organic mental disorders precipitated by (2) 34: 5
Anger
  as antidepressant side effect (2) 59: 15
  in stress-response syndromes (1) 41: 11
  suppressed, coronary heart disease related to (2) 126: 4–5
Angiotensin, and limbic-hypothalamic-pituitary axis dysregulation in melancholia (3) 54: 8
Anhedonia
  in children (2) 30: 2
  in depression (2) 30: 2
Animal models (3) **46: 1–18**
  of anxiety disorders (3) 14: 4
  of attention deficit disorder (2) 36: 5
  categories (3) 46: 1–2
    empiric or "assay" (3) 46: 1
    etiologic (3) 46: 2
    treatment-induced (3) 46: 1–2
  of depression
    behavioral despair in (3) 55: 7
    learned helplessness in (3) 55: 7
    separation (3) 55: 7
  dreaming (3) 60: 8
  of electroconvulsive therapy (3) 68: 5–6
  of hallucinogens (3) 46: 12–18
    face validity (3) 46: 17–18
    parallels between effects on humans (3) 46: 16
    treatment validity (3) 46: 16–17
  of limbic-hypothalamic-pituitary axis dysregulation in mel melancholia (3) 54: 4–8
  new directions in (3) 46: 4–5
    bidirectional development of modes (3) 46: 4
    drug-induced behaviors as models (3) 46: 4–5
    emphasis on symptoms or behavioral dimensions (3) 46: 4
  sleep requirements (3) 60: 8
  stimulant-induced psychosis (3) 46: 5–12. See also Stimulants, psychosis induced by, animal model for
  validation criteria in (3) 46: 2–3
    common conceptual derivation (3) 46: 3
    face validity (3) 46: 3
    treatment validity (3) 46: 2–3
Anomia, suicide related to (1) 71: 2
Anonymity, of psychotherapist (1) 8: 4
Anorexia, stimulants causing (3) 66: 19–20
Anorexia nervosa (2) 40: 7–8; **102: 1–9**
  bulimia in (2) 40: 7; 102: 5
  clinical description (2) 40: 7; 102: 3–4
  definition (2) 40: 7; 102: 1
  depression distinguished from (2) 40: 7
  differential diagnosis (2) 40: 7
  DSM-III diagnostic criteria (2) 102: 1
  endocrine correlates (2) 9: 10
  epidemiology (2) 102: 2; (3) 12: 19
  etiology (2) 40: 7; 102: 5–6
  family dynamics in (2) 110: 4–5
  historical background (2) 102: 1
  hypothalamic function in (1) 28: 7; (2) 102: 3–4

menstrual function in (2) 102: 3
  prognosis (2) 102: 9
  psychopathology in (2) 102: 4
  starvation effects in (2) 102: 3
  treatment (2) 40: 7–8; 102: 7–9
    behavior therapy (2) 40: 8; 102: 7–8
    drugs (2) 102: 8
    enhancing adolescent deficits (2) 102: 8
    hospitalization (2) 102: 7–8
    as outpatient (2) 102: 8–9
    psychotherapy (2) 40: 8; 102: 8
    results (2) 102: 9
    weight gain methods (2) 102: 7–8
  triangulation of family in (2) 110: 5
  weight loss in (2) 102: 3
Anosognosia (1) 28: 9; (2) 87: 11
Antabuse. See Disulfuram
Anthropology, in psychiatry (3) 2: 1–2. See also Cross-cultural psychiatry; Culture
Antiandrogens, for sexually dangerous offender (3) 28: 23–25
Antianxiety drugs. See also Hypnotics; Sedatives
  in children (2) 39: 8; 59: 16–18
    pharmacokinetics (2) 59: 17
    side effects (2) 59: 17
    tolerance and dependence after use (2) 59: 17
  withdrawal syndrome (2) 90: 10–11
Antibiotics, psychiatric side effects (2) 91: 6
Antibodies (2) 128: 1–2. See also Immune system
  in brain lesions (2) 128: 8
  in schizophrenia (2) 128: 13–14
Anticholinergic drugs
  in Alzheimer's disease (2) 119: 3
  in depression (3) 55: 5
  interactions with other drugs (2) 111: 3
  mood effects (3) 55: 4–5
  psychiatric side effects (2) 91: 5
  toxic hallucinatory state due to (2) 90: 8
  tricyclic antidepressants (2) 111: 5–6. See also Antidepressants, tricyclic
Anticoagulants, in cerebrovascular disease (2) 87: 9
Anticonvulsants
  in antisocial personality disorder (1) 10: 3
  in attention deficit disorder (3) 66: 20–21
  in behavior disorders in children (2) 59: 18
  interaction with tricyclic antidepressants (2) 111: 6–7
  organic mental disorders precipitated by (2) 34: 6
  psychiatric side effects (2) 91: 7
Antidepressants. See also Imipramine
  in Alzheimer's disease (2) 119: 3
  in borderline personality disorders (1) 17: 12
  in cancer (2) 104: 3–4
  cardiac effects (2) 99: 5–6
  caution when used by suicidal patient (1) 71: 9
  in children and adolescents (2) 59: 10–11, 14–16
    in attention deficit disorder (2) 59: 8, 14
    in depression (2) 59: 8, 14–15
    in enuresis (2) 59: 8, 14

Antidepressants, in children and adolescents *(continued)*
follow-up in (2) 59: 11
interactions with other drugs (2) 59: 11
mechanism of action (2) 59: 14
medical workup prior to use (2) 59: 10, 19
pharmacokinetics (2) 59: 14
side effects (2) 59: 10–11, 15–16
tapering dosage at end of therapy (2) 59: 16
in chronic depression (1) 10: 4–5
in depression, in elderly (2) 119: 4–5
in depressive pseudodementia (2) 87: 8
heterocyclic (1) 61: 8–11
in depression (1) 61: 8–11
interactions with other drugs (1) 61: 10–11
maintenance treatment in depression (1) 61: 12
pharmacology (1) 61: 8–11
side effects (1) 61: 9
in treatment-resistant chronic depression (1) 61:
17
tricyclics compared with (1) 61: 9
mechanism of action (3) 50: 10–11
down-regulation of receptors (3) 55: 6
in medically ill (2) 99: 5–6
monoamine oxidase inhibitors. *See* Monoamine
oxidase inhibitors
in obsessive-compulsive disorder (1) 10: 7; 34: 9
organic mental disorders in children precipitated
by (2) 34: 6
for pain disorder in depression (2) 104: 10–11
psychiatric side effects (2) 91: 2–3
and receptors
of beta-adrenergic agonists (1) 64: 9–10
of neurotransmitters (3) 50: 10–11
in schizoaffective disorder (1) 70: 7
serotonin-norepinephrine dichotomy explaining
different response of depression to (3) 55:
6
side effects (2) 99: 5–6
tapering dosage at end of therapy (2) 59: 16
terminology (1) 61: 8
tricyclic. *See also under* heterocyclic *above*
adverse effects (2) 111: 6
in agoraphobia without panic attacks (1) 10: 6–
7
in agoraphobia with panic attacks (1) 33: 11
anticholinergic action (2) 111: 5–6
anticonvulsants, interaction with (2) 111: 6–7
antihypertensive drugs, interaction with (2) 111:
6
in anxiety disorders (1) 32: 12
arrhythmias related to (2) 111: 6
in attention deficit disorder (2) 36: 11; (3) 66:
20
bipolar disoder induced by (1) 59: 8
catecholamine effects of (3) 55: 2
in children (2) 30: 7; 59: 10–11, 14–16
chlorvynol, interaction with (2) 111: 1, 2
circadian rhythm effects (3) 59: 5

controversy on benefit versus liability of (3) 72:
1
in depression (1) 61: 7–10
in children (2) 30: 7
in generalized anxiety disorder (1) 10: 5
heterocyclics compared with (1) 61: 9
interaction with other drugs (2) 111: 5–7
locus ceruleus inhibition by (1) 32: 7
mechanism of effect (2) 111: 4–5
in myocardial infarction (2) 118: 3
in narcolepsy (3) 61: 13
and norepinephrine and serotonin (3) 50: 10
in panic disorder (1) 10: 6; 32: 7, 11
side effects
psychiatric (2) 91: 2
receptor interactions related to (3) 50: 12–13
muscarinic-cholinergic interactions (3) 50:
12
noradrenergic alpha-receptor interactions
(3) 50: 12–13
timing of drug administration based on biological rhythms (3) 59: 13
in treatment-resistant chronic depression (1) 61:
17–18
use of monoamine oxidase inhibitors with (1)
61: 11
Antigens (2) 128: 1
in affective disorders (3) 53: 7
histocompatibility. *See* Histocompatibility antigens
Antihistamines
in extrapyramidal side effects of neuroleptics (1)
55: 24
as hypnotics (3) 61: 15
organic mental disorders precipitated by (2) 34: 6–
7
as sleep inducers in children (2) 59: 18
Antihypertensive drugs
antipsychotic drugs, interaction with (2) 111: 4
monoamine oxidase inhibitors interacting with (2)
111: 8
psychiatric side effects (2) 91: 5; 118: 8
tricyclic antidepressants interacting with (2) 111: 6
Anti-inflammatory agents, psychiatric side effects (2)
91: 4
Antilirium. *See* Physostigmine
Antimalarials
organic mental disorders precipitated by (2) 34: 5
psychiatric side effects (2) 91: 6–7
Antineoplastic drugs, organic mental disorders precipitated by (2) 34: 5
Antipsychotic drugs. *See also* Neuroleptics *and under
specific agent*
in Alzheimer's disease (2) 119: 3
with anticholinergic properties (2) 111: 3
and attention in schizophrenia (3) 65: 9–10
in borderline personality disorder (1) 10: 2
in cancer (2) 104: 4
classes of (1) 55: 3–5

comparison of compounds with differing efficacy (3) 50: 3
drugs comprising (2) 111: 2
in generalized anxiety disorder (1) 10: 5
informed consent for (3) 30: 12–13
  in acute setting (3) 30: 13
  explaining tardive dyskinesia (3) 30: 13
  information required to be disclosed in (3) 30: 4
interactions with other drugs (2) 111: 2–5
malpractice related to adverse effects (3) 29: 10
organic mental disorders precipitated by (2) 34: 6
in paranoid disorders (1) 68: 15
  paranoid personality disorder (1) 10: 4
patients' right to refuse (3) 35: 5–7
psychiatric side effects (2) 91: 3
in schizoaffective disorder (1) 70: 7
in schizoid personality disorder (1) 10: 4
in schizophrenia, evidence for efficacy (1) 55: 5–7
in schizophreniform disorder (1) 70: 10
sedatives interacting with (2) 111: 2–3
structure (1) 55: 4–7
Antisocial behavior. *See also* Conduct disorder; Juvenile delinquency
antisocial personality distinguished from (1) 23: 2, 3, 4
diagnostic evaluation (2) 37: 7–8
EEG in (1) 23: 4
and extraversion (1) 2: 20
in frontal lobe syndrome (1) 28: 10
psychotherapy benefit in (1) 11: 5
Antisocial personality (1) **23: 1–10**
age related to (3) 19: 5
  at onset (3) 19: 10–11
antisocial behavior distinguished from (1) 23: 2, 3, 4
anxiety and (3) 19: 7
association with other diagnoses (3) 19: 6–7
biochemical findings (1) 23: 4
in children and adolescents (1) 23: 2
children of patient with (3) 19: 12
classification (1) 23: 2
clinical correlates (1) 23: 4–7
community programs for (1) 23: 8
conduct disorder in children related to (3) 19: 4–5
consequences of laws dealing with (1) 23: 10
course and prognosis (1) 23: 6–7
creativity related to (1) 23: 6
criminal behavior distinguished from (1) 23: 3
criminality associated with (1) 23: 6
and dangerousness (1) 23: 10
definition (1) 23: 2; (3) 19: 1
depression and (1) 23: 6–7; (3) 19: 7
diagnosis (1) 23: 2–4
differential diagnosis (1) 23: 3–4
drug abuse and alcoholism related to (2) 90: 5; (3) 19: 6
EEG in (1) 23: 4
emigration and (3) 19: 3

emotional development related to (1) 23: 4–5
epidemiology (3) **19: 1–13**
  association with other diagnoses (3) 19: 6–7
  evidence for rising rate (3) 19: 5–6
  natural history (3) 19: 7–13
  social correlates (3) 19: 3–5
  study designs and methods of ascertainment (3) 19: 1–2
family of (1) 23: 9
genetics (1) 23: 5–6
historical background (1) 23: 1–2
hospital care for
  general psychiatric institution (1) 23: 9
  special programs (1) 23: 7–8
hysteria related to (1) 23: 5
impairment in (3) 19: 11
marriage partners in (3) 19: 11–12
medroxyprogesterone or cyproterone injections for (1) 23: 9
in narcissistic personality disorder (1) 18: 4
natural history (3) 19: 7–13
neurologic correlates in (1) 23: 4
prevalence in various sites (3) 19: 2–3
in prisoners (3) 19: 2–3
psychodynamic correlates (1) 23: 5
psychosurgery for (1) 23: 9
race related to (3) 19: 4–5
remission (3) 19: 12–13
reproductive activity in (3) 19: 11–12
rising rate of (3) 19: 5–6
schizophrenia related to (3) 19: 6–7
sex differences in (3) 19: 3
social class related to (3) 19: 3–4
social correlates (1) 23: 6; (3) 19: 3–5
  age (3) 19: 5
  emigration (3) 19: 3
  race (3) 19: 4–5
  sex differences (3) 19: 3
  social class (3) 19: 3–4
  urbanization (3) 19: 4
somatization disorder related to (3) 19: 7
suicide attempts in (1) 71: 3
symptom frequency in (3) 19: 8–10
treatment (1) 23: 7–9
urbanization and (3) 19: 4
wilderness programs for (1) 23: 8–9
Antisocial personality disorder
affective disorders associated with (1) 3: 4
attention deficit disorder related to (3) 66: 9
drug treatment (1) 10: 3–4
narcissistic personality disorder distinguished from (1) 18: 8
and substance abuse in adolescents (2) 35: 2
Anxiety. *See also* Anxiety disorders; Stress
alcohol abuse associated with (3) 18: 14–15
animal studies (3) 14: 4
arrhythmias related to (2) 118: 5
in avoidant personality (1) 24: 9

Anxiety *(continued)*
  behavioral theories of (2) 39: 1
  benzodiazepine receptors and (1) 32: 8–9
  biological theories (1) 3: 6–8; 32: 6–9; (2) 39: 2,
    5–6
  castration, in surgical patient (2) 121: 2
  in childhood (2) 39: 2–3
  Children's Manifest Anxiety Scale for (2) 23: 7
  cognitive learning approach to (1) 2: 17
  in coronary bypass surgery (2) 118: 3
  danger situations causing (1) 1: 8–9
  definition (3) 14: 1
  denial related to (2) 118: 1
  depression associated with (1) 59: 10; (3) 14: 11
  depression distinguished from (1) 32: 10; 40: 2–3
  in elderly (2) 119: 6–7
    clinical features (2) 119: 6
    treatment (2) 119: 6–7
  fear distinguished from (3) 14: 1
  future research on (3) 14: 11
  hallucinations in children due to (2) 20: 10–11
  hypertension related to (2) 118: 7
  in hyperthyroidism (2) 88: 7
  learning theories (1) 2: 12; 32: 5–6; (2) 39: 5
  measures of (3) 14: 1
  in menopause (2) 120: 8
  in myocardial infarction (2) 118: 2
  panic attacks. *See* Panic disorder
  personality disorders associated with (1) 14: 3
  in phobias. *See also* Phobia
    simple (1) 33: 5
    social (1) 33: 6
  physical appearance as clue to (2) 20: 4
  physical illnesses distinguished from (1) 32: 9–10
  psychic versus somatic manifestations (3) 14: 1
  psychoanalytic concepts (1) 32: 5; (2) 39: 1–2, 4–
    5
  psychological tests in (1) 7: 8
  self-report tests of (1) 7: 8
  separation (2) 39: 4, 5
    behavior therapy (2) 39: 7
    biophysiologic mechanism for (1) 3: 7–8
    conversion disorder distinguished from (2) 47: 6
    depressive illness in children distinguished from
      (2) 30: 5
    development (2) 39: 5
    endogenous versus exogenous (2) 39: 5–6
    epidemiology (3) 12: 16
    in hospitalized patient (2) 121: 2
    imipramine for (1) 32: 6
    panic disorder due to abnormality of (1) 32: 6
    school phobia distinguished from (2) 39: 5
    as somatization disorder (2) 47: 1
    transsexualism related to conflict with (1) 46:
      13–14
  stranger (2) 39: 5
  as symptom of psychiatric and medical illness (3)
    14: 1
  symptoms (1) 32: 2

temperament related to (2) 39: 5
Anxiety disorders (1) **32: 1–12;** (2) **39: 1–9.** *See also*
    Anxiety; Panic disorder
  agoraphobia. *See* Agoraphobia
  and antisocial personality (3) 19: 7
  avoidant disorder (2) 39: 3–4
  catecholamines in (1) 32: 7
  in childhood (2) 39: 2–3
    drug treatment (2) 59: 17
  classification (2) 39: 2
  clinical description (1) 32: 4; (2) 39: 3–4
  community surveys (3) 14: 3
  conduct disorder distinguished from (2) 39: 6
  conversion reactions (2) 95: 12–13. *See also* Con-
    version disorders
  definition (1) 32: 2; (2) 39: 2; (3) 14: 5–6
  diagnosis (1) 32: 10–11; (2) 39: 6
  differential diagnosis (1) 32: 9–11; (2) 39: 6–7
  in drug abuse (2) 90: 9
  DSM-III on (1) 32: 1; (2) 39: 2; (3) 14: 2, 5–6
  emergency management (2) 95: 11–13
  epidemiology (1) 32: 2; (2) 39: 2–3; (3) **14: 1–11**
    community studies (3) 14: 9
    familial patterns (3) 14: 4, 10
    prevalence rates (3) 14: 2, 3, 6–10
    risk factors (3) 14: 4–5, 10–11
    survey from epidemiologic catchment areas (3)
      14: 6–8
    survey of psychotherapeutic drug use (3) 14: 7
    Zurich panel study of young adults (3) 14: 8–9
  etiology (1) 32: 4–9; (2) 39: 4–6
  familial patterns (3) 14: 4, 10
  generalized
    drug therapy (1) 10: 5–6
    DSM-III on (3) 14: 6
  genetics (1) 32: 9
  historical background (2) 39: 1–2; (3) 14: 1–2
  hyperthyroidism distinguished from (2) 88: 7
  hyperventilation (2) 95: 12
  medical illness distinguished from (2) 39: 7
  mitral valve prolapse related to (3) 14: 10–11
  obsessive-compulsive disorder. *See* Obsessive-com-
    pulsive disorder
  over-anxious disorder (2) 39: 3
  panic disorder (2) 95: 11–12. *See also* Panic dis-
    order
  phobias. *See* Phobia
  posttraumatic stress disorder (2) 95: 12
  prevalence rates (3) 14: 2, 3, 6–10
  prevention (2) 39: 8–9
  psychophysiologic symptoms in (2) 39: 3
  reliability of tests for (3) 14: 6
  risk factors for (3) 14: 4–5, 10–11
  secondary problems in (2) 39: 3
  stress-response syndromes. *See* Stress-response syn-
    dromes
  after surgery (2) 121: 6
  transient reactive disturbances distinguished from
    (2) 39: 6–7

treatment (1) 32: 11–12; (2) 39: 7–8
  behavior therapy (1) 32: 12; (2) 39: 7
  in children (2) 59: 17
  in drug abuse (2) 90: 9
  drug therapy (1) 32: 12; (2) 39: 8
  emergency management (2) 95: 11–13
  family therapy (2) 39: 8
  in obsessive-compulsive disorder (1) 34: 5–6
  psychodynamic psychotherapy (1) 32: 12; (2) 39: 7–8
  twin studies (3) 14: 4, 10
Anxiety management training (1) 32: 12
Anxiety neurosis (3) 14: 1–2. *See also* Panic disorder
Anxiolytics. *See* Antianxiety drugs
Apathy
  in frontal lobe syndrome (1) 28: 10
  in Huntington's disease (1) 73: 11–12
  in hydrocephalic dementia (1) 73: 10, 11
  in hyperthyroidism (2) 88: 8
  in Korsakoff's syndrome (1) 73: 19
Aphasia (2) 87: 11; (3) 52: 5. *See also* Language; Language disorder
  in Alzheimer's disease (1) 73: 6–7
  Broca's (3) 52: 5
  childhood (2) **49: 1–10.** *See also* Language disorders
  classification (3) 52: 5–6
  depression in (2) 99: 4
  developmental (3) 67: 1. *See also* Language, developmental disorders
  tests for (3) 52: 8
  Wernicke's (3) 52: 5
Aphonia, causes (2) 20: 9
Apnea, sleep. *See* Sleep apnea
Appetite suppressants, psychiatric side effects (2) 91: 4
Apraxia (2) 87: 11
Aprosodia (2) 99: 4–5
  in right hemisphere syndrome (1) 28: 9–10
Arithmetic abilities, tests (3) 52: 8–9
Arousal, in attention deficit disorder (3) 66: 5–7
Arrhythmias
  biofeedback in (2) 109: 7
  in electroconvulsive therapy (2) 99: 6
  phenothiazines related to (2) 111: 4
  psychiatric aspects in heart disease (2) 118: 5
  tricyclic antidepressants related to (2) 111: 6
Arson (1) 25: 4–5
Articulation
  disorders in childhood (2) 49: 2
    prognosis (2) 49: 2
  tests of (2) 49: 8
Arylcyclohexylamine abuse (3) 17: 14. *See also* Phencyclidine
  in adolescents (2) 35: 5. *See also* Phencyclidine
Asendin. *See* Amoxapine
Asocial character, antisocial personality distinguished from (1) 23: 3
Assessment. *See* Neuropsychological assessment; Psychological tests

Associations, in psychodynamic mental status examination (1) 6: 10
Asthma
  monoamine oxidase inhibitors interacting with drugs used in (2) 111: 8
  systematic desensitization in (2) 109: 9–10
Ataxia, Friedreich's, psychosis in (1) 69: 7
Atherogenesis, pathogenesis in coronary heart disease (2) 126: 5–6
Attachment
  childbirth experience related to parents ability for (2) 39: 9
  development in mother during first few months of infant's life (2) 120: 5
  disorder of infancy (2) 40: 5
  importance in later psychiatric difficulty (3) 12: 23
  in masochistic personality (1) 27: 4
  medication during delivery influencing mother's capacity for (2) 120: 4–5
  reactive disorder, epidemiologic studies (3) 12: 12–13
  role in family development (2) 5: 2
Attention
  in attention deficit disorder (3) 66: 4–5. *See also* Attention deficit disorder
  and brain function (3) 52: 4
  continuous performance tasks and (3) 65: 5–6
  definition (3) 65: 3
  in delirium (1) 73: 13
  determination (3) 52: 4–5
  developmental delay in attention deficit disorder (3) 66: 4
  drugs effect on (3) 65: 9–10
  evaluation in mental status examination (2) 20: 7
  event-related potentials related to (3) 62: 6–8
  as marker in remitted schizophrenia (3) 65: 10
  in psychiatric disorders (3) **65: 1–11.** *See also* Schizophrenia, cognitive function in
  reaction time as determinant of (3) 65: 4
  research on (3) 65: 3–8
  selective (3) 62: 6–8
    in schizophrenia (3) 62: 7–8
  selective deficit in attention deficit disorder (3) 66: 5
  signal detection methodology for (3) 65: 9
  smooth pursuit eye movements (3) 65: 6–7
Attention deficit disorder (2) **36: 1–12;** (3) **66: 1–22**
  activity levels in (3) 66: 7
  adult disorders associated with (3) 66: 9
  adult variants (3) 66: 9
  alcoholism related to (2) 89: 6
  animal models (2) 36: 5
  antisocial personality in (1) 23: 4
  arousal in (3) 66: 5–7
  attentional deficits in (3) 66: 4–5
  borderline personality disorder related to (1) 3: 6; 10: 2
  classification (2) 36: 2; (3) 66: 2–3
  clinical features (2) 36: 5–8; (3) 66: 2–9

Attention deficit disorder *(continued)*
  conduct disorder overlapping but distinct from (3)
        66: 14
  developmental delay in attention in (3) 66: 4, 8
  diagnosis (2) 36: 6–8; (3) 66: 13–15
    criteria for (2) 36: 5–6
    history-taking (2) 36: 6–7
    laboratory tests (2) 36: 8
    neurological examination (2) 36: 7
    physical examination (2) 36: 7
    psychological tests (2) 36: 7–8
  differential diagnosis (3) 66: 14
  dopamine role in (3) 66: 11–12
  drug abuse risk in (3) 66: 20
  DSM-III on (2) 36: 2, 6; (3) 66: 2–3
  EEG in (3) 66: 14
  environmental and psychosocial factors in (2) 36:
        4
  epidemiology (2) 36: 2; (3) 12: 16; 66: 2
  epilepsy distinguished from (2) 36: 6
  etiology (2) 36: 2–4; (3) 66: 9–13
  event-related potentials in (3) 62: 7
  familial and genetic factors in (3) 66: 10
  food additives role in (3) 66: 12–13
  genetics of (2) 36: 4
  head trauma and (2) 36: 3
  hearing loss distinguished from (2) 36: 6
  historical background (2) 36: 1
  hyperactivity in (3) 66: 7
  infant characteristics (3) 66: 7–8
  infections causing (2) 36: 3
  intelligence tests in (3) 66: 14
  lead intoxication and (2) 34: 10; 36: 3; (3) 66: 12
  learning disability associated with (2) 36: 8–9; 48:
        2; (3) 66: 8
  maternal alcohol ingestion and (2) 36: 3
  mental retardation distinguished from (2) 36: 6
  minor physical anomalies in infants associated
        with (3) 66: 8, 10
  neurochemistry (3) 66: 11–12
  neurological factors in (3) 66: 10–11
  pathogenesis (2) 36: 4–5
  peer relationships in (3) 66: 8
  perinatal insult causing (2) 36: 2–3
  pervasive developmental disorders distinguished
        from (2) 36: 6
  prevalence (2) 36: 2
  prognosis (2) 36: 11–12
    in adolescents (3) 66: 9
  progression with age (3) 66: 7–9
  rating scales for (3) 66: 14–15
  Reye's syndrome and (2) 36: 3
  seizure disorders and (2) 36: 4
  sleep disorders in (3) 66: 7
  stimulants in (1) 10: 3
  terminology in (2) 36: 1; (3) 66: 1–2
  Tourette's disorder related to (2) 38: 3
  toxic factors in (2) 36: 3; (3) 66: 12–13

  treatment (2) 36: 8–11; (3) 66: 15–22
    anticonvulsants (3) 66: 20–21
    antidepressants (2) 59: 8, 14
    behavior therapy (2) 36: 9; (3) 66: 21
    caffeine (3) 66: 20
    diet (2) 160: 1–2; (3) 66: 13
    drug management issues (3) 66: 21
      drug holiday (2) 59: 9
    educational (2) 36: 8–9
    lithium (3) 66: 20
    neuroleptics (2) 59: 12; (3) 66: 20
    psychotherapy (3) 66: 21–22
    stimulants (2) 36: 9–11; 59: 4, 6; (3) 66: 15–
        20
      in adults (3) 66: 18
      behavior therapy with (3) 66: 21
      distinguishing good from poor responders (3)
            66: 16
      electronic pupillography after (3) 66: 16
      evoked cortical response to (3) 66: 16
      indications (3) 66: 15–16
      issues in (3) 66: 21
      mechanism of action (3) 66: 6, 11–12
      methylphenidate compared with amphetamine
            (3) 66: 17–18
      as paradoxic response (3) 66: 16–17
      pemoline compared with other agents (3) 66:
            18
      side effects (3) 66: 18–20
      Tourette's disorder precipitated by (3) 66: 19
    tricyclic antidepressants (2) 36: 11; (3) 66: 20
Attribution
  causal (2) 17: 6–7
  in social cognition (2) 17: 4–7
  of success and failure (2) 17: 5–6
Auditory perception, tests of (3) 52: 10–11
Autism. *See also* Developmental disorders, pervasive
  behavioral characteristics (2) 27: 5
  behavior therapy in (2) 27: 9
  clinical description (2) 27: 3–6
  cognitive development in (2) 27: 4
  deafness distinguished from (2) 27: 8
  diagnosis (2) 27: 8–9
  differential diagnosis (2) 27: 8
  DSM-III on (2) 27: 2–3
  in early development (2) 27: 3–4
  epidemiology (2) 27: 3
  etiology (2) 27: 7–8
  event-related potentials in (3) 62: 11
  historical background (2) 27: 1
  immunity in (2) 128: 14
  infantile, epidemiologic studies (3) 12: 13
  language development in (2) 27: 4
  mental retardation distinguished from (2) 27: 8
  neurobiological factors in (2) 27: 7–8
  perceptual development in (2) 27: 4–5
  prenatal insult to nervous system causing (3) 12:
        21

prevention (2) 27: 9
prognosis (2) 27: 6–7
psychotherapy benefit in (1) 11: 5
schizophrenia distinguished from (2) 29: 2
    EEG features (2) 29: 5
    epidemiologic features (2) 29: 3
social development in (2) 27: 5
treatment (2) 27: 9
Autogenic training (2) 109: 3
in Raynaud's disease (2) 109: 7
Autohypnosis
amnesia due to (1) 39: 5
in multiple personality (1) 39: 9
Autoimmune disorders
schizophrenia as (2) 128: 13–14
stress related to (2) 128: 3–4
Autonomic nervous system
adrenergic-cholinergic balance hypothesis of affect-
    ive disorders (3) 55: 3–5
in anxiety disorders (1) 32: 2
classical and operant conditioning of (2) 109: 4
in conversion disorder (1) 35: 6
in mitral valve prolapse (2) 118: 6–7
overactivity in panic disorder (3) 14: 11
sensitivity to stress in children (2) 9: 9–10
sympathetic nervous system. *See* Sympathetic nerv-
    ous system
Autonomy
in adolescence
    in early stage (2) 4: 7
    in late stage (2) 4: 8
psychoanalytic concepts (1) 1: 9–10
Autopagnosia (1) 28: 9
Autopsy, psychological (3) 20: 1
Aversion therapy, in paraphilias (1) 46: 10
Avoidant disorder
in children (2) 39: 3–4
schizoid personality disorder distinguished from (2)
    39: 6
Avoidant personality (1) **24: 1–11**
affective disorders in (1) 24: 9
anxiety disorders in (1) 24: 9
biosocial learning theory for (1) 24: 3
borderline personality distinguished from (1) 24: 8
clinical description (1) 24: 4–6
conflicts in (1) 24: 5–6
constitutional theories on (1) 24: 1–2
dependent personality distinguished from (1) 24: 8
diagnostic criteria (1) 24: 3–4 ‹
differential diagnosis (1) 24: 7–8
disorders coexisting with (1) 24: 9–10
dissociative disorders in (1) 24: 9
DSM-III definition (1) 24: 1, 3–4
epidemiology (1) 24: 4
etiology (1) 24: 6–7
genetic factors in (1) 24: 6
historical forerunners (1) 24: 1–3
infantile fearful patterns in (1) 24: 6

parental rejection and deprecation in (1) 24: 6–7
peer group alienation causing (1) 24: 7
phobias in (1) 24: 9
psychoanalytic conceptions (1) 24: 2–3
psychodynamics (1) 24: 2–3, 6
restricted social experiences in (1) 24: 7
schizoid personality distinguished from (1) 24: 2,
    7–8
schizophrenia in (1) 24: 9–10
schizotypal personality distinguished from (1) 24:
    8
treatment (1) 24: 10–11
Avoidant personality disorder
anxiety causing (2) 39: 4
schizoid personality disorder distinguished from (1)
    16: 3
social phobia distinguished from (1) 33: 7
Axis I codes, in child psychiatry (2) 19: 11
Axis II codes
in child psychiatry (2) 19: 11
circumflex model as integrating framework for (1)
    15: 8–11
sex ratios in (1) 24: 5
Axis III codes, in child psychiatry (2) 19: 11
Axis IV codes, in child psychiatry (2) 19: 11
Axis V codes, in child psychiatry (2) 19: 11
Axons (3) 42: 2, 5–7
diffuse versus specific projections (3) 42: 6
in myelin and saltatory conduction (3) 42: 6–7
myelinated (3) 42: 5–6

Back pain (2) 104: 8–9
biofeedback and relaxation therapy in (2) 109: 8
clinical description (2) 104: 8
epidemiology (2) 104: 8
hospitalization for (2) 104: 9
treatment and prevention (2) 104: 9
Bandura, A., contribution to social learning theory
    (1) 2: 16–17
Barbiturates
abuse by adolescents (2) 35: 3–4
interactions with other drugs (2) 111: 2
psychiatric side effects (2) 91: 4
withdrawal syndrome from (2) 90: 10–11
Basal ganglia disorders
behavioral syndromes (1) 28: 6–7, 11–12
    Huntington's disease (1) 28: 11–12
    Parkinson's disease (1) 28: 11
movement and emotional disorders related to (1)
    28: 7
psychosis related to (1) 69: 5–6
Basal metabolic rate, in puberty (2) 9: 5
Bateson, G., contributions to strategic therapy model
    (1) 9: 4
Bayley Scales of infant development (2) 21: 2

B cells
  early experience effect on (2) 128: 6–7
  in humoral immunity (2) 128: 1–2
Beck, A.T., contributions to behavior therapy (1) 9: 4
Bed-wetting. *See* Enuresis
Behavior
  assessment (2) **23: 1–9**. *See also* Behavioral assessment
  basal ganglia correlates (1) 28: 6–7
  brain correlates (1) 28: 4–7
  contributions to illness (2) **79: 1–8**
    accidents (2) 79: 1
    contradictory messages about (2) 79: 4–5
    cost-effectiveness of psychotherapy on medical care costs (2) 79: 6–8
    costs attributable to preventable disease or injuries (2) 79: 1–2
    delay in seeking help (2) 79: 1
    leading causes of death (2) 79: 1
    public beliefs about (2) 79: 4–5
    strategies for cost reduction after disease occurs (2) 79: 6
    strategies for disease prevention (2) 79: 5–6
  coronary bypass surgery effects on change (2) 118: 4
  description of (2) 23: 1
  emotional (1) 2: 17–18
  global, in schizophrenia (1) 53: 12–13
  health. *See* Health behavior; Illness behavior
  learning theory in explanation of (1) 2: 1–25. *See also* Social learning
  limbic system correlates (1) 28: 6
  psychopathology related to (1) 6: 10
  sexual. *See* Sexual behavior; Sexuality
  tests of. *See* Behavioral assessment; Psychological tests
Behavioral assessment (2) **23: 1–9**
  of children (2) 11: 9; **23: 1–9**
  in classification (2) 23: 2–3
  description (2) 23: 1
  of drug-induced changes (3) 45: 11–13
  interviews (2) 23: 7–9
  need for (2) 23: 1–2
    in classification (2) 23: 1–2
    in describing behavior (2) 23: 1
    in etiologic hypotheses (2) 23: 2
    in evaluating treatment (2) 23: 2
    in prognosis (2) 23: 2
  parents compared with teachers in (2) 11: 8–9
  rating scales (2) **23: 3–7**. *See also* Rating scales
  selection of informants for (2) 11: 8–9
  sources of interest in (2) 23: 2–3
Behavioral inventory, in assessing drug response (3) 45: 10–11
Behavioral medicine (2) **76: 1–7**. *See also* Consultation-liaison psychiatry; Psychosomatic medicine

consultation-liaison psychiatry differences from (2) 76: 5
consultation-liaison psychiatry overlap with (2) 76: 5–6
coronary heart disease related to psychological risk factors (2) **126: 1–8**
definition (2) 76: 2–3
historical aspects (2) 76: 4–5
intellectual tradition in (2) 76: 5–6
psychosomatic medicine differences from (2) 76: 5
psychosomatic medicine overlap with (2) 76: 5–6
Behavioral pediatrics (2) 72: 4
Behavior disorders
  antisocial behavior. *See* Antisocial behavior
  epidemiologic studies in preschool child (3) 12: 13
  in major psychiatric syndromes (2) 95: 2
  parent rating scales for (2) 23: 5
  violent behavior. *See* Violent behavior
Behavior exchange, in family therapy (2) 110: 8
Behavior generalization, and self-perpetuation of abnormal social learning (1) 2: 8–9
Behaviorism (1) 2: 11
  Watson's contributions (2) 1: 4
Behavior potential (1) 2: 15
Behavior Screening Questionnaire (3) 12: 9–10
  for behavior disorders in preschool child (3) 12: 13
Behavior therapy (2) **77: 1–12**
  in agoraphobia (1) 33: 12–13
    without panic attacks (1) 10: 6–7
  in anorexia nervosa (2) 40: 8
  in anxiety disorders (2) 39: 7
  in attention deficit disorder (2) 36: 9; (3) 66: 21
  in back pain (2) 104: 9
  basic principles (2) 77: 1–3
  in borderline personality disorder in children (2) 42: 6
  in bulimia (2) 102: 9
  of children (2) **61: 1–9**
    advances in (2) 61: 7–8
    assessment of outcome (2) 61: 8
    characteristics (2) 61: 1–3
    cognitive therapy (2) 61: 5–6
    conceptual views (2) 61: 1–2
    in conduct problems (2) 61: 3–7
    directive and active treatment prescriptions (2) 61: 2–3
    DSM-III application to (2) 61: 8
    focus of treatment (2) 61: 8–9
    in inpatient programs (2) 64: 14
    limitations (2) 61: 6–9
    meditational versus nonmeditational views (2) 61: 2
    parent and family variables in (2) 61: 7
    parent management training (2) 61: 3–5
    primacy of behavior in (2) 61: 2
    response covariation in (2) 61: 7–8
    scope of (2) 61: 3

social learning theory (2) 61: 2
use of paraprofessionals (2) 61: 2
choice among other orientations (1) 9: 7
cognitive approaches in (1) 9: 4
cognitive social learning theory (2) 77: 4–8
    environment-person-behavior dimensions in (2) 77: 5–7
    implications for therapeutic programs (2) 77: 7–8
    therapies based on (2) 77: 6
for compliance in hypertension therapy (2) 118: 8
consequent control (2) 77: 11–12
contingency arrangements in (2) 77: 5
definition (2) 56: 2; 77: 4
efficacy expectations influence on (2) 77: 6–7
of enuresis (2) 43: 3–4
environmental sources of influence (2) 77: 5
in family therapy (1) 9: 8; (3) 7: 8–9
goals (1) 9: 4
in group therapy of children and adolescents (2) 63: 4
historical background (1) 9: 3–4; 52: 11; (2) 77: 3
learning distinguished from performance in (2) 77: 7
of mentally disordered offenders (3) 28: 15
in mental retardation (2) 28: 6
in migraine headache (2) 104: 7–8
modeling and rehearsal (2) 77: 8–9
in obesity
    mild form (2) 103: 11
    moderate form (2) 103: 9, 10
in obsessive-compulsive disorder (1) 10: 7; 34: 9
in panic and anxiety disorders (1) 32: 12
paradoxical intention (2) 39: 7
personal sources of influence (2) 77: 5–7
in pervasive developmental disorders (2) 27: 9
in phobias (2) 39: 7
rationale for (1) 9: 4
relaxation training (2) 77: 9–10. See also Relaxation training
scope of (2) 61: 1, 3
self-management (2) 77: 6–8
setting for (1) 9: 4
in sexual disorders (1) 47: 10–11
of sexually dangerous offender (3) 28: 23
in social phobia (1) 33: 13
specific treatment approaches in (2) 77: 1–3
stimulus arrangements in (2) 77: 5
stimulus control (2) 77: 10–11
systematic desensitization (2) 109: 1–2
techniques (1) 9: 4; (2) 77: 8–12
    consequent control (2) 77: 11–12
    modeling and rehearsal (2) 77: 8–9
    relaxation training (2) 77: 9–10. See also Relaxation training
    stimulus control (2) 77: 10–11
in Tourette's disorder (2) 38: 6

of type A behavior (2) 126: 6–7
variables potentially useful in producing immediate and maintained change (2) 77: 6
variety of techniques in (2) 77: 3–4
verbal therapy compared for effectiveness with (1) 11: 4
vicarious reinforcement in (2) 77: 5
for weight gain in anorexia nervosa (2) 102: 7–8
Benadryl. See Diphenhydramine
Bender Gestalt test (2) 20: 5–7
of perceptual motor function (3) 52: 12
Benton-Iowa battery (3) 52: 15
Benton Visual Retention Test (3) 52: 12
Benzodiazepines. See also Diazepam
agonists and antagonists (3) 50: 10
alprazolam. See Alprazolam
in antisocial personality disorder (1) 10: 3
in anxiety disorders (1) 32: 12
in children (2) 59: 16–17
cimetidine interaction with (2) 111: 1–2
comparison of various agents (3) 61: 16
in conversion disorder (1) 10: 8
daytime hangover due to (3) 61: 15
depression due to (2) 91: 3
in generalized anxiety disorder (1) 10: 5
half-life of (2) 90: 10
in insomnia (2) 105: 6
interactions with other drugs (2) 111: 2
in myocardial infarction (2) 118: 2
organic mental disorders precipitated by (2) 34: 6
other hypnotics compared with (3) 61: 16
psychiatric side effects (2) 91: 3–4
    in elderly (2) 91: 3–4
receptors for
    and anxiety (1) 32: 8–9
    subtypes (3) 50: 9–10
in schizophrenia (3) 61: 15
in sleep-related myoclonus (2) 105: 8; (3) 61: 11
withdrawal syndrome (1) 32: 12; (2) 90: 10–11; 91: 3; (3) 61: 7
Benztropine mesylate (Cogentin)
in dystonic reactions (2) 95: 7
for extrapyramidal symptoms during rapid tranquilization (2) 95: 5
Bereavement. See also Grief reaction
grief and mourning distinguished from (2) 95: 13
latency-aged child response to (2) 3: 5
suicide during mourning for spouse (3) 20: 6
uncomplicated (1) 41: 8
Beta-adrenergic blockers. See also Propranolol
in anxiety disorders (1) 32: 11
in panic disorder (1) 32: 7
in schizophrenia, improved cognition in (3) 72: 2–3
in social phobia (1) 33: 13–14
Beta-adrenergic nervous system, in panic disorder (1) 32: 6–7
Binge eating. See Bulimia

Bioavailability, of neuroleptics (1) 55: 9
Biobehavioral factors, in cardiovascular disease (2) **126: 1–8.** *See also* Neurobiology
Biochemistry. *See* Neurochemistry; Neurotransmitters
Biofeedback (2) **109: 4–11.** *See also* Relaxation therapy
  in arrhythmias (2) 109: 7
  in blepharospasm (2) 109: 8
  in cancer (2) 109: 10–11
  clinical applications (2) 109: 5–11
  in conversion disorder (1) 35: 8
  definition (2) 109: 4
  in diabetes management (2) 109: 10
  EEG feedback in (2) 109: 5
  electrodermal feedback in (2) 109: 5
  EMG feedback in (2) 109: 5
  in fecal incontinence (2) 109: 9
  in gastrointestinal disorders (2) 109: 9
  in headache (2) 109: 5–6
  in hypertension (2) 109: 6–7
  in insomnia (2) 109: 10; (3) 61: 5–6
  in irritable bowel syndrome (2) 109: 9
  learning model of (2) 109: 4
  mechanism of action (2) 109: 4–5
  methods (2) 109: 5
  in migraine headache (2) 104: 7–8
  negative side effects (2) 109: 11
  in neuromuscular rehabilitation (2) 109: 7–9
  origins of (2) 109: 4–5
  in pain disorders (2) 109: 8–9
  in panic and anxiety disorders (1) 32: 12
  in rheumatoid arthritis (2) 109: 7
  systems approach to (2) 109: 4–5
  in temporomandibular joint syndrome (2) 109: 8–9
  thermal feedback in (2) 109: 5
  in torticollis (2) 109: 8
Biogenic amines
  in affective illness (1) 64: 8–9
  as neurotransmitters (3) 43: 2. *See also* Acetylcholine; Catecholamines; Dopamine; Neurotransmitters; Serotonin
Biological endowment, role in child development (2) 2: 2
Biological learning theory (1) 2: 18–22
Biological markers. *See* Markers
Biological model. *See also* Brain; Neurobiology; Neurochemistry
  of affective disorders (1) 3: 2–5; **64: 1–2, 7–15**
  in borderline personality disorders (1) 3: 5–6
  in disorders with neuroanatomical determinants (1) 3: 9–10
  historical background (1) 52: 4
  improvements in knowledge (1) 64: 1
  in lithium-responsive labile or explosive personality (1) 3: 8–9
  of memory (3) **71: 1–6**

from molecular biological simplification to more realistic central nervous system dynamics (3) 72: 1–6
  in panic anxiety and agoraphobia (1) 3: 6–7
  of personality disorders (1) **3: 1–10**
  of schizophrenia (1) **64: 1–2, 4–7, 13–15**
Biological psychiatry
  applications of neuropsychology in (3) 52: 15–21
  decline and rebirth (1) 52: 6–7
Biological rhythms (3) **59: 1–14**
  biorhythm theory (3) 59: 7
  circadian rhythms (3) **59: 1–6.** *See also* Circadian rhythms
  circannual rhythms (3) 59: 7–11
    internal (3) 59: 11
  classification (3) 59: 1
  clinical applications (3) 59: 11–14
  definitions in (3) 59: 14
  and drug-related behavioral effects (3) 45: 7
  infradian rhythms (3) 59: 7
  in insomnia (3) 59: 11–12
  in jet lag (3) 59: 12–13
  light therapy of disorders (3) 59: 13–14
  menstrual cycle (3) 59: 7. *See also* Menstrual cycle
  neuroanatomy of oscillators and photoperiodism (3) 59: 8–10
  neuropharmacology of seasonal rhythms (3) 59: 10–11
  photoperiodism (3) 59: 7–8
  seasonal rhythms, in mental disorders (3) 59: 11. *See also* Seasonal variations
  in shift workers (3) 59: 12
  in sleep (3) 60: 1–7. *See also* Sleep
  in timing of clinical sampling (3) 59: 13
  in timing of psychotropic medication (3) 59: 13
  ultradian rhythms (3) 59: 6–7
Biomedical model (2) 116: 1
Biopsychosocial model (2) 76: 1; 108: 1; 116: 1. *See also* Psychosomatic medicine
  in consultation-liaison psychiatry (2) 110: 1–2
  in psychosomatic medicine (2) 78: 3–4
Biopsychosocial spiral (2) 110: 2–4
Biorhythm theory (3) 59: 7
Biosocial learning theory (1) 2: 21–22
Bipolar disorder
  age as risk factor for (1) 60: 10; (3) 13: 10
  atypical (1) 59: 4–5
    clinical features (1) 59: 8
    terminology (1) 61: 22–23
  classification (1) 59: 3; 60: 2, 7–8; (3) 13: 2
    before DSM-III (1) 59: 5–7
    genetic considerations (1) 62: 18–19
  clinical course in (1) 59: 7
  clinical description (1) 59: 7–8
  colorblindness related to (1) 62: 17
  complications (1) 59: 8
  consequences (3) 13: 12

cyclic effects in (1) 59: 7, 8
definition (1) 60: 2; (3) 13: 1
depressive neurosis distinguished from (1) 40: 6
DSM-III on (1) 60: 2
epidemiology (1) 60: 7–11; (3) 13: 8–12
etiology (1) 59: 8
genetic factors in (1) 60: 10–11; (3) 13: 11–12
  adoption studies (1) 62: 15–16
  biological markers and linkage study (1) 62: 17–18
  heterogeneity (1) 62: 18–19
  mode of inheritance (1) 62: 16–17
  population and family studies (1) 62: 12–14
  twin studies (1) 62: 14–15
hospitalization for (1) 60: 9; (3) 13: 9–10
incidence rates (1) 60: 9; (3) 13: 9–10
insulin insensitivity in (1) 64: 12
lifetime risk (1) 60: 8–9; (3) 13: 10
lithium transport in (1) 64: 10
manic-depressive illness related to (1) 60: 8
marital status in (1) 60: 10; (3) 13: 11
premorbid personality in (1) 59: 7–8
prevalence rates (3) 13: 8, 9
prevention (1) 61: 24–25
primary versus secondary (1) 59: 7
prognosis (1) 59: 8; 60: 11
race as risk factor for (1) 60: 10; (3) 13: 11
rapid cyclers (1) 61: 23–24
risk factors for (1) 60: 10–11; (3) 13: 10–12
seasonal variation in (3) 59: 11
season of birth and (3) 13: 12
sex as risk factor for (1) 60: 10; (3) 13: 10
social class in (1) 60: 10; (3) 13: 10–11
thyrotropin-releasing hormone in (1) 64: 11
treatment
  atypical disorder (1) 61: 22–23
  carbamazepine (1) 61: 21–22
  chronic mania (1) 61: 24
  cyclothymic disorder (1) 61: 23
  depressive phase (1) 61: 18
  drug holidays (1) 61: 22
  light therapy (1) 61: 22
  lithium (1) 59: 8; 61: 18–21
    compliance and psychotherapeutic issues (1) 61: 20–21
    workup prior to use (1) 61: 18
  maintenance phase (1) 61: 19–20
  manic phase (1) 61: 19
  rapid cyclers (1) 61: 23–24
  sleep deprivation (1) 61: 22
  in woman desiring pregnancy (1) 61: 22
tricyclic antidepressants inducing (1) 59: 8
twin studies in (3) 13: 11–12
types of onset in (1) 61: 24, 25
Bipolar I disorder (1) 59: 7–8. *See also* Bipolar disorder

Bipolar II disorder (1) 59: 4, 8; 61: 22–23. *See also* Bipolar disorder, atypical
Bipolar III disorder (1) 61: 12
Birth injury, schizophrenia related to (1) 54: 13–14; (3) 15: 7–8
Bitemporal amnesia (2) 13: 4
Blackmail, in forensic situations (3) 36: 8–9
Blacks, schizophrenia in (1) 54: 13; (3) 15: 8. *See also* Race
Bleeding disorder, factitious (2) 101: 4
Blepharospasm, biofeedback in (2) 109: 8
Bleuler, E., on schizophrenia (1) 53: 1–2, 10
Blindness, and puberty (2) 9: 5
Blink reflex, habituation to strong stimuli in schizophrenia (3) 65: 6
Block Design test (3) 52: 11, 22
Blood, in neurochemistry studies on children (2) 12: 2
Blood pressure, measurement (2) 109: 6. *See also* Hypertension
Body image
  in adolescence
    chronic impact effect on (2) 4: 14
    in early stage (2) 4: 6
    in middle stage (2) 4: 8
  disturbance in obesity (2) 103: 3
  improvement after surgery for obesity (2) 103: 8
Bonding. *See* Attachment
Borderline
  definition of term (1) 17: 2–7
  as denoting spectrum case of schizophrenia or manic-depression (1) 17: 6–7
  as dynamic constellation (1) 17: 5–6
  historical background of use of term (1) 17: 1–2
    after psychoanalysis (1) 17: 1–2
  as level of function (1) 17: 3–4
  as personality type (1) 17: 5
  as prognostic statement (1) 17: 6
  as syndrome (1) 17: 4–5
Borderline personality
  antisocial personality distinguished from (1) 23: 3
  avoidant personality distinguished from (1) 24: 8
  definition (2) 82: 6–7
  impact of medical illness in (2) 82: 7–8
  in medical setting (2) 82: 7–8
  psychodynamics (2) 82: 7
  treatment approach in medical illness (2) 82: 8
Borderline personality disorder (1) **17: 1–13**
  affective disorders related to (1) 3: 6
  agreement and disagreement between diagnostic systems (1) 17: 8–9
  attention deficit disorder overlap with (1) 10: 2
  attention deficit disorder related to (1) 3: 6
  biological markers in (1) 17: 11–12
  biological model (1) 3: 5–6
  in children and adolescents (2) **42: 4–7**
    clinical features (2) 42: 5

Borderline personality disorder, in children and
    adolescents *(continued)*
      drugs (2) 42: 7
      treatment (2) 42: 5–7
        behavior therapy (2) 42: 6
        parent involvement (2) 42: 7
        psychotherapy (2) 42: 5–6
        termination (2) 42: 7
    classification (1) 17: 2
    clinical description (1) 17: 8–10
    controversy on nature (1) 10: 2
    definition (1) 3: 5; 10: 1–2; 17: 2–7. *See also* Bor-
      derline
    dependent personality disorder distinguished from
      (1) 26: 3
    depressive neurosis distinguished from (1) 40: 7
    dexamethasone suppression test in (1) 17: 11
    diagnostic criteria for (1) 3: 5–6; 17: 4–5
    differential diagnosis (1) 17: 10–11
    drug therapy (1) 10: 2–3
    DSM-III on (1) 17: 5; (2) 101: 7
    epidemiology (1) 17: 7–8
    etiology (1) 17: 10
    in factitious illness (2) 101: 7
    function in (1) 17: 3–4
    genetics of (1) 3: 6
    historical background (1) 17: 1–2
      after psychoanalysis (1) 17: 1–2
    histrionic personality disorder overlap with (1) 19:
      2
    incest relationship to (1) 17: 8
    manic depressive psychosis distinguished from (1)
      17: 11
    monoamine oxidase levels in (1) 17: 11
    narcissistic personality disorder distinguished from
      (1) 18: 9
    natural history (1) 17: 9–10
    neurosis distinguished from (1) 17: 3, 10
    in premenstrual syndrome (1) 17: 8
    prevalence (1) 17: 7
    prognosis (1) 17: 9–10
    psychoanalytic concept (1) 17: 1–3; (2) 42: 5
    psychodynamics (1) 17: 5–6
    psychological tests in (1) 17: 11–12
    psychosis in (1) 3: 6
    REM sleep latency in (1) 17: 11
    schizophrenia distinguished from (1) 17: 10–11
    schizotypal personality disorder distinguished from
      (1) 16: 7
    sex ratio in (1) 17: 7–8
    suicide in (1) 17: 9–10
    traits typical of (1) 3: 5
    transference in (2) 101: 7
    treatment (1) 17: 12–13
      drugs (1) 17: 12
      organic overlay patient (1) 17: 12
      psychoanalysis (1) 17: 12–13

      psychotherapy (1) 17: 12–13
Boston Process Approach (3) 52: 14
Boxers, dementia of (1) 73: 6
Brain. *See also* Neurobiology
    and aggression (1) 45: 3–4
    in Alzheimer's disease (1) 73: 5–7; (2) 87: 8
    amino acids in (3) 43: 2
    in amnesia (3) 71: 7–8
    anatomic correlations for personality change (1)
      28: 4–7
    antibody levels related to lesions (2) 128: 8
    in arousal (3) 66: 5–6
    and behavior (1) 28: 4–7; (3) **42: 1–18**
      future research on (3) 42: 17–18
    benzodiazepine receptor and anxiety (1) 32: 8–9
    biogenic amines in (3) 43: 2
    biologic aspects of psychiatric disorder. *See* Biologi-
      cal model; Neurobiology; Neurochemistry
    Brodmann's diagram of cerebral cortex (3) 42: 13
    chemical communication in (3) **43: 1–7**. *See also*
      Neurochemistry; Neurotransmitters
    circadian rhythm oscillator in (3) 59: 2–3, 8–10
    clonidine effect on (2) 38: 4–5
    comparing left-right hemispheric abilities (1) 72: 3,
      9–10
    in decision making (1) 28: 6
    in delirium (1) 73: 13; (2) 87: 6
    depression in disorders of (2) 99: 4–5
    development
      hyperactivity and (2) 13: 7–8
      by latency (2) 3: 3–4
      neuronal systems (2) 13: 7–8
    electrical activity measurements in (1) 64: 3
    in electroconvulsive therapy (3) 68: 3–5
    event-related potentials in (1) 64: 3
    evoked potentials and function of (3) **62: 1–14.**
      See also Evoked potentials
    extracellular fluid space significance in (1) 64: 4
    function and dysfunction in neurologic and psy-
      chiatric disorders (3) 42: 9–18
      corticostriatal projection (3) 42: 11
      dopaminergic transmission (3) 42: 9–10
      future of research in (3) 42: 17–18
      inhibitory network of neostriatum (3) 42: 15
      neostriatium and psychiatric disorders (3) 42: 17
      neostriatium role in movement (3) 42: 15–17
      neostriatium structure and function (3) 42: 10–
        15
      spiny I neuron of neostriatum (3) 42: 10–11
      synaptic action of neostriatal afferents (3) 42: 11–
        15
    and gender identity (1) 45: 3–4
    hemispheric lateralization of functions (1) 72: 3, 9–
      10
      declarative memory (3) 52: 13–14
      dominance for verbal and nonverbal functions
        (3) 67: 10–13

event-related potentials in study (3) 62: 11
left hemispheric deficit in schizophrenia (1) 72:
    15
neuropsychological assessment (2) 21: 9
right hemisphere syndromes (1) 28: 9–10
    deficit in affective disorders (1) 72: 14
sex differences in fetal development (2) 9: 8
in specific developmental language disorders (2)
    49: 6
in speech and language (3) 67: 10–13
verbal and nonverbal functions (3) 67: 10–13
imaging techniques in psychiatry (3) **51: 1–7**
    cautions and methodologic standards (3) 51: 7
    computed tomography (3) 51: 3
    emission tomography (3) 51: 3–4
    image reconstruction from projections (3) 51: 1–
        2
    magnetic resonance imaging (3) 51: 4–6
    studies with psychiatric patients (3) 51: 6
and immune system (2) 128: 7–9
    cell-mediated immunity (2) 128: 9
    humoral immunity (2) 128: 7–9
in impulse control (1) 25: 2
infections related to psychosis (1) 69: 4–5
in Korsakoff's syndrome (1) 73: 19–20
in language disorders (2) 49: 6–7
and learning (2) 13: 3–4
    developmental aspects (2) 13: 7–8
localization of function in psychiatric disorders
    left hemispheric deficit in schizophrenia (1) 72:
        15
    neuropsychological assessment (1) 72: 9
    right hemispheric deficit in affective disorders
        (1) 72: 14
locus ceruleus role in panic disorder (1) 32: 7–8
mapping electrical activity in (1) 64: 3
mapping neural activity in (1) 64: 3
in memory (2) 13: 3–4; (3) **71: 1–6**
    and education (3) 71: 10
    implications for psychiatry (3) 71: 10
    lesions related to dysfunction (3) 71: 11
metabolic function
    in affective disorders (1) 64: 13
    cerebral blood flow and (1) 64: 13
minimal dysfunction (3) 66: 1–2, 4. *See also* At-
    tention deficit disorder
monoamine neural systems in (3) **44: 1–13.** *See
    also* Monoamine neural systems
in movement (3) 42: 15–17
neurochemical strategies for assessment of function
    (2) 12: 1–5. *See also* Neurochemistry
neuroleptics sites and actions in (1) 55: 14–20
neuropeptides in (3) 43: 2–3
neuropsychological assessment (1) **72: 1–15;** (2)
    21: 7–9; (3) **52: 1–25.** *See also* Neuropsy-
    chological assessment; Neuropsychology
abstraction (3) 52: 8–10

attention (3) 52: 4–5
language (3) 52: 5–8
memory (3) 52: 12–14
perceptual motor abilities (3) 52: 10–12
reaction time (3) 52: 3–4
neurotransmitter pathways in (1) 64: 2–3
in obsessive-compulsive disorder (1) 34: 6
organic syndromes (2) **89: 1–17.** *See also* Organic
    mental disorders; Psychoses, symptomatic
lesions causing psychiatric disorders (1) **69: 1–
    14**
pathological studies in schizophrenia (1) 64: 6–7
in personality. *See* Personality, neurologic disease
    causing changes in
psychiatric disorders in children related to dis-
    orders of (2) 11: 11–12
psychological tests as indirect measure of function
    (3) **52: 1–25.** *See also* Psychological tests
    in impairment (1) 7: 6–7
psychosis related to location of lesion (1) 69: 9–10
    in brain injury (1) 69: 2–3
in sexual response cycle (1) 45: 2
sleep-wake cycle regulation by (3) 60: 1–2, 7
symptoms related to location of lesion (1) 69: 10
syphilis of (1) 69: 5
in visual information processing (3) 71: 4–6
Brainstem reticular system. *See* Reticular activating
    system
Brain tumor
    cell-mediated immunity in (2) 128: 9
    organic mental disorders in children due to (2) 34:
        8
    personality change due to (1) 28: 4
    psychosis in (1) 69: 3–4
Brazelton neonatal assessment scale (2) 21: 2
Briquet's syndrome (1) **35: 14–16;** (2) **100: 7–9**
    acute medical presentations (2) 100: 8
    brief reactive psychosis distinguished from (1) 70:
        13
    clinical description (1) 35: 15
    confused terminology in (2) 100: 7
    conversion disorder distinguished from (1) 35: 4, 5
    danger of prescribing medications in (2) 100: 9
    definition (1) 35: 14–15
    diagnostic criteria (2) 100: 7–8
    DSM-III criteria for (1) 35: 14
    epidemiology (1) 35: 15; (2) 100: 8
    etiology (1) 35: 15; (2) 100: 8–9
    group psychotherapy in (2) 100: 9
    historical background (1) 35: 14; (2) 100: 7
    hypochondriasis distinguished from (1) 35: 15
    original description (2) 47: 1
    treatment (1) 35: 16; (2) 100: 9
Bromocriptine
    personality changes caused by (1) 28: 11
    psychiatric side effects (2) 91: 7
Bromosis, delusions of (2) 100: 5

Bruxism, biofeedback and relaxation therapy in (2)
    109: 9
Bulimia (2) 40: 6–7; **102: 1–10**
    in anorexia nervosa (2) 102: 5
    binge eating in (2) 102: 4–5
    clinical description (2) 40: 6; 102: 4–5
    complications of vomiting in (2) 40: 6
    definition (2) 102: 1–2
    differential diagnosis (2) 40: 6
    DSM-III diagnostic criteria (2) 102: 1–2
    endocrine correlates (2) 9: 10
    epidemiology (2) 102: 2–3
    etiology (2) 40: 6; 102: 6–7
    historical background (2) 102: 1
    in obesity (2) 103: 3
    physiologic complications (2) 102: 5
    psychopathology in (2) 102: 5
    treatment (2) 40: 6–7; 102: 9–10
        cognitive behavioral therapy (2) 102: 9
        drugs (2) 102: 9–10
        group therapy (2) 102: 9
    vomiting and laxative use in (2) 102: 5
Bulimia nervosa (2) 102: 1
Burn-out syndrome
    in antisocial personality (1) 23: 6
    in drug abuse (1) 23: 6
    in schools (2) 70: 4
Buspirone
    in anxiety disorders (1) 32: 12
    in generalized anxiety disorder (1) 10: 5
Butanediol, as marker in alcoholism (3) 53: 11
Butyrophenones. *See also* Antipsychotic drugs; Neu-
        roleptics
    efficacy related to affinity for dopamine receptors
        (3) 50: 3–4
    in schizophrenia
        dosage (1) 55: 12
        preparations (1) 55: 13

Caffeine
    in attention deficit disorder (3) 66: 20
    irritability due to (1) 32: 9
    organic mental disorders precipitated by (2) 34: 6
CAGE questions, in alcoholism (2) 89: 6
Calcium. *See also* Hypercalcemia; Hypocalcemia
    in electroconvulsive therapy (3) 68: 3
    in learning neurophysiology (2) 13: 4–5
    and panic attack (1) 32: 8
Cancer
    consultation-liaison psychiatry in (2) 117: 4
    course of disease disability in (2) 117: 1–3
    depression in (2) 99: 1–2
    hypnosis in (2) 112: 3–4
    nausea and vomiting due to chemotherapy in (2)
        117: 4

    pain in (2) 104: 2–4; 117: 4. *See also* Pain
    personality characteristics and (2) 128: 6
    pre-illness psychopathology in (2) 117: 3
    psychiatric disorders in (2) 104: 3
    psychosocial problems in (2) 117: 4
    psychotherapy in (2) 104: 4
    relaxation therapy and biofeedback in (2) 109: 10–
        11
    stress related to (2) 128: 6
Cannabinoids, toxicity of (2) 90: 4. *See also* Mari-
        juana
Capgras' syndrome (1) 68: 12
Carbamazepine (Tegretol)
    in antisocial personality disorder (1) 10: 3
    in bipolar disorder (1) 61: 21–22
    lithium interaction with (2) 111: 10
    receptor stabilization effects (1) 64: 10
    in temporal lobe epilepsy (1) 28: 8
Carbon monoxide poisoning, organic mental dis-
        orders in children due to (2) 34: 10
Cardiac transplantation. *See* Heart, transplantation
Cardiovascular disease
    biobehavioral factors in (2) **126: 1–8**
    psychiatric aspects (2) **118: 1–9**. *See also* Heart dis-
        ease; Hypertension
Case-control studies (2) 11: 2
Case formulation (1) 6: 12
Case identification, in child psychiatry (3) 12: 3
Case management
    for chronic mental patients (3) 6: 10–11
    political issues in funding for chronic mental pa-
        tients (3) 6: 13
Case register, utilization of mental health services
        studied by (3) 22: 2
Castration anxiety
    in paraphilias (1) 46: 8–9
    research on (1) 1: 15
Cataplexy, in narcolepsy (2) 52: 8; 105: 13; (3) 61:
        12
Catapres. *See* Clonidine
Catathymic crisis (1) 25: 5
Catatonia (2) 95: 6
    in schizophrenia (1) 53: 12–13, 15
Catecholamines. *See also* Dopamine; Epinephrine;
        Monoamine neural systems; Norepineph-
        rine
    in affective disorders (3) 55: 2–3
    in anxiety disorders (1) 32: 6
    in attention deficit disorder (2) 36: 4–5; (3) 66:
        11
    in biological stress response systems (1) 41: 13
    in depression (3) 50: 10–11
    in memory and learning (2) 13: 6–7
Catechol-O-methyl transferase, as marker in affective
        disorders (3) 53: 8
Categorical classification system. *See* Classification,
        categorical system

Categorical perspective (1) 6: 6
Category Test, of nonverbal abstraction ability (3) 52: 9
Cathartic method, Freud's use (1) 1: 3
Cattell infant intelligence scale (2) 21: 2–3
Causal attribution (2) 17: 6–7
  behavioral causality (2) 17: 6–7
  causal direction (2) 17: 6
  likeness of causal elements (2) 17: 6
Cell-mediated immunity. *See* Immune system, cell-mediated
Central nervous system. *See also* Brain; Neurological disorders
  in behavior (1) 28: 4–7
  and personality change (1) **28: 1–12.** *See also* Personality, neurologic disease causing change in
Cerebral blood flow
  and brain metabolism (1) 64: 13
  in schizophrenia (1) 64: 6–7
Cerebrospinal fluid (CSF), in neurochemistry studies on children (2) 12: 2
  special considerations in obtaining specimen (2) 12: 9
Cerebrovascular disease
  biofeedback in rehabilitation (2) 109: 8
  clinical manifestations (1) 73: 9–10
  dementia in (1) 73: 8–10; (2) 87: 9
  diagnosis (1) 73: 9–10
  emotional problems in (1) 73: 9
  neuropathology in (1) 73: 9
  personality change due to (1) 28: 4
  psychosis in (1) 69: 9
  treatment (1) 73: 10
Cerebrum. *See* Brain
Challenge tests, methodologic considerations (2) 12: 6–8
Character disorder. *See* Antisocial personality
Character-spectrum disorder (1) 61: 15
  depressive neurosis distinguished from (1) 40: 8
Chemotherapeutic agents
  organic mental disorders precipitated by (2) 34: 5
  psychiatric side effects (2) 91: 6
Chief complaint (1) 6: 2, 12. *See also* Patient, perspective of problem
Child abuse
  conversion disorder confused with (2) 47: 6
  parental disorder in (2) 50: 4
  reporting statutes on (3) 31: 15–16
Child Assessment Schedule (3) 12: 10
Child Behavior Checklist (2) 23: 6–7; (3) 12: 6–8, 26
  in epidemiologic studies in child psychiatry (2) 11: 6–7
Childbirth. *See also* Postpartum period; Pregnancy
  attachment of infant to parents related to (2) 39: 9
  natural (2) 120: 4

pain determinants in (2) 120: 4, 5
physical symptoms related to ambivalence and conflict in (2) 120: 3
Child development. *See* Development
Child guidance clinics (3) 12: 26, 27
  historical background (2) 69: 2
  modifications and improvements to reach poor people (2) 69: 3–4
Child molestation, offenders (3) 28: 23
Child psychiatry. *See also* Children
  assessment in (2) **20: 1–15.** *See also* Children, psychiatric assessment in
  for children not living in stable environment (2) 56: 7–8
  classification in (2) **19: 1–15;** (3) 12: 26–27. *See also* Classification, in child psychiatry
    diagnosis and (2) 19: 3–5
    DSM-III in (2) 19: **9–14;** (3) 12: 4–5
    DSM-IV prospects (2) 19: 14–15
    epidemiologic findings and (2) 11: 12–13
    historical background (2) 19: 1–2
    improvements in (2) 11: 4
    theoretic approaches (2) 19: 5–9
  community (2) **69: 1–9**
    concepts in (2) 69: 2–3
    definition (2) 69: 1
    historical aspects (2) 69: 1–2
    service programs in (2) 69: 3–7
      child guidance clinics (2) 69: 3–4
      consultation (2) 69: 6–7
      mental health education (2) 69: 7
      neighborhood and comprehensive health centers (2) 69: 4–5
      in public schools (2) 69: 6
      targeted to specific populations (2) 69: 5–6
    training in (2) 69: 7–8
  epidemiologic studies in (2) **11: 1–14;** (3) **12: 1–28**
    accuracy of data collection (3) 12: 5
    in adolescence
      early (3) 12: 16–17
      late (3) 12: 18–19
      middle (3) 12: 17–18
    applications to patterns of service utilization (3) 12: 25–26
    assessment instruments (2) 11: 6–8
    biologic factors in (3) 12: 20–22
    case definition in (2) 11: 4; (3) 12: 4–5, 7, 12
    case identification (3) 12: 3
    and causation (2) 11: 10–12; (3) 12: 4, 20–23
    choosing sample (2) 11: 3–4
    clarification of disorder (3) 12: 4–5, 7, 12
    in classification (2) 11: 12–13
    cohort studies (3) 12: 27–28
    in cross-cultural research (3) 12: 27
    developmental issues (2) 11: 13–14
    diagnostic approaches (3) 12: 5, 7

Child psychiatry, epidemiologic studies in *(continued)*
  in elementary school-age disorders (3) 12: 14–16
  evaluation of studies (3) 12: 11–12
  family influences (3) 12: 4
  future directions (3) 12: 26–28
  genetics (3) 12: 28
  historical overview (3) 12: 2–4
  information gathering techniques (3) 12: 6–11
  interaction of biological and psychosocial factors in (3) 12: 22
  interview methods (3) 12: 8–10
  natural history studies (3) 12: 3–4
  normal development and deviations from normality (3) 12: 3
  observational methods (3) 12: 10–11
  official records used in (3) 12: 11
  one versus two stage assessment procedure (2) 11: 4–6
  overall indices of prevalence at different ages (3) 12: 19–21
  in preschool disorders (3) 12: 12–14
  prevalence studies (2) 11: 9–10; (3) 12: 4, 19–21
  prevention (3) 12: 23–25
  problems in studying (3) 12: 2
  psychosocial factors (3) 12: 22–23
  purposes (3) 12: 1–2
  questionnaires and checklists (3) 12: 6–8
  selecting informants for behavioral assessment (2) 11: 8–9
  selection of strategy (2) 11: 2
  in treatment selection (3) 12: 27
 group therapy (2) **63: 1–7.** *See also* Group therapy, for children and adolescents
 historical background (2) **1: 1–5; 69:** 1–2
  child guidance clinics (2) 1: 3–4
  child study movement (2) 1: 1–2
  and juvenile delinquency (2) 1: 2–3
  and mentally retarded child (2) 1: 2
  pediatrics impact (2) 1: 4–5
  psychoanalytic concepts (2) 1: 4
  training programs (2) 1: 5
  World War II influence (2) 1: 5
 hospital and residential treatment in (2) **64: 1–19.** *See also* Hospitalization
 legal issues in (2) **71: 1–4**
  children's needs and rights (2) 71: 2–3
  role of clinical expert (2) 71: 3–4
  role of state and role of parents (2) 71: 1–2
 mental hygiene movement in (3) 12: 2
 neurochemical strategies in (2) **12: 1–12.** *See also* Neurochemistry; Neurotransmitters
  brain function studies (2) 12: 1–5
  methodologic considerations
   clinical (2) 12: 5–9
   development (2) 12: 9–11
   laboratory (2) 12: 12
 organizations for (2) 1: 5
 parent-child interactions in (3) 12: 23
 pediatric consultation in (2) **72: 1–7.** *See also* Pediatric consultation
 personality disorders in (2) **42: 1–7.** *See also* Personality disorders, in children
 prevalence of psychiatric disorders (2) 11: 9–10
 psychodynamic factors in (2) **18: 1–8**
  developmental considerations (2) 18: 4–5
  theoretic assumptions (2) 18: 2
  vulnerability and risk (2) 18: 5–8
 psychodynamic therapies in (2) **57: 1–6.** *See also* Psychoanalysis, in child psychiatry
  infants and preschool children (2) 57: 4–5
  range of therapies (2) 57: 4–6
  therapeutic situation (2) 57: 2–3
  transference (2) 57: 3–4
 questionnaires used in (3) 12: 6–8
 research in (2) 1: 1
 school consultation (2) **70: 1–9.** *See also* School, consultation in
 sleep disorders in (2) **52: 1–11.** *See also* Sleep disorders, in children
 spectrum of services required in (2) 64: 3–5
 underutilization of services (3) 12: 25–26
Child rearing, and family development (2) 5: 6
Children. *See also* Adolescents; Child psychiatry; Infants
 adjustment disorders in (2) **51: 1–6.** *See also* Adjustment disorders
 advocacy for proper treatment (2) 56: 9
 affective disorders in (2) **30: 1–8.** *See also* Affective disorders; Depression, in children
 antianxiety drugs in (2) 39: 8
 antisocial personality in (1) 23: 2
 anxiety disorders in (2) **39: 1–9**
  clinical description (2) 39: 3–4
  definition (2) 39: 2
  diagnosis (2) 39: 6–7
  epidemiology (2) 39: 2–3
  etiology (2) 39: 4–6
  prevention (2) 39: 8–9
  treatment (2) 39: 7–8
 attention deficit disorder in (3) **66: 1–22.** *See also* Attention deficit disorder
 avoidant disorder in (2) 39: 3–4
 bed-wetting in (3) 61: 13–14. *See also* Enuresis
 behavioral assessment in (2) **23: 1–9.** *See also* Behavioral assessment
  interviews (2) 23: 7–9
  rating scales (2) 23: 3–7
   by observer (2) 23: 6–7
   by parents (2) 23: 4–6
   by self (2) 23: 7
   by teachers (2) 23: 6
 behavior therapy of (2) **61: 1–9.** *See also* Behavior
 civil commitment of (3) 32: 4
 community mental health services for (3) 5: 10

conduct disorder in (2) **37: 1–9.** *See also* Conduct
disorder
depression in (1) 59: 11. *See also* Depression, in
children
conduct disorder linked to (2) 30: 5
development determining (2) 30: 2
epidemiology (2) 30: 5
grief reaction distinguished from (2) 30: 5
low self-esteem in (2) 30: 3
nonbipolar disorder (1) 60: 6; (3) 13: 7
parental depression related to (2) 30: 6
predisposing to depressive neurosis in adult life
(1) 40: 10
psychomotor retardation in (2) 30: 3
school failure (2) 30: 3
separation anxiety distinguished from (2) 30: 5
separation role in (2) 30: 6
sleep disorder in (2) 30: 3, 7
social withdrawal in (2) 30: 2–3
socioeconomic factors related to (2) 30: 6
treatment (2) 30: 7–8
developmental issues. *See* Development; Developmental disorders
developmental milestones (2) 2: 4–5
difficulty of diagnosis in (2) 2: 3, 6
eating disorders in (2) **40: 1–8.** *See also* Eating disorders, in children and adolescents
event-related potentials in (3) 62: 10–11
family therapy of (2) **62: 1–11.** *See also* Family
therapy, of children and adolescents
gender identity disorders in (1) 46: 16–18; (2) 41:
2–4
group psychotherapy for (2) **63: 1–7.** *See also*
Group therapy, for children and adolescents
hallucinations in (2) 20: 10–11
in anxiety (2) 20: 10–11
drugs causing (2) 20: 10
in infections (2) 20: 10
metabolic disorders causing (2) 20: 10
schizophrenia causing (2) 20: 11
in seizure disorder (2) 20: 10
as stress response (2) 20: 10
history-taking in (2) 20: 2
histrionic personality disorder in (1) 19: 6
hospitalization in psychiatric emergencies (2) 62:
11
hysterical personality disorder in (1) 19: 6
importance of early attention to psychiatric disturbances in (2) 2: 1
insomnia in (2) 52: 7–8
interviewing in assessment (2) 23: 8
language and speech disorders in (2) **49: 1–10;**
(3) **67: 1–13.** *See also* Language disorders;
Speech disorders
learning in
disabilities (2) **48: 1–8.** *See also* Learning disabilities

neurobiology (2) **13: 1–9**
legal rights (2) 71: 2–3
manic-depressive illness in (2) 30: 4–5
memory in, neurobiology (2) **13: 1–9**
mental health services for (3) 12: 25–26
of mentally ill parents (3) 7: 10–12. *See also* Family
mental retardation in (2) **28: 1–8.** *See also* Mental
retardation
mental status examination in (2) 20: 4–12. *See
also* Mental status examination
mutual storytelling in (2) 39: 8
obsessions in (1) 34: 8
obsessive-compulsive disorder in (1) 34: 4
organic mental disorders in (2) **34: 1–11.** *See also*
Organic mental disorders, in children
classification (2) 34: 1–3
clinical characteristics suggesting (2) 34: 1
epidemiology (2) 34: 3
other disorders with physical manifestations in (2)
43: 1–9
encopresis (2) 43: 4–6
enuresis (2) 43: 1–4
night terrors (2) 43: 7–8
sleepwalking (2) 43: 6–7
stuttering (2) 43: 8–9
over-anxious disorder in (2) 39: 3
paradoxical response to stimulants in, neurotransmitters role in (2) 12: 11
of paranoid disorder (1) 68: 4–5
personality inventory for (2) 23: 6
pharmacology of psychotropic medications in (2)
59: 1–22. *See also* Psychopharmacology,
in children and adolescents
prevention of mental illness in children at risk (3)
7: 11–12
projective tests in (2) 21: 6
psychiatric assessment in (2) **20: 1–15**
clinical methods (2) 20: 1–12
concluding evaluation (2) 20: 12
documentation of findings (2) 20: 12
history-taking (2) 20: 2
interviewing (2) 20: 2–4, 13, 15
mental status examination (2) 20: 4–12
fantasies and inferred conflicts (2) 20: 11
intelligence (2) 20: 9
language and speech (2) 20: 8–9
memory (2) 20: 9
nervous system functioning (2) 20: 5–8
physical appearance (2) 20: 4–5
positive attributes (2) 20: 12
thinking processes (2) 20: 9–11
psychological tests (2) 20: 14, 15. *See also* Psychological tests
structured interviews (2) 20: 13, 15
types of (2) 20: 1
psychiatric disorders in
age and (2) 11: 10

Children, psychiatric disorders in *(continued)*
  biologic factors in (3) 12: 20–22
  brain disorders related to (2) 11: 11–12
  demographic factors in (2) 11: 10
  epidemiology (3) **12: 1–28.** *See also* Child psy-
        chiatry, epidemiolgic studies in
  etiology (2) 11: 10–12
  intellectual deficit related to (2) 11: 12
  interaction of biological and psychosocial factors
        in (3) 12: 22
  postnatal insult causing (3) 12: 21–22
  prenatal insult causing (3) 12: 21
  prevalence rates (2) 11: 9–10
  prevention (3) 12: 23–25
  psychosocial factors (3) 12: 22–23
  sex factor in (2) 11: 10
  psychiatric emergencies in (2) 62: 9–11
  psychological assessment in (2) 19: 4–5; 20: 14,
        15; **21: 1–10.** *See also* Psychological tests
    early childhood (2) 21: 3–6
      adaptive behavior (2) 21: 6
      cognitive assessment (2) 21: 3–6
      personality (2) 21: 6
    in infancy (2) 21: 2–3
    instrument issues in (2) 21: 1
    middle childhood and adolescents (2) 21: 6–10
      academic achievement (2) 21: 10
      adaptive behavior (2) 21: 9–10
      cognitive assessment (2) 21: 6–7
      neuropsychological assessment (2) 21: 7–9
      personality (2) 21: 10
  psychologic reactions to illness in (2) 72: 4–5
  psychoses in, classification (2) 29: 2–3
  psychosexual disorders in (2) **41: 1–7.** *See also*
        Psychosexual disorders
  at risk for mental illness (3) 7: 10–12
    interventions for (3) 7: 11
    joint hospitalization with mentally ill parent (3)
        7: 11
    prevention (3) 7: 11–12
  schizophrenia in (2) **29: 1–8**
    clinical description (2) 29: 3–4
    definition (2) 29: 1–3
    epidemiology (2) 29: 3
    etiology (2) 29: 4–6
    future prospects in (2) 29: 7–8
    organic factors (2) 29: 5
    psychodynamics (2) 29: 5
    treatment and prognosis (2) 29: 7
  self behavioral assessment by (2) 11: 9
  self-report anxiety measures in (2) 23: 7
  sleep apnea in (2) 105: 11; (3) 61: 9
  sleep disorders in (2) **52: 1–8.** *See also* Sleep dis-
        orders, in children
  somatoform disorders in (2) **47: 1–7.** *See also* Con-
        version disorders, in children and adoles-
        cents
  structured interviews in (2) 20: 13, 15

substance abuse in (2) **35: 1–6.** *See also* Substance
        abuse
  suicidal behavior in (2) 30: 3–4
    attempted suicide in (1) 71: 15
  therapy
    characteristics (2) 61: 1–3
    in conduct problems (2) 61: 3–7
    current limitations (2) 61: 8–9
    recent advances in (2) 61: 7–8
  tics in (2) 38: 1–2
  treatment planning for
    not living in stable environment (2) 56: 7–8
    parent considerations (2) 56: 7
Children's Apperception Test (2) 21: 6
Children's Manifest Anxiety Scale (2) 23: 7
Child study movement (2) 1: 1–2
China, depression definition in (3) 2: 5–6
Chloral hydrate, interactions with other drugs (2)
        111: 2
Chlordiazepoxide. *See* Benzodiazepines
Chloroquine, psychiatric side effects (2) 91: 6
Chlorpromazine (Thorazine). *See also* Antipsychotic
        drugs; Neuroleptics; Phenothiazines
  blood levels versus route of administration (1) 55:
        8–9
  blood levels versus therapeutic response (1) 55: 10
  in borderline personality disorder (1) 10: 2
  convulsion threshold during treatment with (2)
        111: 4
  half-life (1) 55: 8
  historical perspective (1) 55: 2
  in impulse disorders (2) 59: 7
  interactions with other drugs (2) 111: 2–5
  lithium interaction with (1) 55: 11
  in schizophrenia
    dosage (1) 55: 12
    preparations (1) 55: 13
  in severe agitation (2) 59: 7
  structure (1) 55: 4
Chlorprothixene, structure (1) 55: 4
Choline, depression due to (3) 55: 4
Cholinergic-adrenergic balance hypothesis (3) 55: 3–
        5
Cholinergic neurons. *See also* Acetylcholine
  in dreaming (3) 60: 11–12
  localization in forebrain and neocortex (3) 44: 12
  in REM sleep (3) 60: 7–8, 11–12
Cholinesterase inhibitors, depression due to (3) 55: 3–
        4
Chorea
  Huntington's. *See* Huntington's disease
  Sydenham's, psychosis related to (1) 69: 5
Chronic mental patients (3) **6: 1–14**
  advocacy for (3) 35: 13–15
  appropriate source of care for (3) 6: 12
  birth rate among (3) 7: 12
  changes in concepts leading to community care for
        (3) 6: 2–3

clinical description (3) 6: 5
community fears of (3) 6: 10
community mental health services for (3) 4: 15; 5: 9–10
continuity between inpatient and outpatient phases (3) 6: 6–7
cost of care considerations (3) 6: 12–13
crisis management (3) 6: 7
current issues in (3) 6: 12–14
custodial care (3) 6: 6
day treatment programs for (3) 6: 8
definition (3) 6: 3–4
deinstitutionalization (3) 4: 12–13; 6: 3
    community mental health services after (3) 5: 7
    patients' rights to aftercare (3) 35: 10–13
    politics (3) 5: 6–7
disability in (3) 6: 4
epidemiology (3) 6: 4
family planning for (3) 7: 12
government role in care for. *See also* Government
historical background of care for (3) 6: 1–3
hospitals for (3) 6: 5–7; 22: 5
housing for (3) 6: 10
income assistance for (3) 6: 10
institutions for (3) 6: 1–2
location of (3) 6: 4–5
medical care for (3) 6: 8
political issues in funding care for (3) 6: 12–13
President's Commission on Mental Health for (3) 4: 12–13
psychiatric disorders in (3) 6: 3
psychiatrist role in care (3) 6: 14
rights of (3) **35: 1–15**. *See also* Patients' rights
treatment (3) 6: 5–12
    case management responsibility (3) 6: 10–11
    crisis management (3) 6: 7
    drugs (3) 6: 7
    family services (3) 6: 9
    hospitalization (3) 6: 5–7
    levels of care required for comprehensive management (3) 6: 11–12
    medical and mental health services (3) 6: 5–9
    outpatient care in community (3) 6: 7–9
    psychosocial skill training (3) 6: 8
    using community facilities (3) 6: 10
    vocational training (3) 6: 10
    welfare and social services (3) 6: 9–10
young adult population (3) 6: 4–5
Chronobiology. *See* Biological rhythms
Cigarette smoking. *See* Smoking
Cimetidine
    benzodiazepines interaction with (2) 111: 1–2
    psychiatric side effects (2) 91: 4–5
Cingulate cortex, and alerting reactions (3) 54: 3. *See also* Limbic system
Circadian rhythms (3) **59: 1–6**. *See also* Biological rhythms
birth and death related to (3) 59: 1

of body temperature (3) 59: 1–2
in brain (3) 59: 2–3
brain role as oscillator (3) 59: 8–10
definition (3) 59: 1
delayed sleep phase syndrome (3) 61: 7–8
disturbance in sleep disorders (3) 61: 6
and drug effects (3) 45: 7; 59: 3
drugs effect on (3) 59: 5, 13
free-running rhythms (3) 59: 3–4
of hormones (3) 59: 2; 60: 5–6
internal desynchronization (3) 59: 4–5
light-dark cycle synchronization (3) 59: 5
lithium effect on (3) 59: 5
melatonin as timing transmitter in (3) 59: 9–11
neural system controlling (3) 60: 1–2
neuroanatomy of oscillators and photoperiodism (3) 59: 8–10
phase advance hypothesis for depression (3) 59: 5–6
sleep-wake cycle (3) 59: 3; 60: 1–2. *See also* Sleep-wake cycle
in sleep-wake schedule disorders (3) 61: 7–8
Circannual rhythms (3) 59: 7–11. *See also* Biological rhythms
    internal (3) 59: 11
Circumplex
    as integrating framework for DSM-III Axis II diagnosis (1) 15: 8–11
    personality traits described by (1) 15: 8–10
    in Structural Analysis of Social Behavior test (1) 15: 7
Cirrhosis. *See* Liver cirrhosis
Civil commitment (3) 32: **1–16**
    APA Model Law on (3) 32: 8–9
    attorney behavior in (3) 32: 12
    of children (3) 32: 4
    clinical aspects (3) 32: 13–16
    confidentiality in proceedings (3) 31: 4
    contemporary critiques of law for (3) 32: 7–11
    continued confinement (3) 32: 5–6
    court hearings for (3) 32: 12–13
    current status of law for (3) 32: 3–11
    dangerousness standard for (3) 32: 5–6
        criticisms of (3) 32: 7–8
    as detention (3) 32: 10
    difficulty in assessing patient suitability for (3) 32: 13–15
    empiric research on (3) 32: 11–13
    evolution of system for (3) 32: 1–3
    of forensic patient (3) 27: 9–10
    influence on criminal justice system (3) 32: 11–12
    of insanity acquittee (3) 27: 10
    involving patient in decision-making process after (3) 32: 15
    Lanterman-Petris-Short Act for (3) 32: 5
    as least restrictive alternative (3) 32: 6–7
    Lessard v. Schmidt case on (3) 32: 3
    liberty concerns (3) 32: 3–4

Civil commitment *(continued)*
maintaining therapeutic alliance after (3) 32: 15
malpractice related to (3) 29: 6–7
O'Connor v. Donaldson case on (3) 32: 5–6
opposition to (3) 32: 9–10
and outcome of mentally ill (3) 32: 13
in paranoid disorders (1) 68: 15
parens patriae function of state as consideration in
(3) 32: 4–5, 9
patient characteristics (3) 32: 13
patient satisfaction after recovery (3) 32: 13
patients' rights (3) **35: 1–15.** *See also* Patients'
rights
predictions of future dangerousness (3) 28: 13
procedural standards for (3) 32: 3–4
psychiatric decision-making in (3) 32: 12
resistance to externally imposed changes (3) 32:
11
resolution of conflicts between legal and ethical
demands on therapist (3) 32: 15–16
and right to refuse treatment (3) 32: 10–11
splitting roles of therapist from person responsible
for (3) 32: 15
statistics on (3) 32: 9–10
substantive standards for (3) 32: 4–7
therapeutic alliance in (3) 36: 12
for treatment (3) 32: 9–10
of violent patient (2) 95: 10
Civilization, mental illness related to. *See* Cross-cultural psychiatry; Culture
Clarification
in psychodynamic life narrative (2) 108: 5–7
in psychotherapy (2) 108: 2
Classification (2) **19: 1–15**
of adjustment disorders (1) 41: 7
of affective disorders (1) 59: 1–2; 60: 2; 64: 7; (3)
13: 1
before DSM-III (1) 59: 5–7
genetic considerations (1) 62: 18–19
relevant to treatment (1) 61: 2–5
of anxiety disorders (2) 39: 2
of attention deficit disorder (2) 36: 2; (3) 66: 2–3
behavioral assessment in (2) 23: 2–3
categorical (2) 19: 5–6
psychological tests in (1) 7: 3–4
in child psychiatry (3) 12: (2) 11: 4; **19: 1–15**
categorical approach to (2) 19: 5–6, 9
cluster analysis in (2) 19: 6–8
construct validity in (2) 19: 8
content validity in (2) 19: 8
diagnosis and (2) 19: 3–5
dimensional approach to (2) 19: 6–9
DSM-III in (2) 19: 9–14; (3) 12: 4–5
ICD-9 compared with (2) 19: 1–2, 12
DSM-IV prospects (2) 19: 14–15
epidemologic findings and (2) 11: 12–13
factor analysis in (2) 19: 6
Group for Advancement of Psychiatry system (2)
19: 2

historical background (2) 19: 1–2
instruments contributing to (2) 19: 4–5
predictive validity in (2) 19: 9
psychoanalytic-based system of Anna Freud (2)
19: 2
purposes (2) 19: 2–3
theoretic approaches (2) 19: 5–9
in treatment planning (2) 19: 2–3
comparison of DSM-III with ICD-9 (2) 19: 1–2
of conduct disorder (2) 37: 1, 3
of depression (1) 59: 8–9
dimensional approach (2) 19: 6–9
of personality disorders (1) 14: 4–5
psychological tests in (1) 7: 3, 5–9
DSM-III system (2) 19: 9–14. *See also* DSM-III
of eating disorders in children and adolescents (2)
40: 1
epidemiology related to (3) 12: 5
producing advances in (3) 11: 7–8
of family therapy (2) 62: 2–3
of fictitious disease (2) 101: 2
of groups (2) 63: 4–6
historical background, in child psychiatry (2) 19: 1–
2
labeling versus (2) 19: 3
of language disorders (3) 67: 2
medical model for (1) 51: 2–4
of mental retardation (2) 19: 13; 28: 3
of neuroses (1) 31: 2
of obesity (2) 103: 5–6
of organic mental disrders, in children (2) 34: 1–3
of paranoid disorders (1) 68: 6–7, 11–12
of personality disorders (1) 14: 4–5; (2) 42: 1–2
in children (2) 42: 1–2
of pervasive developmental disorders (2) 27: 2–3
of phobias (1) 33: 1, 2
of psychiatric disorders (1) 14: 4
of psychoses (1) 69: 13–14; 70: 1
in childhood (2) 29: 2–3
of psychosexual disorders (2) 41: 2
of schizoaffective disorder (1) 70: 2–4
of schizophrenia (1) 53: 15–16; 54: 3–4; 69: 13–
14
of sleep disorders (2) 52: 2; 105: 1–3
stigma resulting from (2) 19: 3
taxonomy distinguished from (3) 12: 5
Cleft lip and palate, speech disorder in (2) 49: 3
Client-centered psychotherapy (1) 9: 6
Clinical analysis questionnaire, in personality disorders (1) 15: 5–6
Clinical data systems (2) **23: 1–9.** *See also* Interviewing; Rating scales
Clinical evaluation (1) **6: 1–13**
behavioral hypotheses in (1) 6: 10
biomedical hypotheses in (1) 6: 8
categorical versus individualistic perspectives (1) 6:
6
in clinical record (1) 6: 12
clinical value of eliciting (1) 6: 3–4

clinician's perspective of problem (1) 6: 5–11
conflict in (1) 6: 11–12
interview as hypothesis testing (1) 6: 7–8
multidimensional perspective (1) 6: 6–7
as negotiation (1) 6: 11–12
patient's perspective of problem (1) 6: 1–5. *See also* Patient, perspective of problem
classification (1) 6: 2
eliciting patient request (1) 6: 3–5
requests for desired methods of treatment (1) 6: 2–5
resistance to expressing request (1) 6: 5
psychodynamic hypotheses in (1) 6: 8–9
psychodynamic mental status examination (1) 6: 10–11
sociocultural hypotheses in (1) 6: 9–10
subjective response of clinician (1) 6: 11
Clomipramine. *See also* Antidepressants
developmental pharmacokinetics (2) 59: 3
in obsessive-compulsive disorders (1) 10: 7
Clonazepam. *See* Benzodiazepines
Clonidine
in anxiety (1) 10: 6
effect on brain (2) 38: 4–5
in panic disorder (1) 32: 11
and receptors of depressed patients (1) 64: 10
side effects in children (2) 59: 18
in Tourette's disorder (2) 38: 6; 59: 18
in withdrawal states (2) 91: 5
Clorgyline, circadian rhythm effects (3) 59: 5. *See also* Monoamine oxidase inhibitors
Clozapine
as antipsychotic agent (1) 55: 4, 5
receptor actions and minimal extrapyramidal side effects with (3) 50: 13–14
Cloze technique (1) 53: 10
Cluster analysis, in classification (2) 19: 6–8
Cocaine abuse (3) 17: 11–13
in adolescents (2) 35: 4
clinical features (2) 35: 4
comparative rates with other drugs (3) 17: 12
demographic trends (3) 17: 12–13
nasal septum perforation due to (2) 90: 3
temporal trends in (3) 17: 12
Coercion theory, of conduct disorders (2) 61: 3–4
Cogentin. *See* Benztropine mesylate
Cognitive development
in pervasive developmental disorders (2) 27: 4
Piaget's stages in adolescence (2) 4: 2
and psychosomatic disorders (2) 78: 5
social perspective on (2) **17: 1–8.** *See also* Cognitive social learning theory
attribution theory (2) 17: 4–7
causal attribution (2) 17: 6–7
behavioral causality (2) 17: 6–7
causal direction (2) 17: 6
discounting, in causal attribution (2) 17: 7
likeness of causal elements (2) 17: 6
formal operations (2) 17: 3–4

Kohlberg's scheme of moral development (2) 17: 2, 3
morality (2) 17: 1–3
perspective and role taking (2) 17: 2–3
Piagetian orientation (2) 17: 1–4
schema theory (2) 17: 7–8
scripts (2) 17: 7–8
success and failure (2) 17: 5–6
thinking in adolescents (2) 17: 3–4
Cognitive dysfunction. *See also* Cognitive development; Cognitive function; Dementia
alcohol use and (3) 21: 7–8
in amnesic syndrome (2) 87: 10–11
in dementia (1) 73: 3–4
epidemiologic studies on etiology (3) 21: 7–9
genetics (3) 21: 7
iron deficiency related to (2) 160: 3
nutrition and (3) 21: 7
in pervasive developmental disorders (2) 27: 4
underlying behavior problems (2) 61: 5
Cognitive enhancing drugs, in Alzheimer's disease (2) 119: 3–4
Cognitive function. *See also* Cognitive development; Cognitive dysfunction; Intelligence
in adolescence
in early stage (2) 4: 7
in middle stage (2) 4: 8
in alcohol abuse (1) 72: 12
attention (3) 65: 3
classification (2) 21: 4
definitions (3) 65: 2–3
in depressive neurosis (1) 40: 10
distortion as self-perpetuation of abnormal social learning (1) 2: 8
in elderly (3) **21: 1–11**
in epilepsy (1) 72: 12
evaluation in children (2) 20: 9–12
evoked potentials and (3) **62: 1–12.** *See also* Evoked potentials
habituation (3) 65: 2–3
Halstead-Reitan Neuropsychological Test Battery for (1) 72: 4–6
hot versus cold (2) 4: 7
in Huntington's disease (1) 73: 11–12
in hypochondriasis (1) 35: 12
information processing (3) 65: 3
intelligence tests of (1) 7: 6
in latency (2) 3: 4–5
medical illness impact on (2) 78: 6
memory (3) **71: 1–14.** *See also* Memory
neuropsychological assessment (1) 72: 3–4. *See also* Neuropsychological assessment
in psychiatric disorders (3) **65: 1–11**
in relaxation training (2) 77: 9–10
research on (3) 65: 3–8
in schizophrenia, chronic illness (1) 53: 14
skill underlying social behavior (2) 61: 5
tests of. *See also* Intelligence tests; Psychological tests

Cognitive function, tests of *(continued)*
  in early childhood (2) 21: 3–6
  in middle childhood and adolescence (2) 21: 6–
    7
  in neurologic disorders (1) 7: 6–7
Cognitive quotient (2) 21: 4
Cognitive social learning theory (1) 2: 15–18; (2)
    77: 4–8
  behavioral sources of influence (2) 77: 7
  environmental sources of influence (2) 77: 5
  implications for therapeutic programs (2) 77: 7–8
    behavioral self-management (2) 77: 7–8
    learning and performance (2) 77: 7
    modeling and behavioral rehearsal (2) 77: 7
    therapeutic flexibility (2) 77: 8
  personal sources of influence (2) 77: 5–7
Cognitive therapy (1) 9: 3–4. *See also* Behavior ther-
    apy
  background and underlying rationale (2) 61: 5
  in bulimia (2) 102: 9
  characteristics of treatment (2) 61: 5–6
  choice among other orientations (1) 9: 7
  in conduct disorders (2) 61: 5–6
  definition (2) 56: 2
  efficacy (2) 61: 6
  in family therapy (2) 110: 8
  in group therapy of children and adolescents (2)
    63: 4
  historical aspects (1) 9: 3–4
  limitations in (2) 61: 6–7
  rationale for (1) 9: 4
Cohort effect
  in depression (3) 13: 6
  in suicide (3) 20: 10–11
Cohort studies (2) 11: 2
  advantages and disadvantages (2) 11: 2
  in child psychiatry (3) 12: 27–28
  of psychiatric disorders in elderly (3) 21: 6–7
Colorblindness, bipolar disorder related to (1) 62: 17
Commitment (3) **32: 1–16.** *See also* Civil commit-
    ment
Communication
  in administration (2) 64: 9, 10
  family styles role in social learning (1) 2: 5
  Sequenced Inventory of Communication Develop-
    ment test of (2) 21: 3
  tests of (2) 49: 9
Communication disorders. *See* Language disorders;
    Speech disorders
Community, definition for mental health services (2)
    69: 3
Community child psychiatry (2) **69: 1–9.** *See also*
    Community mental health services
  concepts in (2) 69: 2–3
  definition (2) 69: 1
  historical aspects (2) 69: 1–2
  service programs in (2) 69: 3–7
    child guidance clinics (2) 69: 3–4

    consultation (2) 69: 6–7
    mental health education (2) 69: 7
    neighborhood and comprehensive health centers
      (2) 69: 4–5
    in public schools (2) 69: 6
    targeted to specific populations (2) 69: 5–6
  training in (2) 69: 7–8
Community Mental Health Centers (3) 6: 3
  for children (2) 69: 4
  financing of (3) 3: 10–11
  JCAH accreditation of (3) 5: 11
  legislation for (3) 5: 3–4, 10
  relation to outside systems of care (3) 5: 8–9
  subsystems within (3) 5: 9–10
  three types according to structure (3) 5: 9
Community Mental Health Centers Act of 1963 (3)
    4: 10
Community mental health services (3) **5: 1–13**
  accountability to community (3) 5: 6
  for antisocial personality (1) 23: 8
  for children (2) **69: 1–9;** (3) 5: 10. *See also* Com-
    munity child psychiatry
  for chronic mental patients (3) 4: 15; 5: 6–7, 9–
    10
  consultation in (2) 69: 6–7
  consultation-liaison psychiatry in (2) 116: 8
  cost containment effects on (3) 5: 11–13
  definition (3) 5: 9
  dilemmas in (3) 5: 10–13
  education in (2) 69: 7
  funding for (3) 5: 10–11
    for systems rather than clinical episodes (3) 5: 6
  future prospects in (3) 5: 13
  government regulation (3) 5: 11
  historical background (3) 4: 9–12; 5: 1–5; 6: 2–3
    in late 1940s through 1950s (3) 5: 2–3
    in mid 1970s through mid 1980s (3) 5: 4–5
    in 1960s through mid 1970s (3) 5: 3–4
    in World War II era (3) 5: 2
  legislation on (2) 69: 2; (3) 5: 3–4, 10
  for mentally disordered offenders (3) 28: 18–19
  movement away from (3) 5: 13
  National Institute of Mental Health Community
    Support Program (3) 4: 12
  political-professional context and issues (3) 5: 5–7
    accountability to community (3) 5: 6
    deinstitutionalization and chronically ill (3) 5: 6–
      7
    focus on treatment organization rather than
      practitioner (3) 5: 5
    funding of systems rather than clinical episodes
      (3) 5: 6
    increasing numbers of professionals (3) 5: 5
  precursors leading to (3) 6: 2–3
  in prevention (3) 5: 10
  in schools (2) 69: 6
  social and political background (3) 5: 1–5
  systems of care (3) 5: 7–10

targeted to special populations (2) 69: 5–6
Community organizations, health promotion in (2) 129: 4–5
Community Support Program (3) 4: 12
Community surveys
  of schizophrenia (3) 15: 4–6
  types of (3) 15: 4, 5
Compazine. *See* Prochlorperazine
Competency
  to be sentenced (3) 27: 6
  to give informed consent (2) 121: 9; (3) 30: 5–7; 36: 4
    after restoration of incompetent patient (3) 30: 6–7
  to plead guilty (3) 27: 6
  standards for evaluation (3) 30: 5
  to stand trial (3) 27: 3–6; 28: 2–5, 7; 36: 7. *See also* Competency to stand trial
  for tolerating courtroom procedure (3) 36: 6
  in trial proceedings (3) 27: 6
Competency proceedings, testimonial privilege in (3) 31: 5
Competency to stand trial (3) 27: 3–6; 28: 2–5, 7; 36: 7
  amnesia and (3) 27: 6
  evaluation procedures and special concerns (3) 27: 5–6
  legal standards for (3) 27: 3–4
  malingering distinguished from incompetency (3) 27: 6, 13
  other competencies (3) 27: 6
  psycholegal criteria (3) 27: 4–5
  suicide ideation and (3) 27: 6
Competency to Stand Trial Instrument (3) 27: 5
Competition, in mental health care (3) 4: 14
Competitiveness, in hysterical personality disorder in women (1) 19: 3–4
Complementary reframing, in family therapy (2) 62: 9
Compliance
  in adolescents (2) 4: 14
  in bipolar disorder (1) 61: 20–21
  costs of failure (2) 79: 4
  in hypertension treatment (2) 118: 8
Comprehension, test for (3) 52: 7
Comprehensive health center, mental health services for children in (2) 69: 5
Compulsion (1) 34: 1, 3–4. *See also* Obsessive-compulsive disorder
  impulse distinguished from (1) 25: 1
Compulsive personality
  characteristics (2) 82: 2
  impact of medical illness in (2) 82: 2–3
  in medical setting (2) 82: 2–3
  psychodynamics (2) 82: 2
Compulsive personality disorder (1) **22: 1–8.** *See also* Obsessive-compulsive disorder
  clinical description (1) 22: 3–4

constitutional factors in (1) 22: 5
course and prognosis (1) 22: 4–5
definition (1) 22: 2
depression in (1) 22: 7
diagnosis (1) 22: 6
differential diagnosis (1) 22: 6–7
DSM-III criteria for (1) 22: 2
epidemiology (1) 22: 2
etiology (1) 22: 5–6
genetic factors in (1) 22: 5
historical aspects (1) 22: 1, 3–4
obsessional personality traits as premorbid personality (1) 22: 6–7
obsessive compulsive disorder distinguished from (1) 22: 6
personality disorders coexisting with (1) 22: 7
psychoanalysis for (1) 22: 7
psychodynamics (1) 22: 5–6
schizoid personality disorder distinguished from (1) 16: 3
treatment (1) 22: 7–8
Computed tomography. *See* Tomography, computed
Computers
  in identifying psychosocial problems related to chronic illness (2) 81: 9–10
  in psychological testing (1) 7: 5
Conditioned reflex (1) 2: 10–11
Conditioned stimulus (1) 2: 10–11
Conditioning
  adaptive (2) 13: 2
  anxiety explained by (1) 32: 5–6
  and asthmatic attack (2) 128: 10
  of autonomic nervous system (2) 109: 4
  aversive (2) 13: 2
  classical (2) 13: 2; 109: 4
  definition (2) 13: 2
  and drug-related behavioral effects (3) 45: 9
  of immune processes (2) 128: 9–10
  neurophysiology of (3) 71: 3, 4
  operant (1) 2: 2–3; (2) 13: 2; 109: 4
    and biofeedback action (2) 109: 4
  and tuberculin reaction (2) 128: 10
  vicarious (1) 2: 16, 17
Conduct disorders (2) **37: 1–9.** *See also* Hyperactivity
  antisocial personality related to (3) 19: 4–5
  anxiety disorder distinguished from (2) 39: 6
  attention disorder overlapping but distinct from (3) 66: 14
  behavior therapy in (2) 61: 3–7
    cognitive therapy (2) 61: 5–6
    limitations (2) 61: 6–7
    parent management training (2) 61: 3–5
  classification (2) 37: 1, 3
  clinical characteristics (2) 37: 5–7
  coercion theory (2) 61: 3–4
  definition (2) 37: 1
  depression related to (2) 30: 5; 37: 6
  diagnostic evaluation (2) 37: 7–8

Conduct disorders *(continued)*
  differential diagnosis (2) 37: 7–8
  endocrine correlates (2) 9: 10–11
  epidemiology (2) 37: 3–4; (3) 12: 15–16
  epilepsy related to (2) 37: 5
  etiology (2) 37: 4–5
  historical background (2) 37: 1–3
    psychodynamic tradition (2) 37: 1–2
    sociologic tradition (2) 37: 2
    typologic tradition (2) 37: 2–3
  history-taking in (2) 37: 8
  intelligence in (2) 37: 7
  in mania (2) 37: 6–7
  medical illness in (2) 37: 5
  neurologic disorders in (2) 37: 5
  overlapping disorders (3) 12: 15
  paranoid ideation in (2) 37: 6, 8
  parental factors in (2) 37: 4
  prevention (3) 12: 24–25
  prognosis (2) 37: 8
  psychiatric signs and symptoms in (2) 37: 6–7
  psychoanalytic concepts (2) 37: 1–2
  psychoeducational factors in (2) 37: 7
  reading retardation associated with (3) 12: 15
  treatment (2) 37: 8–9; 61: 3–7
    antianxiety drugs in (2) 59: 17
    behavior therapy (2) 61: 3–7
Confabulation, in Korsakoff's syndrome (1) 73: 19
Confidentiality (3) **31: 1–16**
  in civil commitment proceedings (3) 31: 4
  in criminal cases (3) 31: 8–9
  divulgence to safeguard the patient or others (3)
        31: 13–14; 36: 12. *See also* Tarasoff case
  duty of physician-patient relationship (3) 31: 2
  duty to report threat to third party (3) 36: 12
  ethical principle underlying (3) 31: 1
  in examinations on behalf of third party (3) 31: 4
  of hospital records (3) 31: 5
  informed consent regarding breaking of (3) 30: 14
  outside litigation (3) 31: 10–16
  within litigation (3) 31: 1–10
  of minors' records (3) 31: 12
  nonapplicable situations (3) 31: 2. *See also* Testi-
        monial privilege
  patient access to records (3) 31: 11–13
  reportable situations (3) 31: 13–16
  in research (3) 31: 11
  in supervision (3) 31: 11
  and testimonial privilege (3) **31: 1–10.** *See also*
        Testimonial privilege
  to third-party payors (3) 31: 10–11
  in treating mentally disordered offenders (3) 28:
        10–11, 18
  violation to protect injury to third person (3) 29: 9–
        10
  writing about patients (3) 31: 13
Conflict
  approach versus avoidance (1) 2: 14
  as basis for psychopathology (1) 2: 14

  inner, recognition by free association (1) 8: 6
  psychic (1) 1: 2; (2) 57: 2
    structural model (1) 1: 7–8
    topographical model (1) 1: 7
  in psychosomatic disorders (2) 78: 3–4, 7–8
  in school (2) 70: 4
  in treatment
    classification (1) 6: 11
    displacement of (1) 6: 11
    negotiation (1) 6: 12
Confounding, in epidemiologic studies (3) 13: 12
Confrontation
  in psychotherapy of medically ill (2) 108: 8–9
  with unexpressed affect (2) 108: 8–9
Confusion, delirium distinguished from (1) 73: 12.
        See also Delirium
Congenital anomalies, minor physical anomalies as-
        sociated with attention deficit disorder (3)
        66: 8, 10
Conjugal paranoia (1) 68: 7–8
Connors' questionnaire, in child psychiatry (3) 12: 6–
        8
Consciousness, impairment in. *See* Delirium
Consent, informed (3) **30: 1–14**
  for antipsychotic drugs (3) 30: 4, 12–13
  competency to give (2) 121: 9; (3) 30: 5–6; 36: 4
    in organic brain syndromes (2) 87: 16
  in confidentiality intentions (3) 30: 14
  in decision-making (3) 30: 2
  by defendant in forensic evaluation (3) 27: 12
  in elderly (3) 30: 13
  in electroconvulsive therapy (3) 30: 4, 12
    patient understanding after (3) 30: 9
  in emergencies (3) 30: 6
  empirical studies on (3) 30: 8–9
  essential components of (3) 36: 4
  ethical considerations (3) 30: 2
  exceptions to (3) 30: 6–7
  in forensic evaluation (3) 27: 12
  historical background (3) 30: 1–3
  in hospitalization (3) 30: 4, 13–14
  in human experimentation (3) 30: 11–12
    in Alzheimer's disease (3) 30: 13
    competency to give (3) 30: 5
    federal regulations on (3) 30: 11–12
    physician acceptance of (3) 30: 8
  informed. *See* Informed consent
  justification for not disclosing information (3) 29:
        6
  legal doctrine development in (3) 30: 2–3
  legislation on (3) 30: 4
  malpractice related to (3) 29: 5–6
  materiality of information to be disclosed (3) 29:
        6; 30: 3–4
  materiality standard for (3) 30: 3
  memory of (2) 121: 8–9
  method of obtaining (3) 30: 9–10
  nature of information to be disclosed (3) 29: 6;
        30: 3–4

obligation of physician to determine competency
to give (3) 29: 6
in pharmacotherapy of children (2) 59: 20–21
physician disclosure standard for (3) 29: 5–6
professional reaction to (3) 30: 7–8
professional standard for (3) 29: 5–6; 30: 2–3
by proxy (3) 30: 10–11
in psychiatry (3) 30: 4, 11–14
in psychotherapy (3) 30: 14
purposes (3) 30: 2
refusal (3) 29: 6
in resolution of agency conflict (3) 36: 4
stress related to (2) 121: 8–9
in surgery (2) 121: 8–9
therapeutic privilege to withhold (3) 30: 7
valid (3) 30: 4–6
voluntary nature of (3) 30: 4–5
waiver by patient to exclude information (3) 30: 7
Consequent control, in behavior therapy (2) 77: 11–
12
Consequential theory, in psychosomatic medicine (2)
78: 7–8
Constructs, in cognitive development (2) 17: 1
Construct validity (1) 15: 4
in classification (2) 19: 8
Consultation-liaison psychiatry (2) **76: 1–7; 117: 1–
8.** *See also* Behavioral medicine; Consultation psychiatry; Psychosomatic medicine
advantage to psychiatric residents (2) 116: 8
behavioral medicine differences from (2) 76: 5
behavioral medicine overlap with (2) 76: 5–6
in cancer (2) 117: 4
contraindications to inpatient evaluation (2) 72: 7
defining leadership of patient care team (2) 117: 7
definition (2) 76: 2
depression in medically ill (2) **99: 1–7.** *See also*
Depression, in medically ill
drug abuse evaluation and treatment (2) **90: 1–12.**
See also Substance abuse
drug-drug interactions (2) **111: 1–11.** *See also*
Drugs, interactions
in dying and grief (2) 110: 5–7
in eating disorders (2) **102: 1–10**
and education (2) 115: 5–6; 117: 6–8
medical personnel (2) 116: 5–7
in end-stage renal disease (2) 117: 4–5
engagement of nonmotivated patient (2) 108: 11–
12
family approaches in (2) **110: 1–9.** *See also* Family
therapy, in consultation-liaison psychiatry
functions of psychiatrist in (2) 117: 1–2
in heart disease (2) **118: 1–7.** *See also* Heart disease
historical aspects (2) 76: 4, 6
in hypertension (2) 118: 7–9. *See also* Hypertension
hypnosis in (2) 112: 3–4. *See also* Hypnosis
intellectual tradition in (2) 76: 5–6
isolation from other psychiatrists in (2) 116: 8

medical model in psychiatric care (1) **51: 1–7.** *See
also* Medical model
neurologic disorders causing personality changes
(1) **28: 1–12.** *See also* Personality, neurologic disease causing changes in
in obstetrics gynecology (2) **120: 1–10.** *See also*
Obstetrics-gynecology
organic brain syndromes in (2) **87: 1–17.** *See also*
Organic mental disorders
pain (2) **104: 1–12;** 117: 4. *See also* Pain
parent consultation (2) 72: 7
in patient evaluation (2) 117: 3–4
in pediatrics (2) **72: 1–7.** *See also* Pediatric consultation
personality types and impact of medical illness (2)
82: 1–11
borderline personality (2) 82: 6–8
compulsive personality (2) 82: 2–3
depressive-masochistic personality (2) 82: 5–6
histrionic personality (2) 82: 3–5
narcissistic personality (2) 82: 8–9
paranoid personality (2) 82: 9–10
physician-patient relationship in (2) 82: **81: 1–10.**
See also Physician-patient relationship
in primary care medicine (2) **116: 1–8.** *See also*
Primary care medicine
psychiatric manifestations of physical illness (2)
88: 1–15. *See also* Medical illness
in psychosomatic illness (2) 110: 4–5
psychosomatic medicine differences from (2) 76: 1–
2, 5
psychosomatic medicine overlap with (2) 76: 5–6
psychotherapeutic approaches in medically ill (2)
108: 1–12. *See also* Medical illness, psychotherapy in
relaxation therapy and biofeedback in medical
practice (2) **109: 1–11.** *See also* Biofeedback; Relaxation therapy
requirements of psychiatrist in (2) 117: 2–3
in research (2) 117: 8
resolving medical staff conflicts (2) 117: 6, 7
somatoform disorders (2) **100: 1–10.** *See also* Psychosomatic medicine; Somatoform dis-
orders
in spinal cord injury (2) 117: 5–6
staff consultation (2) 72: 6–7
supervising counseling by other health staff (2)
117: 4
supportive intervention
with hospitalized drug addict (2) 108: 10–11
of self-esteem in narcissistic character (2) 108:
10
with suspicious and angry patient (2) 108: 10–
11
in surgery (2) **121: 1–9.** *See also* Surgery
in team maintenance (2) 117: 7
technique (2) 72: 6
therapeutic stance in (2) 108: 11–12
wish to no longer live (2) 117: 5

Consultation psychiatry (2) 115: **1–8.** *See also* Consultation-liaison psychiatry
  adverse attitudes of patients or staff in (2) 115: 6–7
  case formulation in (2) 115: 3–4
  in community child psychiatry (2) 69: 6–7
    coordination problems in (2) 69: 6–7
    goals (2) 69: 6
    models for (2) 69: 6
    role definition problems in (2) 69: 7
    in schools (2) 69: 6
  data collection in (2) 115: 1–3
  discomfort in medical milieu (2) 115: 8
  educational issues in (2) 115: 5–6
  follow-up in (2) 115: 5
  intervention in (2) 115: 4–5
  introduction to patient (2) 115: 2
  lack of control in (2) 115: 7–8
  mechanics of (2) 115: 1–5
  objectives of (2) 115: 1
  parent consultation (2) 72: 7
  in psychoanalysis (1) 8: 9
  in schools (2) **70: 1–9.** *See also under* School
  special problems in (2) 115: 6–8
  staff-oriented approach (2) 115: 8
  systems analysis in (2) 115: 3–4
  time pressure in (2) 115: 7
  training in, for schools (2) 70: 8–9
  uncertainty in (2) 115: 7
  written response to consultee (2) 115: 4–5
Content validity, in classification (2) 19: 8
Contextual therapy (3) 7: 9–10
Contiguity learning (1) 2: 2
Contingency arrangements (2) 77: 5
Contingent negative variation (3) 62: 4–5
Contingent reward methods, negative impact on social learning (1) 2: 4–5
Continuous performance tasks, in schizophrenia (3) 65: 5–6
Continuous Performance Test (3) 52: 5
Contraception
  needs of mentally ill patient (3) 7: 12
  psychiatry role in (3) 7: 12
Contract
  therapeutic
    ambiguity in forensic setting (3) 36: 8
    basic model (3) 36: 8
    in forensic psychiatry (3) 36: 8–9
    problems in practice (3) 36: 8–9
      blackmail (3) 36: 8–9
      contracts with God (3) 36: 9
      unsigned contract (3) 36: 9
    unsigned (3) 36: 9
Contracts with God (3) 36: 9
Conversion disorders (1) **35: 3–8;** (2) **100: 5–7.** *See also* Somatoform disorders
  attitude toward disability in (1) 35: 5
  autonomic nervous system involvement (1) 35: 6
  Briquet's syndrome distinguished from (1) 35: 4, 5

changing terminology of (2) 100: 5
in children and adolescents (2) **47: 1–7**
  anxiety disorders distinguished from (2) 47: 6
  child abuse distinguished from (2) 47: 6
  clinical description (2) 47: 3–4
  consequences of symptom removal in (2) 47: 6–7
  diagnosis (2) 47: 5
  differential diagnosis (2) 47: 5–6
  epidemiology (2) 47: 2–3
  etiology (2) 47: 4–5
  family dynamic in (2) 47: 4–5
  hystrionic personality disorder in (2) 47: 5
  learning theory of (2) 47: 4, 5
  masked depression distinguished from (2) 47: 6
  predominant disorders in children (2) 47: 1–2
  psychoanalytic concept of (2) 47: 4
  psychoses distinguished from (2) 47: 6
  sociocultural factors in (2) 47: 5
  treatment (2) 47: 6–7
clinical description (1) 35: 5–6
  in children and adolescents (2) 47: 3–4
consequences of symptom removal in (2) 47: 6–7
convulsions (1) 35: 5–6
definition (1) 35: 3; (2) 47: 2
diagnosis (1) 35: 7
  in children and adolescents (2) 47: 5
differences between children and adults (2) 47: 2
differential diagnosis (1) 35: 7
drug therapy (1) 10: 8
DSM-III criteria for (1) 35: 3, 4; (2) 100: 5–6
epidemiology and incidence (1) 35: 4–5
  in children (2) 47: 2–3
etiology (1) 35: 6–7; (2) 100: 7
  in children and adolescents (2) 47: 4–5
historical aspects (1) 35: 3–4
identification with another ill person (1) 35: 5
incidence (2) 100: 6
interpersonal communication and psychosocial adaptation in (1) 35: 7
masked depression distinguished from (2) 47: 6
motivations involved in (1) 35: 7
motor disturbances (1) 35: 6
neurologic disease associated with (2) 100: 6
pain in (2) 100: 6
phenomenology of conversion in (1) 35: 5–6
prognosis (2) 100: 6–7
psychodynamic concept (1) 35: 7
psychopathology associated with (2) 100: 6
psychosomatic disorders distinguished from (1) 35: 3
sensory disturbances (1) 35: 6
somatic compliance in (1) 35: 5
suggestive treatment (2) 100: 7
symptoms (2) 100: 6
treatment (1) 35: 7–8
Conversion reactions (2) 95: 12–13. *See also* Dissociative disorders; Hysteria
  cultural relativism applied to (3) 2: 3

emergency treatment (2) 95: 13
symptoms (2) 95: 12–13
Convulsions. *See also* Epilepsy
hallucinations in children due to (2) 20: 10
hysterical (1) 35: 5–6
neuroleptic-induced (2) 59: 13
phenothiazines influence on threshold for (2) 111:
    4
stimulants causing (2) 90: 8
in temporal lobe epilepsy (1) 28: 8
in therapy (3) **68: 1–9.** *See also* Electroconvulsive
    therapy
Coping strategies. *See also* Adaptation
biological reactions to stress related to (2) 121: 1–
    2
in depressive neurosis (1) 40: 6
development of (2) 2: 3
endocrine correlates in children (2) 9: 9–10
instrumental learning role in (1) 2: 3
learning of (1) 2: 18
in organic brain syndromes (2) 87: 3–4
in surgery (2) 121: 8
Coprolalia, in Tourette's disorder (2) 38: 2
Coronary artery disease
atherogenesis mechanism in (2) 126: 5–6
behavior therapy in (2) 126: 6–7
lipids role in etiology (2) 126: 1–2
prevention (2) 126: 7–8
risk factors for (2) 126: 1–2
    psychological (2) 126: 2–5
type A behavior related to (2) 78: 3; 126: 2–5
    and atherogenesis (2) 126: 5–6
    behavior therapy for (2) 126: 6–7
    hostility and suppressed anger (2) 126: 4–5
    implications for treatment (2) 126: 6–8
    initial studies showing relationship (2) 126: 3
    studies not showing relationship (2) 126: 3–4
Coronary bypass surgery
affective aspects (2) 118: 3
behavioral aspects (2) 118: 4–5
cognitive aspects (2) 118: 3–4
delirium after (2) 118: 3–4
psychiatric aspects (2) 118: 3–5
return to work after (2) 118: 4–5
Correctional institution, antisocial personality treat-
    ment in (1) 23: 7–8
Corticosteroids. *See also* Cortisol
in affective illness (1) 64: 10–11. *See also* Dexa-
    methasone suppression test
in biological stress response systems (1) 41: 12–
    13; (2) 9: 9
and immune system
    in depression (2) 128: 12
    stress effects (2) 128: 10–11
organic mental disorders precipitated by (2) 34: 5
psychiatric side effects (2) 91: 4
psychosis of (2) 88: 9
and stress response in children (2) 9: 9
suicidal behavior related to (1) 71: 12

Corticostriatal projection (3) 42: 11
Cortisol. *See also* Corticosteroids
in anorexia nervosa (2) 102: 4
atherogenesis related to (2) 126: 6
delinquency related to (2) 9: 9
in depression (1) 64: 11. *See also* Dexamethasone
    suppression test
in electroconvulsive therapy (3) 68: 3
and immune system
    in depression (2) 128: 12
    stress effects (2) 128: 10–11
limbic system role in adrenal release (3) 54: 1–2
negative feedback on anterior pituitary (3) 54: 1
and sleep-wake cycle (3) 60: 5
in type A behavior (2) 126: 6
Cost-benefit analysis
cost-effectiveness analysis distinguished from (3) 3:
    5
in mental health care (3) 3: 5–6
of psychiatric intervention in surgery (2) 121: 9
Cost containment, of mental health care (3) 4: 14;
    5: 11–13
Cost-effectiveness
cost benefit analysis distinguished from (3) 3: 5
in mental health care (3) 3: 5–6
of psychotherapy (1) 11: 6–7
Costs
of alcohol-related disease (2) 79: 1–2; (3) 3: 3–5
of chronic mental patient care (3) 6: 12–13
of cigarette-related disease (2) 79: 2
of diseases related to lifestyle (2) 79: 2
of drug abuse (3) 3: 3–5
illness behavior as factor in (2) 79: 3–4
insurance company role in cutting (2) 79: 6
of mental illness (3) 3: 2–6
    benefits of mental health care versus (3) 3: 5–6
    direct (3) 3: 2–5
of pollution-related disease (2) 79: 2
for psychoanalysis (1) 8: 11–12
psychotherapy influence on medical care (2) 79: 6–
    8
strategies for reduction after disease occurs (2) 79: 6
of suicide attempt (2) 79: 1
Counseling, of cancer patient (2) 117: 4
Countertransference
in antisocial personality psychotherapy (1) 23: 7
basic concept (3) 36: 9–10
definition (3) 36: 9–10
in dependent personality disorder (1) 26: 4
of depressive-masochistic personality in medical
    caretakers (2) 82: 6
in forensic issues (3) 36: 9–10
    common problems in (3) 36: 10
    resolution (3) 36: 10
maintaining neutrality in (1) 8: 4
with mentally disordered offenders (3) 28: 10, 18
Creativity
antisocial personality related to (1) 23: 6
in schizophrenia (3) 65: 8–9

Criminal behavior. *See also* Antisocial personality
  antisocial personality associated with (1) 23: 6
  antisocial personality distinguished from (1) 23: 3
  in children (2) **37: 1–9.** *See also* Conduct disorders
    epidemiology (2) 37: 3–4
    genetic factors in (2) 37: 4–5
    mental illness related to (3) 28: 1–2, 11, 12
    rising rate of (3) 19: 5–6
    treatment of mentally disordered offenders (3) **28: 1–26.** *See also* Mentally disordered offenders
  XYY genotype and (1) 23: 6
Criminality. *See* Criminal behavior
Criminal justice system
  forensic evalution in (3) **21: 1–14**
    competency to stand trial (3) 27: 3–6
    insanity, criminal responsibility and related issues (3) 27: 6–14
    mental health professionals role (3) 27: 1–3
  mentally disordered offenders and (3) 28: 2, 3
Criminal responsibility
  definition (3) 27: 6–7
  legal standards for (3) 27: 6–9
Crisis
  developmental (1) 6: 9
  of medically ill (2) 108: 4
Crisis intervention
  of chronic mental patients (3) 6: 7
  in family therapy (2) 62: 10
  in medical illness (2) 108: 4
  in stress response systems (1) 41: 15
  treatment planning for (2) 56: 6
Cross-cultural psychiatry (3) **2: 1–14.** *See also* Culture
  cultural relativism in (3) 2: 2–3
  epidemiologic investigations (3) 2: 6–10. *See also* Epidemiology
    depression (3) 2: 9–10
    neurotic disorders (3) 2: 8–10
    schizophrenia (3) 2: 7–8
  future prospects in (3) 2: 13–14
  historical background (3) 2: 1–2
  insanity definitions (3) 2: 3–4
  outcome studies (3) 2: 10–13
    neurotic disorders (3) 2: 12–13
    schizophrenia (3) 2: 10–12
  problem of variable definitions in (3) 2: 2–6
    depression (3) 2: 5–6
    schizophrenia (3) 2: 3–5
Cross-dressing (1) 46: 5
  in transsexualism (1) 46: 11
Cross-gender disorders (1) **46: 10–18.** *See also* Gender identity disorders
Crossover design (3) 45: 8–9
Cross-sectional studies (2) 11: 2
CT scan. *See* Tomography, computed
Cultural relativism (3) 2: 2–3
Culture. *See also* Cross-cultural psychiatry; Social class

epidemiologic studies in child psychiatry (3) 12: 27
  in hysterical and histrionic personality disorder (1) 19: 8
  insanity definitions (3) 15: 2
  latency characteristics (2) 3: 1–2
  and mental retardation (3) 12: 14
  and physician-patient relationship (2) 81: 2–3
  psychopathology related to (1) 6: 9
  schizophrenia definition by (3) 15: 2
  schizophrenia related to (1) 54: 11–13; (3) 15: 11–12
    and prognosis (3) 15: 11–12
  and utilization of mental health services (3) 22: 9–10
  variable definitions of mental illness related to (3) 2: 2–5
Cushing's syndrome
  behavioral correlates (2) 9: 11
  depression in, limbic system role (3) 54: 9–10
  organic mental disorders in children due to (2) 34: 8
  psychiatric manifestations (2) 88: 8–9
Custodial care, of chronic mental patients (3) 6: 6
Cyclic AMP
  dopamine stimulation of (1) 55: 17
  in electroconvulsive therapy (3) 68: 4
Cyclobenzaprine, psychiatric side effects (2) 91: 2
Cycloserine, psychiatric side effects (2) 91: 6
Cyclothymia, affective disorders associated with (1) 3: 4
Cyclothymic disorder
  definition (1) 59: 3
  DSM-III criteria for (1) 59: 3, 4
  treatment (1) 61: 23
Cyclothymic personality, depressive neurosis distinguished from (1) 40: 7–8
Cylert. *See* Pemoline
Cyproterone acetate
  for antisocial personality (1) 23: 9
  for sexually dangerous offender (3) 28: 23, 25
  side effects (3) 28: 23
Cytomegalovirus infections, organic mental disorders after (2) 34: 4

Dangerousness. *See also* Violent patient
  antisocial personality related to (1) 23: 10
  controversy in determination of (3) 32: 6
  criticisms as criteria for commitment (3) 32: 7–8
  difficulty in predicting (3) 32: 7–8, 13–14
  in insanity acquittee (3) 27: 10
  predicting (2) 95: 10; (3) 28: 13
  recidivism and (3) 28: 11–13
  risk factors for (3) 32: 14
  standard for commitment (3) 32: 5–6
Data systems (2) **23: 1–9.** *See also* Interviewing; Rating scales

Day treatment, for chronic mental patient (3) 6: 8
Deafness. *See* Hearing; Hearing loss
Death
  family reactions to (2) 110: 5–7
  grief reaction to (1) 41: 8. *See also* Grief reaction
  impending (2) 119: 8–9
  pathologic mourning after (2) 110: 6–7
  stress reactions in survivors (1) 41: 9–10
Death instinct (1) 27: 5
Decision-making
  cerebral cortex role in (1) 28: 6
  difficult decisions attented by psychosomatic proc-
     esses (2) 78: 7–8
  informed consent role in (3) 30: 2
Defense mechanisms
  danger situations producing (1) 1: 8–9
  evaluation in mental status examination in chil-
     dren (2) 20: 11
  Freud's concept (1) 1: 3–4
  in neuroses (1) 31: 5
Deinstitutionalization (3) 4: 11–12
  of chronic mental patient (3) 6: 3
  government role (3) 4: 11–12
  historical background (3) 4: 11–12
  impact on acute and intermediate care for chronic
     mental patient (3) 6: 6
  location of chronic mental patients after (3) 6: 4
  patients' rights to aftercare (3) 35: 10–13
  politics of (3) 5: 6–7; 6: 13
Delinquency, definition (2) 37: 2. *See also* Antisocial
     personality; Conduct disorders; Juvenile
     delinquency
Delirium (1) **73: 12–17;** (2) 87: 4–6
  alcohol withdrawal (2) 35: 3. *See also* Delirium
     tremens
  behaviors in (1) 73: 14–15
  brain in (1) 73: 13
  in children (2) 34: 1
  clinical manifestations (1) 73: 13–15; (2) 87: 5;
     95: 1–2
  consciousness in (1) 73: 13–14
  definition (1) 73: 12–13; (2) 87: 1
  in dementia (2) 87: 5
  diagnostic process in (1) 73: 12
  differential diagnosis (1) 73: 15–16; (2) 87: 5
  drug abuse causing (2) 90: 8–9
  EEG in (1) 73: 15
  in elderly (2) 87: 5; 119: 5–6
    causes (2) 119: 6
    management (2) 119: 6
    sundowning (2) 119: 6
  etiology (2) 87: 5
  evaluation (2) 95: 2–3
  hallucinations in (1) 73: 14
  after heart surgery (2) 118: 3–4
  neurochemistry of (1) 73: 16
  neurological findings in (2) 87: 5
  pathogenesis (1) 73: 16
  pathophysiology (2) 87: 5–6

  perception in (1) 73: 14
  schizophrenia distinguished from (2) 87: 5
  signs and symptoms (2) 87: 5; 95: 2
  stimulants causing (2) 90: 8–9
  terminology in (1) 73: 12–13; (2) 87: 4
  treatment (1) 73: 16–17; (2) 87: 6
Delirium tremens (2) 35: 3
  prevention in alcoholic detoxification (2) 89: 8
Delusional perception (1) 53: 8
Delusions. *See also* Organic mental disorders
  in Alzheimer's disease (1) 73: 7
  autochthonous (1) 53: 8
  of bromosis (2) 100: 5
  cultural definition of abnormality (3) 15: 2
  cultural relativism of (3) 2: 2–3
  definition (1) 68: 1; (2) 87: 1
    psychotherapy in (2) 87: 17
  grandiose (1) 68: 10
  hallucinogens causing (2) 35: 5
  hypochondriac (1) 68: 9–10
  of jealousy (1) 68: 7–8
  marijuana causing (2) 35: 5
  measurement of (1) 68: 14
  as multidimensional phenomenon (1) 68: 14
  obsessions distinguished from (1) 34: 4
  organic (2) 87: 13–14. *See also* Psychoses, sympto-
     matic
    in children (2) 34: 2
  in paranoid disorder (1) 68: 1, 7, 16
  paranoid distinguished from paranoic (1) 68: 2
  of parasitosis (2) 100: 5
  prognosis in paranoid disorders (1) 68: 16
  as result of close relationship with paranoid pa-
     tient (1) 68: 10
  in schizophrenia
    acute illness (1) 53: 8
    chronic illness (1) 53: 13
Dementia (1) **73: 2–12;** (2) 87: 6–10. *See also* Cog-
     nitive dysfunction; Organic mental dis-
     orders
  aging process distinguished from (1) 72: 11
  alcoholism causing (2) 87: 8–9
  Alzheimer's disease (1) 73: 5–8. *See also* Alzhei-
     mer's disease
  of boxers (1) 73: 6
  in cerebrovascular disease (1) 73: 8–10
    clinical manifestations (1) 73: 9–10
    diagnosis (1) 73: 9–10
    emotional problems in (1) 73: 9
    neuropathology (1) 73: 9
    treatment (1) 73: 10
  in children (2) 34: 2
  classification (2) 87: 6
  clinical manifestations (1) 73: 3–4; (2) 87: 7
  definition (1) 73: 2–3; (2) 87: 1, 6
  delirium distinguished from (1) 73: 15
  delirium in (2) 87: 5
  depression distinguished from (1) 59: 4–5, 12; (2)
     99: 4

Dementia *(continued)*
  depression in (1) 73: 4
  diagnosis (1) 73: 3–5; (2) 87: 7–8
  differential diagnosis (1) 72: 11; 73: 4; (2) 87: 6–
      8; (3) 21: 2
  difficulty in diagnosis (3) 21: 2
  EEG in (1) 73: 5
  in elderly (2) 119: 1–4
      coexisting illnesses (2) 119: 2–3
      diagnostic issues (2) 119: 1–2
      epidemiology (2) 119: 1
      pharmacologic treatment (2) 119: 3–4
      supportive treatment (2) 119: 4
  epidemiology (2) 87: 2
  etiology (2) 87: 6, 8–9
      in elderly (3) 21: 7
  evaluation (2) 95: 2–3
  event-related potentials in (3) 62: 10
  genetics (3) 21: 7
  in Huntington's disease (1) 73: 11–12
  in hydrocephalus (1) 73: 10–11; (2) 87: 10
      diagnosis (1) 73: 11
      frontal lobe syndrome related to (1) 73: 11
      treatment (1) 73: 11
  incidence in elderly (3) 21: 5–7
  Korsakoff's syndrome distinguished from (1) 73: 2,
      18
  laboratory tests in (1) 73: 4–5
  medical illness influence on (1) 73: 5
  Mental Status Questionnaire in (2) 119: 2
  multi-infarct (1) 73: 8–10
  neurologic diagnosis (1) 73: 4–5
  neuropsychological assessment in (1) 72: 10–11
  Parkinson's disease distinguished from (1) 28: 11
  pathophysiology (2) 87: 8
  personality change due to (1) 28: 4
  Pick's disease. *See also* Pick's disease
  presenile, abandonment of terminology (1) 73: 6
  prognosis (2) 87: 7
  pseudodementia distinguished from (1) 59: 12; (2)
      87: 7–8
  psychiatric disorders in (1) 73: 4
  psychoses in (1) 69: 7
  psychotherapy in (2) 87: 17
  reversible (2) 87: 9–10
  senile, of Alzheimer type (1) 73: 6
  signs and symptoms (2) 95: 2; 119: 2
  sleep disorder in (2) 119: 8
  subcortical (1) 73: 10–11
  tests of mental capacity in (1) 73: 4
  treatment (1) 73: 5
      in elderly (2) 119: 3–4
  variability of pathology and prognosis in (1) 73: 3
  vascular causes (2) 87: 9
Dementia praecox (1) 53: Schizophrenia
Demerol. *See* Meperidine
Demoralization (1) 10: 4; (2) 99: 2–3
  definition (1) 40: 3
Demyelinating disease, psychosis in (1) 69: 8

Dendrites (3) 42: 2
  dopamine release from (3) 42: 7
Denial
  anxiety related to (2) 118: 1
  in myocardial infarction (2) 118: 1–2
  by narcissistic personality (2) 82: 9
  positive and negative aspects (2) 118: 1–2
  of psychiatric illness (3) 22: 10
  in right hemisphere syndrome (1) 28: 9
  of stressful life event (1) 41: 2–6
Dependence, substance (2) 35: 1
Dependency, in mental retardation (2) 28: 5
Dependent personality, avoidant personality distin-
      guished from (1) 24: 8
Dependent personality disorder (1) **26: 1–4**
  affective disorders in (1) 26: 3
  agoraphobia distinguished from (1) 26: 3
  definition (1) 26: 2
  diagnosis (1) 26: 2–4
  differential diagnosis (1) 26: 3–4
  epidemiology (1) 26: 2
  etiology (1) 26: 2–3
  historical aspects (1) 26: 1
  prevention (1) 26: 4
  psychodynamics (1) 26: 1
  reaction formation in (1) 26: 3
  separation process in (1) 26: 3
  treatment (1) 26: 4
Depersonalization (1) **39: 10–11**
  definition (1) 39: 10
  differential diagnosis (1) 39: 11
  epidemiology (1) 39: 10
  etiology (1) 39: 10
  after marijuana use (2) 35: 5
  treatment (1) 39: 11
Depersonalization disorder, panic disorder distin-
      guished from (1) 32: 11
Depression (1) **59: 8–12.** *See also* Affective disorders
  absence of intimate relationship as factor in (1)
      60: 7; (3) 13: 8
  acetylcholine in (3) 55: 3–5
  in adjustment disorder (1) 59: 5
  in adolescents (1) 59: 11–12
      differential diagnosis (1) 59: 11–12
      epidemiologic studies (3) 12: 16–17
      mood fluctuations and misery distinguished from
          (2) 4: 11–12
      prevalence (2) 4: 9–10
      sleep disorder in (2) 52: 10
  adversity role in (1) 63: 5–9
  age as risk factor in (1) 60: 6; (3) 13: 5–6
  agoraphobia distinguished from (1) 33: 6
  alcohol abuse associated with (1) 59: 9–10; (3)
      18: 11–14
  alcoholism complicated by (1) 59: 10
  Alzheimer's disease coexisting with (2) 119: 3
  analogy to hibernation (3) 59: 10
  animal models
      behavioral despair in (3) 55: 7

learned helplessness in (3) 55: 7
  separation (3) 55: 7
anorexia nervosa distinguished from (2) 40: 7
antihypertensive drugs causing (2) 91: 5; 118: 8
and antisocial personality (1) 23: 6–7; (3) 19: 7
anxiety associated with (1) 59: 10; (3) 14: 11
anxiety disorders distinguished from (1) 32: 10;
    40: 2–3
in aphasia (2) 99: 4
arrhythmias related to (2) 118: 5
atypical (1) 59: 4–5; 61: 13
  panic attacks in (1) 33: 6
benzodiazepines causing (2) 91: 3
biological vulnerability to (3) 55: 8
in bipolar disorder (1) 60: 7–11; (3) 13: 8–12. *See*
    also Bipolar disorder
in brain-damaged patient (2) 99: 4–5
brief reactive, drug therapy (1) 10: 5
in cancer (2) 99: 1–2
catecholamines in (3) 55: 2–3
characterologic (1) 3: 3–4
childhood experiences and (1) 60: 6; (3) 13: 7
in children (1) 59: 11
  anhedonia in (2) 30: 2
  conduct disorder linked to (2) 30: 5
  development determining (2) 30: 2
  grief reaction distinguished from (2) 30: 5
  juvenile manic-depressive illness (2) 30: 4–5
  longitudinal course and outcome (2) 30: 4
  low self-esteem in (2) 30: 3
  nonbipolar disorder (1) 60: 6; (3) 13: 7
  parental depression related to (2) 30: 6
  predisposing to depressive neurosis in adult life
    (1) 40: 10–11
  prevalence (2) 30: 5
  psychomotor retardation in (2) 30: 3
  school failure (2) 30: 3
  separation anxiety distinguished from (2) 30: 5
  separation role in (2) 30: 6
  sleep disorder in (2) 30: 3, 7
  social withdrawal in (2) 30: 2–3
  socioeconomic factors related to (2) 30: 6
  treatment (2) 30: 7–8
    antidepressants (2) 59: 14–15
chronic
  laboratory procedures and selective medical
    workup in (1) 61: 16–17
  overlap with other diagnoses (1) 10: 4
  pathways to (1) 61: 14
  psychiatric evaluation of patients resistant to
    treatment (1) 61: 16
  treatment (1) 61: 13–18
    characterologic depression (1) 61: 14–15
    drug-free baseline in (1) 61: 16
    drugs (1) 10: 4–5
    major depressions with chronicity (1) 61: 13–
      14
    secondary dysphorias (1) 61: 15–16
    treatment-resistant patients (1) 61: 16

chronic characterologic (1) 10: 4
circadian rhythms in (3) 59: 5–6
classification (1) 59: 2, 8–9; 60: 2, 7–8; 61: 4;
    (3) 13: 1–2
  attempts before DSM-III (1) 59: 5–7
  genetic considerations (1) 62: 19
clonidine effect on adrenergic receptors in (1) 64:
    10
cohort effect in (3) 13: 6
communication of suicidal intent in (1) 71: 7
comparison of affect between pathologic and nor-
    mal forms (1) 40: 3
in compulsive personality disorder (1) 22: 7
in coronary bypass surgery (2) 118: 3
cortisol metabolism in (1) 64: 11. *See also* Dexa-
    methasone suppression test
course of (1) 59: 9
cross-cultural definitions (3) 2: 5–6
culture and (3) 2: 5–6
  epidemiologic studies (3) 2: 9–10
in Cushing's syndrome (2) 88: 8
  limbic system role (3) 54: 9–10
in cyclothymic disorder (1) 59: 3, 4
definitions in (1) 40: 2–5
  affect (1) 40: 2–3
  culture determining (3) 2: 5–6
  demoralization (1) 40: 3
  endogenous versus reactive (1) 40: 3–4
  mood (1) 40: 2–3
dementia distinguished from (1) 59: 4–5, 12; (2)
    99: 4
dementia with (1) 73: 4; (2) 119: 3
demoralization reaction distinguished from (2) 99:
    2–3
developmental considerations (3) 55: 8
dexamethasone suppression test in (3) 53: 5; 54:
    10–11
diagnosis
  in children (2) 30: 1–4
  drug treatment in (1) 3: 3
differential diagnosis (1) 40: 6–8; (2) 30: 5
in drug abuse (2) 90: 5
DSM-III on (1) 59: 2–3; (2) 30: 1–2; (3) 13: 2
  depressive episode (1) 59: 2, 3
in elderly (1) 59: 12; (2) 119: 4–5
  prevalence (3) 21: 3–5
  social factors influencing (3) 21: 8–9
electroconvulsive therapy for (3) 68: 6–7. *See also*
    Electroconvulsive therapy
endogenous, reactive versus (1) 59: 9; 61: 3–4
epidemiology (1) 60: 2–7; (3) 13: 1–8
  in adolescents (3) 12: 16–17
  in children (2) 30: 5
  cross-cultural studies (3) 2: 9–10
  in nonbipolar disorder (1) 60: 2–7; (3) 13: 1–8
etiology (1) 59: 9
  in children (2) 30: 6–7
  stressful life events (1) 63: 5–9
  vulnerability (1) 63: 6–8

Depression *(continued)*
  evaluation of suicidal potential in (1) 61: 6
  family studies (1) 60: 6; (3) 13: 7
  genetic factors (3) 13: 7
    adoption studies (1) 62: 15–16
    biological markers and linkage study (1) 62: 17–
        18
    heterogeneity (1) 62: 18–19
    mode of inheritance (1) 62: 16–17
    population and family studies (1) 62: 13–14
    twin studies (1) 62: 14–15
  grief reaction distinguished from (1) 40: 8–9; (2)
        95: 13; 99: 3
  Hamilton Rating Scale for (1) 7: 8
  historical background (1) 52: 18–20; 59: 1
    classification (1) 52: 18–19
  hostility related to (1) 52: 20
  in Huntington's disease (1) 28: 11
  hypersomnia in (2) 105: 9
  in hypertensive disease (2) 118: 9
  in hyperthyroidism (2) 88: 8
  in hypochondriasis (1) 35: 13; (2) 100: 4–5
    caution in confronting patient with diagnosis (2)
        100: 4
    psychosis in (2) 100: 4–5
  after hysterectomy (2) 120: 9
  in hysterical personality disorder (1) 19: 8–9
  immunity in (2) 128: 12–13
  incidence rates (1) 60: 3–5; (3) 13: 3–5
  in insomnia (3) 61: 5
  insulin insensitivity in (1) 64: 12
  lifetime prevalence (1) 59: 9
  lifetime risk (1) 60: 2–3; (3) 13: 4–6
  limbic-hypothalamic-pituitary-adrenal axis dysreg-
        ulation in (3) **54: 1–11**
    acetylcholine and (3) 54: 6–7
    anatomical substrate of affectual state (3) 54: 2–
        4
    angiotensin and (3) 54: 8
    dexamethasone suppression test as marker (3)
        54: 10–11
    future studies (3) 54: 11
    GABA and (3) 54: 7
    neurotransmitters and (3) 54: 4–8
    norepinephrine and (3) 54: 4–5
    opiates and (3) 54: 7–8
    physiology (3) 54: 1–2
    serotonin and (3) 54: 5–6
    vasopressin and (3) 54: 8
  linkage studies in (1) 63: 8
  loss in childhood related to (1) 63: 11
  lymphocytes in (2) 128: 12
  major (1) **59: 8–11.** *See also under other subentries
        in this heading*
    depressive neurosis distinguished from (1) 40: 6–
        7
  marital status and (1) 60: 6
  markers in, dexamethasone suppression test (3) 53:
        5. *See also* Affective disorders, markers in

marriage related to (1) 63: 12–13
masked (1) 59: 12; (2) 30: 1; 99: 4; 100: 4–5
  in conduct disorder (2) 37: 6
  conversion disorder distinguished from (2) 47: 6
masochistic personality distinguished from (1) 27:
        7
medical disorders associated with (1) 59: 12
in medically ill (2) **99: 1–7**
  alexithymia (2) 99: 3
  brain-damaged patients (2) 99: 4–5
  cancer (2) 99: 1–2
  demoralization reactions (2) 99: 2–3
  difficulty in diagnosis (2) 99: 1, 2
  drugs for (2) 99: 5–6
  in elderly (2) 99: 4
  electroconvulsive therapy (2) 99: 6–7
  epidemiology (2) 99: 1
  grief reaction (2) 99: 3
  organic syndromes (2) 99: 2
  psychotherapy for (2) 99: 5
  somatic complaints (2) 99: 4
memory complaints in (3) 71: 13–14
in menopause (1) 60: 6; (2) 120: 8; (3) 13: 6
mood-congruent symptoms in (1) 59: 2
in myocardial infarction (2) 118: 2–3
neuroendocrine studies in (1) 3: 3
neurotic (1) 3: 3; **40: 1–13.** *See also* Neurosis, de-
        pressive
  controversy of relationship to affective disorder
        (1) 40: 1
  definition (1) 40: 5
  major depression distinguished from (1) 61: 13
  terminology (1) 61: 13
neurotransmitters in (1) 61: 4; (3) **55: 1–8.** *See
        also* Affective disorders, neurotransmitters
        in
nonbipolar
  DSM-III on (3) 13: 2
  incidence (1) 60: 3–5; (3) 13: 3–5
  lifetime risk (1) 60: 2–3; (3) 13: 4–6
  prevalence (1) 60: 3, 4; (3) 13: 2–3
  risk factors (1) 60: 5–7; (3) 13: 5–8
norepinephrine role in (1) 64: 8–9
obsessive-compulsive disorder associated with (1)
        34: 4, 5
obsessive-compulsive disorder distinguished from
        (1) 34: 7
opioid hypothesis in (3) 55: 6
oral contraceptives causing (2) 88: 14; 91: 7
in other psychiatric disorders (1) 59: 10
pain in (2) 104: 10–11
  clinical description (2) 104: 10
  epidemiology (2) 104: 10
  treatment and prevention (2) 104: 10–11
in pancreatic carcinoma (2) 88: 13
in panic disorder (1) 32: 10–11; 33: 6
Parkinson's disease distinguished from (1) 28:
        11
pathoplasty view of (1) 40: 4

personality attributes and (1) 40: 4–5; 60: 6–7;
(3) 13: 7–8
predisposing to (3) 55: 8
phase advance hypothesis for (3) 59: 5–6
physiologic stresses predisposing to (3) 55: 8
in postpartum period (1) 60: 7; (2) 88: 14–15;
120: 6; (3) 13: 6
prevalence (1) 59: 9; 60: 3, 4; (3) 13: 2–3
prevention (1) 61: 25–26
primary versus secondary (1) 59: 6
prognosis (1) 60: 11
pseudounipolar (1) 61: 12
psychoanalysis impact on (1) 52: 19–20
psychobiological final common pathway hypothesis (3) 55: 7–8
psychological tests in (1) 7: 8
race as risk factor for (1) 60: 6; (3) 13: 7
reactive
brief, drug therapy (1) 10: 5
endogenous versus (1) 59: 9; 61: 3–4
recent life events and (1) 60: 7; (3) 13: 8
receptors for adrenergic agonists in (1) 64: 9–10
down-regulation hypothesis (3) 55: 3, 6
recurrent, treatment (1) 61: 12–13
REM sleep in (3) 53: 5
risk factors for (1) 40: 2; 60: 5–7; (3) 13: 5–8;
55: 8
schizoaffective disorder distinguished from schizophrenia with (1) 70: 6
schizophrenia associated with (1) 59: 10
chronic illness (1) 53: 13–14
in schizotypal personality disorder (1) 16: 7
seasonal variation in (3) 59: 11
secondary (1) 61: 2–3
depressive neurosis distinguished from (1) 40: 7
self-esteem loss related to (1) 40: 9
serotonin-norepinephrine dichotomy in (3) 55: 6
serotonin role in (1) 64: 8–9; (3) 55: 5–6
sex and (1) 60: 5–6; (3) 13: 5, 6
signs and symptoms (2) 95: 2
in sleep disorders (3) 61: 5
social class and (1) 60: 6; (3) 13: 6–7
social phobia distinguished from social withdrawal
in (1) 33: 7
social support systems in (3) 13: 8
somatization disorder associated with (1) 59: 10
in somatoform disorders (2) 100: 2. *See also*
Somatoform disorders
historical aspects (1) 35: 1
in spinal cord injury (2) 117: 5–6
stressful life events in (3) 55: 8
mode of action (1) 63: 11–12
stress in elderly related to (3) 21: 8–9
suicide in (1) 59: 9–11; 71: 2–4; (3) 20: 12–14
risk in (1) 71: 10
after surgery (2) 121: 6
in thyroid disease (1) 59: 12
thyrotropin-releasing hormone in (1) 64: 11
treatment (1) **61: 5–18**

acute melancholic episode (1) 61: 6–7
anxiety component (1) 61: 11
in atypical variant (1) 61: 13–18
in bipolar disorder (1) 61: 18
drugs (1) 61: 7–12
dysthymic and atypical variants (1) 61: 13
electroconvulsive therapy (1) 61: 7
enlisting family support (1) 61: 7
evaluation of suicidal potential in (1) 61: 6
health education about nature of disorder (1)
61: 6
heterocyclic antidepressants (1) 61: 8–11
hospitalization (1) 61: 7–8
lithium (1) 61: 12, 18
maintenance for recurrent major depression (1)
61: 12–13
medical work-up in (1) 61: 5
monoamine oxidase inhibitors (1) 61: 11–12
primary care physician role (1) 61: 5–6
psychotherapy, in acute melancholic episode (1)
61: 7
suicide risk during (1) 61: 6–7
treatment patterns in (1) 60: 11, 12
TSH response to TRH in (3) 53: 6
amphetamine challenge (3) 53: 6–7
catechol-O-methyl transferase levels (3) 53: 8
cholinergic rapid eye movement induction test
(3) 53: 7
REM sleep (3) 53: 5
skin conductance-electrodermal activity (3) 53:
8
TSH response to TRH (3) 53: 6
tyramine levels in urine (3) 53: 9
twin studies on (3) 13: 7
undertreatment by primary care physician (1) 61:
5–6
unipolar (1) 60: 2; (3) 13: 2
vulnerability to (1) 63: 6–8
work related to (1) 63: 12–13
Depressive affect
definition (1) 40: 2–3
endogenous, reactive depression distinguished from
(1) 40: 3–4
reactive, endogenous depression distinguished from
(1) 40: 3–4
Depressive disorders (1) **59: 8–12.** *See also under*
Depression
Depressive equivalents (2) 30: 1
Depressive-masochistic personality. *See also* Masochistic personality disorder
clinical features (2) 82: 5
countertransference in medical caretakers of (2)
82: 6
help-rejection in (2) 82: 5
hysterical personality disorder distinguished from
(1) 19: 8, 9
impact of medical illness in (2) 82: 5–6
in medical setting (2) 82: 5–6
psychodynamics (2) 82: 5

Depressive neurosis (1) **40: 1–13.** *See also* Neurosis, depressive
Depressive personality, drug therapy (1) 10: 4–5
Depressive position (1) 1: 10
Deprivation dwarfism (2) 40: 4
Deprivation syndrome. *See* Psychosocial deprivation
Derailment, in schizophrenia (1) 53: 10
Derogatis Stress Profile (1) 7: 9
Desensitization
    historical aspects (1) 2: 11, 12
    systematic (1) 2: 12; (2) 109: 1–2
        alternative explanations for (2) 77: 3–4
        in asthma (2) 109: 9–10
        in obsessive-compulsive disorder (1) 34: 9
        in simple phobia (1) 33: 10
Desipramine. *See also* Antidepressants, tricyclic
    in depression of elderly (2) 119: 5
    in panic disorder (1) 10: 6
    receptors for, and mechanism of action (3) 50: 11
Desire phase disorders (1) 47: 5
Desynchronize, definition (3) 59: 14
Desyrel. *See* Trazodone
Determinism, psychic (1) 1: 1
Detoxification
    in alcoholism (2) 89: 8
    in narcotic addiction (2) 90: 12
Devaluation, in narcissistic personality disorder (1) 18: 4
Development
    adaptation in (2) 2: 3
    in adolescence (2) **4: 1–15.** *See also* Adolescence
        chronic illness impact and (2) 4: 14–15
        and drug abuse (2) 4: 13–14
        psychopathology related to (2) 4: 11–15
        sexual behavior and (2) 4: 12–13
    of affects (2) 2: 6–7
    assessment in pre-school child (2) 20: 2, 3
    in autism (2) 27: 3–5
    of brain (2) 13: 7–9
    child's endowment role in (2) 2: 2
    cognitive (2) **17: 1–8.** *See also* Cognitive development
    and depression in children (2) 30: 2
    and depressive neurosis (1) 40: 10–11
    and dreaming (3) 60: 11
    in early childhood **1–7**
    epidemiologic studies relating age to psychiatric disorders (2) 11: 13–14
    of family (2) **5: 1–10.** *See also* Family, development of
    Gesell's contribution to (2) 1: 3
    in group therapy considerations (2) 63: 5–6
    and immune system (2) 128: 6–7
    importance of directing therapy to momentum of (2) 2: 1
    of impulse control (1) 25: 1–2, 7
    of language (2) 2: 4–5
    of learning, neurobiology (2) 13: 7–9

        learning role in (2) 2: 3
        and manifestations of psychologic disorder (2) 2: 3, 6
        in mental retardation (2) 28: 4
        milestones of (2) 2: 4–5
        neuroanatomical aspects (1) 64: 2
        and neurochemistry research (2) 12: 9–11
        neuropsychological stages (1) 2: 21–22
        norepinephrine effects on memory and learning during (2) 13: 8–9
        object relationships in (2) 2: 2
        observational assessment (3) 12: 11
        parent-child relationship related to (2) 50: 2–3
        of personality (2) 42: 2–4
            biological origins (2) 42: 2
            psychological origins (2) 42: 3–4
            psychosocial factors (2) 42: 4
        and pharmacokinetics (2) 59: 2–4
        phase-specific tendencies in (2) 2: 2
        play role in (2) 2: 2–3
        and psychodynamic factors in children (2) 18: 3–5, 8
        psychological maturation in (2) 2: 2
        psychosexual disorders in (2) **41: 1–7.** *See also* Psychosexual disorders
        at school age (2) **3: 1–6.** *See also* Latency
        screening and mapping of (2) 2: 4–5, 7
        sexual. *See also* Sexual differentiation
        of sleep patterns (2) 52: 1–2
        of social learning (1) 2: 21–22. *See also* Social learning, theories of
        tests for (2) 2: 4–7; 20: 14
            in early childhood (2) 21: 3–6
            in infants (2) 21: 2–3
            language milestones (3) 67: 3, 4
            in middle childhood and adolescents (2) 21: 6–10
            in newborn (2) 21: 2
        theories on (2) 2: 1–3
        and toxicology of psychotropic medications (2) 59: 1
    in treatment planning (2) 56: 4
Developmental crisis (1) 6: 9
Developmental disorders
    in attention deficit disorder (3) 66: 8
    language and speech (2) **49: 1–10;** (3) **67: 1–13.** *See also* Language disorders; Speech disorders
        causes (2) 20: 8, 9
        clinical description (3) 67: 2–3
        definition (3) 67: 1–2
        epidemiology (3) 67: 3
        research on (3) 67: 3, 5–13
        signs (2) 20: 8
    learning disorders (2) **48: 1–8.** *See also* Learning disabilities
    pervasive (2) **27: 1–9.** *See also* Autism

attention deficit disorder distinguished from (2) 36: 6
behavioral characteristics (2) 27: 5
behavior therapy in (2) 27: 9
classification (2) 27: 2–3
clinical description (2) 27: 3–6
cognitive development in (2) 27: 4
definitions (2) 27: 2–3
diagnosis (2) 27: 8–9
differential diagnosis (2) 27: 8
DSM-III on (2) 27: 2–3
in early development (2) 27: 3–4
epidemiology and demography (2) 27: 3; (3) 12: 14–15
etiology (2) 27: 7–8
historical background (2) 27: 1–2
language development in (2) 27: 4
neurobiological factors in (2) 27: 7–8
perceptual development in (2) 27: 4–5
prevention (2) 27: 9
prognosis (2) 27: 6–7
social development in (2) 27: 5
treatment (2) 27: 9
phonic behaviors and stereotypies in (2) 38: 7
psychodynamic therapy for (2) 57: 4
Dexamethasone suppression test
in affective disorders (1) 64: 11
in borderline personality disorder (1) 17: 11
in childhood depression (2) 30: 6–7
in depression (3) 53: 5; 54: 10–11
in elderly (2) 119: 5
after electroconvulsive therapy (3) 68: 6
false-positive and false-negative results (3) 54: 10–11
and limbic-hypothalamic-pituitary-adrenal dysregulation in melancholia (3) 54: 10–11
sensitivity and specificity in depression (3) 54: 10
Dexedrine. See Amphetamines
Diabetes mellitus
relaxation therapy and biofeedback and control in (2) 109: 10
symptoms in (2) 88: 13
Diagnosis. See also Classification; DSM-III
in children (2) 19: 3–5; 20: 1–15. See also Children, psychiatric assessment in
clinical methods (2) 20: 1–12
difficulty in young children (2) 2: 3, 6
DSM-III in (2) 19: 9–14. See also DSM-III
instruments contributing to (2) 19: 4–5
interview in (2) 19: 5; 20: 13, 15
mental status examination (2) 20: 4–12
processes involved in (2) 18: 1–2
psychological tests (2) 19: 4–5; 20: 14, 15. See also Psychological tests
questions to be answered in (2) 19: 4
treatment planning related to (2) 19: 4
treatment results related to (2) 19: 6
and classification in child psychiatry (2) 19: 3–5

clinical evaluation (1) 6: 1–13. See also Clinical evaluation
epidemiologic studies producing advances in (3) 11: 7–8
in family therapy (3) 7: 5
of high-risk for medical disease (2) 88: 4–5
international differences in (3) 11: 7
interview as hypothesis testing (1) 6: 7–8
medical alliance in (3) 36: 5–6
medical model for psychiatric disorders (1) 51: 2–4
patient's perspective of problem (1) 6: 1–5. See also Patient, perspective of problem
of patient's response to clinician's elicitation of request for treatment (1) 6: 3
process of (2) 56: 2
quantitative assessment of personality disorders (1) 15: 1–12. See also Psychological tests
role in treatment planning (2) 56: 1–2
sources of variance in process (3) 11: 7–8
validity of (3) 11: 8
Diagnostic and Statistical Manual of Mental Disorders. See DSM-III
Diagnostic Interview for Children and Adolescents (3) 12: 6, 9, 10
in epidemiologic studies in child psychiatry (2) 11: 7–8
Diagnostic Interview Scale, in personality disorders (1) 15: 2–3
Diagnostic Interview Schedule
in epidemiologic studies (3) 11: 9
for mental disorder concurrence with alcohol abuse (3) 18: 10
Diagnostic Interview Schedule for Children, in epidemiologic studies in child psychiatry (2) 11: 8
Dialysis, in sedative overdose (2) 90: 6–7
Diarrhea, factitious (2) 101: 4
Diazepam, in alcoholism during detoxification (2) 89: 8. See also Benzodiazepines
Dibenzodiazepine (1) 55: 4, 5
Diencephalic amnesia (2) 13: 4
Diencephalon, in amnesia (3) 71: 7
Diet
in attention deficit disorder (2) 160: 1–2
cognitive dysfunction related to (3) 21: 7
and drug-related behavioral effects (3) 45: 8
emotional responses to (2) 103: 3, 6, 7
in hypoglycemia (2) 160: 2
in obesity
mild form (2) 103: 9–11
moderate form (2) 103: 8–9
severe form (2) 103: 6
protein-sparing-modified fast (2) 103: 9
in psychiatric therapy (2) 160: 1–2
Differentiation, in family with schizophrenic offspring (3) 7: 3

Digitalis
  lithium interaction with (2) 111: 10
  psychiatric side effects (2) 91: 6
Dihydroergotoxine mesylate, in Alzheimer's disease
    (2) 119: 3–4
Dilantin. See Phenytoin
Dimensional classification system, approach. See
    Classification, dimensional
Diminished capacity (3) 27: 9
Diphenhydramine (Benadryl)
  in dystonic reactions (2) 95: 7
  for extrapyramidal symptoms during rapid tran-
    quilization (2) 95: 5
Disability
  in chronic mental patient (3) 6: 4
  grave, predictors for (3) 32: 14–15
Discounting, in causal attribution (2) 17: 7
Discovery procedures (3) 31: 9–10
Disease
  definition (1) 51: 1–2
  psychiatric disorders as (1) 51: 2; 73: 1–2. See also
    Medical model
Disengagement
  around dying and grief (2) 110: 5–6
  in family functioning (2) 62: 4
    in illness (2) 110: 2–4
Dissociative disorders (1) **39: 1–11**
  amnesia (1) 39: 2–6. See also Amnesia
  in avoidant personality (1) 24: 9
  classification (1) 39: 2
  depersonalization (1) 39: 10–11. See also Deper-
    sonalization
  different concepts of (1) 39: 1–2
  DSM-III definition (1) 39: 2
  fugue (1) 39: 6–7
  historical aspects (1) 39: 1–2
  multiple personality (1) 39: 8–10. See also Person-
    ality, multiple
  in post-traumatic stress disorder (1) 41: 6
  schizophrenia confused with (1) 39: 2
  in temporal lobe epilepsy (1) 39: 7
  varying definition in different versions of DSM (1)
    39: 2
Distractibility. See also Attention; Attention deficit
    disorder
  in attention deficit disorder (3) 66: 4–5
  in schizophrenia (3) 65: 5
Disulfiram (Antabuse)
  in alcoholism (2) 89: 10–12
  organic mental disorders precipitated by (2) 34: 5
  psychiatric side effects (2) 91: 7
Diuretics, lithium pharmacokinetics related to (2)
    111: 10
Diurnal (3) 59: 14
Divorce
  latency-aged child response to (2) 3: 5
  stress-response syndrome after (1) 41: 10
DNA, recombinant, application to psychiatric genetics
    research (2) 10: 3–4

Doctor-patient relationship. See Physician-patient re-
    lationship
Dollard J., contribution to learning theory (1) 2: 14
L-Dopa
  antipsychotic drugs interaction with (2) 111: 3–4
  psychiatric side effects (2) 91: 7
  and reversal of dopamine binding after chronic
    neuroleptic use (3) 50: 7
  and reversal of manifestations of supersensitivity to
    dopamine receptors (3) 50: 6–7
Dopamine. See also Monoamine neural systems; Neu-
    rotransmitters
  in affective disorders (1) 64: 11–12
  in attention deficit disorder (3) 66: 11–12
  dendritic release in neuronal regulation (3) 42: 7
  developmental considerations (2) 12: 10
  in electroconvulsive therapy (3) 68: 4, 5
  in hyperactive states (3) 66: 12
  receptors for (1) 64: 5
    in assay of neuroleptics (1) 55: 9–10
    comparison of neuroleptic actions at (3) 50: 12
    efficacy of neuroleptics related to affinity for (3)
      50: 3–6
    interactions of neuroleptics with (1) 55: 16–18
    in schizophrenia (3) 50: 7–8
    side effects of neuroleptics related to (1) 55: 20–
      25; (3) 50: 12
      extrapyramidal effects (3) 50: 13–14
    subtypes (3) 50: 9
    supersentivity and tardive dyskinesia (3) 50: 6–
      7
    up-regulation (3) 50: 6
  in schizophrenia etiology (1) 64: 4–5
  striatal neuron effects of (3) 44: 7
  in Tourette's disorder (2) 38: 4–5
Dopamine beta-hydroxylase
  as marker in alcoholism (3) 53: 11
  as marker in schizophrenia (3) 53: 14
Dopamine radioreceptor assay, for neuroleptics (1)
    55: 9–10
Dopaminergic challenge test, in affective disorders
    (1) 64: 12
Dopaminergic neural system (3) 44: 6–8. See also
    Dopamine; Monoamine neural systems
  anatomy and physiology in brain (3) 44: 6–8
  in diencephalon (3) 44: 7
  in mesotelencephalic system (3) 44: 6–8
  and neuropsychiatric dysfunction (3) 42: 9–10
  periventricular system (3) 44: 7
  in substantia nigra (3) 44: 7
  tuberohypophyseal system (3) 44: 7
Dose-response, and behavioral effect of drugs (3) 45:
    3
Double-bind (1) 2: 5
  in family dynamics (3) 7: 7
  in family with schizophrenic offspring (3) 7: 3–4
Doxepin, in depression of elderly (2) 119: 5
Draft Act Governing Hospitalization of the Mentally
    Ill (3) 32: 3

Dreaming. *See also* REM sleep
  in animals (3) 60: 8
  bizarreness of (3) 60: 10–11
  developmental aspects (3) 60: 11
  Freud's contributions to understanding of (3) 60:
      11
  meaning of (3) 60: 11
  ontogeny of (3) 60: 11
  phenomenology of (3) 60: 10–12
  psychoanalytic theory of (1) 1: 5–6
  recall of (3) 60: 9–10
  REM sleep and (3) 60: 11–12
DRG. *See* Prospective reimbursement
Drive behaviors (1) 1: 1–2
  evaluation in mental status examination in chil-
      dren (2) 20: 11
  hypothalamus role in (1) 28: 5–6
  psychoanalytic concept (2) 57: 1
Droperidol
  as antipsychotic agent (1) 55: 3
  in schizophrenia (1) 55: 13
Drug abuse (2) **90: 1–12**. *See also* Substance abuse
Drug Abuse Warning Network (DAWN), survey on
      drug abuse (3) 17: 5
Drug addiction (2) 90:
Drug challenge tests, methodologic considerations (2)
      12: 6–8
Drug interactions. *See* Drugs, interactions
Drugs. *See also* Pharmacotherapy; Psychopharmacol-
      ogy; *and under specific agent*
  with abuse liability (2) 90: 1, 2
  abuse of (2) **90: 1–12**. *See also* Substance abuse
  animal models for (3) 46: 4–5
  in anorexia nervosa (2) 102: 8
  attention influenced by (3) 65: 9–10
  circadian rhythm effects (3) 59: 3, 13
  for depression in medically ill (2) 99: 5–6
  in elderly (3) 21: 10
  endocrine side effects (2) 9: 11–12
  epidemiologic studies producing advances in use
      (3) 11: 7
  factors influencing behavioral effects (3) 45: 2–10
    constitutional and trait-state factors (3) 45: 5–8
      age differences (3) 45: 6–7
      cyclical variations (3) 45: 7
      genetically related (3) 45: 5
      individual differences (3) 45: 5–6
      physiologic abnormality (3) 45: 8
      sex differences (3) 45: 6
      state of health (3) 45: 7–8
      strains of species (3) 45: 5
    experimental factors (3) 45: 8–10
      manipulations (3) 45: 8
      placebo effect (3) 45: 8–9
      situational factors (3) 45: 9–10
      state dependency or conditioning studies in
          animals (3) 45: 9
    procedural factors (3) 45: 2–5
      chronicity (3) 45: 4

    dose-response analyses (3) 45: 3
    drug-drug interactions (3) 45: 4–5
    route of administration (3) 45: 4
    time-response analyses (3) 45: 3–4
    training variables (3) 45: 5
  general principles in therapy (1) 10: 1
  generic versus trade names (2) 111: 11
  hallucinations due to (2) 87: 13
    in children (2) 20: 10
  interactions (1) 55: 11; (2) **111: 1–11;** (3) 45: 4–
      5
    antipsychotic agents (2) 111: 2–4
    lithium (2) 111: 9–11
    monoamine oxidase inhibitors (2) 111: 7–9
    sedatives (2) 111: 1–2
    tricyclic antidepressants (2) 111: 4–7
  interpreting behavioral changes due to (3) 45: 10–
      13
    assessing extent of behavioral change (3) 45: 11–
        13
    behavioral inventory (3) 45: 10–11
    selection of behavioral measures (3) 45: 11
  neuroleptics (1) 55: 1–2. *See also* Antipsychotic
      drugs; Neuroleptics
  neurotransmitter effects (2) 12: 8–9
  organic brain syndromes precipitated by (2) 34: 5–
      7
  pharmacokinetics, developmental aspects (2) 59:
      2–4
  psychiatric side effects (2) **91: 1–8.** *See also under*
      side effects *below*
  radioreceptor binding assays for (3) 50: 1–3
  for rapid tranquilization (2) 95: 5–6
  receptors and (3) **50: 1–14.** *See also* Receptors
  in schizotypal personality disorder (1) 16: 8
  side effects of psychotropic medications (2) 95: 6–
      7. *See also* Neuroleptics, side effects
    acute dystonia (2) 95: 7
    akathisia (2) 95: 7
    developmental aspects (2) 59: 1
    endocrine (2) 9: 11–12
    neuroleptic malignant syndrome (2) 95: 7
    psychiatric (2) **91: 1–8**
      antianxiety and sedative-hypnotic agents (2)
          91: 3–4
      antibiotics (2) 91: 6
      anticholinergics (2) 91: 5
      anticonvulsants (2) 91: 7
      antidepressants (2) 91: 2–3
      antihypertensive drugs (2) 91: 5
      anti-inflammatory agents (2) 91: 4
      antimalarials (2) 91: 6–7
      antipsychotics (2) 91: 3
      antituberculous agents (2) 91: 6
      chemotherapeutic agents (2) 91: 6
      cimetidine (2) 91: 4–5
      digitalis (2) 91: 6
      lithium (2) 91: 3
      major offenders (2) 91: 1–6

Drugs, side effects of psychotropic medications, psychiatric *(continued)*
　　minor offenders (2) 91: 6–7
　　narcotics (2) 91: 6
　　oral contraceptives (2) 91: 7
　　stimulants and weight loss agents (2) 91: 4
　　sympathomimetics (2) 91: 4
　receptor interactions related to (3) 50: 11–14
　　blockage by multitransmitter receptor interactions (3) 50: 13–14
　　in multitransmitter receptor interactions (3) 50: 11–12
　　psychotomimetic action of opiates (3) 50: 13
　　tricyclic antidepressants (3) 50: 12–13
　therapeutic use. *See* Pharmacotherapy
　timing administration according to biological rhythms (3) 59: 13
Drug therapy. *See* Pharmacotherapy
DSM-III. *See also* Classification
　on adjustment disorders (1) 41: 7
　on affective disorders (1) 59: 1–4
　on agoraphobia (1) 33: 2
　　without panic attacks (3) 14: 5
　on alcohol abuse (2) 89: 2–3
　on amnesia (1) 39: 2–3
　on anorexia nervosa and bulimia (2) 102: 1–2
　on antisocial behavior (2) 37: 7
　on antisocial personality (1) 23: 2
　on anxiety disorders (1) 32: 1; (2) 39: 2; (3) 14: 2, 5–6
　on attention deficit disorder (2) 36: 2, 6; (3) 66: 2–3
　on autism (2) 27: 2–3
　on avoidant personality (1) 24: 1, 3–4
　and behavior therapy (2) 61: 8
　on bipolar disorder (1) 60: 2
　on borderline personality disorder (1) 17: 5; (2) 101: 7
　on brief reactive psychosis (1) 70: 12
　on Briquet's syndrome (1) 35: 14
　in child psychiatry (2) **19: 9–14**
　　adaptation and (2) 19: 11, 13
　　axes in (2) 19: 11
　　critiques of (2) 19: 12–14
　　on mental retardation (2) 19: 13
　　operational criteria in (2) 19: 10–11
　　in overlapping disorders (2) 19: 14
　　physical disorders and (2) 19: 11
　　psychosocial stressors and (2) 19: 11, 13
　　reliablity of (2) 19: 9–10
　　validity of (2) 19: 10
　circumplex model for integrating Axis II diagnosis (1) 15: 8–11
　on compulsive personality disorder (1) 22: 2
　on conduct disorder (2) 37: 7
　on conversion disorder (1) 35: 3, 4; (2) 100: 5–6
　critiques of (2) 19: 12–14
　on depersonalization (1) 39: 10
　on depression (2) 30: 1–2; (3) 13: 2

　on depressive episode (1) 59: 2, 3
　on depressive neurosis (1) 40: 2
　on dissociative disorders (1) 39: 2
　on dyspareunia (1) 47: 6
　on eating disorders in childhood (2) 40: 1
　on factitious illness (1) 35: 16
　on gender identity disorders (1) 46: 16; (2) 41: 2
　historical background (2) 19: 1–2
　on histrionic personality disorder (1) 19: 2
　on homosexuality (1) 45: 5
　on hypochondriasis (1) 35: 10–11; (2) 100: 2
　ICD-9 compared with (2) 19: 1–2, 12
　on impaired female excitement (1) 47: 5
　on impaired female orgasm (1) 47: 2
　on impotence (1) 47: 4
　on impulse disorders (1) 25: 2
　on impulsive personality disorder (1) 25: 6
　influence on epidemiologic studies (1) 54: 15; (3) 15: 3
　on inhibited male orgasm (1) 47: 2–3
　on inhibited sexual desire (1) 47: 5
　on intermittent explosive disorder (1) 25: 5
　on kleptomania (1) 25: 3–4
　on language delay (3) 67: 1–2
　on learning disabilities (2) 48: 2
　on manic episode (1) 59: 2
　on masochistic personality (1) 27: 1
　on mental retardation (2) 28: 2–3
　on multiple personality (1) 39: 8
　on neurosis (1) 31: 1–2, 7–8
　on obsessive-compulsive disorder (1) 34: 2; (3) 14: 6
　odd cluster (1) 16: 1
　on organic mental disorders (1) 6: 8
　on other disorder with physical manifestations (2) 43: 1, 2
　on pain disorders (2) 104: 2
　on panic disorder (1) 32: 1, 2; (3) 14: 5–6
　on paranoid disorders (1) 68: 1–2, 11
　on paranoid personality disorder (1) 16: 8
　on paraphilias (1) 46: 3–4
　on pathologic gambling (1) 25: 3
　on personality disorders (1) 14: 1, 2, 4; (2) 42: 1
　　limitations (1) 14: 1, 2
　on pervasive developmental disorders (2) 27: 2–3
　on phobias (1) 33: 1–3; (3) 14: 5
　on post-traumatic stress disorder (3) 14: 6
　on premature ejaculation (1) 47: 3
　on psychogenic pain (1) 35: 8; (2) 104: 9
　on psychoses not elsewhere classified (1) 70: 1
　on psychosexual dysfunction (1) 47: 1
　on pyromania (1) 25: 4
　on reactive psychosis (1) 68: 12
　on schizoid personality disorder (1) 16: 1–2
　on schizophrenia (1) 53: 6, 15
　on schizophreniform disorder (1) 68: 12; 70: 8–9
　on schizotypal personality disorder (1) 16: 4–5
　on simple phobia (1) 33: 3
　on sleep disorders (2) 109: 10

on social phobia (1) 33: 2
on somatization disorder (1) 35: 14
on vaginismus (1) 47: 6
DSM-IV, future prospects in child psychiatry (2) 19: 14–15
Durkheim, E., on suicide (1) 71: 1–2
Dwarfism
  hypopituitary, behavioral correlates (2) 9: 11
  psychosocial (2) 40:
Dwindles (2) 119: 7
Dying patient
  disengagement by family in (2) 110: 5–6
  family therapy for (2) 110: 6–7
Dynamic unconscious (1) 1: 1, 7
Dysarthria, causes (2) 20: 9
Dysesthesia, pain in (2) 104: 5
Dyskinesia
  in schizophrenia, chronic illness (1) 53: 14
  tardive
    in children (2) 59: 13
    definition (1) 55: 21, 22
    dopaminergic transmission in (3) 42: 10
    explanation in informed consent (3) 30: 13
    pathogenesis (1) 55: 22–23
    receptor supersensitivity to neuroleptics and (3) 50: 6–7
    risk factors for (1) 55: 24–25
    treatment (1) 55: 23–24
Dyslexia. See also Learning disabilities
  clinical description (2) 48: 1–2
  definition (2) 48: 2; (3) 52: 6
  error patterns in (2) 20: 8
  perceptual difficulties in (2) 48: 4
  research on (2) 48: 4
  sequential processing abilities in (3) 67: 6
  treatment, optometric training (2) 160: 3–4
Dysmenorrhea
  etiology (2) 120: 2–3
  treatment (2) 120: 3
Dysmorphophobia (2) 100: 5
Dysnomia (2) 87: 11
Dyspareunia (1) 47: 6
  DSM-III criteria for (1) 47: 6
Dysphasia (2) 87: 11
Dysphoria
  chronic. See also Depression, chronic
    classification (1) 10: 4
    treatment (1) 61: 13–18
  hysteroid, depressive neurosis distinguished from (1) 40: 7
  secondary (1) 61: 15–16
Dysrhythmia, causes (2) 20: 9
Dyssocial character, antisocial personality distinguished from (1) 23: 3
Dysthymia (1) 2: 19–20
Dysthymic character, depressive neurosis distinguished from (1) 40: 7–8
Dysthymic disorder (1) 40: 2, 4. See also Depression, chronic; Neurosis, depressive

DSM-III criteria for (1) 59: 3–5
laboratory procedures and selective medical workup in (1) 61: 16–17
psychiatric evaluation of patients resistant to treatment (1) 61: 16
sleep profile in (1) 61: 14
treatment (1) 61: 13–18
  in characterologic depression (1) 61: 14–15
  drug-free baseline in (1) 61: 16
  in major depressions with chronicity (1) 61: 13–14
  secondary dysphorias (1) 61: 15–16
  treatment-resistant patients (1) 61: 16
Dystonia
  drug reaction causing (2) 95: 7
  neuroleptics causing (1) 55: 23

Eating behavior
  behavior modification in mild obesity (2) 103: 11
  mass media influence on (2) 129: 4
  after surgery for obesity (2) 103: 8
Eating disorders (2) **40: 1–8; 102: 1–10.** See also Anorexia nervosa; Bulimia
  in children and adolescents (2) **40: 1–8**
    anorexia nervosa (2) 40: 7–8. See also Anorexia nervosa
    bulimia (2) 40: 6–7. See also Bulimia
    classification (2) 40: 1
    differences from adults (2) 40: 1
    DSM-III on (2) 40: 1
    excessive weight gain (2) 40: 3. See also Obesity
    insufficienct weight gain (2) 40: 4–6
    nonorganic failure to thrive (2) 40: 5–6. See also Failure to thrive
    pica (2) 40: 2–3
    psychosocial dwarfism (2) 40:
    rumination (2) 40: 4–5
    treatment
      multidisciplinary approach (2) 40: 1–2
      parent-child separation in (2) 40: 2
  clinical description (2) 102: 3–5
  definition (2) 102: 1–2
  endocrine correlates (2) 9: 10
  epidemiology (2) 102: 2–3
  etiology (2) 102: 5–7
  historical aspects (2) 102: 1
  treatment (2) 102: 7–10
Echolalia, in Tourette's disorder (2) 38: 2
Economics
  costs versus benefits for mental health services (3) 3: 2–6
  financing mental health care (3) 3: 6–11
  income assistance to chronic mental patients (3) 6: 9
  insurance issues (3) 3: 1
  manpower issues (3) 3: 1–2, 11–12

Economics *(continued)*
of mental health (3) **3: 1–12.** *See also* Costs; Financing
public systems of care (3) 3: 10–11
suicide and (3) 20: 7–8
ECT. *See* Electroconvulsive therapy
Education. *See also* Learning disability; Training
in community child psychiatry (2) 69: 7
consultation-liaison psychiatry role in (2) 117: 6–8
in family therapy (2) 110: 8
government role in (3) 4: 6–9
health. *See* Health education
on interviewing psychiatric patient (2) 116: 6, 7
level of, and illness behavior (3) 22: 10
memory concepts influence on (3) 71: 10
methods used in (2) 69: 7
psychiatry for primary care medicine (2) 116: 5–7
effectiveness (2) 116: 7
formats for (2) 116: 6–7
objectives (2) 116: 5
in research in mental health (3) 4: 4
special programs for learning disabled (2) 48: 5–6
EEG. *See* Electroencephalogram
Effeminacy, in homosexuality (1) 45: 6
Efficacy expectations, and behavior therapy (2) 77: 6–7
Ego
marijuana effect on functions of (2) 4: 13
psychoanalytic concept (1) 1: 7–8; (2) 57: 1
modern model (1) 1: 8–10
Ego ideal (1) 1: 9
Ego psychological model (1) 1: 8–10
Ego supportive psychotherapy. *See also* Psychotherapy, supportive
Ejaculation
pain on (1) 47: 6
partially retarded (1) 47: 3
premature (1) 47: 3–4
DSM-III definition (1) 47: 3
reactions of male and partner to (1) 47: 4
retarded (1) 47: 2–3
Elavil. *See* Antidepressants
Elderly (2) **119: 1–9.** *See also* Aging
abuse of (2) 119: 9
affective disorders in (2) 119: 4–5
anxiety in (2) 119: 6–7
benzodiazepines side effects in (2) 91: 3–4
cognitive function in (3) **21: 1–11**
in affective disorders (2) 87: 7
delirium in (2) 87: 5; 119: 5–6
dementia in (2) 119: 1–4. *See also* Dementia
etiology (3) 21: 7
incidence (3) 21: 5–7
depression in (1) 59: 12; (2) 119: 4–5
clinical features (2) 119: 4
dexamethasone suppression test in (2) 119: 5
epidemiology (2) 119: 4

hospitalization in (2) 119: 5
management (2) 119: 4–5
in medical illness (2) 99: 4
prevalence (3) 21: 3–5
social factors influencing (3) 21: 8–9
determining mental health in (3) 21: 1–2
epidemiology of psychiatric disorders in (3) **21: 1–11**
cohort studies (3) 21: 6–7
difficulty in studying (3) 21: 2
distribution of cases in population (3) 21: 2–6
and estimating need, demand, supply and utilization of services (3) 21: 9–10
and etiology (3) 21: 7–9
failure to thrive (2) 119: 7
impending death in (2) 119: 8–9
increase in numbers of (3) 21: 2–3
informed consent for psychiatric treatment in (3) 30: 13
insomnia in (2) 119: 7–8
life expectancy of (3) 21: 3
medical illness associated with psychiatric symptoms in (2) 88: 4
mental health in (2) 119: 1
neuropsychological assessment (1) 72: 8
normal aging process (2) 119: 1
organic brain syndromes in. *See also* Organic mental disorders
paranoid disorders in (1) 68: 13; (2) 119: 5
pseudohypochondriasis in (1) 35: 13
psychiatric disorders in, decreased incidence (3) 21: 4–5
psychotropic drug use in (3) 21: 10
sleep disorders in (2) 105: 4–5; 119: 7–8; (3) 21: 3
sleep apnea (3) 61: 9
sleep in (3) 60: 9; 61: 3
sleeping pills in (2) 119: 8
suicide in (3) 21: 3, 4
sundowning in (2) 119: 6
suspiciousness in (3) 21: 4
transient hypochondriasis in (2) 100: 4
underuse of psychiatric services (2) 119: 1
Electricity, characteristics of stimulus in electroconvulsive therapy (3) 68: 7–8
Electrocardiogram, nocturnal recording in sleep disorders (3) 61: 4
Electroconvulsive therapy (ECT) (2) 160: 4; (3) **68: 1–9**
amnesia after (2) 87: 10–11
anesthesia in (3) 68: 1, 7
animal studies (3) 68: 5–6
arrhythmias associated with (2) 99: 6
basic clinical issues in (3) 68: 6–8
brain in (3) 68: 3–5
calcium metabolism in (3) 68: 3
contraindications (2) 99: 6; (3) 68: 7
cortisol secretion in (3) 68: 3

in depersonalization disorder (1) 39: 11
in depression
    in acute melancholic episode (1) 61: 7
    in medically ill (2) 99: 6–7
dexamethasone suppression test after (3) 68: 6
electrode placement in (3) 68: 7
frequency and number of treatments in (3) 68: 8
future prospects in (3) 68: 8–9
hospitalization for (1) 61: 7
hypertensive crisis in (2) 99: 6–7
hypothalamic-pituitary axis in (3) 68: 5
indications for (3) 68: 6–7
informed consent for (3) 30: 12
    information required to be disclosed in (3) 30: 4
    method of giving (3) 30: 10
    patient understanding after (3) 30: 9
intracranial events following (3) 68: 1–2
malpractice related to injuries in (3) 29: 10
in medical conditions (1) 61: 7, 8; (2) 99: 6–7
neurotransmitters and neuroreceptors in (3) 68: 4,
    5
peripheral events in (3) 68: 2–3
research problems in (3) 68: 1–2
risks (2) 99: 6–7
safety of (1) 61: 7, 8
in schizoaffective disorder (1) 70: 7
in schizophrenia (1) 55: 2
stimulus characteristics in (3) 68: 7–8
surface phenomena in (3) 68: 3–4
termination of (3) 68: 8
Electrodermal feedback, in biofeedback (2) 109: 5
Electrodermal skin conductance, habituation to mild
    stimuli in schizophrenia (3) 65: 6
Electrodes, placement in electroconvulsive therapy
    (3) 68: 7
Electroencephalogram (EEG)
all-night sleep recordings
    in infants and toddlers (2) 52: 2–3
    in sleep disorders (3) 61: 4
in antisocial personality (1) 23: 4
in attention deficit disorder (3) 66: 14
atypical alpha intrusions in insomnia (2) 105: 8–9
in biofeedback (2) 109: 5
brain electrical activity measurements as more so-
    phisticated evaluation of (1) 64: 3
in delirium (1) 73: 15
in dementia (1) 73: 5; (2) 119: 2
evoked potentials (3) **62: 1–14.** *See also* Event-re-
    lated potentials; Evoked potentials
in schizophrenia (3) 65: 7–8
in meditation (2) 109: 3
in organic brain syndromes (2) 87: 14–15
in schizophrenic children (2) 29: 5
in sleep (3) 60: 2, 3, 4
in Tourette's disorder (2) 38: 3, 5
Electromyogram (EMG)
and biofeedback (2) 109: 4
feedback in relaxation therapy (2) 109: 5

nocturnal recording in sleep disorders (3) 61: 4
Electrophysiology, and neurotransmitter function (3)
    43: 5–6
Electroshock therapy. *See* Electroconvulsive therapy
Electrotherapy, in depression of medically ill (2) 99:
    6–7. *See also* Electroconvulsive therapy
Ellis, A.
contribution to behavior therapy (1) 9: 4
contribution to social learning theory (1) 2: 17–18
Embedded Figures Test (3) 52: 11
Emergencies, psychiatric (2) **95: 1–14**
anxiety (2) 95: 11–13. *See also* Anxiety
catatonia and mutism (2) 95: 6
in children and adolescents (2) 62: 9–11
conversion reactions (2) 95: 12–13. *See also* Con-
    version disorders
definition (2) 95: 1; (3) 30: 6
grief reaction (2) 95: 13. *See also* Grief reaction
hyperventilation (2) 95: 12
incidence of (2) 95: 1
informed consent exception in (3) 30: 6
narcotic overdose (2) 90: 7
opiate withdrawal (2) 90: 12
panic disorder (2) 95: 11–12
posttraumatic stress disorder (2) 95: 12. *See also*
    Stress-response syndromes
psychosis (2) 95: 1–7. *See also* Psychoses
reactions to psychotropic drugs (2) 95: 6–7
sedative and anxiolytic withdrawal (2) 90: 10–11
sedative overdose (2) 90: 6–7
sexual assault (2) 95:
situational disturbances (2) 95: 13–14
suicide (2) 95: 10–11. *See also* Suicide
telephone calls (2) 95: 14
toxic delirium due to drugs (2) 90: 8–9
violent patient (2) 95: 7–10. *See also* Violent pa-
    tient
in Wernicke-Korsakoff syndrome (1) 73: 20
Emission tomography. *See* Tomography, emission
Emotional behavior (1) 2: 17–18
Emotionally unstable (1) 23: 3
Empathy, and parent-child relationship (2) 50: 6
Empiric approach (3) 12: 5
Employee health, health promotion in (2) 129: 3–4
Employment, after coronary bypass surgery (2) 118:
    4–5
Enactment, in family therapy (2) 62: 7–8
Encephalitis
organic mental disorders after (2) 34: 3–4
psychosis related to (1) 69: 4–5
Encephalitis lethargica (1) 69: 5
Encopresis (2) 43: 4–6
clinical features (2) 43: 5
definition (2) 43: 4
diagnosis (2) 43: 2, 5
DSM-III diagnostic criteria (2) 43: 2, 4
epidemiology (2) 43: 4–5
etiology (2) 43: 5

Encopresis *(continued)*
  historical aspects (2) 43: 4
  organic causes (2) 43: 5
  psychological characteristics in (2) 43: 5
  toilet training and (2) 43: 5
  treatment (2) 43: 5–6
Endemiology (1) 54: 2
Endocrine disorders. *See also* Hormones; Neuroendo-
      crinology
  depression due to (1) 61: 2
  factitious (2) 101: 5
  psychiatric manifestations (2) **88: 5–15**
    Addison's disease (2) 88: 10
    adrenogenital syndrome (2) 88: 10
    androgens (2) 88: 15
    Cushing's syndrome (2) 88: 8–9
    estrogens (2) 88: 14–15
    hyperadrenocorticism (2) 88: 8–9
    hyperglycemia (2) 88: 13
    hyperparathyroidism (2) 88: 11
    hyperthyroidism (2) 88: 7–8
    hypoadrenocorticism (2) 88: 9–10
    hypoglycemia (2) 88: 12–13
    hypoparathyroidism (2) 88: 11–12
    hypothyroidism (2) 88: 5–7
    pancreatic carcinoma (2) 88: 13
    pancreatitis (2) 88: 13
    pheochromocytoma (2) 88: 10
    pituitary (2) 88: 13–14
    sex hormones (2) 88: 14–15
    steroid psychosis (2) 88: 9
Endorphins
  and childbirth pain (2) 120: 5
  in electroconvulsive therapy (3) 68: 5
  limbic system dysregulation in depression (3) 54:
      8, 9
  in schizophrenia (1) 64: 5–6
End-stage renal disease. *See* Kidney, end-stage dis-
      ease
Engagement, in family consultation (2) 110: 7
Engel, G.
  on conversion disorder (1) 35: 6, 7
  on psychogenic pain disorder (1) 35: 9
Enkephalins, in schizophrenia (1) 64: 5–6
Enmeshment
  in family dynamics in illness (2) 110: 2–4
  in family functioning (2) 62: 4
  in psychosomatic illness (2) 110: 4–5
Enuresis (2) **43: 1–4;** 52: 7; (3) 61: 13–14
  classification (2) 43: 1–2
  definition (2) 43: 1–2
  developmental immaturity causing (2) 43: 2–3
  diagnosis (2) 43: 2, 3
  DSM-III diagnostic criteria (2) 43: 2
  etiology (2) 43: 2–3
  historical aspects (2) 43: 1
  organic causes (2) 43: 3
  other sleep disorders related to (2) 43: 3
  prevalence (2) 43: 2

  psychodynamics in (2) 43: 3
  treatment (2) 43: 3–4
    behavioral-conditioning approach (2) 43: 3–4
    bell-and-pad method (2) 52: 7
    imipramine (2) 43: 4; 52: 7
    psychotherapy (2) 43: 4
    supportive (2) 43: 3
    tricyclic antidepressants (2) 43: 4; 52: 7; 59: 8,
        14
Envy, in narcissistic personality disorder (1) 18: 4
Epidemiologic Catchment Area (3) 11: 9–10; 15: 5–
        6
  concurrence of mental disorder with alcohol abuse
        in (3) 18: 10–11
  drug abuse survey in (3) 17: 6–7
  objectives (3) 11: 9
Epidemiology (3) **11: 1–13**
  accuracy of data collection in (3) 12: 5
  of affective disorders (1) **60: 1–12;** (3) **13: 1–13**
    bipolar disorder (1) 60: 7–11; (3) **13: 8–12.** *See
        also* Bipolar disorder
    depression (1) 60: 2–7; (3) **13: 1–8.** *See also*
        Depression
    unsolved problems (3) 13: 12–13
  of alcohol abuse (2) 89: 3–4; (3) **18: 1–16.** *See
      also* Alcohol abuse; Alcoholism
    concurrence between mental illness and alcohol
        use (3) 18: 9–16
    estimating prevalence rates (3) 18: 3–9
      community survey approach (3) 18: 7–9
      by mortality from cirrhosis (3) 18: 3–5
      by per capita consumption (3) 18: 5–6
  of amnesia (1) 39: 5
  of anorexia nervosa (3) 12: 19
  of antisocial personality (3) **19: 1–13.** *See also* An-
      tisocial personality, epidemiology
    study designs and methods of ascertainment (3)
        19: 1–2
  of anxiety disorders (1) 32: 2; (2) 39: 2–3; (3)
      14: 1–11. *See also* Anxiety disorders
  of attention deficit disorder (2) 36: 2; (3) 12: 16;
      66: 2
  of autism (3) 12: 13
  of avoidant personality (1) 24: 4
  avoiding bias in ascertainment of samples (1) 54: 6–
      7
  of behavior problems in preschool children (3) 12:
      13
  of borderline personality disorder (1) 17: 7–8
  of Briquet's syndrome (1) 35: 15; (2) 100: 8
  causal studies (2) 11: 10–12; (3) 11: 2; 12: 4, 20–
      23
  in child and adolescent psychiatry (2) **11: 1–14;**
      (3) **12: 1–28.** *See also* Child psychiatry,
      epidemiologic studies in
    accuracy of data collection (3) 12: 5
    in adolescence
      early (3) 12: 16–17
      late (3) 12: 18–19

middle (3) 12: 17–18
applications to patterns of service utilization (3) 12: 25–26
assessment instruments (2) 11: 6–8
biologic factors in (3) 12: 20–22
case definition in (2) 11: 4; (3) 12: 4–5, 7, 12
and causation (2) 11: 10–12; (3) 12: 4, 20–23
choosing sample (2) 11: 3–4
in classification (2) 11: 12–13
cohort studies (3) 12: 27–28
considerations in conducting studies (2) 11: 1–9
in cross-cultural research (3) 12: 27
developmental issues (2) 11: 13–14
diagnostic approaches (3) 12: 5, 7
in elementary school-age disorders (3) 12: 14–16
evaluation of studies (3) 12: 11–12
future directions (3) 12: 26–28
genetics (3) 12: 28
historical overview (3) 12: 2–4
information gathering techniques (3) 12: 6–11
interaction of biological and psychosocial factors in (3) 12: 22
interview methods (3) 12: 8–10
issues in clarification of psychiatric disorder (3) 12: 4–5, 7, 12
observational methods (3) 12: 10–11
official records used in (3) 12: 11
one versus two stage assessment procedure (2) 11: 4–6
overall indices of prevalence at different ages (3) 12: 19–21
in preschool disorders (3) 12: 12–14
prevalence studies (2) 11: 9–10; (3) 12: 4, 19–21
prevention (3) 12: 23–25
psychosocial factors (3) 12: 22–23
purposes (3) 12: 1–2
questionnaires and checklists (3) 12: 6–8
selecting informants for assessment of child's behavior (2) 11: 8–9
selection of strategy (2) 11: 2
in treatment selection (3) 12: 27
of chronic mental illness (3) 6: 4; 11: 3
classification related to (3) 12: 5
of CNS disorders with psychotic symptoms (1) 69: 2–9
cohort studies (2) 11: 2; (3) 12: 27–28; 21: 6–7
of compulsive personality disorder (1) 22: 2
of conduct disorder (2) 37: 3–4; (3) 12: 15–16
confounding in (3) 13: 12
considerations in conducting studies (2) 11: 1–9
contributions to psychiatry (1) 60: 1
of conversion disorder (1) 35: 4–5
in children and adolescents (2) 47: 2–3
cross-cultural investigations (3) 2: 6–10; 12: 27. *See also* Cross-cultural psychiatry; Culture
definition (2) 11: 1; (3) 11: 1
terminology in (1) 54: 2–3; 69: 1–2

of dementia in elderly (2) 119: 1
of depersonalization disorder (1) 39: 10
of depression (1) 60: 2–7; (3) 13: 1–8
in adolescents (3) 12: 16–17
in childhood (2) 30: 5
cross-cultural studies (3) 2: 9–10
in elderly (2) 119: 4
in medically ill (2) 99: 1
of depressive neurosis (1) 40: 2
in diagnosis (3) 11: 1
domain of (3) 21: 1
of drug abuse (3) **17: 1–16**. *See also under* of substance abuse *below*
DSM-III influence on (3) 15: 3
of eating disorders (2) 102: 2–3
of elderly psychiatric disorders (3) **21: 1–11**. *See also* Elderly
empiric approach in (3) 12: 5
of epidemic hysteria (3) 12: 17
etiology determined by (3) 21: 7–9
of factitious illness (1) 35: 16–17
of fugue (1) 39: 6
genetic (1) 62: 1–4; (3) 11: 12. *See also* Genetics
in affective disorders (1) 62: 12–19
adoption studies (1) 62: 15–16
biological markers and linkage study (1) 62: 17–18
population and family studies (1) 62: 12–14
twin studies (1) 62: 14–15
in schizophrenia (1) 62: 4–12
adoption studies (1) 62: 8–10
biological markers and linkage study (1) 62: 11–12
population and family studies (1) 62: 4–6
twin studies (1) 62: 6–8
historical background in psychiatry (3) **11: 2–6**
achievements and limitations of post-World War II studies (3) 11: 6
pre-World War II (3) 11: 3–4
during World War II (3) 11: 4–5, 6
of hypochondriasis (1) 35: 11; (2) 100: 2–3
of hysterical and histrionic personality disorders (1) 19: 2–3
in infectious diseases (3) 11: 3
of language delay (3) 12: 13–14
of masochistic personality (1) 27: 2
medical illness in psychiatric patients (2) 88: 2–4
of mental retardation (3) 12: 14
methodology (2) 11: 1–9; (3) 11: 2
assessment instruments (2) 11: 6–8
case-control studies (2) 11: 2
case-definition in (2) 11: 4; (3) 12: 4–5, 7, 12
choosing sample (2) 11: 3–4
cohort studies (2) 11: 2; (3) 12: 27–28; 21: 6–7
cross-sectional studies (2) 11: 2
interviewing tests (2) 11: 4–8
one versus two stage assessment procedure (2) 11: 4–6

Epidemiology, methodology *(continued)*
  sampling in (2) 11: 1, 3—4
    control group (2) 11: 4
    geographic (2) 11: 3
    school (2) 11: 3
    select groups (2) 11: 3—4
  selecting informants for assessment of child's
      behavior (2) 11: 8—9
  selection of research strategy (2) 11: 2
  self-report questionnaires in (2) 11: 6—7
  steps in investigation (1) 54: 2
of multiple personality (1) 39: 8
of narcissistic personality disorder (1) 18: 3
of neuroses (1) 31: 4—5
  cross-cultural studies (3) 2: 8—10
of obesity (2) 103: 2
of obsessive-compulsive disorder (1) 34: 2—3
of organic brain syndromes (2) 87: 2
of panic disorder (1) 32: 2
parameters related to variation in risk estimate (1)
      60: 1
of paranoid disorder (1) 68: 3—4
of paranoid personality disorder (1) 16: 8—9
of paraphilias (1) 46: 4
of pervasive developmental disorder (2) 27: 3; (3)
      12: 14—15
of phobias (1) 33: 3—4
in psychiatry (1) 54: 1—2
  achievements and limitations (3) 11: 6
  community studies (3) 11: 4—6
  current trends in (3) 11: 8—11
  definition problems (1) 54: 3—4
  Diagnostic Interview Schedule in (3) 11: 9
  DSM-III influence on (1) 54: 15
  Epidemiologic Catchment Area program (3) 11:
      9—10
  future prospects (1) 54: 14—15; (3) 11: 12—13
  and genetic and neurobiologic advances (3) 11:
      6—7
  historical background (3) 11: 3—6
  impact of development in research (3) 11: 6—8
  international developments (3) 11: 10—11
  military studies (3) 11: 4—5
  problem areas in (3) 11: 11—12
  World Health Organization role (3) 11: 10, 11
of psychogenic pain disorder (1) 35: 8
of psychoses in adolescents (3) 12: 18
purposes (1) 60: 1; (3) 11: 1—2; 12: 1—2, 11—12
of reactive attachment disorder (3) 12: 12—13
of reading retardation (3) 12: 15
in research (3) 11: 1
of schizoid personality disorder (1) 16: 2
of schizophrenia (1) **54: 1—15**
  in adulthood (3) **15: 1—12**
  age factor (1) 54: 13; (3) 15: 8
  in childhood (2) 29: 3
  community survey studies (3) 15: 4—6
  cross-cultural studies (3) 2: 7—8
  detection problems in (3) 15: 4—6

  family environment factor (1) 54: 8—9; (3) 15: 8-
      9
  genetic factors (1) 54: 6—8; (3) 15: 6—7
  incidence rates (1) 54: 4—5
  perinatal factors (1) 54: 13—14; (3) 15: 7—8
  prevalence rates (1) 54: 4
  problem of definition in (3) 15: 1—3
  problem of determining incidence and preva-
      lence rates (1) 54: 3
  race factor (1) 54: 13; (3) 15: 8
  risk factors (1) 54: 5—14; (3) 15: 6—12
  sex factor (1) 54: 13; (3) 15: 8
  social causation versus social selection (1) 54: 9—
      10; (3) 15: 10—11
  social class factor (1) 54: 9—10; (3) 15: 10—11
  societal factors (1) 54: 11—13; (3) 15: 11—12
  stressful life events (1) 54: 10—11; (3) 15: 9—10
  treated prevalence versus true prevalence (3) 15:
      4
of schizotypal personality disorder (1) 16: 5
sensitivity and specificity in (2) 11: 5
of separation anxiety (3) 12: 16
of sexual disorders (1) 47: 1
of sleep disorders (2) 105: 3—5; (3) 61: 2
and social theories in psychiatry (1) 63: 1
steps in investigation (1) 54: 2
of stress-response syndromes (1) 41: 8—10
of substance abuse (3) 12: 17—18; **17: 1—16**
  amphetamines and other stimulants (3) 17: 13—
      14
  cocaine (3) 17: 11—13
  comparison of heroin use in U.S. soldiers in Vi-
      etnam and those on U.S. mainland (3)
      17: 2—3
  Epidemiologic Catchment Areas data (3) 17: 6—
      7
  hallucinogens (3) 17: 15
  high-school survey (3) 17: 4, 9
  household survey (3) 17: 4, 8
  marijuana (3) 17: 15—16
  narcotics (3) 17: 10—11
  natural history (3) 17: 2—4
  phencyclidine (3) 17: 14—15
  risk factors (3) 17: 2
  sedatives hypnotics tranquilizers (3) 17: 7—8, 10
  social control functions and (3) 17: 1—3
  special problems in estimating (3) 17: 4—6
  surveys on use (3) 17: 4—6
  temporal factors (3) 17: 2
of suicide (3) 12: 18, 19; **20: 1—14.** *See also* Sui-
      cide
of suicide attempt (3) 12: 18
in syndrome identification (3) 11: 2
terms used in (1) 54: 2—3; 60: 2; 69: 1—2
treated prevalence of psychiatric disorder and use
      of mental health services (3) **22: 1—11**
in treatment selection (3) 12: 27
uses of (3) 11: 1—2
of violent deaths in adolescents (3) 12: 19

Epilepsy
  amnesia distinguished from (1) 39: 6
  attention deficit disorder distinguished from (2)
      36: 6
  attention deficit disorder related to (2) 36: 4
  cognitive function in (1) 72: 12
  neuropsychological assessment in (1) 72: 12
  psychomotor. *See under* temporal lobe *below*
  psychoses in (1) 69: 2
    in interictal period (2) 87: 14
  sleep-related myoclonus distinguished from (2)
      105: 7–8
  temporal lobe
    chronic depression in (1) 61: 17
    clinical presentation (1) 28: 7–8
    depersonalization (1) 39: 11
    differential diagnosis (1) 28: 8
    dissociative phenomena in (1) 39: 7
    interictal behavior syndrome (1) 28: 7–8
    multiple personality distinguished from (1) 39:
        9
    personality changes in (1) 3: 9–10; 28: 1–2, 4,
        6
      clinical presentation (1) 28: 7–8
      physiologic aspects (1) 28: 6
    psychosis in (1) 69: 2
    psychosurgery for (2) 160: 4–5
    sleepwalking distinguished from (2) 105: 14–15
  Tourette's disorder distinguished from (2) 38: 5
  in violent adolescent (2) 37: 5
Epinephrine
  in anxiety disorders (1) 32: 6
  in biological stress response systems (1) 41: 13
  as neurotransmitter (3) 44: 12
Episodic dyscontrol syndrome (2) 87: 12
Erikson, E.
  on adolescence (2) 4: 2
  on life cycle of stages (1) 1: 9–10
Erikson, M.H., contributions to strategic therapy
      model (1) 9: 4
Erotic paranoia (1) 68: 8–9
Eskalith. *See* Lithium
Estriol, and postpartum disturbances (2) 88: 15
Estrogens (2) 9: 2. *See also* Sex hormones
  in menopause therapy (2) 120: 8
  psychiatric manifestations (2) 88: 14–15
  and sexual differentiation in prepubescent child
      and adolescent (2) 9: 4
Ethanol, acute reaction as marker in alcoholism (3)
      53: 11. *See also* Alcohol; Alcohol abuse;
      Alcoholism
Ethanol-metabolizing enzymes, in alcoholism (3) 53:
      10
Ethchlorvynol, interaction with tricyclic antidepres-
      sants (2) 111: 1, 2
Ethics
  of confidentiality (3) 31: 1
  difficult decisions attended by psychosomatic proc-
      esses (2) 78: 7–8

  of informed consent (3) 30: 2. *See also* Consent,
      informed
  in physician-patient relationship (2) 81: 6–7
  of psychiatric participation in forensic matters (3)
      27: 2–3
  of psychopharmacology in children (2) 59: 20–21
Ethnic group. *See* Race
Ethology, modern psychoanalytic concepts influenced
      by (1) 1: 13
Event-related potentials (3) **62: 1–14;** 64: 3. *See also*
      Evoked potentials
  in attention deficit disorder (3) 62: 7
  in autism (3) 62: 11
  in children (3) 62: 10–11
  cognitive function and (3) 62: 3–12
    in preparatory interval (3) 62: 3–6
  contingent negative variation (3) 62: 4–5
  definition (3) 62: 2
  expectancy and decision making associated with
      (3) 62: 8–10
  in information processing (2) 13: 3
  and language (3) 62: 11–12
  as marker in affective disorders (3) 53: 8
  movement-related (3) 62: 3–4
    in neurologic disorders (3) 62: 4
  nonspecific correlations (3) 62: 12
  P300 component (3) 62: 8–10
  postimperative negative variation (3) 62: 5–6
  psychiatric applications (3) 62: 12–13
  in psychoses (3) 62: 12–13
  readiness potential (3) 62: 3–4
  in schizophrenia (3) 62: 7–8, 11–13; 65: 7–8
  selective attention related to (3) 62: 6–8
Evoked cortical response. *See also* Evoked potentials
  in schizophrenia (3) 65: 7–8
  to stimulants in attention deficit disorder (3) 66:
      16
Evoked potentials (3) **62: 1–14.** *See also* Event-re-
      lated potentials
  abnormalities in neurologic disorders (3) 62: 3
  anatomic origins of (3) 62: 3
  clinical uses of sensory components (3) 62: 3
  cognitive function and (3) 62: 3–12
  consistency within individual (3) 62: 1
  definition (3) 62: 1
  descriptions of (3) 62: 1–2
  endogenous component (3) 62: 1–2
  late component (3) 62: 2
  as marker in schizophrenia (3) 53: 13
Examination. *See* Mental status examination; Neuro-
      logical examination
Excitement phase disorders (1) 47: 4–5
  in female (1) 47: 5
  impotence (1) 47: 4
Exercise
  health promotion at worksite (2) 129: 4
  menarche related to (2) 9: 5
  obesity related to (2) 103: 5
Exhibitionism (1) 46: 6

Existential alliance (3) 36: 6
Expectancy
    dysfunctional (1) 2: 17
    event-related potentials related to (3) 62: 8–10
    generalized (1) 2: 16
    in social learning (1) 2: 15–16
Expectancy learning (1) 2: 2, 15–16
Experiential psychotherapy (1) 9: 5–6
    choice among other orientations (1) 9: 7
    goals (1) 9: 6
    group therapy format (1) 9: 9
    rationale for (1) 9: 5–6
    techniques (1) 9: 6
Exploration, hallucinogens effect on (3) 46: 14–16
Expressed emotion
    measurement of (1) 63: 14
    and schizophrenia (1) 63: 14–17
Expressive aphasia. *See* Language disorders, expressive
Extension test (2) 20: 7
Extinction (1) 2: 6–7; (2) 13: 2
    difficulty for early learnings (1) 2: 6
    of generalized learning (1) 2: 7
    of random learning (1) 2: 6
    by reciprocal inhibition (1) 2: 12
Extrapyramidal system
    akathisia (2) 95: 7
    dystonia (2) 95: 7
    neuroleptic toxicity to (1) 55: 20–25
        malignant syndrome (1) 55: 25
        pathogenesis (1) 55: 22–23
        risk factors for (1) 55: 24–25
        treatment (1) 55: 23–24
Extraversion (1) 2: 19
    and antisocial behavior (1) 2: 20
    and neurosis (1) 2: 19–20
Eye
    biofeedback for disorders of (2) 109: 8
    neuroleptic toxicity to (1) 55: 26
Eye movements
    blinking rate as marker in schizophrenia (3) 53: 13
    nocturnal recording in sleep disorders (3) 61: 4
    rapid. *See* REM sleep
    smooth pursuit in schizophrenia (1) 62: 11; (3) 53: 14–15; 65: 6–7
Eye tracking, evaluation in neurological evaluation (2) 20: 7
Eysenck, H. J., contribution to social learning theory (1) 2: 19–20

Facilitating interneuron (2) 13: 5
Factitious illness (1) **35: 16–19**; (2) **101: 1–8.** *See also* Malingering; Munchausen's syndrome
    borderline personality in (2) 101: 7

classification (2) 101: 2
clinical description (1) 35: 17–18
death (2) 101: 5
definition (1) 35: 1, 16
diagnosis (1) 35: 19; (2) 101: 5
differential diagnosis (1) 35: 19
difficulty in diagnosis, consultation and treatment (2) 101: 9–10
DSM-III criteria for (1) 35: 16; (2) 101: 3
endocrine diseases (2) 101: 5
epidemiology (1) 35: 16–17
etiology (1) 35: 18–19; (2) 101: 6
fever (1) 35: 17; (2) 101: 3
gastrointestinal (2) 101: 4–5
hematological (2) 101: 4
historical background (2) 101: 1–2
malingering distinguished from (1) 35: 16; (2) 101: 1, 8
modes of presentation (2) 101: 3–5
mothers producing syndrome in child (2) 101: 5
Munchausen's syndrome distinguished from (2) 101: 2–3
personality characteristics in (1) 35: 18
psychodynamics (2) 101: 7–8
self-induced infection (1) 35: 17
of skin (2) 101: 3–4
somatoform disorder distinguished from (2) 101: 1
spectrum of disease presentation in (2) 101: 6–8
of thyroid (2) 101: 5
treatment (1) 35: 19
Failure
    ambition and (2) 17: 5
    attributions related to (2) 17: 5–6
    development of feelings related to (2) 17: 5
Failure to thrive (2) 40: 5–6
    classification (2) 40: 5
    clinical description (2) 40: 5
    differential diagnosis (2) 40: 6; 119: 7
    in elderly (2) 119: 7
        differential diagnosis (2) 119: 7
        evaluation (2) 119: 7
    epidemiologic studies (3) 12: 12–13
    etiology (2) 40: 5–6
    predisposing factors (2) 40: 5
    psychosocial deprivation causing (2) 40: 5–6
    treatment (2) 40: 6
False patient (2) **101: 1–8.** *See also* Factitious illness; Malingering; Munchausen syndrome
Family. *See also* Family therapy; Parents
    alcohol abuse impact on (3) 18: 2–3
    in alcoholism (2) 89: 9–10
    analysis of origin, in family therapy (2) 110: 8
    in anorexia nervosa (2) 110: 4–5
    of antisocial personality (1) 23: 9
    in borderline personality disorder etiology (1) 17: 10
    boundaries of (2) 62: 4; (3) 7: 6–7
    children at risk for mental illness (3) 7: 10–12

of chronic mental patient, services for (3) 6: 9
communication within (2) 62: 4–5
  and social learning (1) 2: 5
in conversion disorder in children (2) 47: 4–5
depressive neurosis related to dynamics in (1) 40: 11
development of (2) **5: 1–10**
  attachment role (2) 5: 2
  basic concepts (2) 5: 1–4
  death of child or parent impact on (2) 5: 2
  parent subsystem role (2) 5: 3–4
  psychoanalytic concept (2) 5: 2–4
  in reconstitution (2) 5: 10
  separation role (2) 5: 2
  stages (2) 5: 4–9
    adolescence and confluence of generational change (2) 5: 8
    aging and death (2) 5: 9
    couple formation and mating (2) 5: 4
    first childbearing (2) 5: 5
    first year of infant's life (2) 5: 5–6
    latency, school and outer world (2) 5: 7–8
    mating and marriage of offspring and coming of grandparenthood (2) 5: 8–9
    oedipal constellation (2) 5: 7
    toddler (2) 5: 6–7
disengagement in (2) 62: 4
  during physical illness (2) 110: 2–4
double bind in (3) 7: 7
of dying patient
  disengagement in (2) 110: 5–6
  family therapy for (2) 110: 6–7
dysfunctional (2) 62: 5
of end-stage renal disease patient (2) 117: 5
enmeshment in (2) 62: 4
  during physical illness (2) 110: 2–4
epidemiologic study in child psychiatry related to (3) 12: 4
existential evaluation of (3) 7: 5
expressed emotion in (3) 15: 9
in gender identity disorders (2) 41: 2
historical perspectives on contribution to mental illness (3) 7: 13–14
in histrionic personality disorder (1) 19: 8
of hospitalized child (2) 64: 16–17
in hysterical personality disorder (1) 19: 7–8
interactional evaluation of (3) 7: 5
lines of authority in (2) 62: 5–6
loyalties and fairness in (3) 7: 9–10
marital skew, marital schism and schizophrenia (1) 54: 8; (3) 15: 8
as mediator of response to stress (2) 121: 2
mental illness impact on (3) 7: 10–12
mourning in (2) 5: 2
in organic brain syndromes (2) 87: 16–17
in paraphilias (2) 41: 4–7
parent-child relationship disorders (2) **50: 1–6**. *See also* Parent-child relationship

physical illness in
  biopsychosocial model of (2) 110: 1–2
  disengagement spiral in (2) 110: 2–4
  enmeshment spiral in (2) 110: 2–4
  systems theory for (2) 110: 1–2
problem solving by (3) 7: 7
prognosis of schizophrenia related to (3) 15: 9
in psychosocial dwarfism (2) 40: 4
in psychosomatic disorders (2) 50: 5; 110: 4–5
reconstitution of (2) 5: 10
role structure in (3) 7: 6–7
as schizophrenia risk factor (1) 54: 8–9; (3) 15: 8–9
with schizophrenic offspring (3) 7: 2–5, 12–13
  differentiation in (3) 7: 3
  double bind in (3) 7: 3–4
  family thinking in (3) 7: 3
  group therapy for (3) 7: 13
  pseudomutual relationships in (3) 7: 3, 7
  role allocation in (3) 7: 2–3
  therapist sensations in working with (3) 7: 3
  thinking processes in (3) 7: 13
of spinal cord injury patient (2) 117: 6
studies in genetics of psychiatric disorders (2) 10: 2–3
subsystems of (2) 62: 4
support groups in alcoholism (2) 89: 10
as support system in depression (1) 61: 7
triangulation in (2) 110: 5
Family consultation (2) 110: 7–9. *See also* Family therapy
Family medicine. *See* Primary care medicine
Family planning
  importance in prevention of mental illness (3) 7 11:
  need in mentally ill population (3) 7: 12
  psychiatry role in (3) 7: 12
Family psychiatry (3) **7: 1–15**. *See also* Family; Family therapy
  definition (3) 7: 1
  historical background (3) 7: 1–2
  schizophrenia studies (3) 7: 2–5. *See also* Family, with schizophrenic offspring
Family therapy (1) 9: 7–8; (2) **62: 1–11**; (3) **7: 4–10**. *See also* Family; Parents
  in anorexia nervosa (2) 110: 4–5
  in anxiety disorders (2) 39: 8
  behavior therapy in (3) 7: 8–9
  biopsychosocial model and (2) 110: 1–2
  changing vicious cycles (2) 110: 8
  of children and adolescents (2) **62: 1–11**
  choice among other formats (1) 9: 10
  classification (2) 62: 2–3
  in conflict resolution (2) 62: 4–5
  in consultation-liaison psychiatry (2) **110: 1–9**
    biopsychosocial spirals (2) 110: 2–4
    dying and grief (2) 110: 5–7
    enmeshment and disengagement spirals (2) 110: 2–4

Family therapy, in consultation-liaison psychiatry
    (continued)
    family consultation (2) 110: 7–9
    psychosomatic spirals (2) 110: 4–5
    systems theory (2) 110: 1–2
  contextual therapy (3) 7: 9–10
  contraindications (1) 9: 10
  crisis intervention in (2) 62: 10
  definition (2) 56: 2
  in depressive neurosis (1) 40: 12
  determining interactions in (3) 7: 5
  distinction between symptom etiology and symp-
      tom maintenance in (2) 62: 3
  double bind in (3) 7: 7
  in emergencies (2) 62: 9–11
  evaluation and diagnosis in (2) 62: 5–7; (3) 7: 5,
      10
    child-parent relationship (2) 62: 6
    communication styles (2) 62: 6
    conflict resolution (2) 62: 6
    flexibility and clarity of boundaries (2) 62: 6
    initial interview (2) 62: 5
    lines of authority (2) 62: 5–6
    parental relationship (2) 62: 6
    technique (3) 7: 10
  evolution of (3) 7: 4–5
  experiential (2) 62: 2–3
  goals (1) 9: 8
  historical background (1) 9: 8; (2) 62: 1–2; (3) 7:
      4–5
  identifying vicious cycles (2) 110: 7–8
  indications for (3) 7: 6
  intervention in (3) 7: 6, 10
    technique (3) 7: 10
  joining process in (2) 110: 7
  loyalities and fairness in (3) 7: 9–10
  objectives of (2) 62: 3, 7
  in paranoid disorders (1) 68: 15
  problem solving in (3) 7: 7
  projective identification in (3) 7: 9
  pseudomutuality in (3) 7: 7
  in psychosomatic illness (2) 110: 4–5
  rationale for (1) 9: 8
  reinforcing virtuous cycles (2) 110: 8–9
  in schizophrenia (3) 7: 4–5, 13
  setting (1) 9: 8
  stages (2) 110: 7
  structural (2) 62: 3–4; (3) 7: 6–7
  in suicidal behavior (2) 62: 10–11
  systems theory in (2) 110: 1–2; (3) 7: 5
  technique
    in evaluation (3) 7: 10
    for facilitating change (2) 110: 8
    in intervention (3) 7: 10
  theoretical aspects (2) 62: 3; (3) 7: 6–10
  transformational approaches between psychoana-
      lytic and behavioral therapies in (3) 7:
      8–9
  treatment process in (2) 62: 7–9
    complementary reframing (2) 62: 9
    emergency management (2) 62: 9–11
    enactment (2) 62: 7–8
    hospitalization (2) 62: 9–11
    joining (2) 62: 7
    phases of (2) 62: 7
    redefinition (2) 62: 8–9
    termination (2) 62: 7
    therapeutic tasks (2) 62: 9
    unbalancing (2) 62: 8
  varieties of (2) 62: 2–3
Fantasies, evaluation in mental status examination in
    children (2) 20: 11
Fathers, and antisocial personality of offspring (1)
    23: 5. *See also* Parents
Fears
  in agoraphobia (1) 33: 4
  anxiety distinguished from (3) 14: 1
  in childhood (2) 39: 2–3
  differential diagnosis (1) 33: 6–7
  in hospitalization and surgery (2) 121: 2–3
  obsessional (1) 34: 3
  in simple phobia (1) 33: 5
  in social phobia (1) 33: 5
Fecal incontinence, biofeedback in (2) 109: 9
Federal government. *See* Government
Feingold diet (2) 160: 1–2
Females. *See* Sex; Women
Femininity. *See also* Obstetrics-gynecology
  in boys (1) 46: 16–18
  concepts related to childbearing capacity (2) 120:
      1
Fenfluramine
  in obesity (2) 103: 9
  psychiatric side effects (2) 91: 4
Fetishism (1) 46: 5; (2) 41: 4–6
  clinical description (2) 41: 4–6
  development (2) 41: 4
Fetus, sexual differentiation (2) 9: 2–3
  gonadal sex hormones (2) 9: 2–3
  gonad differentiation (2) 9: 2
  gonadotropin releasing hormone and gonadotro-
      pins (2) 9: 2
Fever, factitious (1) 35: 17; (2) 101: 3
Fibroblast skin cultures, in neurochemistry studies on
    children (2) 12: 3
Financial assistance, for chronic mental patients (3)
    6: 9
Financing
  conflict between mental health systems and reim-
      bursing for treatmemt of episodes of ill-
      ness (3) 5: 6
  of mental health care (3) 3: 6–11; 4: 13–14
    community mental health centers (3) 3: 10–11
    discriminatory coverage (3) 3: 7–10
    DRG payment mechanism (3) 3: 10
    importance in determining treatment (3) 3: 6–7

insurance (3) 3: 7
public systems (3) 3: 10
regulation of health care spending (3) 5: 11–13
Finland, community organizations in health promotion in (2) 129: 5
Fire setting (1) 25: 4–5
Flashbacks (2) 90: 3–4
Fluency, test for (3) 52: 7–8
Fluphenazine (Prolixin)
blood levels versus therapeutic response (1) 55: 10
half-life (1) 55: 8
injectable preparation (1) 55: 11–12
in schizophrenia
dosage (1) 55: 12
preparations (1) 55: 13
structure (1) 55: 7
Flurazepam. See Benzodiazepines
Focal therapy
choice among other orientations (1) 9: 6
goals (1) 9: 3
historical aspects (1) 9: 2
rationale (1) 9: 2–3
setting for (1) 9: 3
technique (1) 9: 3
Follicle-stimulating hormone (2) 9: 1
Food, likes and dislikes after surgery for obesity (2) 103: 8
Food additives
in attention deficit disorder (3) 66: 12–13
hyperactivity related to (2) 34: 11
Forensic psychiatry (3) **36: 1–13**
agents and agency issues (3) 27: 2; 36: 1–5
informed consent in resolution of conflict in (3) 36: 4
management of conflict in (3) 36: 4
mixed agency (3) 36: 2–3
allegiance of psychiatrist in (3) 27: 2
conflicts in (3) 36: 3
alliance in
existential (3) 36: 6
medical (3) 36: 5–6
rational (3) 36: 6–7
situational (3) 36: 8
therapeutic (3) 36: 4–8
avoidance of forensic patient (3) 36: 10
blackmail in (3) 36: 8–9
civil commitment. See Civil commitment
contracts with God in (3) 36: 9
countertransference in (3) 36: 9–10
common problems (3) 36: 10
resolution (3) 36: 10
definition (3) 36: 1
ethical considerations in (3) 27: 2–3
evaluation in criminal justice system (3) **27: 1–14**
agents and agency issues (3) 27: 2; 36: 1–5
informed consent in resolution of conflict in (3) 36: 4
management of (3) 36: 4

civil commitment (3) 27: 9–10
competency to stand trial (3) 27: 3–6; 28: 2–5, 7; 36: 7
evaluation procedures and special concerns (3) 27: 5–6
legal standards for (3) 27: 3–4
other competencies (3) 27: 6
psycholegal criteria (3) 27: 4–5
for criminal responsibility (3) 27: 12–13
diminished capacity (3) 27: 9
ethical considerations (3) 27: 2–3
guilty but mentally ill (3) 27: 9; 28: 4, 6, 8
informed consent by defendant (3) 27: 12
in resolution of agency conflict (3) 36: 4
insanity defense (3) 27: 7–9; 28: 4, 5, 7–8
for malingering (3) 27: 13
mental health professional role (3) 27: 1–3
not guilty by reason of insanity (3) 28: 4, 5, 7–8
privacy (3) 27: 11
procedures for (3) 27: 11–14
psychological tests (3) 27: 13
refusal (3) 27: 12
reviewing background material (3) 27: 11–12
for substance abuse (3) 27: 13
transfer of mentally ill prisoners to hospitals (3) 27: 10–11
existential alliance in (3) 36: 6
guardianship problems in (3) 36: 12
historical background (3) 27: 1
insanity, criminal responsibility and related issues (3) 27: 6–14
institutions for mentally disordered offenders (3) 28: 14–15
interaction as n-of-1 experiment in (3) 36: 5
irrational alliance in (3) 36: 7
Lamb warning (3) 36: 4
medical alliance in (3) 36: 5–6
medicolegal issues in therapeutic setting (3) 36: 11–13
involuntary commitment in alliance (3) 36: 12
involuntary interventions other than commitment (3) 36: 13
problems with guardianship (3) 36: 12
special issues in inpatient milieu (3) 36: 11–12
threats to third parties (3) 36: 12
mentally disordered offenders (3) **28: 1–26.** See also Mentally disordered offenders
mixed agency in (3) 36: 2–3
patients' rights (3) **35: 1–15.** See also Patients' rights
rational alliance in (3) 36: 6–7
rescue fantasy in (3) 36: 10
seclusion and restraints (3) 36: 13
sharing uncertainty in (3) 36: 4–5
situational alliance in (3) 36: 8
therapeutic alliance application in (3) 36: 4–8
therapeutic contract in (3) 36: 8–9

Forensic psychiatry *(continued)*
  threats to third parties (3) 36: 12
  unsigned contracts in (3) 36: 9
  use of patient to reform system (3) 36: 10
Free association. *See also* Psychoanalysis
  explicitness of agreement for (1) 8: 7
  Freud's concept (1) 1: 4
  interferences in (1) 8: 2
  in psychoanalysis (1) 8: 2–3
  recognizing determinants (1) 8: 5–7
    completion of interrupted mourning (1) 8: 6
    delineation and tolerance of affects (1) 8: 6
    expansion of condensation (1) 8: 5–6
    inner conflict (1) 8: 6
    learning and identification (1) 8: 7
    transference (1) 8: 6–7
    unconscious determinants (1) 8: 5
  and theories of cure (1) 8: 3
Freud, Sigmund
  on anxiety disorder (1) 32: 5
  on compulsive personality disorder (1) 22: 3
  on conversion disorder (1) 35: 7
  on defense (1) 1: 3–4
  on dreams (1) 1: 5–6; (3) 60: 11
  on free association (1) 1: 4
  on grief (1) 41: 5
  influences allowing discovery of psychoanalysis (1)
      1: 2–3
  on latency (2) 3: 2
  on libido theory (1) 1: 7
  on masochistic personality (1) 27: 5
  on neuroses (1) 31: 4
  on Oedipus complex (1) 1: 6
  on panic disorder (1) 32: 5
  on paranoid disorders (1) 68: 2, 5
  on phobias (1) 33: 1, 8
  psychoanalysis development by (1) 1: 3–8
  on regression (1) 1: 7
  on repression (1) 1: 5
  on resistance (1) 1: 3
  on sexual development (1) 1: 6–7
  on transference (1) 1: 4–5
Friedreich's ataxia, psychosis in (1) 69: 7
Frigidity (1) 47: 5
Frontalis muscle, in biofeedback (2) 109: 5, 6
Frontal lobe, in decision making (1) 28: 6
Frontal lobe syndromes (1) 28: 10–11
  causes (1) 28: 11
  clinical description (2) 87: 11–12
  dorsolateral (1) 28: 10
  hypofrontality in schizophrenia (1) 64: 7
  orbital (1) 28: 10
  pathophysiology (2) 87: 12
  personality changes after injury (1) 28: 1
  treatment (2) 87: 12
  ventromedial (1) 28: 10
Fugue (1) **39: 6–7.** *See also* Dissociative disorders
  amnesia distinguished from (1) 39: 3
  clinical description (1) 39: 6–7

  differential diagnosis (1) 39: 7
  DSM-III definition (1) 39: 6
  epidemiology (1) 39: 6
  etiology (1) 39: 7
  multiple personality distinguished from (1) 39: 9
Functional psychiatric disorders
  historical background (1) 52: 14–15
  neuropsychological assessment in (1) 72: 12–15
  organic mental disorders distinguished from (1)
      72: 2, 13–14

GABA
  in electroconvulsive therapy (3) 68: 4
  in extrapyramidal toxicity of neuroleptics (1) 55:
      21–22
  and limbic-hypothalamic-pituitary axis dysregula-
      tion in melancholia (3) 54: 7
  receptor-drug interactions (3) 50: 8
Gait, as clue to underlying disorder (2) 20: 5
Galvanic skin response, in biofeedback (2) 109: 5
Gambling, pathologic (1) 25: 2–3
  DSM-III definition (1) 25: 3
  natural history of (1) 25: 3
  psychodynamics (1) 25: 3
  psychotherapy in (1) 25: 3
Gamma-aminobutyric acid. *See* GABA
Ganser syndrome, definition (2) 101: 1
Gastric bypass surgery
  emotional response to (2) 103: 6, 7
  positive effects (2) 103: 6, 8
Gastrointestinal tract
  biofeedback and relaxation therapy for disorders c
      (2) 109: 9
  biopsy in studying peptides (2) 12: 3
  factitous disease involving (2) 101: 4–5
Gender disorders (1) **46: 1–18.** *See also* Gender iden
      tity disorders; Paraphilias
  sexual disorders distinguished from (1) 46: 2
Gender dysphoria (1) 46: 10
Gender identity
  brain role in (1) 45: 3–4
  homosexuality related to childhood disturbance in
      (1) 45: 6
  in male pseudohermaphroditism (2) 9: 6
  in prenatal virilization of female fetus (2) 9: 6–7
    in congenital adrenal hyperplasia (2) 9: 6–7
    after prenatal treatment with progestins (2) 9: 7
  sex hormones effects on (2) 9: 6–7
  sex reassignment of normal male, effect on (2) 9:
Gender identity disorders (1) **46: 10–18;** (2) 41: 2–
  in childhood (1) 46: 16–18
    clinical course (1) 46: 17
    clinical description (1) 46: 16–17
    definition (1) 46: 16
    diagnosis and differential diagnosis (1) 46: 18
    epidemiology (1) 46: 16
    etiology (1) 46: 17–18
    prognosis (1) 46: 17

treatment (1) 46: 18
clinical description (2) 41: 3–4
definition (1) 46: 10
DSM-III definition (2) 41: 2
family dynamics in (2) 41: 2
female transsexualism (1) 46: 15–16
male transsexualism (1) 46: 10–15
paraphilias distinguished from (1) 46: 9
prognosis (2) 41: 3
Gender-role behavior (1) 46: 2
areas comprising (2) 9: 7
in congenital adrenal hyperplasia (2) 9: 7
after prenatal treatment with progestins (2) 9: 7
sex hormones effects on (2) 9: 7
in transsexualism (1) 46: 11
Gender-role identity (1) 46: 2
General appearance, in psychodynamic mental status examination (1) 6: 10
Generalized anxiety disorder. *See* Anxiety disorder, generalized
Genetic counseling, in mental retardation (2) 58: 4
Genetic epidemiology (1) 62: 1–4. *See also* Genetics
Genetic marker (1) 62: 4
Genetics
of affective disorders (1) 3: 3; **62: 12–19;** (3) 53: 4–5
adoption studies (1) 62: 15–16
biological markers and linkage study (1) 62: 17–18; (3) 53: 4–9
heterogeneity (1) 62: 18–19
mode of inheritance (1) 62: 16–17
population and family studies (1) 62: 12–14
schizophrenia and (1) 62: 19–20
of alcoholism (3) 53: 9–10
of Alzheimer's disease (1) 73: 8
of antisocial personality (1) 23: 5–6
of anxiety disorders (3) 14: 4, 10
of attention deficit disorder (2) 36: 4; (3) 66: 10
in avoidant personality (1) 24: 6
in bipolar disorder (1) 60: 10; (3) 13: 11–12
of borderline personality disorder (1) 3: 6
of compulsive personality disorder (1) 22: 5
of conduct disorder (2) 37: 4–5
definitions in (2) 10: 1
of dementia (3) 21: 7
in depression (1) 60: 6; (3) 13: 7
and drug-related behavioral effects (3) 45: 5
epidemiologic studies (3) 11: 12
producing advances in (3) 11: 6–7
generalized single major locus model (1) 62: 3
of hysterical and histrionic personality disorder (1) 19: 6
linkage studies
in affective disorders (1) 62: 17–18
in schizophrenia (1) 62: 12
major directions in (1) 62: 1
mapping of genome in (1) 62: 4
markers in (3) 53: 1–2. *See also* Markers
in affective disorders (1) 62: 4, 17–18; (3) 53: 4–9

association versus linkage (3) 53: 2–3
dichotomous versus continuous (3) 53: 2
methodologic considerations in study (3) 53: 2–4
possible uses (3) 53: 2
requirements to be ideal (3) 53: 3
of masochistic personality (1) 27: 4–5
of mental retardation, and prevention (2) 28: 6–7
methods used in (1) 62: 2–4
mixed model in (1) 62: 3
multifactorial-polygenic model (1) 62: 2–3; (2) 10: 4–5
in neurochemistry (2) 12: 5
of obesity (2) 103: 4
of obsessive-compulsive disorder (1) 34: 2–3
of panic disorder (1) 3: 7; 32: 9
of paranoid personality disorder (1) 16: 9–10
path analysis (1) 62: 3–4
pedigree analysis in (2) 10: 6–7
of personality (2) 42: 2
of phobias (1) 33: 9
of puberty onset (2) 9: 4
research designs in (2) 10: 1–4
of schizophrenia (1) 54: 6–8; **62: 1, 4–12;** (3) 15: 6–7, 12; 53: 12
adoption studies (1) 62: 8–10
affective disorders and (1) 62: 19–20
biological markers and linkage study (1) 62: 11–12
heterogeneity (1) 62: 10
mode of inheritance (1) 62: 10
polygenic-multifactorial models (1) 62: 11
population and family studies (1) 62: 4–6
single gene models (1) 62: 10–11
twin studies (1) 62: 6–8
of schizotypal personality disorder (1) 16: 6–7
segregation analysis in (2) 10: 6–7
and sleep requirements (3) 61: 1
strategies for study in psychiatry (2) **10: 1–9**
adoption studies (2) 10: 2
complicating factors in (2) 10: 7–9
diagnostic imprecision as limitation in (2) 10: 7–8
family studies (2) 10: 2–3
hypothesis testing in (2) 10: 8–9
linkage studies (2) 10: 3–4
mixed model (2) 10: 7
models and analytic methodologies (2) 10: 4–9
multifactorial-polygenic model (2) 10: 4–5
pedigree analysis (2) 10: 6–7
research approaches in childhood behavioral disorders (2) 10: 9
restriction fragment length polymorphisms (2) 10: 3–4
segregation analysis (2) 10: 6–7
single-major-locus or two-allele autosomal model (2) 10: 5–7
twin studies (2) 10: 2
of suicidal behavior (1) 71: 6

Genetics *(continued)*
  of symptomatic psychoses (1) 69: 11–12
  terminology used in (1) 62: 2
  tetrachoric correlation coefficient in (1) 62: 2–3
  of Tourette's disorder (2) 38: 3–4
Genotype (1) 62: 2; (2) 10: 1
Geographical factors
  in mental illness. *See* Cross-cultural psychiatry;
      Culture
  in suicide rates
    international (3) 20: 6, 8
    regional within U.S. (3) 20: 8–9
Geophagia (2) 40: 2
Geriatric psychiatry (2) **119: 1–9.** *See also* Elderly
Gesell, Arnold
  contributions to child development (2) 1: 3
  on latency (2) 3: 1
Gestalt therapy (1) 9: 6
Glucose, utilization in brain
  in schizophrenia (3) 51: 6
  studied by positive emission tomography (3) 51: 4
Glue sniffing, toxic effects (2) 90: 4
Golgi type I and II neurons (3) 42: 7
Gonadotropin releasing hormones (2) 9: 1
  in fetus (2) 9: 2
Gonadotropins (2) 9: 1–2
  in anorexia nervosa (2) 102: 3–4
  in fetus (2) 9: 2
  follicle-stimulating hormone (2) 9: 1
  in infants (2) 9: 3
  luteinizing hormone (2) 9: 2
  in prepubescent children and adolescents (2) 9: 3
  in sleep (3) 60: 5
Gonads, differentiation in fetus (2) 9: 2
Government. *See also* Legislation
  in community mental health services (3) **5: 1–13.**
      See also Community mental health ser-
      vices
  mental health centers program (3) 4: 10
  organization of mental health services influencing
      utilization (3) 22: 8–9
  political issues in funding care for chronic mental
      patients (3) 6: 12–13
  psychiatrist role in public policy formulation (3) 4:
      16
  reimbursement for chronic mental patient care (3)
      6: 12–13
  in research (3) 4: 3–6
  role in mental health (3) **4: 1–16**
    in community treatment programs (3) 4: 9–12;
        5: 1–13
    critical issues in mental health services in 1980s
        (3) 4: 13–15
    deinstitutionalization (3) 4: 11–12
    in education and training (3) 4: 6–9
    in financing mental health services (3) 3: 10–
        11; 4: 13–14; 6: 12–13
    historical background (3) 4: 1–2

  and manpower development (3) 4: 7–8
  National Institute of Mental Health (3) 4: 2–6
  in new federalism program of President Reagan
      (3) 4: 13
  President's Commission on Mental Health (3) 4:
      12–13
  in research (3) 4: 3–6. *See also* Research
  in services (3) 4: 9–15
  in training and education (3) 4: 6–8
Graft rejection, stress related to (2) 128: 5–6
Grave disability, predictors for (3) 32: 14–15
Graves' disease (2) 88: 7–8. *See also* Hyperthyroidism
Grief reaction (2) 78: 6
  bereavement and mourning distinguished from (2)
      95: 13
  circumstances likely to increase severity or dura-
      tion (1) 41: 8
  depression distinguished from (1) 40: 8–9; (2) 95:
      13
  in children (2) 30: 5
  emergency department management (2) 95:
      13
  family therapy in (2) 110: 6–7
  immediately after death (2) 110: 6
  in medical illness (2) 99: 3
  normal reaction (2) 99: 3
  normal versus pathologic (1) 41: 5–6
  pathologic (2) 78: 6–7; 99: 3
  in recovery from chronic illness or handicap (1)
      41: 6
  resolution therapy for (2) 110: 6–7
  stages of (1) 41: 5–6
  stress-response syndrome after (1) 41: 9–10
  treatment (2) 95: 13
Group for Advancement of Psychiatry, classification
      system in child psychiatry (2) 19: 2
Group homes. *See also* Residential treatment
  comparison with hospital and residential treatment
      (2) 64: 2, 3
  historical background (2) 64: 3
  spectrum of services in (2) 64: 5
Groups. *See also* Group therapy
  in alcoholism (2) 89: 9–10
    for family (2) 89: 10
    for patient (2) 89: 9
  for weight control (2) 103: 11–12
Group therapy (1) 9: 8–10. *See also* Groups
  in Briquet's syndrome (2) 100: 9
  children and adolescents (2) **63: 1–7**
    age and gender in (2) 63: 2–3
    behavior therapy (2) 63: 4
    classification (2) 63: 4–6
    cognitive therapy (2) 63: 4
    composition of group (2) 63: 2
    contraindication to (2) 63: 3
    curative factors basic to (2) 63: 3–4
    developmental stages and (2) 63: 5–6
    duration of session (2) 63: 3

early school-age children (2) 63: 6
family contact in (2) 63: 3
frequency of sessions (2) 63: 3
goals and definitions (2) 63: 1–2
group leader in (2) 63: 3
homogeneity of group (2) 63: 2
individual interviewing prior to (2) 63: 2
in inpatient programs (2) 64: 15
preadolescents (2) 63: 6
preschool children (2) 63: 5–6
psychoanalytic (2) 63: 4
relationships within group (2) 63: 4–5
rules in (2) 63: 3
setting for (2) 63: 2
size of group (2) 63: 2
technical considerations (2) 63: 2–4
termination (2) 63: 3
theoretic orientation (2) 63: 4
therapeutic outcome (2) 63: 6–7
transactional analysis (2) 63: 4
choice among other formats (1) 9: 10–11
classification (2) 63: 4–6
curative factors basic to (2) 63: 3–4
definition (2) 56: 2
for family with schizophrenic offspring (3) 7: 13
goals (1) 9: 9
heterogeneous (1) 9: 9
   indications (1) 9: 10
historical aspects (1) 9: 8–9
homogeneous (1) 9: 9
   indications (1) 9: 11
in hypochondriasis (2) 100: 3
indications (1) 9: 10–11
outcome measures (2) 63: 6–7
setting for (1) 9: 9
techniques (1) 9: 9–10
testimonial privilege in (3) 31: 5
Growth
methylphenidate effect on (2) 36: 11
neuroendocrine correlates (2) 9: 1–2
   gonadotropins (2) 9: 1–2
   hypothalamic releasing hormones (2) 9: 1
   sex hormones (2) 9: 2
stimulants effect on (3) 66: 19–20
Growth hormone
in affective disorders (1) 64: 11–12
in anorexia nervosa (2) 102: 4
behavioral correlates of deficiency (2) 9: 11
in electroconvulsive therapy (3) 68: 5
in growth (2) 9: 4
and immune system, stress effects (2) 128: 11
in sleep (3) 60: 5
Guanethidine, psychiatric side effects (2) 91: 5
Guardianship, problems in forensic psychiatry (3) 36:
   12
Guilt
interventions to alleviate (2) 108: 9
reactivation in physically ill patient (2) 121: 2

in survivor of loved one (1) 41: 11
Guilty but mentally ill (3) 27: 9; 28: 4, 6, 8. See also
   Mentally disordered offenders
   treatment considerations (3) 28: 21
Gunderson, J., on borderline disorders (1) 17: 4–5
Gynecology. See Obstetrics-gynecology

Habituation (2) 13: 1–2. See also Learning
of blink response in schizophrenia (3) 65: 6
definition (3) 65: 2–3
of electrodermal response in schizophrenia (3) 65:
   6
in memory (3) 71: 2–3
model in Aplysia california (2) 13: 4–5
molecular basis (2) 13: 4–5
in psychiatric disorders (3) **65: 1–11**
Hair analysis, therapy based on (2) 160: 3
Haldol. See Haloperidol
Haley, J., contributions to strategic therapy model
   (1) 9: 4–5
Half-life, of neuroleptics (1) 55: 8
Half-way house, for chronic mental patient (3) 6: 10
Hall, G. Stanley, contributions in child psychiatry (2)
   1: 1–2
Hallucinations
alcohol causing (2) 35: 3
in Alzheimer's disease (1) 73: 7
in amnesia (1) 39: 5
auditory, in schizophrenia (1) 53: 8–9
in children (2) 20: 10–11
   in anxiety (2) 20: 10–11
   drugs causing (2) 20: 10
   in infections (2) 20: 10
   metabolic disorders causing (2) 20: 10
   schizophrenia causing (2) 20: 11
   in seizure disorder (2) 20: 10
   as stress response (2) 20: 10
in conduct disorder in adolescent (2) 37: 6
cultural definition of abnormality (3) 15: 2
cultural relativism of (3) 2: 2–3
in delirium (1) 73: 14; (2) 87: 5
   auditory (1) 73: 14
   visual (1) 73: 14
drug abuse causing (2) 90: 8, 9
hypnagogic (3) 61: 12
   in narcolepsy (2) 52: 8; 105: 13
organic (2) 87: 13
   in children (2) 34: 2
   definition (2) 87: 1
   etiology (2) 87: 13
   pathophysiology (2) 87: 13
   treatment (2) 87: 13
      drugs (2) 87: 15–16
      psychotherapy in (2) 87: 17
phencyclidine causing (2) 90: 8

Hallucinations *(continued)*
  in schizophrenia
    acute illness (1) 53: 8−9
    chronic illness (1) 53: 13
  in stress-response syndrome (1) 41: 3
  in substance abuse (2) 87: 13
  tactile, in schizophrenia (1) 53: 9
  toxic (2) 90: 8
  true distinguished from pseudo (1) 53: 9
  visual, in schizophrenia (1) 53: 9
Hallucinogens
  abuse of (3) 17: 15
    comparative rates with other drugs (3) 17: 15
    demographic trends (3) 17: 15
    epidemiology (3) 17: 15
    temporal trends (3) 17: 15
  affective disorder (2) 35: 5
  animal models for (3) 46: 12−18
    and exploration (3) 46: 14−16
    face validity (3) 46: 17−18
    parallels between effects on humans (3) 46: 16
    relevance to schizophrenia (3) 46: 12−13
    and spontaneous activity (3) 46: 14
    treatment validity (3) 46: 16−17
  in children (2) 20: 10
  clinical features (2) 35: 5
  complications (2) 90: 3−4
  delusions due to (2) 35: 5; 87: 14
  human effects (3) 46: 12−13
  schizophrenia distinguished from effects of (3) 46: 12−13
  symptoms of overdose (2) 90: 3
Haloperidol (Haldol). *See also* Antipsychotic drugs;
      Neuroleptics
  in Alzheimer's disease (2) 119: 3
  blood levels versus route of administration (1) 55: 8−9
  developmental pharmacokinetics (2) 59: 3
  efficacy related to affinity for dopamine receptors (3) 50: 3−4
  interactions with other drugs (1) 55: 11; (2) 111: 2, 5
  lithium interaction with (1) 55: 11
  in organic brain syndromes (2) 87: 15, 16
  organic mental disorders precipitated by (2) 34: 6
  in rapid tranquilization (2) 95: 5
  in schizophrenia
    dosage (1) 55: 12
    preparations (1) 55: 13
  in severe agitation (2) 59: 7
  structure (1) 55: 4
  in stuttering (2) 43: 9
  in Tourette's disorder (2) 38: 6; 59: 7
Halstead Impairment Index (1) 72: 4
Halstead-Reitan Neuropsychological Battery (1) 7: 7;
      72: 4−6; (3) 52: 14
  allied procedures in (1) 72: 4, 6
  for broad view of cognitive and emotional func-
      tioning (1) 72: 2

  in children (2) 21: 8
  individual tests in (1) 72: 5
  use of (1) 72: 6
Hamilton Rating Scale for Depression (1) 7: 8
Headache
  biofeedback in (2) 109: 5−6
  migraine (2) 104: 6−8. *See also* Migraine headache
  relaxation therapy in (2) 109: 5−6
Head banging
  in sleep (2) 52: 4−5
  treatment (2) 52: 5
Head trauma
  amnesia after (1) 72: 10; (3) 71: 7
  attention deficit disorder related to (2) 36: 3
  behavioral effects (1) 72: 11
  neuropsychological assessment in (1) 72: 10−11
  organic mental disorders due to (2) 34: 7
  personality change due to (1) 28: 3−4
  psychosis after (1) 69: 2−3
Health behavior (2) **129: 1−6.** *See also* Health pro-
      motion; Illness behavior
  decisions about seeking medical attention (2) 79: 3−4
  factors influencing illness behavior (3) 22: 9−11
  physician-patient relationship determining (2) 81: 5
  psychotherapy effect on (2) 129: 11
  as risk factors for leading causes of death (2) 129: 1, 5−6
  and somatization reactions (1) 35: 2
Health care. *See* Medical care; Mental health care
Health education
  contradictory messages in (2) 79: 4−5
  definition (2) 129: 2
  effectiveness of (2) 129: 3
  experimental studies on (2) 129: 2−3
  in health promotion (2) 129: 2
  in hypertension (2) 129: 2−3
  lifecycle approach to (2) 129: 2
  lifestyle changes and reduction of heart disease
      deaths (2) 79: 4
  role in disease or injury prevention (2) 79: 5−6
  on smoking (2) 129: 3
Health insurance. *See* Insurance
Health Professions Educational Assistance Act (3) 4: 7
Health promotion (2) **129: 1−6.** *See also* Health be-
      havior
  in alcohol abuse prevention (2) 129: 5−6
  definition (2) 129: 2
  health education in (2) 129: 2
  lifestyle construct in (2) 129: 6
  mass media role in (2) 129: 4
  settings and channels for (2) 129: 2−5
    community organizations (2) 129: 4−5
    mass communication (2) 129: 4
    medical care settings (2) 129: 2−3
    schools (2) 129: 3
    worksites (2) 129: 3−4

in smoking prevention (2) 129: 5–6
Healy, W., contributions to juvenile delinquency (2) 1: 2–3
Hearing
    evaluation in language disorders (2) 49: 9
    event-related potentials in selective attention (3) 62: 6
Hearing loss
    attention deficit disorder distinguished from (2) 36: 6
    pervasive developmental disorders distinguished from (2) 27: 8
Heart. *See also* Heart disease
    antidepressants effect on (2) 59: 15–16; 99: 5–6
    transplantation, psychiatric aspects (2) 118: 5
Heart disease. *See also* Coronary artery disease
    arrhythmias and sudden death (2) 118: 5
    biobehavioral factors in (2) **126: 1–8**
        mechanisms (2) 126: 5–6
    cardiac transplantation in (2) 118: 5
    coronary bypass surgery in (2) 118: 3–5
    mitral valve prolapse syndrome (2) 118: 5–7
    myocardial infarction (2) 118: 1–3
    psychiatric aspects (2) 126: (2) **118: 1–7**
Heart surgery, anxiety levels and outcome (2) 121: 5. *See also* Coronary bypass surgery
Hebephrenic schizophrenia (1) 53: 15
Helplessness, learned (2) 78: 4; (3) 55: 7
Hematologic disorders
    factitious (2) 101: 4
    neuroleptics causing (1) 55: 25–26
Hemispheric specialization (1) 72: 3, 9–10
    declarative memory (3) 52: 13–14
    event-related potentials in study of (3) 62: 11
    left hemispheric deficit in schizophrenia (1) 72: 15
    neuropsychological assessment (2) 21: 9
    right hemisphere syndromes (1) 28: 9–10
        deficit in affective disorders (1) 72: 14
    sex differences in fetal development (2) 9: 8
    in specific developmental language disorders (2) 49: 6
    in speech and language (3) 67: 10–13
    verbal and nonverbal functions (3) 67: 10–13
Hemodialysis, in schizophrenia (1) 55: 2–3. *See also* Kidney, end-stage disease
Hemolysis, sleep-related (2) 105: 16
Hepatolenticular degeneration
    organic mental disorders in children due to (2) 34: 7–9
    psychosis in (1) 69: 6–7
Heredity. *See* Genetics
Heroin. *See also* Substance abuse
    comparison of use in U.S. soldiers in Vietnam and those on U.S. mainland (3) 17: 2–3
    epidemiology of abuse (3) 17: 10–11
    renal failure related to (2) 90: 3
Herstedvester prison treatment program (3) 28: 15
Heterocyclic antidepressants. *See* Antidepressants, heterocyclic

Higher-order schemata, in attention deficit disorder (3) 66: 5
Hippocampus. *See* Limbic system
Histamine receptors, neuroleptics interaction with (1) 55: 19–20
    and side effects (1) 55: 25
Histocompatibility antigens (HLA)
    in affective disorders (1) 62: 17–18; (3) 53: 7
    in schizophrenia (1) 62: 12; (3) 53: 13
Historical background (1) **52: 1–21**
    of adolescence (2) 4: 2
    of affective disorders (1) 52: 18–19, 20; 59: 1, 5–7
        in children (2) 30: 1
        classification (1) 52: 18–19
            attempts before DSM-III (1) 59: 5–7
            psychoanalysis impact (1) 52: 19–20
    of antisocial personality (1) 23: 1–2
    of anxiety disorders (2) 39: 1–2; (3) 14: 1–2
    of attention deficit disorder (2) 36: 1
    of autism (2) 27: 1–2
    of avoidant personality (1) 24: 1–3
    of behavioral medicine (2) 76: 4–5
    of behavior therapy (1) 52: 11; (2) 77: 3
    of biofeedback (2) 109: 4–5
    of biological theory (1) 52: 4
    of borderline personality disorder (1) 17: 1–2
    of Briquet's syndrome (1) 35: 14
    of care for chronic mental patients (3) 6: 1–3
    of child psychiatry (2) **1: 1–5**; 19: 1–2
    of civil commitment (3) 32: 1–3
    of classification
    of community child psychiatry (2) 69: 1–2
    of community mental health services (3) 4: 9–12; 5: 1–5; 6: 2–3
    of compulsive personality disorder (1) 22: 1, 3–4
    of conduct disorder (2) 37: 1–3
    of consultation-liaison psychiatry (2) 76: 4, 6
    of conversion disorder (1) 35: 3–4
    of cross-cultural psychiatry (3) 2: 1–2
    decline and rebirth of biological psychiatry (1) 52: 6–7
    of dependent personality disorder (1) 26: 1
    of depressive neurosis (1) 40: 1–2
    of descriptive phenomenology paradigm (1) 52: 11–14
    of dissociative disorders (1) 39: 1–2
    of eating disorders (2) 102: 1
    of epidemiology (3) 11: 2–3
        in child and adolescent psychiatric disorders (3) 12: 2–4
        in psychiatry (3) 11: 3–6
    of family psychiatry (3) 7: 1–2
    of family therapy (2) 62: 1–2
    of fictitious disease (2) 101: 2
    of functional disorders (1) 52: 14–15
    of government role in mental health (3) 4: 1–2
    of hospitals, for children (2) 64: 1–3
    of hypnosis (2) 112: 1–2

Historical background *(continued)*
  of hypochondriasis (1) 35: 10
  influence of Adolf Meyer (1) 52: 5–6
  influence of Sigmund Freud. *See* Freud, Sigmund
  of informed consent (3) 30: 1–3
  of interpersonal psychiatry (1) 52: 10–11
  of latency (2) 3: 2
  of learning disabilities (2) 48: 3–4
  of learning theories (1) 2: 9–23
  of mental health care system (3) 4: 9–13
  mental hospital movement (1) 52: 3–4
  of mental retardation (2) 28: 1–2
  of narcissistic personality disorder (1) 18: 1–2
  of neuropsychology (3) 52: 1–3
  of neuroses (1) 31: 2–4; 52: 4–5
    experimental (1) 2: 13–14
  of neurotransmitters (1) 52: 15
    research strategies (3) 43: 1–2
  of obesity (2) 103: 1
  of obsessive-compulsive disorder (1) 34: 1–2
  of organic brain disorders (1) 52: 14–16
  of pain concepts (2) 104: 1
  paradigms in psychiatry (1) 52: 1–3, 6–14
  of paranoid disorder (1) 68: 2–3
  of paranoid personality disorder (1) 16: 8
  of patients' rights (3) 35: 1–2
  of personality changes associated with neurologic
    disease (1) 28: 1–2
  of pervasive developmental disorders (2) 27: 1–2
  of phobias (1) 33: 1
  of physician-patient relationship (2) 81: 1–3
  of psychiatry in primary care medicine (2) 116: 1
  of psychoanalysis (1) 1: 2–5; 52: 7–8
  of psychological tests (1) 15: 1–3; 72: 1–2
  of psychosomatic medicine (2) 76: 3–4; 78: 1–3;
    126: 2
  reform movements (1) 52: 5
  of relaxation therapy (2) 109: 1
  of research in mental health (3) 4: 3–6
  of residential treatment (2) 64: 1–3
  of schizoaffective disorder (1) 70: 1–2
  of schizoid personality disorder (1) 16: 1
  of schizophrenia (1) 52: 16–18; 53: 1–4
    in children (2) 29: 1
    treatment (1) 55: 1–2
  of schizotypal personality disorder (1) 16: 4
  of social psychiatry (1) 52: 9–10
  of somatoform disorders (1) 35: 1–2
  of state hospitals (3) 6: 2
  of suicide (1) 71: 1–2
  18th and 19th century (1) 52: 3–6
  of training in mental health (3) 4: 6–8
History-taking. *See also* Interviewing
  in alcoholism (2) 89: 5–6
  in attention deficit disorder (2) 36: 6–7; (3) 66: 13–
    14
  chief complaint (1) 6: 2
  in conduct disorder (2) 37: 8

  in consultation psychiatry (2) 115: 2–3
  education on (2) 116: 6
  on impotence (1) 47: 4
  interviewing in (2) 20: 2–4
  patient's perspective of his problem (1) **6: 1–5**. *See
    also* Patient, perspective of problem
  to predict violent behavior (2) 95: 7–8
  in psychiatric assessment of children (2) 20: 2
  in sexual disorders (1) 47: 8–9
  in sleep disorders (2) 105: 3; 119: 8; (3) 61: 2–4
  on suicidal behavior (1) 61: 6
Histrionic personality. *See also* Hysteria
  antisocial personality distinguished from (1) 23: 3
  in Briquet's syndrome (2) 100: 8
  characteristics (2) 82: 3–4
  in conversion disorder (2) 47: 5
  impact of medical illness in (2) 82: 4–5
  in medical setting (2) 82: 3–5
  psychodynamics (2) 82: 4
Histrionic personality disorder (1) **19: 1–10**
  borderline personality disorder distinguished from
    (1) 19: 9
  borderline personality disorder overlap with (1)
    19: 2
  in children and adolescents (1) 19: 6
  clinical description (1) 19: 5–6
  confused terminology in (1) 19: 1–2
  contraindications to psychotherapy in (1) 19: 9–
    10
  controversies in (1) 19: 2
  cultural factors in (1) 19: 8
  definition (1) 19: 1
  differential diagnosis (1) 19: 9
  epidemiology (1) 19: 2–3
  etiology (1) 19: 6–8
  family dynamics in (1) 19: 8
  genetic factors in (1) 19: 6
  hysterical personality disorder distinguished from
    (1) 19: 5
  in men (1) 19: 5–6
  narcissistic personality disorder distinguished from
    (1) 18: 9
  prognosis (1) 19: 6
  psychoanalytic concepts (1) 19: 7
  treatment (1) 19: 9–10
  in women (1) 19: 5
Holistic medicine (2) 81: 3
Homocystinuria, organic mental disorders in children
    due to (2) 34: 9
Homosexuality (1) **45: 4–7**
  androgen deficiency at critical period related to (1)
    45: 7
  changing concepts in classification (1) 46: 3
  continuum of sexual behavior in (1) 45: 4
  controversy regarding psychopathologic nature (1)
    45: 4–5
  cross gender behavior as child related to (2) 41: 2
  definition (1) 45: 4

DSM-III deletion (1) 45: 5
effeminacy in (1) 45: 6
etiology (1) 45: 6–7
gender identity disturbance in childhood related to
        (1) 45: 6
immutability versus plasticity of sex print in (1)
        45: 7
in paranoid disorder (1) 68: 5
paranoid ideation related to (1) 16: 10
paraphilias distinguished from (1) 46: 9
in psychiatric disorders (1) 45: 5–6
psychoanalytic theory of (1) 45: 7
secondary (1) 45: 5–6
sex hormones and (2) 9: 8
sex print in (1) 45: 5–7
transient transsexual feelings in (1) 46: 11
Homovanillic acid, CSF levels, developmental consid-
        erations (2) 12: 11
Hopelessness, suicide correlation with (1) 71: 4
Hormones. *See also* Endocrine disorders; Neuroendo-
        crinology
    circadian rhythm of blood and tissue levels (3) 59:
        2; 60: 5–6
    and immune system
        in depression (2) 128: 12–13
        stress effects (2) 128: 10–11
    sex (2) 9: 2. *See also* Androgens; Estrogens; Sex
        hormones
Hospitalization. *See also* Hospitals
    in alcoholism (2) 89: 9
    in anorexia nervosa (2) 102: 7–8
    for antisocial personality
        general psychiatric institution (1) 23: 9
        special programs (1) 23: 7–8
    in back pain (2) 104: 9
    in bipolar disorder (1) 60: 9; (3) 13: 9–10
    in child psychiatry (2) **64: 1–19**
        in assessment process (2) 64: 11–12
        behavior therapy (2) 64: 14
        clinical administration and (2) 64: 8–11, 15
        crisis producing change in child and family (2)
            64: 4–5
        design of activities program (2) 64: 13
        design of daily schedule (2) 64: 13
        design of living unit (2) 64: 13
        dismantling apparatus of illness during treatment
            (2) 64: 12
        education (2) 64: 16
        evaluation and follow-up (2) 64: 18
        exploitation of live events (2) 64: 13–14
        family treatment (2) 64: 16–17
        future needs (2) 64: 18–19
        goals (2) 64: 4
        group therapy (2) 64: 15
        historical background (2) 64: 1–3
        individual therapy (2) 64: 17
        isolation versus community orientation (2) 64:
            14–15

        long-term placement (2) 64: 17
        milieu therapy (2) 64: 12–15
        outcome (2) 64: 17–18
        pharamacotherapy (2) 64: 15–16
        planning (2) 64: 6–8
        public policy on (2) 64: 5–6
            certificate of need determination for (2) 64: 5
            insurance coverage (2) 64: 6
            rate setting in (2) 64: 5–6
            service spectrum (2) 64: 6
        regressive or progressive emphasis in (2) 64: 14
        seclusion and restraint (2) 64: 15
        security considerations (2) 64: 13
        spectrum of services (2) 64: 4–5
        termination (2) 64: 12
        treatment components (2) 64: 12–18
    child's reaction to (2) 72: 5
    for chronic mental patients (3) 6: 5–7
        acute level (3) 6: 5–6
        custodial care (3) 6: 6
        intermittent length stay (3) 6: 6
    civil commitment (3) **32: 1–16.** *See also* Civil com-
        mitment
    comparison with group home and residential treat-
        ment (2) 64: 2, 3
    in depression (1) 61: 7–8
        in elderly (2) 119: 5
    informed consent for (3) 30: 13–14
        information required to be disclosed in (3) 30: 4
    joint admission for mentally ill mother and infant
        or child (3) 7: 11
    for mentally disordered offenders (3) 28: 14
    in mental retardation (2) 58: 5
    in paranoid disorders (1) 68: 14–16
    patients' rights during (3) 35: 7–10
        balancing rights of one patient infringing upon
            rights of others (3) 36: 11
    of prisoners (3) 27: 10–11
    of psychotic patient (2) 95: 6
    in pyschiatric emergencies of children and adoles-
        cents (2) 62: 11
    stress of (2) 121: 2
    of suicidal patient (1) 71: 11, 16; (2) 95: 11
    treatment planning for (2) 56: 7
    utilization statistics for psychiatric patient (3) 22: 4–
        5
Hospitals
    for chronic mental patients (3) 22: 5
    clinical administration in (2) 64: 8–11, 15
    corporations role in cost containment (3) 5: 12
    future in mental health (3) 4: 14–15
    historical background (1) 52: 3–4; (3) 6: 1–2; 32:
        1–2
        for children (2) 64: 1–3
    for mental health care (3) 22: 4–5
    mentally disordered offenders treatment in (3) 28:
        14
    private for-profit (3) 4: 15

Hospitals *(continued)*
  psychiatric disorders treated in general facility (3) 22: 6
  residential treatment compared with (2) 64: 2
  specialized units for psychosomatic medicine (2) 78: 8–9
  spectrum of services for children (2) 64: 4–5
Hostility
  coronary heart disease related to (2) 126: 4–5
  depression related to (1) 52: 20
  paranoid ideation related to (1) 16: 10
Hot flashes, in menopause (2) 120: 7
Housing, for chronic mental patients (3) 6: 10
Hull, C., contribution to learning theory (1) 2: 14
Human experimentation, informed consent in (3) 30: 11–12
  in Alzheimer's disease (3) 30: 13
  competency to give (3) 30: 5
  federal regulations on (3) 30: 11–12
  physician acceptance of (3) 30: 8
Human sexual response (1) 45: 1–2. *See also* Sexuality
Humiliation, paranoid personality disorder related to (1) 16: 10
Huntington's disease
  apathy in (1) 73: 11–12
  in children (2) 34: 9
  dementia in (1) 73: 11–12
  depression in (1) 28: 11
  etiology (3) 12: 22–23
  markers in (3) 53: 15
  neostriatum structure and function in (3) 42: 10
  neurotransmitters in (1) 52: 15
  personality changes in (1) 28: 11–12
  psychological disorders in (1) 73: 11
  psychosis in (1) 28: 11–12; 69: 6
Hydergine. *See* Dihydroergotoxine mesylate
Hydrocephalus
  dementia in (1) 73: 10–11; (2) 87: 10
  diagnosis (1) 73: 11
  frontal lobe syndrome related to (1) 73: 11
  treatment (1) 73: 11
    in dementia (2) 87: 10
6-Hydroxydopamine, in schizophrenia etiology (1) 64: 4–5
5-Hydroxyindoleacetic acid. *See also* Serotonin
  CSF levels, developmental considerations (2) 12: 11
  suicidal behavior related to (1) 71: 12
Hydroxyzine
  interactions with other drugs (2) 111: 2
  lithium interaction with (2) 111: 11
Hyperactivity. *See also* Conduct disorders
  age-appropriate overactivity distinguished from (3) 66: 14
  in attention deficit disorder (2) 36: 6; (3) 66: 3, 7
  brain development and (2) 13: 7–8

  dopamine role in (3) 66: 12
  DSM-III criteria for (3) 66: 3
  evaluation in mental status examination (2) 20: 7
  food additives related to (2) 34: 11
  psychotherapy benefit in (1) 11: 5
  stimulants for (3) 66: 15
Hyperadrenocorticism, psychiatric manifestations (2) 88: 8–9
Hypercalcemia
  causes (2) 88: 11
  psychiatric manifestations (2) 88: 11
Hyperglycemia, symptoms (2) 88: 13
Hyperinsulinism (2) 88: 12
Hyperkinesis (3) 66: 1–2. *See also* Attention deficit disorder
Hyperparathyroidism (2) 88: 11
  anxiety disorders distinguished from (1) 32: 9
  behavioral correlates (2) 9: 11
  incidence (2) 88: 11
  organic mental disorders in children due to (2) 34: 8
  physical and psychiatric manifestations (2) 88: 11
Hypersomnia (2) 105: 9–14; (3) 61: 12–13
  in adolescents (2) 52: 9–10
  classification (2) 105: 2, 9
  conditions causing difficulty in initiating and maintaining sleep and (3) 61: 8–11
  in Kleine-Levin syndrome (2) 105: 14
  menstrual cycle associated with (2) 105: 14
  narcolepsy (2) 105: 12–14; (3) 61: 12–13. *See also* Narcolepsy
  psychiatric disorders associated with (2) 105: 9
  psychophysiologic (2) 105: 9
  sleep apnea causing (2) 105: 9–12; (3) 61: 8–9
  stress causing (2) 105: 9
Hypertension
  antihypertensive drug side effects (2) 118: 8
  biofeedback in (2) 109: 6–7
  compliance and treatment issues (2) 118: 8
  costs of noncompliance with therapy (2) 79: 4
  crisis in electroconvulsive therapy (2) 99: 6–7
  health promotion influence on (2) 129: 2–3
  monoamine oxidase inhibitor interactions with food or drugs causing (2) 111: 7–8
  psychiatric aspects (2) 118: 7–9
  psychologic antecedents and concomitants (2) 118: 7–8
  relaxation therapy in (2) 109: 6–7
  stress related to (2) 118: 7–8
Hyperthyroidism. *See also* Thyroid disease
  anxiety disorders distinguished from (1) 32: 9
  behavioral correlates (2) 9: 11
  psychiatric manifestations (2) 88: 7–8
Hyperventilation, in panic disorder (1) 32: 7–8
Hypervigilance, in stress-response syndrome (1) 41: 2–3
Hypnagogic hallucinations (3) 61: 12

Hypnagogic phenomenon, in stress-response syndrome (1) 41: 3–4
Hypnic jerk (3) 61: 11
Hypnopompic phenomenon, in stress-response syndrome (1) 41: 4
Hypnosis (2) **112: 1–8**
  in cancer (2) 112: 3–4
  clinical uses (2) 112: 3–4
  definition (2) 56: 3; 112: 2–3
  in fugue (1) 39: 7
  growing acceptance of (2) 112: 1
  historical background (2) 112: 1–2
  methods of induction (2) 112: 4–6
  in multiple personality (1) 39: 9–10
  in pain management (2) 112: 4
  personality type and (2) 112: 6
  physiologic state in transcendental meditation distinguished from (2) 109: 3
  practical suggestions and precautions in use (2) 112: 6–8
  theories on (2) 112: 2
Hypnotics (3) 61: 14–16. *See also under* Sedative hypnotics
Hypoadrenocorticism, psychiatric manifestations (2) 88: 9–10
Hypocalcemia, psychiatric manifestations in (2) 88: 11–12
Hypochondriac paranoia (1) 68: 9–10
Hypochondriasis (1) **35: 10–14;** (2) **100: 2–5.** *See also* Psychosomatic disorders; Somatoform disorders
  aggression and masochism in (1) 35: 12
  Briquet's syndrome distinguished from (1) 35: 15
  classification (2) 100: 2
  clinical description (1) 35: 11–12
  conflict versus self-pathology in (1) 35: 13
  definition (1) 35: 10–11
  depression causing (1) 35: 13; (2) 100: 4–5
    caution in confronting patient with diagnosis (2) 100: 4
    psychosis in (2) 100: 4–5
  diagnosis (1) 35: 13; (2) 100: 3
  differential diagnosis (1) 35: 11, 13
  disturbed object relations in (1) 35: 12
  DSM-III criteria for (1) 35: 10–11; (2) 100: 2
  dysmorphophobia (2) 100: 5
  epidemiology (1) 35: 11; (2) 100: 2–3
  etiology (1) 35: 12–13
  group psychotherapy in (2) 100: 3
  historical aspects (1) 35: 10
  MMPI test for (1) 7: 5
  monosymptomatic (2) 100: 5
  perceptual or cognitive abnormality causing (1) 35: 12
  primary (2) 100: 3
  psychodynamics (2) 100: 3
  in schizophrenia (1) 35: 13

  secondary (2) 100: 3–5
  social learning theories on (1) 35: 12
  symptoms (2) 100: 3
  transient (2) 100: 4
  treatment (1) 35: 13–14; (2) 100: 3
Hypofrontality, in schizophrenia (1) 64: 7
Hypoglycemia
  anxiety disorders distinguished from (1) 32: 10
  diet therapy in (2) 160: 2
  fasting (2) 88: 12
  organic mental disorders in children due to (2) 34: 8
  pathophysiology (2) 88: 12
  physical symptoms (2) 88: 12
  postprandial (2) 88: 12
  psychiatric manifestations (2) 88: 12–13
Hypokalemia, and lithium toxicity (2) 111: 10
Hypomania
  in cyclothymic disorder (1) 59: 3, 4
  DSM-III criteria for (1) 59: 3
Hypoparathyroidism (2) 88: 11–12
  behavioral correlates (2) 9: 11
  etiology (2) 88: 11
  physical and psychiatric manifestations (2) 88: 11–12
Hypopituitarism, behavioral correlates (2) 9: 11
Hypotension, orthostatic, neuroleptics causing, receptor interactions related to (3) 50: 11–12
Hypothalamic-pituitary-adrenal axis
  in affective disorders (3) 55: 5
  and immune system
    in depression (2) 128: 12
    stress effects and (2) 128: 10–11
  limbic (3) **54: 1–11.** *See also* Limbic system
    anatomical substrate of affectual state and regulation (3) 54: 2–4
    angiotensin effects (3) 54: 8
    dexamethasone suppression test as marker (3) 54: 10–11
    dysregulation in melancholia (3) 54: 4–10
    future studies (3) 54: 11
    neurotransmitter regulation (3) 54: 4–8
      acetylcholine (3) 54: 6–7
      GABA (3) 54: 7
      norepinephrine (3) 54: 4–5
      opiates (3) 54: 7–8
      serotonin (3) 54: 5–6
    physiology (3) 54: 1–2
    vasopressin effects (3) 54: 8
Hypothalamic-pituitary axis. *See also* Hypothalamic-pituitary-adrenal axis; Hypothalamic-pituitary-gonadal axis; Hypothalamus; Pituitary gland
  in affective disorders (1) 64: 10–12; (3) 55: 5
  in electroconvulsive therapy (3) 68: 5
Hypothalamic-pituitary-gonadal axis
  in fetus (2) 9: 2–3

Hypothalamic-pituitary-gonadal axis *(continued)*
  in growth (2) 9: 1
  in infancy (2) 9: 3
  in prepubescent children and adolescents (2) 9: 3–4
Hypothalamus
  and anaphylaxis (2) 128: 8
  and antibody levels (2) 128: 8
  circadian rhythm oscillator in (3) 59: 9
  clinical presentation of lesions (1) 28: 7
  dopaminergic neural system in (3) 44: 7
  and drive behavior (1) 28: 5–6
  dysfunction in anorexia nervosa (2) 102: 3–4
  in electroconvulsive therapy (3) 68: 5
  and immune system (2) 128: 7–12
    cell-mediated immunity (2) 128: 9
    humoral immunity (2) 128: 7–9
    and stress effects (2) 128: 10–11
  releasing hormones (2) 9: 1
  tumor, organic mental disorders in children due to (2) 34: 8
Hypothyroidism. *See also* Thyroid disease
  anxiety disorders distinguished from (1) 32: 9
  behavioral correlates (2) 9: 11
  prevention of mental retardation in (2) 58: 4
  psychiatric manifestations (2) 88: 5–7
    clinical description (2) 88: 5–6
    historical aspects (2) 88: 5
    pathophysiology (2) 88: 6
    treatment (2) 88: 6–7
Hypoxemia, cognitive change in (3) 52: 19
Hysterectomy (2) 120: 8–9
  depression after (2) 120: 9
  impact on woman (2) 120: 8–9
  indications for (2) 120: 8
  psychological reactions after (2) 120: 9
  statistics on (2) 120: 8
Hysteria (1) 35: 3. *See also* Briquet's syndrome; Conversion disorders; Dissociative disorders; Histrionic personality disorder; Hysterical personality disorder; Somatization disorder
  antisocial personality related to (1) 23: 5
  delirium distinguished from (1) 73: 15
  epidemic, in adolescents, epidemiologic studies (3) 12: 17
  suicide attempts in (1) 71: 3
  terminology in
    abandonment in DSM-III (2) 47: 1
    change in (2) 100: 5, 7
    confusion in (1) 19: 1–2
Hysterical personality disorder (1) **19: 1–10**
  in children and adolescents (1) 19: 6
  clinical description (1) 19: 3–5
  confused terminology in (1) 19: 1–2
  controversies in (1) 19: 1–2
  cultural factors in (1) 19: 8
  definition (1) 19: 1
  depressive-masochistic personality disorder distinguished from (1) 19: 8, 9
  diagnosis (1) 19: 8
  differential diagnosis (1) 19: 8–9
  epidemiology (1) 19: 2–3
  etiology (1) 19: 6–8
  family dynamics in (1) 19: 7–8
  genetic factors in (1) 19: 6
  histrionic personality disorder distinguished from (1) 19: 5
  in men (1) 19: 4–5
    narcissistic personality disorder distinguished from (1) 18: 8
  narcissistic personality disorder distinguished from (1) 18: 8; 19: 8–9
  obsessive-compulsive personality distinguished from (1) 19: 8
  prognosis (1) 19: 6
  psychoanalytic concepts (1) 19: 6–7, 9–10
  treatment (1) 19: 9
  in women (1) 19: 3–4
Hysteroid dysphoria (1) 19: 9
  depressive neurosis distinguished from (1) 40: 7
  drug therapy (1) 17: 12

ICU syndrome (2) 121: 7–8
Id
  development of (2) 57: 6
  psychoanalytic concept (1) 1: 7–8; (2) 57: 1
Identification
  hysterical (1) 35: 5
  with lost object (1) 40: 9
  projective, in family therapy (3) 7: 9
Identity
  amnesia of, stages of (1) 39: 3
  gender. *See also* Gender identity disorders
    core-gender (1) 46: 2
    gender-role (1) 46: 2
  sexual (1) 46: 2
Illness. *See* Medical illness; Mental illness
Illness behavior. *See also* Health behavior
  cost of health care related to (2) 79: 3–4
  decisions about seeking medical attention (2) 79: 3–4
  definition (2) 79: 2–3
  factors determining (2) 79: 3; (3) 22: 9–11
  requirements for coping (2) 108: 3
  styles in somatoform disorders (2) 100: 9–10
  and utilization of mental health services (3) 22: 9–11
Imaginal flooding, in simple phobia (1) 33: 10
Imaging techniques, on brain (3) **51: 1–7**. *See also* Brain, imaging techniques in psychiatry

Imipramine. *See also* Antidepressants
   in agoraphobia with panic attacks (1) 33: 11, 12
   in attention deficit disorder (3) 66: 20
   in borderline personality disorder (1) 10: 2
   in bulimia (2) 102: 9–10
   in enuresis (2) 43: 4; 52: 7; (3) 61: 14
   in panic disorder (1) 10: 6; 32: 11; 33: 11, 12
   receptors for, and mechanism of action (3) 50: 11
   in school phobia (2) 39: 8
Imitation, model, historical aspects (1) 2: 11
Immigration, suicide and (3) 20: 7–8
Immune system (2) **128: 1–14**
   brain modulation of (2) 128: 7–9
      in anaphylaxis (2) 128: 8
   cell-mediated (2) 128: 2
      brain modulation of (2) 128: 9
      conditioning effects on (2) 128: 10
      early experiences effect on (2) 128: 7
      psychosocial factors influencing (2) 128: 4–5
      stress effects on (2) 128: 4–6
   conditioning of processes (2) 128: 9–10
   early experiences effect on (2) 128: 6–7
   humoral (2) 128: 1–2
      brain modulation of (2) 128: 7–9
      conditioning effects on (2) 128: 9–10
      early experiences effect on (2) 128: 6–7
      stress effects on (2) 128: 2–4
   lymphocytes in (2) 128: 1–2
   and psychiatric disorders (2) 128: 12–14
      autism (2) 128: 14
      depression (2) 128: 12–13
      schizophrenia (2) 128: 13–14
   relationship between brain, behavior and (2) **128:
      1–14**
   separation and (2) 128: 6–7
   stress effects on (2) 128: 2–6
      adrenocortical activity (2) 128: 11
      asthma (2) 128: 3
      autoimmune disorders (2) 128: 3–4
      cancer (2) 128: 6
      cell-mediated processes (2) 128: 4–6
      death of spouse causing T cell suppression (2)
         128: 4
      graft rejection (2) 128: 5–6
      humoral processes (2) 128: 2–4
      interferon production (2) 128: 5
      mediation of (2) 128: 10–12
      neuroendocrine factors in (2) 128: 10–12
      premature separation (2) 128: 7
      susceptibility to streptococcal infections (2) 128:
         3
      susceptibility to viral infections (2) 128: 5
      T cell suppression (2) 128: 4–5
   techniques for measuring components of (2) 128:
      2
Immunoglobulins (2) 128: 1–2. *See also* Antibodies
Implicit learning (1) 2: 3

Impotence (1) 47: 4
   DSM-III criteria for (1) 47: 4
   history-taking on (1) 47: 4
   women reaction to (1) 47: 4
Impulse
   compulsion distinguished from (1) 25: 1
   definition (1) 25: 1
Impulse control
   cultural factors in (1) 25: 2
   development of (1) 25: 1–2
Impulse disorders (1) **25: 1–7.** *See also* Impulsive
      personality disorder
   attention deficit disorder related to (3) 66: 9
   biological model for (1) 3: 8–9
   classification (1) 25: 2
   developmental issues in (1) 25: 1–2, 7
   DSM-III on (1) 25: 2
   impulsive personality disorder (1) 25: 6–7. *See also*
      Impulsive personality disorder
   intermittent and isolated explosive disorder (1) 25:
      5–6. *See also* Intermittent explosive dis-
      order
   kleptomania (1) 25:
   pathologic gambling (1) 25:
   pyromania (1) 25:
   treatment, neuroleptics (2) 59: 7, 12
Impulsive personality (1) 23: 3–4. *See also* Impulse
      disorders
Impulsive personality disorder (1) 25: 6–7
   associated features (1) 25: 6
   complications (1) 25: 7
   diagnostic criteria (1) 25: 6
   differential diagnosis (1) 25: 7
   epidemiology (1) 25: 6–7
   impairment in (1) 25: 6
   predisposing factors (1) 25: 7
Impulsivity
   in attention deficit disorder (2) 36: 6
   DSM-III criteria for (3) 66: 3
Inattention. *See also* Attention; Attention deficit dis-
      order
   in attention deficit disorder (2) 36: 6
   DSM-III criteria for (3) 66: 3
Incest, borderline personality disorder related to (1)
      17: 8
Incidence rates. *See also* Epidemiology
   of bipolar disorder (1) 60: 9; (3) 13: 9–10
   definition (1) 54: 2; 60: 2; 69: 1; (3) 11: 2
   for depression (1) 60: 3–5; (3) 13: 3–5
   of schizophrenia (1) 54: 4–5
Incompetent. *See* Competency
Incompetent to stand trial (3) 27: 3–6; 28: 2–5, 7.
      See also Competency to stand trial; Men-
      tally disordered offenders
   treatment of offenders (3) 28: 20
Inconsistent behavior control, negative impact on
      social learning (1) 2: 5

Inderal. *See* Propranolol
Individualistic perspective (1) 6: 6
Individual therapy
  advantages and disadvantages (1) 9: 10
  choice among other formats (1) 9: 10
  history and rationale (1) 9: 7
  setting, techniques and goals (1) 9: 7
Individuation. *See also* Separation
  development of (2) 2: 6
  parent-child relationship disorders related to (2) 50: 3
Indulgent behavior control, negative impact on social learning (1) 2: 5
Infantile autism. *See* Autism
Infants
  attachment disorder in (2) 40: 5; 50: 2
  attention deficit disorder in (3) 66: 7–8
  and family development (2) 5: 5–6
  parent-child relationship in (2) 50: 2
  pica in (2) 40: 2–3
  pituitary-gonadal axis in (2) 9: 3
  psychoanalytic theories related to (1) 1: 9–13
  psychodynamic therapy of (2) 57: 4
  psychological tests in (2) 21: 2–3
  psychosis in, schizophrenia distinguished from (2) 29: 2
  sleep in (3) 60: 9
    disorders (2) 52: 2–5
      nightwaking (2) 52: 3–4
      rhythmic motor behaviors (2) 52: 4–5
  weight gain in (2) 40: 3
Infections
  attention deficit disorder due to (2) 36: 3
  in drug abuse (2) 90: 3
  encephalitis related to psychosis (1) 69: 4–5
  organic mental disorders after (2) 34: 3–5
  stress and susceptibility to (2) 128: 3, 5. *See also* Immune system
Information processing. *See also* Cognitive function; Memory
  in attention deficit disorder (3) 66: 6
  definition (3) 65: 3
  event-related potentials in (2) 13: 3
  as functional sequence (2) 13: 3
  in language delay (3) 67: 6–10
    hemispheric specialization and (3) 67: 10–13
  as marker in remitted schizophrenia (3) 65: 10
  matched tasks for (3) 65: 9
  in memory (3) 71: 4–6
  in psychiatric disorders (3) **65: 1–11**. *See also* Schizophrenia, cognitive function in
  research on (3) 65: 3–8
  in schizophrenia (3) 53: 14; 65: 1–11
  vision (3) 71: 4–6
  visual integration in (3) 65: 5
  visual masking as measure (3) 65: 4–5
Informed consent. *See* Consent, informed
Informed refusal (3) 29: 6

Infradian rhythms (3) 59: 7. *See also* Biological rhythms
Inheritance. *See* Genetics
Inhibition, reciprocal (1) 2: 12
Initiative, intracortical (1) 2: 21–22
Inmate, treatment considerations (3) 28: 6–7, 21–22
  legal considerations (3) 28: 8
Insanity
  abolition or retention as defense of criminal behavior (3) 28: 13–14
  cross-cultural definition (3) 2: 3–4; 15: 2
  definition (3) 27: 6–7
  legal standards for (3) 27: 6–9
  not guilty by reasons of (3) 27: 7–9; 28: 4, 5, 7–8
    civil commitment after (3) 27: 9–10
    disposition after (3) 27: 10
    legal issues in treatment (3) 28: 7–8
    treatment considerations (3) 28: 5
  psycholegal problems associated with (3) 28: 2
  test of (3) 28: 5
Insanity defense
  cooperation with evaluation procedures in (3) 27: 12
  legal standard of (3) 27: 7–9
  psychiatry role in (3) 27: 3
Insomnia (2) 105: 5–9. *See also* Sleep disorders
  in adolescents (2) 52: 10–11
  affective disorders associated with (3) 61: 5
  with atypical polysomnographic features (2) 105: 8–9
  biological rhythms role in (3) 59: 11–12
  in children (2) 52: 7–8
  classification (2) 105: 5
  danger in using hypnotics in (3) 61: 5
  drug and alcohol use associated with (3) 61: 6–7
  duration of (3) 61: 2
  familiar sleep setting and bedtime ritual in (3) 61: 6
  frontalis muscle biofeedback in (2) 109: 10
  history-taking in (3) 61: 2–4
  myoclonus causing (2) 105: 7–8
  prevalence (2) 105: 4
  psychiatric disorders in (2) 105: 4
  psychophysiologic (3) 61: 5–6
    persistent (2) 105: 6–7
  relaxation therapy in (2) 109: 10; (3) 61: 5–6
  sleep-wake schedule disorders (3) 61: 7–8
  transient and short-term (2) 105: 6; (3) 61: 2–3
  treatment, beneficial use of hypnotics in transient form (2) 105: 6
Institutionalization
  in mental retardation (2) 28: 7–8
  patients' rights regarding (3) **35: 1–15**. *See also* Patients' rights
Institutions. *See also* Hospitalization; Hospitals
  historical development for mentally ill (3) 6: 1–2
  for mentally disordered offenders (3) 28: 14–15
  for mental retardation (2) 58: 5

prison treatment programs (3) 28: 15
social structure of (1) 52: 10
instrumental learning (1) 2: 2–3
insulin
  hyperinsulinism (2) 88: 12
  insensitivity in affective disorders (1) 64: 12
insurance
  adverse selection in (3) 3: 9–10
  for children in hospitals (2) 64: 6
  confidentiality issues in disclosing information to
        third party carriers (3) 31: 10–11
  for mental health services (3) 3: 7
    discriminatory coverage (3) 3: 7–10
    limitations (3) 3: 1
  moral hazard in (3) 3: 7–9
  procedures implemented to cut health care costs
        (2) 79: 6
  testimonial privilege applying in claims (3) 31: 3
integrative neural defect, in schizophrenia (1) 2: 20
intellectual functioning, in psychodynamic mental
        status examination (1) 6: 11. See also
        Cognitive function
intelligence (2) 21: 4
  childhood psychiatric disorders related to (2) 11:
        12
  classification (2) 21: 4
  in conduct disorder (2) 37: 7
  evaluation in children (2) 20: 9
  in expressive language disorder (2) 49: 5
  and sex hormones (2) 9: 8–9
intelligence tests (1) 7: 5–6; (2) 20: 14. See also Psy-
        chological tests
  in attention deficit disorder (2) 36: 7–8; (3) 66:
        14
  Bayley Scales for infants (2) 21: 2
  Cattell Scale for infants (2) 21: 2–3
  classification of scales for (2) 21: 4
  in diagnosis (1) 7: 6
  in expressive language disorder (2) 49: 5
  Kaufman assessment battery for children (2) 21: 5
  in language disorders (2) 49: 8
  McCarthy scales of children's abilities (2) 21: 5
  in middle childhood (2) 21: 3–6
  Stanford-Binet test (2) 21: 4
  Wechsler Adult Intelligence Scales-Revised (2) 21:
        6–7
  Wechsler preschool and primary scale of intelli-
        gence (2) 21: 4–5
intensive care units, psychiatric disorders associated
        with (2) 121: 7–8
interferon, stress related to production of (2) 128: 5
interictal behavior syndrome (1) 28: 7–8
intermittent explosive disorder (1) 25: 5–6; (2) 87:
        12
  clinical description (1) 25: 6
  drug treatment (1) 25: 6
  DSM-III criteria for (1) 25: 5
  predisposing factors (1) 25: 6

Internalization, transmuting (1) 18: 7
International Classification of Diseases, DSM-III com-
        pared with (2) 19: 1–2, 12
International psychiatry. See also Cross-cultural psy-
        chiatry; Culture
  comparing epidemiologic findings between coun-
        tries (3) 11: 10–11
  differences in diagnosis (3) 11: 7
  epidemiologic developments (3) 11: 10–11
  suicide rates (3) 20: 6, 8
Interpersonal behavior, self-report tests of (1) 7: 9
Interpersonal psychiatry (1) 52: 10–11
Interpersonal psychoanalysis (1) 1: 12–13
Interpretation
  Freud's concept (1) 1: 4
  in psychodynamic life narrative (2) 108: 5–7
  in psychotherapy (1) 8: 4–5; (2) 108: 2
Interviewing. See also History-taking
  of adolescents (2) 20: 2–4
  in behavioral assessment (2) 23: 7–9
    with children (2) 23: 8
    with parents (2) 23: 7–8
  Behavior Screening Questionnaire (3) 12: 9–10
  Child Assessment Schedule (3) 12: 10
  clinical evaluation (1) **6: 1–13.** See also Clinical
        evaluation
  in diagnosis of childhood psychiatric disorders (2)
        19: 5
  Diagnostic Interview for Children and Adolescents
        (2) 11: 7–8; (3) 12: 6, 9, 10
  Diagnostic Interview Scale (1) 15: 2–3; (3) 11: 9
    in epidemiologic studies (3) 11: 9
  Diagnostic Interview Schedule for Children (2) 11:
        8
  education on (2) 116: 6, 7
  eliciting patient's request (1) 6: 4–5
  in epidemiologic studies in child psychiatry (2) 11:
        4–8; (3) 12: 8–10
  existential alliance in (3) 36: 6
  in family therapy (2) 62: 5
  in history-taking (2) 20: 2–4
  as hypothesis testing (1) 6: 7–8
  irrational alliance in (3) 36: 7
  Isle of Wight method (3) 12: 6, 8–9
  Kiddie-SADS method (3) 12: 6, 9
  medical alliance in (3) 36: 5–6
  Mental Health Assessment Form (3) 12: 9
  in organic mental disease (2) 95: 6
  of paranoid patient (2) 95: 4–5
  patient request in (1) 6: 2–5
  of pre-school child (2) 20: 2, 3
  in psychiatric assessment of children (2) 20: 2–4
  in psychosis (2) 95: 3–5
    opening up emotional contact to identify pa-
          tient's feelings (2) 95: 4
    setting (2) 95: 4
    of significant others (2) 95: 5
    termination (2) 95: 5

Interviewing *(continued)*
  questionnaires in (2) 20: 13, 15
  rational alliance in (3) 36: 6–7
  of school-aged child (2) 20: 2–3
  situational alliance in (3) 36: 8
  structured interview (1) 7: 4
    in children (2) 20: 13, 15
    child's version of Schedule for Affective dis-
        orders (2) 11: 7
    Diagnostic Interview for Children and Adoles-
        cents (2) 11: 7–8; (3) 12: 6, 9, 10
    Diagnostic Interview Scale (1) 15: 2–3; (3) 11:
        9
    Diagnostic Interview Schedule for Children (2)
        11: 8
    in epidemiologic studies in child psychiatry (2)
        11: 7–8
  of violent patient (2) 95: 8–9
Intimacy, lack of, as depression risk factor, in
        nonbipolar disorder (1) 60: 7; (3) 13: 8
Intracortical initiative (1) 2: 21–22
Introversion (1) 2: 19
  and neurosis (1) 2: 19
Involuntary treatment
  agency in (3) 36: 2
  civil commitment (3) **32: 1–16.** *See also* Civil com-
        mitment
IQ. *See* Intelligence; Intelligence tests
Iron, deficiency related to cognitive dysfunction (2)
        160: 3
Irresistible impulse (3) 27: 7–8
Irritable bowel syndrome, biofeedback and relaxation
        therapy in (2) 109: 9
Isle of Wight interview, in child psychiatric epidemi-
        ology (3) 12: 6, 8–9
Ismelin. *See* Guanethidine
Isolation. *See* Social isolation
Isoniazid, psychiatric side effects (2) 91: 6

Jactatio capitis nocturna (2) 52: 4–5
  treatment (2) 52: 5
Jail. *See* Prison
Jakob-Creutzfeldt disease, personality change in (1)
        28: 4
Jaspers, E., on paranoid disorders (1) 68: 3
Jaundice, cholestatic, neuroleptics causing (1) 55: 25
Jealousy
  alcoholic (2) 87: 14
  delusions of (1) 68: 7–8
Jealousy paranoia (1) 68: 7–8
Jejunoileal bypass (2) 103: 6
Jenkins Activity Survey (1) 7: 9
Jet lag (3) 59: 12–13
  hypnotics effect on (3) 59: 13
  treatment (3) 59: 12–13

Joining
  in family consultation (2) 110: 7
  in family therapy intervention (2) 62: 7
Joint Commission on Accreditation of Hospitals
        (JCAH), standards for Community Mental
        Health Centers (3) 5: 11
Judgment, evaluation in mental status examination
        in children (2) 20: 11–12
Juvenile delinquency (2) **37: 1–9.** *See also* Conduct
        disorders
  child psychiatry involvement in (2) 1: 2–3
  cortisol levels related to (2) 9: 9
  endocrine correlates (2) 9: 10–11
  epidemiology (2) 37: 3–4
  parental factors in (2) 37: 4
  prevention (3) 12: 24–25
  treatment (3) 28: 24–25

Kanner, Leo, contributions to child psychiatry (2) 1:
        4
Kaufman assessment battery for children (2) 21: 5
Kernberg, O., on borderline disorders (1) 17: 3
Kiddie-SADS interview method, in child psychiatric
        epidemiology (3) 12: 6, 9
Kidney
  end-stage disease
    consultation-liaison psychiatry in (2) 117: 4–5
    course of disease disability in (2) 117: 1–3
    organic mental syndrome in (2) 117: 4–5
    pre-illness psychopathology in (2) 117: 3
    stress in (2) 117: 5
    wish to no longer live (2) 117: 5
  hemodialysis in schizophrenia (1) 55: 2–3
  heroin associated with failure (2) 90: 3
Klein, M., on child psychoanalysis (1) 1: 10–11
Kleine-Levin syndrome (1) 28: 7; (2) 105: 14
  psychosis in (1) 69: 8
Kleptomania (1) 25: 3–4
  DSM-III definition (1) 25: 3–4
Kluver-Bucy syndrome
  limbic system lesions causing (3) 54: 3
  personality change in (1) 28: 4, 6, 8
Kohlberg, Lawrence, on moral development (2) 17:
        2, 3
Kohut, H., on self theory (1) 1: 11–12
Korsakoff's syndrome (1) **73: 17–20**
  clinical features and diagnostic criteria in (1) 73:
        18–19
  confabulation in (1) 73: 19
  dementia distinguished from (1) 73: 2, 18
  diencephalic region in (3) 71: 7
  hidden set of basic symptoms in (1) 73: 17
  importance of mental status examination in (1)
        73: 17
  memory disorder in (1) 73: 18–19
  neuropathology (1) 73: 19–20

in nonalcoholic (1) 73: 20
personality in (1) 73: 19
temporal lobe lesions associated with (1) 73: 20
treatment (1) 73: 20
Kraepelin, E.
  on paranoid disorders (1) 68: 2
  on schizophrenia (1) 52: 18; 53: 1, 2
Kretschmer, E.
  on avoidant personality (1) 24: 2
  on paranoid disorders (1) 68: 2–3
Kuru, epidemiologic studies on (3) 2: 10
Kwashiorkor, organic mental disorders in children
      due to (2) 34: 10

Labeling, in psychiatric disorders (1) 51: 4–5
La belle indifference (1) 35: 5
  in conversion disorder (2) 100: 6
  infrequent finding in children with conversion dis-
      order (2) 47: 3, 5
Laboratory tests
  in attention deficit disorder (2) 36: 8
  in chronic depression (1) 61: 16–17
  in dementia (1) 73: 4–5
  in high-risk patient for medical disease (2) 88: 4–
      5
  in medical model (1) 51: 3
  in neurochemical strategies in child psychiatry (2)
      12: 2–3
  in organic brain syndromes (2) 87: 14–15; 95: 2–
      3
  in psychiatric disorders (1) 51: 3
  sources of variable results in (2) 12: 12
  timing of sampling based on biological rhythms
      (3) 59: 13
Lactate, panic disorder attack provoked by (1) 32: 8
Lamb warning (3) 36: 4
Landau-Kleffner syndrome (2) 49: 6
Language. *See also* Language disorders
  assessment of (3) 67: 3, 4
  components of (2) 49: 1–2; (3) 67: 5
  development of (2) 2: 4–5
  disorders associated with impairment (2) 20: 9
  evaluation in mental status examination (2) 20: 8–
      9
  event-related potentials and (3) 62: 11–12
  expressive, tests of (2) 49: 8. *See also* Language
      disorders, expressive
  in pervasive developmental disorders (2) 27: 4
  phonology (2) 49: 2
  pragmatics (2) 49: 1
  receptive (2) 20: 8, 9; 49: 5–6
    tests of (2) 49: 8
  semantics (2) 49: 1
  Sequenced Inventory of Communication Develop-
      ment test of (2) 21: 3

signs of dysfunction (2) 20: 8
speech development relation to (3) 67: 2
syntax (2) 49: 1
Language disorders. *See also* Aphasia; Speech dis-
      orders
  definitions in (2) 49: 1–2
  delay
    causes (2) 20: 8
    epidemiologic studies in preschool child (3) 12:
      13–14
  developmental (3) **67: 1–13**
    auditory perception in (3) 67: 6–10
    classification (3) 67: 2
    clinical description (3) 67: 1–3
    definition (3) 67: 1–2
    delay versus deviance (3) 67: 5
    diagnosis (3) 67: 3, 4
    DSM-III on (3) 67: 1–2
    emotional sequelae in (3) 67: 13
    epidemiology (3) 67: 3
    expressive type (3) 67: 2
    hemispheric asymmetry and (3) 67: 10–13
    neuropsychological approach to (3) 67: 6–13
    prognosis (3) 67: 2–3, 13
    psycholinguistics of (3) 67: 3, 5
    receptive type (2) 49: 5–6; (3) 67: 2
    research on (3) 67: 3, 5–13
    speech disorder distinguished from (3) 67: 2
  diagnosis (2) 49: 7–9
  dysnomia (2) 87: 11
  etiology (2) 49: 6–7
  expressive (2) 49: 3–5
    diagnostic issues in (2) 49: 5
    emotional problems in (2) 49: 4–5
    intelligence in (2) 49: 5
    natural history (2) 49: 4–5
    phonology in (2) 49: 4
    pragmatics in (2) 49: 3–4
    progress (2) 49: 5
    semantics in (2) 49: 3
    syntax in (2) 49: 3
  psychiatrist role in (2) 49: 9–10
  receptive (2) 49: 5–6
    natural history (2) 49: 6
    prognosis (2) 49: 6
  receptive-expressive (2) 49: 6
  specific developmental (2) **49: 1–10**
    articulation. *See also* Speech disorders
    diagnosis (2) 49: 7–9
    dichotic listening studies in (2) 49: 6–7
    etiology (2) 49: 6–7
    expressive (2) 49: 3–5
    intelligence tests in (2) 49: 8
    neurologic abnormalities in (2) 49: 6–7
    perceptual dysfunction in (2) 49: 7
    psychiatrist role in (2) 49: 9–10
    receptive (2) 49: 5–6
    treatment (2) 49: 9

Language disorders *(continued)*
  tests for (3) 52: 6–8
    comprehension (3) 52: 7
    fluency (3) 52: 7–8
    naming (3) 52: 7
    reading (3) 52: 6
    repeating (3) 52: 8
    writing (3) 52: 6–7
  treatment (2) 49: 9
Lanterman-Petris-Short Act (3) 32: 5
Larodopa. *See* L-Dopa
Latency (2) **3: 1–6**
  and bereavement (2) 3: 5
  brain development by (2) 3: 3–4
  cognitive function in (2) 3: 4–5
  cultural similarities (2) 3: 1–2
  definition (2) 3: 1
  development during (2) **3: 1–6**
  and divorce (2) 3: 5
  and family development (2) 5: 7–8
  Gesell's description (2) 3: 1
  historical aspects (2) 3: 2
  in middle class children (2) 3: 3
  morality in (2) 3: 5
  neurologic development by (2) 3: 3–4
  and parent-child relationship (2) 50: 3
  psychopathologic disorders in (2) 3: 2–3
  sexuality in (2) 3: 2
  transition to adolescence (2) 3: 5
Laterality, determination (2) 20: 7. *See also* Hemi-
    spheric specialization
Laughing, pseudobulbar (1) 73: 9
Law. *See also* Legal issues
  prevention of disease or injuries through applica-
    tion of (2) 79: 5–6
  psychiatry of (3) **36: 1–13.** *See also* Forensic psy-
    chiatry
Laxatives
  in bulimia (2) 102: 5
  for weight loss (2) 101: 4
Leadership, in hospital administration (2) 64: 10
Lead intoxication
  in attention deficit disorder (2) 34: 10; 36: 3; (3)
    66: 12
  chelating agents in hyperactivity therapy (2) 160:
    3
  cognitive and behavior disorders in (3) 12: 22
  organic mental disorders in children due to (2) 34:
    9–10
  pica causing (2) 40: 2
  sources in environment (2) 34: 9
Learning
  amnesia related to (3) 71: 7–10
  anatomy of (2) 13: 3–4
  application to behavior therapy (2) 77: 3. *See also*
    Behavior therapy
  associative (2) 13: 2
  basic organization and processes of (2) 13: 1–2

  and biofeedback action (2) 109: 4
  catecholamines in (2) 13: 6–7
  in child development (2) 2: 3
  conditioning (2) 13: 2. *See also* Conditioning
  contiguity (1) 2: 2
  as crucial element in psychological treatment (1)
    2: 2
  definition (2) 13: 1
  in depressive neurosis etiology (1) 40: 9–10
  expectancy (1) 2: 2
  extinction (1) 2: 6–7; (2) 13: 2
  generalized (1) 2: 6–7
  of helplessness (3) 55: 7
  implicit (1) 2: 3
  instrumental (1) 2: 2–3
  marijuana effect on (2) 4: 13
  and memory (3) **71: 1–14.** *See also* Memory
  model in *Aplysia california* (2) 13: 4–5
  molecular basis (2) 13: 4–5
  neurobiology (2) **13: 1–9**
    basic organization and processes in (2) 13: 1–3
    developmental aspects (2) 13: 7–9
    molecular basis (2) 13: 4–5
    neurochemistry (2) 13: 5–7
  neurochemistry (2) 13: 5–7
    changes accompanying early childhood experi-
      ences (2) 13: 9
  neuropeptides in (2) 13: 7
  nonassociative (2) 13: 1–2
  phobia related to (1) 33: 7–8
  presymbolic (1) 2: 6
  procedural versus declarative (3) 71: 8–10
  psychopathology explained by (1) 2: 1–25. *See also*
    Social learning
  random (1) 2: 6
  response (1) 2: 2
  sign (1) 2: 14–15
  skills for performance distinguished from (2) 77: 7
  social (1) **2: 1–25.** *See also* Social learning
  solution (1) 2: 14–15
  state-dependent (3) 45: 9
  testing in amnesic patient (3) 71: 11
  theories (1) 2: 9–23. *See also under* Social learning
    theories of
    of anxiety (1) 32: 5–6; (2) 39: 5
    of avoidant personality (1) 24: 3
    of conversion disorder (2) 47: 4, 5
    of obsessive-compulsive disorder (1) 34: 5–6
    of phobia (1) 33: 7–8
  vicarious (1) 2: 3
Learning disabilities (3) 66: 1. *See also* Attention defi-
    cit disorder
  in attention deficit disorder (2) 36: 8–9; (3) 66: 8
  clinical description (2) 48: 1–2
  in conduct disorder (2) 37: 7
  definition (2) 48: 2–3
  developmental (2) **48: 1–8**
  educational programs for (2) 48: 5–6

epidemiologic studies (3) 12: 15, 22
evaluation for (2) 48: 5
historical perspectives (2) 48: 3–4
impact on child's emotional and social develop-
	ment (2) 48: 7–8
intervention in (2) 48: 5–8
	with children (2) 48: 7–8
	with parents (2) 48: 6–7
	with schools (2) 48: 5–6
legislation on (2) 48: 5
neuropsychological models (2) 48: 4–5
optometric training in (2) 160: 3–4
prevalence (2) 48: 3
research on (2) 48: 4–5
Leber's hereditary optic atrophy, psychosis in (1) 69:
	7
Legal issues. *See also* Forensic psychiatry; Malpractice
abolition of retention of insanity defense (3) 28:
	13–14
in child psychiatry (2) **71: 1–4**
	children's needs and rights (2) 71: 2–3
	role of clinical expert (2) 71: 3–4
	role of state and role of parents (2) 71: 1–2
civil commitment (3) 27: 9–10; **32: 1–16.** *See also*
	Civil commitment
competency to stand trial (3) 27: 3–6
confidentiality (3) **31: 1–16.** *See also* Confidential-
	ity
diminished capacity (3) 27: 9
discovery procedures (3) 31: 9–10
forensic evaluation in criminal justice system (3)
	27: 1–14; 36: 1–13. *See also* Forensic
	psychiatry
guilty but mentally ill (3) 28: 4, 6, 8
incompetent to stand trial (3) 28: 2–5, 7
informed consent (3) **30: 1–14.** *See also* Consent,
	informed
of inmates (3) 28: 8
insanity defense (3) 27: 6–9
in malpractice (3) 29: 2–5
on mentally disordered offenders (3) 28: 7–9
not guilty by reason of insanity (3) 28: 4, 5, 7–8
parens patriae (3) 71: 2
patients' rights (3) **35: 1–15.** *See also* Patients'
	rights
	to aftercare (3) 35: 10–13
	during institutionalization (3) 35: 7–10
	to mental health advocacy (3) 35: 13–15
	to refuse treatment (3) 35: 4–7
	to treatment (3) 35: 2–4
probation and parole (3) 28: 4, 7, 8
testimonial privilege (3) **31: 1–10.** *See also* Testi-
	monial privilege
validity of request for release of information (3)
	31: 3
Legislation. *See also* Government
on community mental health services (3) 5: 3–4,
	10; 6: 3

for children (2) 69: 2
on informed consent (3) 30: 4
on learning disabilities (2) 48: 5
on manpower in psychiatry (3) 4: 7–8
on mental health advocacy (3) 35: 14
on mental health services (3) 5: 2–5
Leigh disease, organic mental disorders in children
	due to (2) 34: 8
Leiter test (2) 21: 5
Lesch-Nyhan disease
organic mental disorders in children due to (2) 34:
	9
self-mutilation in (1) 27: 5
Libido theory (1) 1: 7
decreased (1) 47: 5
definition (1) 18: 2
narcissistic (1) 18: 2
object (1) 18: 2
Lidocaine, psychiatric side effects (2) 91: 6
Life cycle, psychodynamic life narrative in clarifica-
	tion of (2) 108: 4–7
Life events
definition (1) 63: 3
as depression risk factor, in nonbipolar disorder
	(1) 60: 7; (3) 13: 8
exploitation in milieu therapy (2) 64: 13–14
normal and abnormal responses to (1) 41: 2–6.
	See also Stress-response syndromes
severity as potential stressor (1) 41: 4–5
stressful (1) **41: 1–15.** *See also* Stressful life events;
	Stress-response syndromes
in suicide (1) 71: 4
Life insurance, testimonial privilege applying in
	claims (3) 31: 3
Life narrative. *See* Psychodynamic life narrative
Life space (2) 64: 11
Life stressors. *See* Life events; Stressful life events
Lifestyle. *See also* Health behavior
costs of disease related to (2) 79: 2
health promotion related to (2) 129: 6
and illness (2) **79: 1–8.** *See also* Behavior, contri-
	butions to illness
and risk factors for leading causes of death (2)
	129: 6
Lifetime Health Monitoring Program (2) 129: 2
Lifetime morbid risk (1) 54: 3. *See also* Morbid risk
Lifetime prevalence
definition (1) 54: 3
of depression (1) 59: 9
problems with (1) 54: 3
Lifetime risk
of bipolar disorder (1) 60: 8–9; (3) 13: 10
of nonbipolar depression (1) 60: 2, 3; (3) 13: 4–6
of schizophrenia (1) 62: 4–6
Light therapy
in biological rhythm control (3) 59: 10–11
in bipolar disorder (1) 61: 22
in rhythm disorders (3) 59: 13–14

Limbic encephalitis (1) 28: 4

Limbic system. *See also* Temporal lobe syndrome

and adrenal cortisol release (3) 54: 1–2

anatomical substrate of affectual state (3) 54: 2–4

behavior correlates (1) 28: 6

hypothalamic-pituitary-adrenal axis dysregulation in melancholia (3) **54: 1–11**

acetylcholine and (3) 54: 6–7

anatomical substrate of affectual state (3) 54: 2–4

angiotensin and (3) 54: 8

dexamethasone suppression test as marker (3) 54: 10–11

future studies (3) 54: 11

GABA and (3) 54: 7

neurotransmitter regulation (3) 54: 4–8

norepinephrine and (3) 54: 4–5

opiates and (3) 54: 7–8

physiology (3) 54: 1–2

serotonin and (3) 54: 5–6

vasopressin and (3) 54: 8

memory disorder related to (1) 73: 20

memory function role (2) 87: 10

psychoses related to lesions in (1) 69: 9

Linguistics. *See* Language

Linkage studies

in alcoholism (3) 53: 11–12

definition (3) 53: 3

in depression (1) 63: 8

in genetics of psychiatric disorders (2) 10: 3–4

restriction fragment length polymorphisms in (2) 10: 3–4

Lipids, in coronary artery disease etiology (2) 126: 1–2

Lithium

age-related considerations in pharmacology (1) 61: 18

anesthetic agents interaction with (2) 111: 10

in antisocial personality disorder (1) 10: 3

in attention deficit disorder (3) 66: 20

in bipolar disorder (1) 61: 18–21

compliance (1) 61: 20–21

cyclothymic disorder (1) 61: 23

in depressive phase (1) 61: 18

drug-free holidays (1) 61: 22

in maintenance phase (1) 61: 19–20

in manic phase (1) 61: 19

in children and adolescents (2) 59: 8, 16

follow-up in (2) 59: 11

interactions with other drugs (2) 59: 11

medical workup prior to use (2) 59: 10

pharmacokinetics (2) 59: 16

side effects (2) 59: 10–11, 16

circadian rhythm effects (3) 59: 5

in depression (1) 61: 12

in children and adolescents (2) 30: 7

digitalis interaction with (2) 111: 10

diuretics and (2) 111: 10

electrolytes related to pharmacokinetics of (2) 111: 10

endocrine side effects (2) 9: 12

in explosive personality (1) 3: 8–9

hypokalemia and toxicity of (2) 111: 10

in impulse disorders (1) 3: 8–9

interaction with other drugs (2) 111: 9–11

with neuroleptics (1) 55: 11

mechanism of action (2) 59: 16

neuronal sensitivity in children to (2) 59: 2

neuropsychological assessment related to use (1) 72: 14

pharmacokinetics (1) 61: 20; (2) 111: 10

psychiatric side effects (2) 91: 3

receptor stabilization effects (1) 64: 10

in schizomanic patient (1) 70: 7

sodium metabolism and toxicity of (2) 111: 10, 11

supersensitivity of adrenergic receptors influenced by (3) 50: 7

thyroid hormones interaction with (2) 111: 10

timing of drug administration based on biological rhythms (3) 59: 13

toxicity (1) 61: 20; (2) 59: 10–11, 16

endocrine (2) 9: 12

transport in red cells as marker for affective disorders (3) 53: 6

transport mechanisms in bipolar patient (1) 64: 10

in woman desiring pregnancy (1) 61: 22

work-up prior to use (1) 61: 18

Litigious paranoia (1) 68: 7

Liver

drug metabolism in children (2) 59: 2

mortality statistics from cirrhosis to determine alcohol abuse prevalence (3) 18: 3–5

neuroleptics toxicity to (1) 55: 25

Locus ceruleus

in Alzheimer's disease (3) 44: 6

and attention and arousal behavior (2) 13: 8

axon projections from (3) 42: 6

neuronal activity in sleep and wakefulness (3) 44: 5

noradrenergic neural system located in (3) 44: 2–5

in panic disorder (1) 32: 7–8

in Parkinson's disease (3) 44: 6

in psychiatric disorders (3) 44: 5–6

Locus of control (1) 2: 16

Longitudinal studies (2) 11: 2

Long-term exploratory psychotherapy (1) 9: 2, 3

choice among other orientations (1) 9: 6–7

goals (1) 9: 3

rationale (1) 9: 3

setting for (1) 9: 3

technique (1) 9: 3

Loxapine (Loxitane)

in rapid tranquilization (2) 95: 5

structure (1) 55: 4

Loxitane. *See* Loxapine

LSD. *See* Hallucinogens; Lysergic acid diethylamide
Ludiomil. *See* Maprotiline
Lupus erythematosus, organic mental disorders in
children due to (2) 34: 7
Luria-Nebraska Neuropsychological Battery (1) 7: 7;
72: 6–8; (2) 21: 8–9; (3) 52: 14–15
Luteinizing hormone (2) 9: 2
in sleep (3) 60: 5
Lymphocytes
B cells (2) 128: 1–2. *See also* B cells
in depression (2) 128: 12
in immune system (2) 128: 1–2
in schizophrenia (2) 128: 13
stimulation tests (2) 128: 2
stress influence on (2) 128: 4
T cells (2) 128: 1, 2, 4–5
Lysergic acid diethylamide (LSD)
abuse (3) 17: 15
human effects (3) 46: 12–13
schizophrenia distinguished from effects of (3) 46:
12–13
therapeutic use in mutism (2) 35: 5

Magnetic resonance imaging
basic principles (3) 51: 4–6
cautions and methodologic standards (3) 51: 7
in psychiatric patients (3) 51: 6
Mainstreaming
in mental retardation (2) 28: 7
public policy supporting (2) 58: 1
Maladaption, definition (2) 51: 2. *See also* Adaptation; Adjustment disorders
Males. *See* Men
Malingering. *See also* Factitious illness
amnesia distinguished from (1) 39: 6
brief reactive psychosis distinguished from (1) 70:
13
competency to stand trial distinguished from (3)
27: 6, 13
factitious illness distinguished from (1) 35: 16; (2)
101: 1, 8
fugue distinguished from (1) 39: 7
functional amnesia distinguished from (3) 71: 14
multiple personality distinguished from (1) 39: 9
Malnutrition, organic mental disorders in children
due to (2) 34: 10–11
Malpractice (3) **29: 1–13**
breach of contract in physician-patient relationship
(3) 29: 2–3
confidentiality of records of other patients treated
by defendant (3) 31: 7
distinction between errors of judgment and errors
of fact (3) 29: 4
impact on medical care (3) 29: 2
initiation of suits by malingerers (2) 101: 9
injury presence requirement (3) 29: 4

lack of restraint causing attack by one patient on
another (3) 36: 11
legal principles in (3) 29: 2–5
negligence (3) 29: 3
and physician-patient relationship (2) 116: 2; (3)
29: 2–3
prevention (3) 29: 13
proximate cause (3) 29: 4
in psychiatry (3) **29: 1–13**
abandonment (3) 29: 7–8
abuses in professional relationship (3) 29: 11–
12
adverse outcomes of treatment (3) 29: 10
inappropriate treatments (3) 29: 11
informed consent issues (3) 29: 5–6; 30: 7–8
infrequency compared to medical specialties (3)
29: 1–2
injury to third persons (3) 29: 9–10
prevention (3) 29: 13
psychotherapy (3) 29: 12–13
suicide (3) 29: 8–9
types of cases involved (3) 29: 2, 5
vicarious liability (3) 29: 11
wrongful commitment (3) 29: 6–7
res ipsa loquitur (3) 29: 4–5
respectable minority rule in (3) 29: 3
standard of care in (3) 29: 3
statistics on increases in (3) 29: 1–2
Mania. *See also* Affective disorders; Bipolar disorder
aggressive or antisocial acts in (2) 37: 6–7
in bipolar disorder, treatment (1) 61: 19
bipolar disorder distinguished from (1) 60: 8
chronic, treatment (1) 61: 24
classification (1) 59: 2
definition (1) 60: 8
DSM-III criteria for (1) 59: 2
mood-congruent and incongruent symptoms in (1)
59: 2–3
in schizoaffective disorder (1) 70: 6, 7
schizophrenia symptoms in (1) 70: 3
secondary (1) 61: 2–3
signs and symptoms (2) 95: 2
thought disorder in (1) 53: 12
treatment (1) 61: 19, 24
unipolar (1) 59: 8
bipolar versus (1) 60: 8
Manic-depressive illness. *See also* Bipolar disorder
in adolescents (2) 30: 5
bipolar disorder related to (1) 60: 8
borderline (1) 17: 7. *See also* Borderline personality
disorder
borderline personality disorder distinguished from
(1) 17: 11
in children (2) 30: 4–5
classification (1) 60: 7–8
Manipulation, in psychotherapy (2) 108: 2
Manpower
critical issues in 1980s (3) 4: 8–9

Manpower *(continued)*
  economic aspects (3) 3: 1–2, 11–12
  increased numbers for community mental health
      services (3) 5: 5
  legislation on (3) 4: 7–8
MAO inhibitors. *See* Monoamine oxidase inhibitors
Maprotiline, psychiatric side effects (2) 91: 2–3
Marasmus, organic mental disorders in children due
      to (2) 34: 10
Marijuana. *See also* Substance abuse
  adolescent use (2) 4: 13–14; 35: 5
  behavioral effects (2) 4: 13
  clinical manifestations (2) 35: 5
  comparative rates of use with other drugs (3) 17:
      15–16
  demographic trends in use (3) 17: 16
  and ego function (2) 4: 13
  epidemiology of abuse (3) 17: 15–16
  lithium interaction with (2) 111: 11
  problem behaviors of youth related to (2) 4: 13–
      14
  temporal trends in abuse (3) 17: 16
  toxicity of (2) 90: 4
  and use of more addicting substances (2) 35: 5
Marital disorders
  conjugal paranoia (1) 68: 7–8
  in paranoid disorder (1) 68: 5, 7–8
Marital status
  alcohol abuse related to (3) 18: 9
  as bipolar disorder risk factor (1) 60: 10; (3) 13:
      11
  conflict related to emotional difficulties in child (3)
      12: 23
  depression related to (1) 63: 12–13
    in nonbipolar disorder (1) 60: 6
  and illness behavior (3) 22: 10
  suicide rates and (3) 20: 5–6
    during bereavement for spouse (3) 20: 6
    influence of children on (3) 20: 5–6
Marital therapy (1) 9: 7–8
  choice among other formats (1) 9: 10
  contraindications (1) 9: 10
  goals (1) 9: 8
  historical aspects (1) 9: 8
  rationale for (1) 9: 8
  setting (1) 9: 8
Markers (3) **53: 1–16**
  in affective disorders (1) 62: 17–18; (3) 53: 4–9
    antigens in blood (3) 53: 7
    behavioral excitation with amphetamine chal-
        lenge (3) 53: 6–7
    catechol-O-methyl transferase levels (3) 53: 8
    cholinergic hypersensitivity (3) 53: 5
    cholinergic rapid eye movement test (3) 53: 7
    dexamethasone suppression test (3) 53: 5
    event-related potentials (3) 53: 8
    lithium intracellular accumulation in red cells
        (3) 53: 6

    methadone and metoclopramide challenge (3)
        53: 6
    monoamine oxidase levels in platelets (3) 53: 7–
        8
    monoamines (3) 53: 6
    muscarinic cholinergic receptors (3) 53: 8
    neurologic and cognitive deficits (3) 53: 9
    REM sleep (3) 53: 5
    skin conductance-electrodermal activity (3) 53:
        8
    TSH response to TRH challenge (3) 53: 6
    tyramine levels in urine (3) 53: 9
  in alcoholism (3) 53: 9–12
    acute reaction to ethanol (3) 53: 11
    2-butanediol (3) 53: 11
    dopamine beta-hydroxylase (3) 53: 11
    ethanol-metabolizing enzymes and acetaldehyde
        (3) 53: 10
    linkage studies (3) 53: 11–12
    monoamine oxidase (3) 53: 10–11
  association versus linkage (3) 53: 2–3
  in borderline personality disorder (1) 17: 11–12
  characteristics (3) 53: 1–2
  in depression in childhood (2) 30: 6–7
  genetic (3) 53: 1–2
  dichotomous versus continuous (3) 53: 2
  methodological considerations in studies of (3) 53:
      2–4
  in neurologic disorders (3) 53: 15
  pepsinogen for susceptibility to peptic ulcer (2) 78:
      2
  possible use (3) 53: 2
  in psychosomatic medicine (2) 78: 2
  requirements to be ideal (3) 53: 3
  in schizophrenia (1) 62: 11–12; (3) 53: 12–15
    dopamine beta-hydroxylase (3) 53: 14
    evoked potentials (3) 53: 13
    eye blinking rate (3) 53: 13
    histocompatibility antigens (3) 53: 13
    monoamine oxidase (3) 53: 14
    psychological tests (3) 53: 14
    smooth-pursuit eye tracking (3) 53: 14–15
  state (3) 53: 1
    possible uses (3) 53: 2
  trait (3) 53: 1–2
  vulnerability (3) 53: 1
Marriage. *See* Marital status
Masculinity, in girls (1) 46: 16–18
Masochism
  in hypochondriasis (1) 35: 12
  masochistic personality distinguished from (1) 27:
      1, 7
  sexual (1) 27: 1; 46: 5–6
    development in children (2) 41: 6–7
  terminology (1) 27: 1
Masochistic personality disorder (1) **27: 1–9.** *See also*
      Depressive-masochistic personality
  arousal of masochistic actions in objects (1) 27: 3

biology of (1) 27: 4–5
clinical course (1) 27: 3–4
clinical description (1) 27: 2–4
cultural rituals distinguished from (1) 27: 7
definition (1) 27: 1–2
dependent personality disorder distinguished from (1) 26: 3–4
depressive neurosis distinguished from (1) 40: 7
diagnosis (1) 27: 7
differential diagnosis (1) 27: 7
distinction between sexual perversion and (1) 27: 1
epidemiology (1) 27: 2
etiology (1) 27: 4–7
in female (1) 27: 5
Freud's theory of (1) 27: 5
genetics (1) 27: 4–5
narcissistic personality disorder distinguished from (1) 18: 8
passive-aggressive disorder similarity to (1) 26: 4–5
perversion distinguished from (1) 27: 7
psychodynamics of (1) 27: 5–7
psychotherapy for (1) 27: 8–9
self-mutilation in (1) 27: 1
submission in (1) 27: 2–3
suicide in (1) 27: 6–7
treatment (1) 27: 7–9
variation in intensity (1) 27: 3
Masserman J., experimental neurosis studies (1) 2: 13–14
Mass media
contradictory health messages by (2) 79: 4–5
health promotion by (2) 129: 4
and lifestyle changes causing reduction in heart disease (2) 79: 4
Masturbation
paraphilias associated with (2) 41: 6–7
sadomasochism associated with (2) 41: 6–7
Matched tasks, information processing determined by (3) 65: 9
McCarthy scales of children's abilities (2) 21: 5
Measles, subacute sclerosing panencephalitis after (2) 34: 4–5
Media. See Mass media
Medical alliance (3) 36: 5–6
Medical care. See also Physician
for chronic mental patient (3) 6: 8
health promotion in (2) 129: 2–3
mental health services for children combined with (2) 69: 5
psychiatric disorders treated in (3) 22: 6–8
in general hospital (3) 22: 6
in nursing home (3) 22: 6
in outpatient setting (3) 22: 6–8
psychosomatic medicine role in (2) 78: 8–9. See also Psychosomatic medicine

Medical illness
in adolescents (2) 4: 14–15
affective disorder mimicking (2) 87: 12–13
alcohol abuse (3) **18: 1–16.** See also Alcohol abuse
alexithymia in (2) 99: 3
anxiety as symptom of (3) 14: 1
anxiety disorder distinguished from (2) 39: 7
behavior contributions to (2) **79: 1–8.** See also Behavior, contributions to illness
biopsychosocial model (2) 108: 1; 110: 1–2
biopsychosocial spirals in (2) 110: 2–4
in chronic mental patient (3) 6: 8
cognitive change in, psychological tests to monitor (3) 52: 19–21
in conduct disorders (2) 37: 5
crisis model for (2) 108: 4
definition (2) 81: 6
dementia exacerbated in (1) 73: 5
demoralization reaction in (2) 99: 2–3
depression due to (1) 61: 2–3
depression in (1) 59: 12; (2) **99: 1–7.** See also Depression, in medically ill
in brain-damaged patient (2) 99: 4–5
difficulty in diagnosis (2) 99: 1, 2
drugs for (2) 99: 5–6
in elderly (2) 99: 4
electroconvulsive therapy (2) 99: 6–7
organic syndromes (2) 99: 2
psychotherapy for (2) 99: 5
disease distinguished from (2) 81: 6
drug abuse (2) **90: 1–12.** See also Substance abuse
drug-drug interactions (2) **111: 1–11.** See also Drugs, interactions
and drug-related behavioral effects (3) 45: 7–8
drug therapy precipitating organic mental disorder in children (2) 34: 5–7
electroconvulsive therapy in (1) 61: 7, 8
fears in (2) 108: 4
grief reaction in (2) 99: 3
heart disease, psychiatric aspects (2) **118: 1–7; 126: 1–8.** See also Heart disease
heterocyclic antidepressants effects on (1) 61: 10
hypertension, psychiatric aspects (2) 118: 7–9. See also Hypertension
hypnosis used in (2) 112: 3–4
impact on adolescent development (2) 4: 14–15
impact on psychological functions (2) 78: 6
isolation in (2) 108: 4
masked depression in (2) 99: 4
movement disorders (2) **38: 1–7.** See also Movement disorders
neurologic disorders causing personality change (1) **28: 1–12.** See also Personality, neurologic disease causing changes in
obesity (2) **103: 1–12.** See also Obesity
organic mental disorders (1) **73: 1–20;** (2) **87: 1–17.** See also Organic mental disorders
in children due to (2) 34: 7–9

Medical illness *(continued)*
  other childhood disorders with physical manifesta-
        tions (2) 43: **1–9**
    encopresis (2) 43: 4–6
    enuresis (2) 43: 1–4
    night terrors (2) 43: 7–8
    sleepwalking (2) 43: 6–7
    stuttering (2) 43: 8–9
  pain (2) **104: 1–12.** *See also* Pain
  personality disorders in (2) **82: 1–11**
  personality types and impact in (2) 78: 2–3; **82: 1–
       11**
    borderline person (2) 82: 6–8
    compulsive personality (2) 82: 2–3
    depressive-masochistic person (2) 82: 5–6
    histrionic personality (2) 82: 3–5
    narcissistic person (2) 82: 8–9
    paranoid person (2) 82: 9–10
  physician-patient relationship in (2) **81: 1–10.** *See
      also* Physician-patient relationship
  psychiatric manifestations (2) **88: 1–15**
    areas of inquiry in study of (2) 88: 1–2
    in endocrine disorders (2) **88: 5–15.** *See also*
        Endocrine disorders
      adrenal (2) 88: 8–10
      pancreas (2) 88: 12–13
      parathyroid (2) 88: 11–12
      pheochromocytoma (2) 88: 10
      pituitary (2) 88: 13–14
      sex hormones (2) 88: 14–15
      thyroid (2) 88: 5–8
    evaluation of high-risk patient (2) 88: 4–5
    implications for clinical practice (2) 88: 4–5
    incidence (2) 88: 2–4
    pathogenesis (2) 88: 1
    prospective studies (2) 88: 2–4
  psychodynamics in (2) **82: 1–11**
  psychosomatic medicine (2) **78: 1–9.** *See also* Psy-
      chosomatic medicine
  psychotherapy in (2) **108: 1–12**
    alleviating guilt (2) 108: 9
    confrontation (2) 108: 8–9
      with unexpressed affect (2) 108: 8–9
    connecting affect with underlying content (2)
      108: 9
    in drug addict (2) 108: 10–11
    eliciting fears and personal meanings (2) 108: 4
    engagement of nonmotivated patient (2) 108:
      11–12
    goals (2) 108: 3–4
    modalities (2) 108: 2
    psychodynamic life narrative (2) 108: 4–7
    psychodynamic perspective on supportive inter-
      ventions (2) 108: 7–8
    special problems in (2) 108: 9–12
    support of self-esteem in narcissistic character
      (2) 108: 10
    in suspicious and distrustful patient (2) 108: 10–
      11

    therapeutic stance in (2) 108: 11–12
    transference in (2) 108: 2, 6, 7
  regression in (2) 82: 1
  requirements for coping (2) 108: 3
  sleep disorders (2) **52: 1–11; 105: 1–16.** *See also*
      Sleep disorders
  somatoform disorders (2) **100: 1–10.** *See also* Psy-
      chosomatic disorders; Somatoform dis-
      orders
  stress of recovery from (1) 41: 6
  suicide in (1) 71: 3, 5
  surgical patient (2) **121: 1–9.** *See also* Surgery
  systems theory applied to (2) 110: 1–2
Medical model (1) **51: 1–7**
  for classification (1) 51: 2–4
  definition (1) 51: 1
  in diagnosis (1) 51: 2–4
  laboratory tests in (1) 51: 3
  new directions in psychiatry based on (1) 51: 7
  physician-patient relationship in (2) 81: 6
  in psychiatry (1) 6: 6; 63: 1–2
  psychoanalysis contrasted with (1) 51: 5–6
  psychosocial factors as part of (1) 51: 2
  resistance to application in psychiatry (1) 51: 4
Medical record. *See* Records
Medical student illness (2) 100: 2
Medication. *See* Drugs; Pharmacotherapy
Medicine
  primary care (2) 116: 2. *See also* Primary care
    medicine
  psychiatry in (2) **116: 1–8.** *See also* Primary care
    medicine
  relaxation therapy and biofeedback in (2) **109: 1–
    11.** *See also* Biofeedback; Relaxation ther-
    apy
Medicolegal issues. *See also* Legal issues; Malpractice
  forensic psychiatry (3) **36: 1–13.** *See also* Forensic
    psychiatry
    in therapeutic setting (3) 36: 11–13
    guardianship problems (3) 36: 12
    involunary interventions other than commitment
      (3) 36: 13
    seclusion or restraint (3) 36: 13
    threats to third parties (3) 36: 12
Meditation (2) 109: 2–3
  autogenic training (2) 109: 3
  hypnosis distinguished from (2) 109: 3
  integrated physiologic response in (2) 109: 3
  physiologic changes during (2) 109: 3
  technique (2) 109: 2–3
Medroxyprogesterone acetate
  for antisocial personality (1) 23: 9
  for sexually dangerous offender (3) 28: 23, 24
  side effects (3) 28: 23
Meehl, P., contribution to social learning theory (1)
    2: 20–21
Megavitamin therapy (2) 160: 2–3
  in children (2) 160: 2
  in pervasive developmental disorders (2) 27: 9

safety (2) 160: 3
toxicity (2) 34: 11
Melancholia (1) 61: 3. *See also* Depression
acute, treatment (1) 61: 6−7. *See also* Depression,
    treatment
definition (1) 59: 3
DSM-III on (1) 59: 3
limbic-hypothalamic-pituitary-adrenal axis dysreg-
    ulation in (3) **54: 1−11**
    anatomical substrate of affectual state (3) 54: 2−
        4
    dexamethasone suppression test as marker (3)
        54: 10−11
    future studies (3) 54: 11
    neurotransmitters and (3) 54: 4−8
    physiology (3) 54: 1−2
Melatonin, as timing transmitter in circadian rhythm
    (3) 59: 9−11
Mellaril. *See* Thioridazine
Memory (3) **71: 1−14.** *See also* Amnesia; Amnesic
    disorder
amnesia (1) 39: 2−6; (3) 71: 6−10. *See also* Am-
    nesia
anatomy of (2) 13: 3−4
basic organization and processes of (2) 13: 2−3
brain in
    and education (3) 71: 10
    implications for psychiatry (3) 71: 10
    lesions related to dysfunction (3) 71: 11
    organization (3) 71: 3−6
    and psychoanalytic theory (3) 71: 10
catecholamines in (2) 13: 6−7
in children
    evaluation (2) 20: 9
    neurobiology (2) **13: 1−9**
consolidation (2) 13: 6−7
declarative versus procedural (3) 52: 12
definition (2) 13: 1
in dementia (1) 72: 11
depersonalization and loss of (1) 39: 10−11
in depression (3) 71: 13−14
disorders in (3) **71: 1−11.** *See also* Dissociative dis-
    orders
episodic (2) 13: 3
evaluation in children (2) 20: 9
in fugue (1) 39: 6−7. *See also* Fugue
habituation and sensitization in (3) 71: 2−3
in Huntington disease (1) 73: 11
iconic (2) 13: 2
immediate and short-term (3) 52: 12−13
importance in psychiatry (3) 71: 1
in Korsakoff's syndrome (1) 73: 17−19
limbic system lesions associated with disorders in
    (1) 73: 20
long-term, proteins related to (2) 13: 5−6
marijuana effect on (2) 4: 13
in multiple personality (1) 39: 8−10
neurobiology (2) **13: 1−9;** (3) 71: 1−6
    anatomy (2) 13: 3−4

basic organization and processes in (2) 13: 1−3
    neurochemistry (2) 13: 5−7
neurochemistry (2) 13: 5−7
neuropeptides in (2) 13: 7
nonverbal (3) 71: 11
organization in brain (3) 71: 3−6
physiology (2) 87: 10
processing and storage in stress-response syn-
    dromes (1) 41: 14
in psychiatric syndromes (2) 95: 2
remote
    in dementia (1) 72: 11
    test of (3) 71: 12−13
semantic (2) 13: 3
short-term versus long-term (2) 13: 2−3
stages of (2) 13: 2−3
structure of (2) 13: 2−3
as synaptic change (3) 71: 1−3
systems of (3) 52: 12
temporal lobe in (3) 71: 7
tests of (3) 52: 12−14; 71: 10−14
    immediate and short-term (3) 52: 12−13
    lateralization of declarative type (3) 52: 13−14
    long-term (3) 52: 13
    new learning capacity (3) 71: 11
    remote memory (3) 71: 12−13
    self rating scale (3) 71: 13
    verbal and nonverbal memory (3) 71: 11
two systems of (3) 71: 8−10
verbal (3) 71: 11
Men. *See also* Sex
histrionic personality disorder in (1) 19: 5−6
hysterical personality disorder in (1) 19: 4−5
Tanner stages (2) 4: 3, 4
transsexualism in (1) 46: 10−15
Menarche
exercise related to (2) 9: 5
as marker for biological age (2) 4: 3, 4
onset of (2) 9: 4−5
weight related to (2) 9: 5
Meningitis, organic mental disorders after (2) 34: 4
Menopause (2) 120: 6−8
depression in (2) 120: 8
    in nonbipolar disorder (1) 60: 6; (3) 13: 6
hot flashes in (2) 120: 7
osteoporosis in (2) 120: 7
physical symptoms in (2) 120: 6−7
psychoanalytic concepts of symptoms in (2) 120: 7
psychological symptoms in (2) 120: 7−8
sexual function in (2) 120: 7
treatment of symptoms of (2) 120: 8
Menstrual cycle (2) 120: 2−3
behavioral effects (2) 88: 14
as biological rhythm (3) 59: 7
in bulimia (2) 102: 5
difficulties in studying (2) 120: 2
dysmenorrhea (2) 120: 2−3
hypersomnia associated with (2) 105: 14
premenstrual syndrome (2) 120: 2, 3

Menstrual cycle *(continued)*
  psychosocial factors in expectation of symptoms
        related to (2) 120: 2–3
  in sexuality (1) 45: 2–3
Mental Health Assessment Form (3) 12: 9
Mental health professionals. *See* Psychiatrists
Mental health services (3) **4: 9–15**
  for adolescents (3) 12: 26
  for antisocial personality (1) 23: 7–9
  categorical support for (3) 4: 13
  for children (3) 12: 25–26
    child guidance clinics (3) 12: 26
    hospital and residential treatment (2) **64: 1–19**
    spectrum of services required (2) 64: 3–5
  for chronic mental patient (3) 4: 15; **6: 1–14;** 22:
        5. *See also* Chronic mental patients
    appropriate source of care (3) 6: 12
    historical aspects (3) 6: 1–3
  Community Mental Health Centers Act and (3) 4:
        10
  community mental health services (3) **5: 1–13;** 6:
        2–3. *See also* Community mental health
        services
  competition in (3) 4: 14
  confederacy of services in system (3) 22: 3–4
  cost containment measures (3) 4: 14
  cost-effectiveness (3) 3: 5–6
  critical issues in 1980s (3) 4: 13–15
  day treatment (3) 6: 8
  deinstitutionalization (3) 4: 11–12; 6: 3. *See also*
        Deinstitutionalization
  economics of (3) **3: 1–12.** *See also* Costs; *and*
        under financing *below*
  epidemiologic applications to (3) 12: 25–26
    in determining needs in elderly (3) 21: 9–10
  financing of (3) 3: 6–11; 4: 13
    community mental health centers (3) 3: 10–11
    discriminatory coverage (3) 3: 7–10
    DRG payment mechanism (3) 3: 10
    importance in determining treatment (3) 3: 6–7
    insurance (3) 3: 7
    public systems (3) 3: 10
  focus on treatment organization rather than indi-
        vidual practitioner (3) 5: 5
  in general health care setting (3) 4: 15
  government role in (3) **4: 1–16.** *See also* Govern-
        ment
  historical background (3) 5: 1–5; 6: 1–3
    in late 1940s through 1950s (3) 5: 2–3
    in mid 1970s through mid 1980s (3) 5: 4–5
    in 1960s through mid 1970s (3) 5: 3–4
    in World War II era (3) 5: 2
  hospital and residential treatment in (2) **64: 1–19;**
        (3) 6: 1–2. *See also* Hospitalization; Hos-
        pitals
    future prospects (3) 4: 14–15
    in late 1970s (3) 4: 11
  informed consent in (3) 29: 6
  insurance for, limitations on coverage (3) 3: 1

  legislation on (3) 5: 2–5
  methods of studying utilization (3) 22: 2
  National Institute of Mental Health Community
        Support Program (3) 4: 12
  nursing homes in (3) 4: 11
  out-of-home services (2) 64: 1
  outpatient setting (3) 22: 5–6. *See also* Ambulatory
        care
  political issues in (3) 5: 5–7
  President's Commission on Mental Health (3) 4:
        12–13
  private for-profit sector in (3) 4: 15
  for private office-based care (3) 22: 5–6
  psychiatric case register in study of (3) 22: 2
  public policy affecting organization of (3) 22: 8–9
  reimbursement for (3) 4: 13–14
    in 1970s (3) 4: 10–11
    in 1950s and 1960s (3) 4: 9–10
  social and political background (3) 5: 1–5
  systems of care (3) 5: 7–10; 22: 3–4
    historical background (3) 4: 9–13
    medical care sector (3) 22: 6–8
    mental health specialty sector (3) 22: 4–6
  treated prevalence and use of (3) **22: 1–11.** *See*
        also Prevalence, treated
  treatment planning for (2) **56: 1–9.** *See also* Treat-
        ment planning
  utilization (3) 22: 8–11
    administrative procedures and treatment prac-
          tices affecting (3) 22: 9
    in ambulatory setting (3) 22: 5–6
    ecologic factors in (3) 22: 9
    factors influencing (3) 22: 8, 11
    geographic factors in (3) 22: 8–9
    in hospitals (3) 22: 4–5
    illness behavior influence on (3) 22: 9–11
    in office-based private practice (3) 22: 5–6
    social class and race influence on (2) 69: 4; (3)
          22: 9, 10
    among various subsystems (3) 5: 8–9
Mental Health Systems Act (3) 4: 8, 12–13; 5: 4–5
Mental hygiene movement, in child psychiatry (3)
        12: 2
Mental illness. *See also* Psychiatric disorders; Psycho-
        pathology
  alcohol abuse related to (3) 18: 9–16
  children at risk for (3) 7: 10–12
  chronic (3) **61: 1–14.** *See also* Chronic mental pa-
        tients
  criminal behavior related to (3) 28: 1–2, 11, 12
  culture role in (3) **2: 1–14.** *See also* Cross-cultural
        psychiatry; Culture
  economic costs (3) **3: 1–12**
    cost-effectiveness of care (3) 3: 5–6
    direct and indirect (3) 3: 2–5
  family impact of (3) 7: 10–12
  insurance coverage for (3) 3: 7–10
  urbanization role in (1) 52: 9–10
  variety of approaches and definitions of (1) 2: 9

Mentally disordered offenders (3) **28: 1–26**
  abolition of retention of insanity defense in (3) 28: 13–14
  adolescents (3) 28: 24–25
  ambulatory treatment (3) 28: 16–18
  classes of (3) 28: 1
  and criminal justice system (3) 28: 2, 3
  definition (3) 28: 1
  descriptive statistics on (3) 28: 2
  guilty but mentally ill
    legal considerations (3) 28: 8
    treatment considerations (3) 28: 4, 6, 21
  incompetent to stand trial (3) 28: 2–5, 7
    legal considerations (3) 28: 7
    treatment considerations (3) 28: 2–4, 20
  inmates (3) 28: 4, 6–8
    legal considerations in treatment (3) 28: 8
    treatment considerations (3) 28: 4, 6, 21–22
  institutions for (3) 28: 14–15
  mentally retarded (3) 28: 23–24
  not guilty by reason of insanity
    legal considerations (3) 28: 7–8
    treatment considerations (3) 28: 4, 5, 20–21
  prediction of future dangerousness in (3) 28: 13
  prison treatment programs for (3) 28: 15
  probation and parole (3) 28: 4, 7, 8
    legal considerations in treatment (3) 28: 8
    treatment considerations (3) 28: 4, 7, 22
  prognosis (3) 28: 12–13
  psycholegal controversy in (3) 28: 2
  public policy considerations and (3) 28: 11–14
  recidivism and prediction of future dangerousness (3) 28: 11–13
  sexually dangerous offender (3) 28: 22–23
  treatment
    ambulatory (3) 28: 16–18
    community programs (3) 28: 18–19
    confidentiality issues in (3) 28: 10–11, 18
    countertransference in (3) 28: 10, 18
    court order request for (3) 28: 16
    general clinical issues in (3) 28: 9–11
    mentally retarded offenders (3) 28: 23–24
    modalities (3) 28: 19–22
    motivation versus apathy (3) 28: 10, 17–18
    psychological health versus stabilization (3) 28: 9–10, 17
    role-agency problem of psychiatrist in (3) 28: 10–11, 18
    security versus
      in ambulatory setting (3) 28: 16–17
      in inpatient setting (3) 28: 9
    settings for (3) 28: 14–19
    sexually dangerous offender (3) 28: 23–25
    specialized programs (3) 28: 18–19
Mental retardation (2) **28: 1–8**
  attention deficit disorder distinguished from (2) 36: 6
  autism disorders distinguished from (2) 27: 8
  child psychiatry involvement in (2) 1: 2
  classification (2) 19: 13; 28: 3
  definition (2) 28: 2–3
  developmental versus difference approach to (2) 28: 4
  DSM-III on (2) 28: 2–3
    critique of (2) 19: 13
  epidemiology (3) 12: 14
  etiology (2) 28: 3–4; (3) 12: 14
  failure and its effects in (2) 28: 5–6
    heightened expectancy of failure (2) 28: 5
    lowered effectiveness motivation (2) 28: 6
    outerdirectedness (2) 28: 5–6
    wariness (2) 28: 5
  genetic counseling in (2) 58: 4
  historical background (2) 28: 1–2
  after infection (2) 34: 4
  mentally disordered offenders with (3) 28: 23–24
  motivation in (2) 28: 4–6
  parental reaction to birth (2) 58: 2–3
  patients' rights for treatment (3) 35: 2–3. *See also* Patients' rights
    for aftercare following institutionalization (3) 35: 11–12
  prevalence (2) 28: 3
  prevention (2) 28: 6–7; 58: 3–5
    early recognition of medical disorders (2) 58: 4
    genetic counseling (2) 58: 4
    in hypothyroidism (2) 58: 4
    in perceptual-motor dysfunction (2) 58: 4–5
    in phenylketonuria (2) 58: 4
    in psychosocial deprivation (2) 58: 5
    in psychosociocultural etiology (2) 58: 3–4
    reducing pregnancy complications (2) 58: 4
  psychological disorders in (2) 58: 5–6
  research in (2) 28: 2
  social deprivation and dependency in (2) 28: 5
  treatment approaches (2) 28: 6–8; **58: 1–7**
    behavioral intervention (2) 28: 6
    genetic counseling and prenatal screening (2) 28: 6–7
    hospitalization and institutionalization (2) 28: 7–8; 58: 5
    mainstreaming (2) 28: 7
    parental reaction (2) 58: 2–3
    patterning (2) 160: 3
    prevention (2) 58: 3–5
    psychotherapy (2) 58: 5–6
    public policy in (2) 58: 1
Mental status examination
  in children (2) **20: 4–12**
    adaptive capacities (2) 20: 12
    affects (2) 20: 11
    attention (2) 20: 7
    defense organization (2) 20: 11
    drive behavior (2) 20: 11
    fantasies and inferred conflicts (2) 20: 11
    hallucinations (2) 20: 10–11
    hyperactivity (2) 20: 7
    intelligence (2) 20: 9

Mental status examination, in children *(continued)*
    judgment and insight (2) 20: 11–12
    language and speech (2) 20: 8–9
    laterality (2) 20: 7
    manner of relating (2) 20: 5
    memory (2) 20: 9
    nervous system functioning (2) 20: 5–8
    neurological soft signs (2) 20: 5–8
    object relations (2) 20: 11
    orientation to time and place (2) 20: 5
    outline for (2) 20: 4
    physical appearance (2) 20: 4–5
    positive attributes (2) 20: 12
    reading (2) 20: 7, 8
    self-esteem (2) 20: 12
    separation (2) 20: 5
    thinking processes (2) 20: 9–11
  in Korsakoff's syndrome (1) 73: 17
  psychodynamic (1) 6: 10–11
    affect and mood (1) 6: 10–11
    associations (1) 6: 10
    content (1) 6: 11
    general appearance (1) 6: 10
    intellectual functioning (1) 6: 11
  questionnaire for (2) 119: 2
Meperidine (Demerol)
  contraindication to use with monoamine oxidase
        inhibitors (2) 111: 8
  monoamine oxidase inhibitors interaction with (2)
        111: 8
Merycism (2) 40:
Mesotelencephalic system (3) 44: 6–8
Meta-analysis
  difficulties as research technique (1) 11: 13
  for effectiveness of psychotherapy (1) 11: 3–4
Metabolic disorders
  hallucinations in children due to (2) 20: 10
  psychosis in (1) 69: 9
Metaprocesses, in attention deficit disorder (3) 66: 5
Meta-therapy (2) 109: 2
Methadone and metoclopramide challenge, in affect-
        ive disorders (3) 53: 6
Methyldopa, psychiatric side effects (2) 91: 5
Methylphenidate (Ritalin)
  in antisocial personality disorder (1) 10: 3
  in attention deficit disorder (2) 36: 10–11; 59: 6;
        (3) 66: 15–20
    amphetamines compared with (3) 66: 17–18
    differential effects on learning and behavior (3)
        66: 17
    pemoline compared with (3) 66: 18
    side effects (3) 66: 18–19
  in depression of medically ill (2) 99: 6
  dose response curves for different effects (2) 59: 5,
        8
  growth effects (2) 36: 11; (3) 66: 19
  in narcolepsy (2) 105: 13–14; (3) 61: 13
  organic mental disorders precipitated by (2) 34: 5–
        6

  pharmacokinetics in children (2) 59: 4
  precipitation of Tourette's disease by (2) 36: 11
  side effects (2) 36: 10–11
    psychiatric (2) 91: 4
  structure (2) 59: 6
Meyer, A., contributions to psychiatry (1) 52: 5–6
Midbrain raphe nuclei
  role in endocrine control (3) 44: 12
  serotonergic innervation (3) 44: 8–12
Mid-life crisis (2) 4: 11
  influence on parent relationship with adolescent
        (2) 4: 11
Midtown Manhattan study, on mental disorder con-
        currence with alcohol abuse (3) 18: 9–10
Migraine headache (2) 104: 6–8
  biofeedback for (2) 104: 7–8; 109: 6
  clinical description (2) 104: 6
  epidemiology (2) 104: 6
  pathophysiology (2) 104: 6–7
  precipitants (2) 104: 6
  relaxation therapy in (2) 104: 7–8; 109: 6
  stress role (2) 104: 7
  treatment and prevention (2) 104: 7–8
    biofeedback and relaxation therapy (2) 104: 7–
        8; 109: 6
    drugs (2) 104: 7
Migration
  antisocial personality and (3) 19: 3
  schizophrenia related to (1) 54: 11; (3) 15: 9
Milieu therapy (2) 64: 12–15
  behavior therapy in (2) 64: 14
  definition (2) 56: 3
  design of activities program in (2) 64: 13
  design of daily schedule in (2) 64: 13
  design of living unit in (2) 64: 13
  exploitation of live events in (2) 64: 13–14
  isolation versus community orientation (2) 64: 14–
    15
  regressive or progressive emphasis in (2) 64: 14
Military
  amnesia in (1) 39: 4, 5
  psychiatric epidemiology in (3) 11: 4–5
  schizophrenia related to service (1) 54: 11
  stress-response syndrome after combat (1) 41: 10
Miller N., contribution to learning theory (1) 2: 14
Millon, T.
  contribution to social learning theory (1) 2: 21–2
  multidimensional system for personality disorders
    (1) 24: 3
Millon Multiaxial Clinical Inventory (1) 7: 4; 15: 7–
    8
Minerals, in psychiatric therapy (2) 160: 3
Minimal brain dysfunction (3) 66: 1–2, 4. *See also*
    Attention deficit disorder
Minnesota Multiphasic Personality Inventory (1) 7:
    5; 15: 5
  diagnostic utility (1) 15: 5
  in Halstead-Reitan Neuropsychological Test Battery
    (1) 72: 4

Mitral valve prolapse (2) 118: 5–7
  anxiety disorders related to (3) 14: 10–11
  clinical characteristics (2) 118: 6
  historical background (2) 118: 5–6
  panic disorder associated with (1) 32: 4, 10; (2) 118: 6
  psychiatric aspects (2) 118: 6
  psychobiologic aspects (2) 118: 6–7
  treatment (2) 118: 7
MMPI. *See* Minnesota Multiphasic Personality Inventory
M'Naghton standard (3) 27: 7–8
Moban. *See* Molindone
Modeling
  participant (1) 33: 10–11
  and rehearsal in behavior therapy (2) 77: 8–9
Model Penal Code, on insanity and criminal responsibility (3) 27: 8
Molecular biology, from simplification to more realistic central nervous system dynamics (3) 72: 1–6
Molindone, structure (1) 55: 4
Monoamine neural systems (3) **44: 1–13.** *See also* Catecholamines; Dopamine; Norepinephrine; Serotonin
  anatomy and physiology in brain
    dopaminergic systems (3) 44: 6–8. *See also* Dopamine
    general features (3) 44: 1–2
    implications (3) 44: 12–13
    noradrenergic systems (3) 44: 2–6. *See also* Norepinephrine
    serotonergic (3) 44: 8–12. *See also* Serotonin
  in attention deficit disorder (2) 36: 4–5
  development (2) 12: 9–11
  development of techniques to visualize cellular distribution (3) 44: 1
  electrophysiologic activity of neurons (3) 44: 2
  general features of (3) 44: 1–2
  localization in brain (3) 44: 1–2
  organization of projections from neurons (3) 44: 2
  target neuron effects (3) 44: 2
Monoamine oxidase
  in anxiety disorders (1) 32: 6
  in borderline personality disorder (1) 17: 11
  developmental considerations (2) 12: 10–11
  as marker in alcoholism (3) 53: 10–11
  as marker in schizophrenia (1) 62: 11; (3) 53: 14
  platelet levels as marker in affective disorders (3) 53: 7–8
  and puberty (2) 12: 10–11
  role in schizophrenia (1) 64: 5
Monoamine oxidase inhibitors
  in agoraphobia without panic attacks (1) 10: 6–7
  in agoraphobia with panic attacks (1) 33: 11, 12
  anesthetic agents interaction with (2) 111: 8–9
  antihypertensive drugs interacting with (2) 111: 8
  in children (2) 59: 16
  classes of (1) 61: 11

  in depression (1) 61: 11–12
  foods to avoid with (1) 61: 11
  hypertensive reaction when combined with other drugs or foods
  hypotension due to (1) 61: 11
    interactions and (2) 111: 8
  interactions with other drugs (1) 61: 11; (2) 111: 7–9
  mechanism of antidepressant action (2) 111: 7
  meperidine interaction with (2) 111: 8
  in obsessive-compulsive disorder (1) 34: 9
  in panic disorder (1) 10: 6; 32: 11
  phenothiazines interacting with (2) 111: 3
  in posttraumatic stress disorder (1) 10: 7
  rich in tyramine (2) 111: 7–8
  safety of (2) 111: 7
  side effects (1) 61: 11
    psychiatric (2) 91: 2
  use with tricyclic antidepressants (1) 61: 11
Monoamines. *See also* Catecholamines; Dopamine; Norepinephrine; Serotonin
  of affective illness (1) 64: 8–9
  in attention deficit disorder (3) 66: 11
  as markers in affective disorders (3) 53: 6
Mood. *See also* Affective disorders; Bipolar disorder; Depression
  in adjustment disorder (1) 59: 5
  definition (1) 40: 2–3
  differential diagnosis of disorders of (1) 59: 4–6
Mood-congruent psychotic symptom (1) 59: 2
Mood-incongruent psychotic symptom (1) 59: 2
Morality
  development of (2) 17: 1–3
  in latency (2) 3: 5
  objective versus subjective (2) 17: 2
Moral treatment movement (3) 6: 1–2
Morbid risk. *See also* Risk factors
  of affective disorders (1) 62: 12–14
  definition (1) 54: 3; 69: 1
  lifetime (1) 54: 3
  of schizophrenia (1) 54: 5; 62: 4–6
    family pedigree studies (3) 15: 6
Morpheme, definition (3) 67: 5. *See also* Language
Mothers. *See also* Parents
  change in relationship with daughter during daughter's pregnancy (2) 120: 5–6
  mental illness impact on child (2) 50: 4–5
  psychiatric hospitalization with child (3) 7: 11
  schizophrenogenic (3) 7: 2
Motivation
  behavior related to (1) 1: 1–2
  effectance (2) 28: 6
    in attention deficit disorder (3) 66: 5
  in mental retardation (2) 28: 4–6
  and neuropsychological assessment (1) 72: 9
  in psychoanalysis (1) 8: 11
  in psychodynamic therapy of children (2) 57: 2
  sex differences in (2) 17: 5

Motor disorders, in conversion (1) 35: 6
Motor neuron disease, psychosis in (1) 69: 7
Mourning
  in family dynamics (2) 5: 2
  family therapy in assistance (2) 110: 6
  free association as means for completion (1) 8: 6
  grief and bereavement distinguished from (2) 95: 13
  pathologic (2) 110: 6–7
  stages of (1) 41: 5–6
Movement
  event-related potentials associated with (3) 62: 3–4
  neostriatum role in (3) 42: 15–17
Movement disorders (2) **38: 1–7**
  basal ganglia diseases causing (1) 28: 11–12
  chronic tic disorder (2) 38: 2
  definitions in (2) 38: 1
  in developmental disorders (2) 38: 7
  differential diagnosis of tics (2) 38: 2, 5
  Huntington's disease (1) 28: 11–12
  Parkinson's disease (1) 28: 11
  phonic behaviors (2) 38: 1, 2, 7
  in schizophrenia (1) 53: 14
  stereotypies (2) 38: 1, 7
  tics (2) 38: 1
  Tourette's disorder (2) **38: 2–7.** *See also* Tourette's disorder
  transient tic disorder (2) 38: 1–2
  treatment, antianxiety drugs in (2) 59: 17
Movement-related potentials (3) 62: 4
Mowrer, O. H., contribution to learning theory (1) 2: 14–15
Multidimensional perspective (1) 6: 6–7
  for personality disorders (1) 24: 3
Multifactorial-polygenic model, of genetic factors in mental illness (2) 10: 4–5
Multiple personality. *See* Personality, multiple
Multiple Risk Factor Intervention Trial (2) 129: 2–3
Multiple sclerosis
  cognitive change in (3) 52: 19
  organic mental disorders due to (2) 34: 7–8
  psychosis in (1) 69: 8
Multiple sleep latency test (2) 105: 3
  in narcolepsy (2) 105: 13
  in sleep apnea (2) 105: 11
Munchausen's syndrome (2) **101: 1–8.** *See also* Factitious illness
  borderline personality in (2) 101: 7
  classification (2) 101: 2
  clinical description (1) 35: 17–18
  definition (1) 35: 16
  diagnosis and differential diagnosis (1) 35: 19
    dilemmas in (2) 101: 5
  epidemiology (1) 35: 16–17
  etiology (1) 35: 18–19; (2) 101: 6
  factitious disease distinguished from (2) 101: 2–3
  historical background (2) 101: 1–2
  malingering distinguished from (2) 101: 1, 8

  modes of presentation (2) 101: 3–5
  mothers producing syndrome in child (2) 101: 5
  personality characteristics in (1) 35: 18
  by proxy (1) 35: 18; (2) 101: 5
  psychodynamics (2) 101: 7–8
  spectrum of disease presentation in (2) 101: 6–8
  treatment (1) 35: 19
Muscle
  psychosis in disorders of (1) 69: 7–8
  tone in relaxation therapy (2) 109: 2
Muscular dystrophy, psychosis in (1) 69: 7–8
Mutism (2) 95: 6
  LSD therapy of (2) 35: 5
  treatment (2) 95: 6
Myelin (3) 42: 5
Myocardial infarction
  anxiety in (2) 118: 2
  denial in (2) 118: 1–2
  depression in (2) 118: 2–3
  emotional aspects (2) 118: 1–3
Myoclonic jerk (3) 61: 11
Myoclonus, sleep-related (2) 105: 7–8; (3) 61: 10–
  clinical features (3) 61: 11
  differential diagnosis (2) 105: 7–8
  evaluation (3) 61: 11
  pathophysiology (3) 61: 10–11
  prevalence (3) 61: 11
  treatment (2) 105: 8; (3) 61: 11
Myotonia congenita, psychosis in (1) 69: 7–8
Myxedema (2) 88: 5–7. *See also* Hypothyroidism

Naloxone, in narcotic overdose (2) 90: 7
Naming, test for (3) 52: 7
Narcan. *See* Naloxone
Narcissism (1) 18: 1. *See also* Narcissistic Personality Narcissistic Personality Disorder
  classification (1) 18: 2
  definition (1) 18: 2
  infantile (1) 18: 2–3
  malignant (1) 18: 4
  pathologic (1) 18: 2–3
  personality disorder
  psychoanalytic versus clinical concept of (1) 18: 2
Narcissistic personality
  antisocial personality distinguished from (1) 23: 1
  denial of illness by (2) 82: 9
  medical illness in (2) 82: 9; 108: 10
  in medical setting (2) 82: 8–9
  psychodynamics (2) 82: 9
  support of self-esteem in (2) 108: 10
Narcissistic personality disorder (1) **18: 1–11**
  in adolescents (1) 18: 5
  antisocial personality disorder distinguished from (1) 18: 8
  atypical features (1) 18: 4–5

borderline personality disorder distinguished from
      (1) 18: 9
   clinical description (1) 18: 3–6
   definition (1) 18: 2–3
   depressive neurosis distinguished from (1) 40: 7
   diagnosis (1) 18: 8–9
   differential diagnosis (1) 18: 8–9
   envy in (1) 18: 4
   epidemiology (1) 18: 3
   etiology (1) 18: 6–8
   historical background (1) 18: 1–2
   histrionic personality disorder distinguished from
      (1) 18: 9
   hysterical personality disorder distinguished from
      (1) 18: 8; 19: 8–9
      in men (1) 18: 8–9
   malignant state in (1) 18: 4
   in middle age (1) 18: 5–6
   object love in (1) 18: 4
   obsessive-compulsive personality distinguished
      from (1) 18: 8
   paranoid personality disorder distinguished from
      (1) 18: 9
   paranoid psychosis distinguished from (1) 18: 9
   prognosis (1) 18: 11
   psychoanalytic concept (1) 18: 6–7, 9–10
   schizoid personality disorder distinguished from (1)
      16: 3; 18: 9
   self-love in (1) 18: 3–4
   sexual promiscuity in (1) 18: 8
   spectrum of functioning in (1) 18: 5
   superego in (1) 18: 4, 7–8
   treatment (1) 18: 9–11
Narcolepsy (2) 105: 12–14; (3) 61: 12–13
   in adolescents (2) 52: 8–9
   cataplexy in (3) 61: 12
   clinical features (2) 52: 8; 105: 12–13; (3) 61: 12
   diagnosis (3) 61: 13
   disorders associated with (2) 105: 13
   multiple sleep latency test in (2) 105: 13
   pathophysiology (3) 61: 12–13
   prevalence (2) 105: 13
   psychosis in (1) 69: 8–9
   sleep apnea distinguished from (2) 105: 12
   sleep-onset REM periods in (2) 105: 13
   sleep paralysis in (3) 61: 12
   treatment (2) 105: 13–14; (3) 61: 13
Narcotics. See also Opiates
   abuse
      by adolescents (2) 35: 4
      comparative rates with other drugs (3) 17: 11
      demographic trends (3) 17: 11
      epidemiology (3) 17: 10–11
      temporal trends (3) 17: 11
   in cancer pain (2) 104: 4
   overdose
      assessment and treatment (2) 90: 7
      pulmonary edema in (2) 90: 7
      symptoms (2) 90: 3, 7

   psychiatric side effects (2) 91: 6
   symptoms of overdose (2) 90: 3, 7
   symptoms of withdrawal (2) 90: 3, 12
   withdrawal syndrome (2) 90: 12
      symptoms (2) 90: 3, 12
      treatment (2) 90: 12
Nardil. See Phenelzine
National Institute of Mental Health
   community support program (3) 4: 12
   historical background (3) 4: 2–3
   in research (3) 4: 3–6
   retrenchment and refocusing (3) 4: 4
   State Manpower Development Program (3) 4:
      8
   in training (3) 4: 6–8
National Mental Health Act of 1946 (3) 4: 6
Nature-nurture problem (2) 51: 1
Nausea
   in cancer patient, desensitization treatment (2)
      117: 4
   relaxation therapy and biofeedback in (2) 109: 10–
      11
Navane. See Thiothixene
Negative difference waves (3) 62: 6–7
Negotiation
   clinical evaluation as (1) 6: 11–12
   in clinical record (1) 6: 13
   of treatment (1) 6: 12
Neighborhood service center, mental health services
      for children in (2) 69: 4–5
Neoplasms
   brain. See Brain tumor
   pancreatic carcinoma (2) 88: 13
   personality change due to (1) 28: 4
   pheochromocytoma (2) 88: 10
Neostriatum
   inhibitory network (3) 42: 15
   organization related to psychiatric disorders (3) 42:
      17
   role in movement (3) 42: 15–17
   spiny I neuron of (3) 42: 10–11
   structure and function of (3) 42: 10–17
   synaptic action of afferents (3) 42: 11–15
Nervous system. See also Brain; Monoamine neural
      systems; Neurobiology; Neurochemistry;
      Neurological disorders; Neurotransmitters
   in alcoholism etiology (2) 89: 6–7
   autonomic. See Autonomic nervous system
   evaluation in mental status examination (2) 20: 5–
      8
   organization in brain (3) 43: 3–4
Neurasthenia
   in China (3) 2: 6
   cross-cultural definition of (3) 2: 6
Neuroanatomy
   of monoamine neural systems (3) **44: 1–13**. See
      also Brain; Monoamine neural systems
   neuron systems and behavior (3) **42: 1–18**. See
      also Neurons

Neurobiology. *See also* Biological model; Brain
  advances in (3) 43: 1
  of affective disorders (1) **64: 1–2, 7–15**
    altered receptor function (1) 64: 9–10
    metabolic function in brain (1) 64: 12–13
    monoamine hypothesis (1) 64: 8–9
    neurotransmitters and neuropeptides in (1) 64:
      10–12
    research advances in (1) 64: 7–8
  of amnesia (3) 71: 7–8
  anatomy and physiology of brain monoamine sys-
    tems (3) **44: 1–13**
  of antipsychotic actions (1) 55: 14–20
    biochemical studies (1) 55: 15–20
    interaction with neurotransmitter receptors (1)
      55: 16–20
      acetylcholine (1) 55: 19
      alpha-adrenergic (1) 55: 20
      dopamine (1) 55: 16–18
      histamine (1) 55: 19–20
    physiologic studies (1) 55: 14–15
  of arousal (3) 66: 5–6
  of atherogenesis in coronary heart disease (2) 126:
    5–6
  of attention in schizophrenia (3) 65: 9–10
  chemical communication in brain (3) **43: 1–7.** *See
    also* Neurochemistry; Neurotransmitters
  circadian rhythms (3) 59: 2–6. *See also* Biological
    rhythms; Circadian rhythms
  of conditioning (3) 71: 3, 4
  development by latency (2) 3: 3–4
  of evoked potentials (3) **62: 1–14.** *See also* Evoked
    potentials
  hierarchical systems of organization (3) 43: 3–4
  immune system related to brain and behavior (2)
    128: 1–14. *See also* Immune system
  limbic-hypothalamic-pituitary-adrenal axis dysreg-
    ulation in melancholia (3) **54: 1–11**
  local circuit neurons role (3) 43: 4
  memory and learning (2) **13: 1–9;** (3) **71: 1–6**
    anatomy (2) 13: 3–4
    basic organization and processes (2) 13: 1–2
    developmental aspects (2) 13: 7–9
    molecular basis (2) 13: 4–5
    neurochemistry (2) 13: 5–7
      changes accompanying early childhood experi-
        ences (2) 13: 9
  from molecular biological simplification to more
    realistic central
  need for change in research orientation (3) 72: 5–
    6
  nervous system dynamics (3) 72: 1–6
  neurochemical strategies in child psychiatry (2) **12:
    1–12**
  neurons, networks and behavior (3) **42: 1–18.** *See
    also* Neurons
  neuropsychological assessment (1) **72: 1–15.** *See
    also* Neuropsychological assessment; Psy-
    chological tests

  neurotransmitters in affective disorders (3) **55: 1–
    8.** *See also* Neurotransmitters
  new ways to think about (3) 72: 5
  of pervasive developmental disorders (2) 27: 7
  in psychosomatic medicine (2) 78: 1–2
  receptors and psychiatric disorders (3) **50: 1–14.**
    See also Receptors
  REM sleep related to cyclicity of hormones and
    body functions (3) 59: 6–7
  of schizophrenia (1) **64: 1–2, 4–7, 13–15**
    brain abnormalities (1) 64: 6
    cerebral blood flow (1) 64: 6–7
    dopamine hypothesis (1) 64: 4–5
    neuropathological studies (1) 64: 6–7
    neuropeptides role (1) 64: 5–6
    viral mechanisms (1) 64: 6
  single-source divergent neurons role (3) 43: 4
  of sleep (3) **60: 1–13.** *See also* Sleep; Sleep dis-
    orders; Sleep-wake cycle
  somatosensory pathway development (1) 64: 2
  synaptic considerations (3) 43: 4–5
  technical and conceptual advances in (1) 64: 2–4,
    14
    functional mapping of neural activity (1) 64: 3
    identification and tracing of neurotransmitter
      pathways (1) 64: 2–3
    mapping electrical activity in brain (1) 64: 3
    in neurochemistry (1) 64: 2–4
    visualizing cellular distribution of monoamines
      (3) 44: 1
  time course of local circuit actions (3) 43: 5
Neurochemical challenge tests, methodologic considerations (2) 12: 6–8
Neurochemistry (3) **43: 1–7.** *See also* Neurotransmitters
  advances in knowledge (1) 64: 14
  of affective disorders
    altered receptor function (1) 64: 9–10
    monoamine hypothesis(1) 64: 8–9
    neurotransmitters and neuropeptides (1) 64: 10
      12
  of Alzheimer's disease (1) 73: 7; (2) 87: 8
  of attention deficit disorder (3) 66: 11–12
  in child psychiatry (2) **12: 1–12**
    brain function determination (2) 12: 1–5
    clinical considerations (2) 12: 5–9
      additional clinical sources of variance (2) 12:
        8
      cerebrospinal fluid samples (2) 12: 9
      diagnostic group mean values (2) 12: 5
      medication effects (2) 12: 8–9
      neurochemical and behavior measures (2) 12:
        9
      neuroendocrine and neurochemical challenge
        tests (2) 12: 6–8
      relationships among measures (2) 12: 8
      sample collection and effects of stress on chil-
        dren (2) 12: 5–6
      stability of variables over time (2) 12: 6

clinical specimens (2) 12: 2–3
developmental considerations (2) 12: 9–11
laboratory considerations (2) 12: 12
methodologic considerations (2) 12: 1, 9–12
   clinical (2) 12: 5–9
   developmental (2) 12: 9–11
   laboratory (2) 12: 12
neural regulation and neuronal systems complexity (2) 12: 3–4
neurogenetics and (2) 12: 5
selections for assay in clinical research (2) 12: 4–5
of circadian rhythms (3) 59: 9–10
clinical research models (2) 12: 1
clinical specimens in (2) 12: 2–3
   blood (2) 12: 2
   cerebrospinal fluid (2) 12: 2
   salivary fluid (2) 12: 2–3
   skin fibroblast culture (2) 12: 3
   tissue biopsy (2) 12: 3
   urine (2) 12: 2
conceptual advances in (1) 64: 3–4
of coronary heart disease-type A behavior link (2) 126: 5–6
of delirium (1) 73: 16
of depression (1) 3: 3
developmental considerations (2) 3: 4; 12: 9–11
dopamine hypothesis for schizophrenia (1) 64: 4–5
of hallucinations (2) 87: 13
identification and tracing of neurotransmitters (1) 64: 2–3
of learning and memory (2) 13: 5–7
   changes accompanying early childhood experiences (2) 13: 9
monoamine neural system in brain (3) **44: 1–13.** *See also* Monoamine neural systems
of neuroleptics actions (1) 55: 15–20
receptors and psychiatric disorders (3) **50: 1–14.** *See also* Receptors
of REM versus NREM sleep (3) 60: 7–8
of seasonal variations (3) 59: 10–11
of Tourette's disorder (2) 38: 4–5
Neuroendocrinology (2) **9: 1–12.** *See also* Endocrine disorders; Neurotransmitters; Sex hormones
abilities (2) 9: 8–9
   sexual orientation (2) 9: 7–8
of affective disorders (2) 9: 10. *See also* Affective disorders, neurotransmitters in
of aggressive conduct disorders (2) 9: 10–11
behavioral correlates of childhood endocrine disorders (2) 9: 11
of eating disorders (2) 9: 10
growth and development correlations (2) 9: 1–2
   gonadotropins (2) 9: 1–2
   hypothalamic releasing hormones (2) 9: 1
   sex hormones (2) 9: 2

hypothalamic-pituitary axis. *See* Hypothalamic-pituitary axis; Hypothalamic-pituitary-adrenal axis; Hypothalamic-pituitary-gonadal axis; Hypothalamus
of immune system
   in depression (2) 128: 12–13
   stress effects (2) 128: 10–12
limbic-hypothalamic-pituitary-adrenal axis dysregulation in melancholia (3) **54: 1–11**
methodologic considerations of challenge tests on children (2) 12: 6–8
onset of puberty (2) 9: 4–5
pituitary-gonadal function in infancy (2) 9: 3
of psychosocial dwarfism (2) 9: 10
of sex-dimorphic behavior (2) 9: 5–9
   gender identity (2) 9: 6–7
   gender-role behavior (2) 9: 7
   intelligence level and sexually differentiated cognitive
sexual differentiation of fetus (2) 9: 2–3
side effects of psychotropic drugs (2) 9: 11–12
of sleep (3) 60: 5–6
of stress (2) 9: 9–10
Neurogenetics (2) 12: 5
Neuroglia (3) 42: 5
Neuroleptic malignant syndrome (1) 55: 25; (2) 95: 7
Neuroleptics. *See also* Antipsychotic drugs; *and under specific agent*
in attention deficit disorder (2) 59: 12; (3) 66: 20
blood levels with
   interindividual variations (1) 55: 8
   route of administration versus (1) 55: 8–9
   therapeutic response versus (1) 55: 10
   toxic effects versus (1) 55: 10–11
in children and adolescents (2) 59: 7, 10–14
   in attention deficit disorder (2) 59: 12; (3) 66: 20
   follow-up in (2) 59: 11
   in impulse disorders (2) 59: 7
   interactions with other drugs (2) 59: 11
   mechanism of action (2) 59: 12
   medical workup prior to use (2) 59: 10, 19
   pharmacokinetics (2) 59: 12–13
   in psychosis (2) 59: 7
   in severe agitation (2) 59: 7
   side effects (2) 59: 10–11, 13
   in Tourette's syndrome (2) 59: 7, 12
comparison of different agents actions at dopamine receptor (3) 50: 12
definition (1) 55: 1–2
in depression (1) 61: 7–8
dopamine radioreceptor assay for (1) 55: 9–10
efficacy related to affinity for dopamine receptors (3) 50: 3–6
endocrine side effects (2) 9: 12
half-life of (1) 55: 8
interactions with other drugs (1) 55: 11
   in children (2) 59: 11

Neuroleptus, interactions with other drugs *(continued)*
  receptor antagonism causing (1) 55: 26
  intramuscular preparations (1) 55: 11–12
  in mania (1) 61: 19
  neuropsychological assessment related to use (1)
    72: 14
  organic mental disorders precipitated by (2) 34: 6
  in pervasive developmental disorders (2) 27: 9
  pharmacokinetics (1) 55: 7–11
    in children (2) 59: 12–13
  prolactin elevation due to (1) 55: 14–15
  in schizophrenia
    dose (1) 55: 12–13
    preparations (1) 55: 13
    sites and actions (1) 55: 14–20
  side effects (1) 55: 20–26; (2) 59: 10–11, 13
    blood abnormalities (1) 55: 25–26
    in children (2) 59: 10–11, 13
    endocrine (2) 9: 12
    liver abnormalities (1) 55: 25
    malignant syndrome (1) 55: 25; (2) 95: 7
    parkinsonism (1) 55: 22–23
    receptor antagonism (1) 55: 26
    from receptor blockade (1) 55: 20–25
      acetylcholine (1) 55: 25
      alpha-adrenergic (1) 55: 25
      antidopaminergic (1) 55: 20–25
      histamine (1) 55: 25
    receptor interactions related to (3) 50: 11–14
    skin and eye abnormalities (1) 55: 26
    tardive dyskinesia (1) 55: 22–23
  sites and actions of (1) 55: 14–20; (3) 50: 3–6
    biochemical studies (1) 55: 15–20
    on brainstem reticular system (1) 55: 14
    chemoreceptor trigger zone (1) 55: 14
    interaction with neurotransmitter receptors (1)
      55: 16–20
      acetylcholine (1) 55: 19
      alpha-adrenergic (1) 55: 20
      dopamine (1) 55: 16–18
      histamine (1) 55: 19–20
    physiologic studies (1) 55: 14–15
  structure (1) 55: 4–7
  supersensitivity to dopamine receptors due to (3)
    50: 6–7
  in Tourette's disorder (2) 38: 6
Neurological disorders. *See also* Organic mental dis-
      orders
  in antisocial personality (1) 23: 4
  in conduct disorders (2) 37: 5
  conversion disorder associated with (2) 100: 6
  conversion disorder distinguished from (2) 47: 5–6
  depression in (1) 61: 3
  focal disorders in organic brain syndromes (2) 87:
    11
  movement-related potentials in (3) 62: 4
  personality changes in (1) **28: 1–12.** *See also*
        Personality, neurologic disease causing
        changes in

psychiatric disorders in children related to (2) 11:
    11–12
  psychological tests in (1) 7: 6–7
Neurological examination
  in attention deficit disorder (2) 36: 7; (3) 66: 13
  attention span (2) 20: 7
  Bender Gestalt test (2) 20: 5–7
  in conduct disorders (2) 37: 5
  in delirium (2) 87: 5
  extension test (2) 20: 7
  laterality (2) 20: 7
  soft signs (2) 20: 5–7
Neurological soft signs
  in attention deficit disorder (2) 36: 7; (3) 66: 10–
    11, 13
  classification (2) 20: 5
  deficiencies associated with (2) 20: 5–7
  evaluation in mental status examination (2) 20: 5
    7
  in schizophrenic children (2) 29: 5
Neuromuscular disorders, biofeedback and relaxation
      therapy in (2) 109: 7–9
Neuronal plasticity, in learning (2) 13: 4–5
Neurons (3) **42: 1–18.** *See also* Monoamine neural
      systems; Neurochemistry; Neurotransmit-
      ters
  anatomic features (3) 42: 1–2
  autonomously active (3) 42: 4
  axon characteristics and neuronal interactions (3)
      42: 5–7
    diffuse versus specific axonal projections (3) 42:
      6
    myelin and saltatory conduction (3) 42: 5–6
    remote versus local action (3) 42: 7
  depolarization and hyperpolarization of (3) 42: 4
  diversity of structure (3) 42: 1, 2
  dopamine release from dendrites (3) 42: 7
  Golgi type I and II (3) 42: 7
  inactivation in (3) 42: 5
  initiation and propagation of action potential (3)
      42: 4–5
  inputs (3) 42: 4
  of neostriatum (3) 42: 10–11
  networks underlying functions (3) 42: 8–9
  occurrence of active potential related to summa-
      tion of synaptic
  resting membrane potential in (3) 42: 4
  structure (3) 42: 1–4
  in synapse (3) 42: 2–4
  synaptic transmission and behavioral plasticity (3)
      42: 4, 7–8
Neuropathology, of schizophrenia (1) 64: 6–7
Neuropeptides. *See also* Neurotransmitters
  in affective disorders (1) 64: 10–12
  electrophysiologic signs of action (3) 43: 6
  and immune system effects of stress (2) 128: 11
  in memory and learning (2) 13: 7
  as neurotransmitters (3) 43: 2–3
  in schizophrenia (1) 64: 5–6

similar structure of (3) 43: 2–3
in sleep (3) 60: 7
Neuropsychological abilities (3) 52: 3–14
Neuropsychological assessment (1) 7: 6–7; **72: 1–15**
  abstraction (3) 52: 8–10
  age and (1) 72: 8
  of aging process (1) 72: 11
  attention (3) 52: 4–5
  in chronic schizophrenia (1) 72: 13–14
  comparing left-right hemispheric abilities (1) 72: 3
  diagnostic prescriptive approach (2) 21: 9
  in distinguishing organic versus functional disorders (1) 72: 2, 13–14
  emotional factors in (1) 72: 10
  functional approach (2) 21: 9
  in functional psychiatric disorders (1) 72: 12–15
  Halstead-Reitan Neuropsychological Battery (1) 72: 4–6; (2) 21: 8
  hemispheric lateralization of functions (1) 72: 3, 9–10
  historical antecedents for (1) 72: 1–2
  of intellectual, sensorimotor and emotional functions (1) 72: 3–4
  language (3) 52: 5–8
  and lithium usage (1) 72: 14
  of localization of functions in brain (1) 72: 9
  Luria-Nebraska Neuropsychological Battery (1) 72: 6–8; (2) 21: 8–9
  memory (3) 52: 12–14
  in middle childhood and adolescence (2) 21: 7–9
  motivation and (1) 72: 9
  and neuroleptic usage (1) 72: 14
  in organic mental disorders (1) 72: 10–12
    alcohol abuse and withdrawal (1) 72: 11–12
    dementia (1) 72: 11
    head injury (1) 72: 10–11
    seizure disorders (1) 72: 12
  pattern analysis (1) 72: 3
  perceptual motor abilities (3) 52: 10–12
  premorbid history and (1) 72: 8–9
  purposes (1) 72: 1
  qualitative approach (1) 72: 3
  quantitative approach (1) 72: 2–3
  reaction time (3) 52: 3–4
  in schizophrenia (1) 72: 10
  substantive issues in (1) 72: 8–10
  theoretical approaches to (1) 72: 2–3
Neuropsychology
  applications in biological psychiatry (3) 52: 15–21
    as adjunct in neuropsychiatric diagnosis (3) 52: 15–17
    confirming treatment effects (3) 52: 21
    determination of deficits in conditions of interest (3) 52: 15
    elucidating natural history of cognitive change in disease (3) 52: 19–21
    mapping patterns of deficit (3) 52: 17–19
  behaviors of interest in (3) 52: 3
  historical background (3) 52: 1–3

of language and speech disorders (3) **67: 6–13**
of learning disabilities (2) 48: 4–5
methodologic considerations in applications to psychiatry (3) 52: 21–25
  age and education effects (3) 52: 21–22
  data reduction (3) 52: 23–25
  repeated measures and practice effects (3) 52: 22–23
  selection of tests (3) 52: 23
tests as indirect measure of brain function (3) **52: 1–25**. *See also* Neuropsychological assessment; Psychological tests
Neuropsychometry (3) **52: 1–25**. *See also* Neuropsychological assessment; Psychological tests
Neuroreceptors. *See* Receptors
Neuroses (1) **31: 1–8**
  anxiety (3) 14: 1–2. *See also* Panic disorder
  borderline personality disorder distinguished from (1) 17: 3, 10
  chronicity of (1) 31: 5
  classification (1) 31: 2, 4
  culture and
    epidemiologic studies (3) 2: 8–10
    outcome studies (3) 2: 12–13
  defense mechanisms and (1) 31: 5
  definition (1) 31: 1–2
  depressive (1) 3: 3; *40: 1–13*
    aggression and (1) 40: 9
    atypical (1) 40: 7
    biological studies on (1) 40: 8
    bipolar disorder distinguished from (1) 40: 6
    character spectrum disorder distinguished from (1) 40: 8
    character structure related to (1) 40: 4–5
    childhood experiences predisposing to (1) 40: 10–11
    clinical description (1) 40: 5–6
    cognitive theory of (1) 40: 10
    controversy of relationship to affective disorder (1) 40: 1
    coping mechanisms in (1) 40: 6
    course of illness (1) 40: 6
    definition (1) 40: 2–5
    differential diagnosis (1) 40: 6–8
    dysthymic character distinguished from (1) 40: 7–8
    early developmental contributions to (1) 40: 10–11
    endogenous depression distinguished from (1) 40: 3–4
    epidemiology (1) 40: 2
    etiology (1) 40: 8–10
    grief related to (1) 40: 8–9
    historical overview (1) 40: 1–2
    laboratory procedures and selective medical workup in (1) 61: 16–17
    learned helplessness causing (1) 40: 9–10
    major depression distinguished from (1) 40: 6–7; 61: 13

Neuroses, depressive *(continued)*
    object relations in (1) 40: 9
    personality disorders distinguished from (1) 40: 7
    psychiatric evaluation of patients resistant to treatment (1) 61: 16
    psychoanalytic concepts (1) 40: 1, 4
    psychodynamics (1) 40: 8–11
    self-esteem and (1) 40: 9
    separation in childhood related to (1) 40: 11
    somatic symptoms in (1) 40: 5–6
    terminology (1) 61: 13
    treatment (1) 40: 12–13; 61: 13–18
      brief psychosocial therapy (1) 40: 12
      characterologic depression (1) 61: 14–15
      drug-free baseline in (1) 61: 16
      drugs (1) 40: 12–13
      family therapy (1) 40: 12
      major depressions with chronicity (1) 61: 13–14
      psychoanalysis (1) 40: 12
      secondary dysphorias (1) 61: 15–16
      treatment-resistant patients (1) 61: 16
  DSM-III on (1) 31: 1–2, 7–8
  dysthymia (1) 2: 19–20
  epidemics of (1) 31: 5
  epidemiology (1) 31: 4–5
    cross-cultural studies (3) 2: 8–10
  etiology (1) 31: 6–7
  extraversion and (1) 2: 19–20
  historical background (1) 31: 4–5; 52: 4–5
  hysteric (1) 2: 19
  influence on development of stress-response syndrome (1) 41: 12
  introversion and (1) 2: 19
  learning role in
    behavioral studies on (1) 2: 11, 12
    psychodynamic studies on (1) 2: 13–15
    solution and sign learning in (1) 2: 14–15
  neurotic process role in (1) 31: 5
  personality disorders related to (1) 31: 5–6
  terminology (1) 31: 1, 7–8
  trauma related to (1) 31: 7
    psychodynamics (2) 18: 7–8
  treatment, drugs (1) **10: 1–8**
Neurotic disorders (1) 31: 2. *See also* Neuroses
Neuroticism (1) 2: 19
Neurotic paradox (1) 2: 15
Neurotic process (1) 31: 2
  and psychopathology (1) 31: 5, 6
Neurotransmitters (3) **55: 1–8**. *See also* Neurochemistry; *and under specific neurotransmitter*
  adrenergic-cholinergic balance hypothesis (3) 55: 3–5
  advances in identification and tracing techniques for (1) 64: 2–3
  advances in knowledge (1) 64: 14
  in affective disorders (1) 61: 4; (3) **55: 1–8**

  adrenergic-cholinergic balance hypothesis (3) 55: 3–5
  catecholamine hypothesis (3) 55: 2–3
  etiologic hypotheses (3) 55: 1
  final common pathway hypothesis (3) 55: 7–8
  models between psychological and biological explanations (3) 55: 7–8
  opioid hypothesis (3) 55: 6
  receptor down-regulation hypothesis (3) 55: 6
  research strategies in (3) 55: 1–8
  serotonin hypothesis (3) 55: 5–6
  serotonin-norepinephrine dichotomy hypothesis (3) 55: 6
amino acids as (3) 43: 2
assay techniques for (1) 64: 2–3
and behavioral plasticity (3) 42: 7–8
catecholamine hypothesis (3) 55: 2–3
challenge tests on, methodologic considerations (2) 12: 6–8
circadian rhythms of (3) 59: 2–3
coding consequences of actions (3) 43: 6
developmental considerations (2) 12: 9–11
disenabling (3) 43: 6
domains of known diversity of (3) 43: 3
dopamine hypothesis for schizophrenia (1) 64: 4–5
in electroconvulsive therapy (3) 68: 4
electrophysiologic signs of functional diversity (3) 43: 5–6
enabling action (3) 43: 5–6
energy domain for (3) 43: 6–7
in extracellular fluid (1) 64: 4
final common pathway hypothesis (3) 55: 7–8
hierarchical systems of organization (3) 43: 3–4
historical background (1) 52: 15; (3) 43: 1–2
and immune system
  in depression (2) 128: 12–13
  stress effects (2) 128: 11
implications of (3) 43: 3
and limbic-hypothalamic-pituitary axis dysregulation in melancholia (3) 54: 4–8
  acetylcholine (3) 54: 6–7
  GABA (3) 54: 7
  norepinephrine (3) 54: 4–5
  opioids (3) 54: 7–8
  serotonin (3) 54: 5–6
local circuit neurons and (3) 43: 4
in memory and learning (2) 13: 6–7
monoamine neural system in brain (3) **44: 1–13.** *See also* Monoamine neural systems
monoamines (3) 43: 2. *See also* Acetylcholine; Ca echolamines; Dopamine; Norepinephrine Serotonin
neural regulation of (2) 12: 3–4
neuroendocrine strategy in study (3) 55: 2
neuroleptics interaction with receptors for (1) 55 16–20
neuropeptides as (3) 43: 2–3

in schizophrenia (1) 64: 5–6
neurotransmitter agonist and antagonist strategies
    in study (3) 55: 2
opioid hypothesis (3) 55: 6
and psychopharmacology (3) **50: 8–14**
    bridge strategy in study of (3) 55: 2
receptors and (3) **50: 1–14.** *See also* Receptors
    down-regulation hypothesis (3) 55: 6
    radioreceptor binding assays (3) 50: 1–3
selection for research (2) 12: 4–5
serotonin hypothesis (3) 55: 5–6
serotonin-norepinephrine dichotomy hypothesis
    (3) 55: 6
single-source divergent neurons and (3) 43: 4
synapse and (3) 43: 4–5
    storage (3) 42: 3
    transmission across (3) 42: 4
time course of local circuit actions (3) 43: 5
Neutrality, of psychotherapist (1) 8: 4
Newborn, Brazelton's neonatal assessment scale for
    (2) 21: 2
Nigeria, schizophrenia outcome studies in (3) 2: 11–
    12
Night-eating syndrome (2) 103: 3
Nightmares (2) 105: 15–16
    etiology (2) 105: 16
    night terrors distinguished from (2) 43: 7; 52: 6;
        105: 15; (3) 61: 14
    in preschool and school-age children (2) 52: 6
    as rebound effect of stopping hypnotics (2) 105: 6–
        7
    treatment (2) 105: 16
Night terrors (2) 43: 7–8; 105: 15; (3) 61: 14
    clinical features (2) 43: 7
    diagnosis (2) 43: 2, 7; 105: 15
    DSM-III diagnostic criteria (2) 43: 2, 7
    etiology (2) 43: 7
    nightmares distinguished from (2) 43: 7; 52: 6;
        105: 15; (3) 61: 14
    in preschool and school-age children (2) 52: 5–6
    prevalence (2) 105: 15
    psychological problems in (2) 43: 7; 52: 6
    sleepwalking similarities to (2) 43: 7
    treatment (2) 43: 7–8; 105: 15; (3) 61: 14
        antianxiety drugs in (2) 59: 17
Nightwaking, in infants (2) 52: 3–4
Noctec. *See* Chloral hydrate
Nocturnal myoclonus (3) 61: 10–11
Nocturnal polysomnogram (3) 61: 4
Node of Ranvier (3) 42: 5
Nonbipolar major depression (1) 60: 2–7; (3) 13: 1–
    8. *See also* Depression
    definition (1) 60: 2; (3) 13: 2
    DSM-III definition (3) 13: 2
    epidemiology (1) 60: 2–7; (3) 13: 1–8
Noncompliance, costs of (2) 79: 4
Nonspecificity hypothesis, in psychotherapy (1) 11:
    9–11

Noradrenergic neural systems (3) **44: 2–6.** *See also*
    Monoamine neural systems
    anatomy and physiology in brain (3) 44: 2–6
    fluorescence methods for (3) 44: 3
    immunochemical methods for (3) 44: 3–4
    localization in locus ceruleus (3) 44: 2–5
    in psychiatric disorders (3) 44: 5–6
Norepinephrine. *See also* Monoamine neural systems;
    Noradrenergic neural systems
    in affective disorders (1) 64: 8–9; (3) 55: 2–3
        serotonin dichotomy with (3) 55: 6
    attention and arousal effects of (2) 13: 8
    in attention deficit disorder (3) 66: 11
    in depression, serotonin dichotomy with (3) 55:
        6
    developmental considerations (2) 12: 10
        effects on neuronal plasticity (2) 13: 8–9
    down-regulation of receptors for (3) 55: 3, 6
    effects on target neurons (3) 44: 5
    in electroconvulsive therapy (3) 68: 4, 5
    electrophysiologic signs of function (3) 43:
        5–6
    and limbic-hypothalamic-pituitary axis dysregula-
        tion in
    melancholia (3) 54: 4–5
    and neuronal plasticity (2) 13: 8–9
    in psychiatric disorders (3) 44: 5–6
    receptors for, side effects of neuroleptics related to
        (3) 50: 11
    in sleep (2) 119: 8
Norpramin. *See* Desipramine
Nose, septal perforation in cocaine abuse (2) 90:
    3
Not competent to stand trial. *See* Competency to
    stand trial
Not guilty by reason of insanity (3) 27: 7–9; 28: 4,
    5, 7–8. *See also* Mentally disordered of-
    fenders
    treatment considerations (3) 28: 20–21
NREM sleep (3) 60: 2
    in animals (3) 60: 8
    characteristics (3) 60: 3, 4
    deprivation effects (3) 60: 12–13
    neurochemistry of (3) 60: 7–8
Nuclear magnetic resonance. *See* Magnetic resonance
    imaging
Nursing homes
    in mental health care (3) 4: 11
    psychiatric disorders treated in (3) 22: 6
Nutritional disorders
    organic mental disorders in children due to (2) 34:
        10–11
    treatment in anorexia nervosa (2) 40: 8
Nutritional therapy (2) **160: 1–3**
    diet (2) 160: 1–2
    megavitamins (2) 160: 2–3
    minerals (2) 160: 3
    in organic brain syndromes (2) 87: 15

Obesity (2) **103: 1–12**
  behavior modification in
    in mild form (2) 103: 11
    in moderate form (2) 103: 9, 10
  body image disturbance in (2) 103: 3
  bulimia in (2) 103: 3. *See also* Bulimia
  classification (2) 103: 5–6
  clinical description (2) 40: 3; 103: 2–4
  complications (2) 103: 5
  consequences of social attitudes toward (2) 103: 1
  definition (2) 103: 1–2
  determinants (2) 103: 4–5
  developmental determinants (2) 103: 4–5
  diet in
    complications (2) 103: 3
    in mild form (2) 103: 9–11
    in moderate form (2) 103: 8–9
    in severe form (2) 103: 6
  differential diagnosis, in infants and children (2)
        40: 3
  drug therapy (2) 103: 9
  elevation of set point for weight regulation causing
        (2) 103: 4
  emotional disturbance in (2) 103: 2–3
  epidemiology (2) 103: 2
  etiology (2) 103: 4–5
  fat cell number in (2) 103: 4–5
  gastric restriction procedures (2) 103: 6–8
  genetic factors (2) 103: 4
  group treatment program (2) 103: 11–12
  historical background (2) 103: 1
  in infants and children (2) 40: 3
    differential diagnosis (2) 40: 3
    etiology (2) 40: 3
    treatment (2) 40: 3
  jejunoileal bypass in (2) 103: 6
  mild, treatment (2) 103: 9–12
  moderate, treatment (2) 103: 8–9
  multiplicity of factors involved with (2) 40: 3
  overeating in (2) 103: 3
  physical activity in (2) 103: 5
  prevalence (2) 103: 2
  prognosis (2) 40: 3
  protein-sparing-modified fast in (2) 103: 9
  psychoanalysis for (2) 103: 12
  severe, treatment (2) 103: 6–8
  sleep apnea in (3) 61: 8, 10
  socioeconomic factors in (2) 103: 2
  surgical treatment (2) 103: 6–8
    benefits (2) 103: 6, 8
    body image after (2) 103: 8
    eating patterns after (2) 103: 8
    emotional response to (2) 103: 6, 7
    food likes and dislikes after (2) 103: 8
  treatment (2) 103: 6–12
    behavior modification (2) 103: 9–11
    in children (2) 40: 3
    diet (2) 103: 8–11
    drugs (2) 103: 9

    group programs (2) 103: 11–12
    mild form (2) 103: 9–12
    moderate form (2) 103: 8–9
    severe form (2) 103: 6–8
    surgery (2) 103: 6–8
Object love, in narcissistic personality disorder (1)
        18: 4
Object relations
  depressive neurosis and (1) 40: 9
  evaluation in mental status examination in chil-
        dren (2) 20: 11
Object relations theory (1) 1: 10–11
Object Sorting Test (1) 7: 7–8
Observation, in child psychiatric epidemiology (3)
        12: 10–11
Obsessional personality, as premorbid personality of
        compulsive personality disorder (1) 22: 6,
        7
Obsessions (1) 34: 1, 3–4. *See also* Obsessive-com-
        pulsive disorder
  categories of behaviors (1) 34: 3
  categories of thoughts (1) 34: 3
  in children (1) 34: 8
  convictions (1) 34: 3
  delusions distinguished from (1) 34: 4
  fears (1) 34: 3
  ideas (1) 34: 3
  images (1) 34: 3
  impulses (1) 34: 3
  rituals (1) 34: 3–4
  ruminations (1) 34: 3
Obsessive-compulsive disorder (1) **34: 1–10.** *See als*
        Compulsive personality disorder
  anxiety reduction role in persistence of symptoms
        (1) 34: 5–6
  avoidance of social situations in (1) 33: 7
  in children (1) 34: 4
  clinical description (1) 34: 3–4
  complications (1) 34: 5
  compulsive personality disorder distinguished fro
        (1) 22: 6
  course of (1) 34: 4–5
  definition (1) 34: 2
  depression associated with (1) 34: 4, 5
  depression distinguished from (1) 34: 7
  diagnosis (1) 34: 7–8
  differential diagnosis (1) 34: 7–8
  DSM-III on (3) 14: 6; 34: 2
  epidemiology (1) 34: 2–3
  etiology (1) 34: 5–7
  family studies (3) 14: 10
  historical background (1) 34: 1–2
  hysterical personality disorder distinguished from
        (1) 19: 8
  incidence and prevalence (1) 34: 1, 2
  masochistic personality distinguished from (1) 27
        7
  narcissistic personality disorder distinguished from
        (1) 18: 8

neurobiology (1) 34: 6
physiology (1) 34: 6
prognostic factors (1) 34: 5
psychoanalytic concepts (1) 34: 6–7
psychotherapy benefit in (1) 11: 5
schizophrenia distinguished from (1) 34: 8
in Tourette's disorder (2) 38: 3
treatment (1) 34: 8–10
    behavior therapy (1) 34: 9
    drugs (1) 10: 7; 34: 9
    psychosurgery (1) 34: 9–10
    psychotherapy (1) 11: 5; 34: 8–9
bstetrics-gynecology
femininity perceived as related to childbearing (2)
        120: 1
hysterectomy (2) 120: 8–9
menopause (2) 120: 6–8
menstrual cycle (2) 120: 2–3
postpartum reactions (2) 120: 6. See also Postpar-
        tum period
pregnancy and childbirth (2) 120: 3–6
psychiatric aspects (2) **120: 1–10**
bstinacy, in compulsive personality disorder (1) 22:
        2
ccupation
schizophrenia related to (1) 54: 10; (3) 15: 10–11
suicide and (3) 20: 10
ccupational health, health promotion in (2) 129: 3–
        4
ddball paradigm (3) 62: 8–10
edipal phase
and family development (2) 5: 7
Freud's theory of (1) 1: 6
neiroid state, in delirium (1) 73: 14
perant conditioning (1) 2: 2–3; (2) 13: 2
in pain (2) 104: 8–9
piates. See also Narcotics
adolescent abuse (2) 35: 4
in affective disorders (3) 55: 6
and limbic-hypothalamic-pituitary axis dysregula-
        tion in melancholia (3) 54: 7–8
receptors for
    psychotomimetic actions of opiates related to (3)
            50: 13
    subtypes (3) 50: 13
treatment (2) 35: 4
withdrawal syndrome (2) 35: 4
otic atrophy, Leber's hereditary, psychosis in (1)
        69: 7
otometric training (2) 160: 3–4
ral contraceptives
depression due to (1) 61: 2; (2) 88: 14
psychiatric side effects (2) 91: 7
rderliness, in compulsive personality disorder (1)
        22: 2
rganic brain syndrome, terminology as distin-
        guished from organic mental disorder (1)
        73: 2. See under Organic mental disorders
rganic delusional syndrome (2) 87:

in children (2) 34: 2
definition (2) 87: 1
psychotherapy in (2) 87: 17
Organic hallucinosis. See Hallucinations, organic
Organicity (1) 72: 2
Organic mental disorders (1) **73: 1–20**; (2) **87: 1–
        17.** See also Neurological disorders
affective syndromes (1) 59: 5; (2) 87: 12–13
    in children (2) 34: 2
    definition (2) 87: 1
agitation in (2) 87: 16
Alzheimer's disease (1) 73: 5–8
amnesia distinguished from (1) 39: 6
amnesic syndrome (2) 87: 10–11. See also Am-
        nesic syndrome
    in children (2) 34: 2
atypical
    in children (2) 34: 3
    definition (2) 87: 2
brief reactive psychosis distinguished from (1) 70:
        13
in cancer (2) 117: 4
in children (2) **34: 1–11**
    affective syndrome (2) 34: 2
    amnesic syndrome (2) 34: 2
    atypical or mixed organic brain syndrome (2)
            34: 3
    classification (2) 34: 1–3
    clinical characteristics suggesting (2) 34: 1
    delirium (2) 34: 1
    delusional syndrome (2) 34: 2
    dementia (2) 34: 2
    drugs precipitating (2) 34: 5–7
    environmental factors causing (2) 34: 9–11
    epidemiology (2) 34: 3
    hallucinosis (2) 34: 2
    personality syndrome (2) 34: 2–3
    physical trauma causing (2) 34: 7
    postinfectious syndromes (2) 34: 3–5
    systemic or metabolic illnesses causing (2) 34: 7–
            9
coping strategies in (2) 87: 3–4
definition (2) 87: 1–2
delirium (1) 73: 12–17; (2) 87: 4–6; 95: 1–2. See
        also Delirium
    in children (2) 34: 1
delusional syndrome (2) 87: 13–14. See also Delu-
        sions
    in children (2) 34: 2
dementia (1) 73: 2–12; (2) 87: 6–10; 95: 2. See
        also Dementia
    in children (2) 34: 2
determining competency to give informed consent
        (2) 87: 16
diagnosis (1) 73: 2, 3; (2) 87: 14–15
DSM-III on (1) 6: 8
in end-stage renal disease (2) 117: 4–5
epidemiology (2) 87: 2–3
    in children (2) 34: 3

Organic mental disorders *(continued)*
  etiology (2) 87: 2–4
  focal neurologic problems (2) 87: 11
  fugue distinguished from (1) 39: 7
  functional disorders distinguished from, neuropsy-
      chological assessment in (1) 72: 2, 13–14
  hallucinosis (2) 87: 13
    in children (2) 34: 2
    definition (2) 87: 1
  historical background (1) 52: 14–16
  Huntington's disease (1) 73: 11–12. *See also* Hunt-
      ington's disease
  in ICU syndrome (2) 121: 7–8
  importance to understanding psychiatric disease
      (1) 73: 1–2
  Korsakoff's syndrome (1) 73: 17–20
  laboratory investigations in (2) 87: 14–15
  mixed, definition (2) 87: 2
  multi-infarct dementia (1) 73: 8–10
  neuropsychological assessment (1) 72: 10–12. *See
      also* Neuropsychological assessment
    alcohol abuse and withdrawal (1) 72: 11–12
    dementia (1) 72: 11
    head injury (1) 72: 10–11
    seizure disorders (1) 72: 12
  in pancreatitis (2) 88: 13
  pathogenesis (2) 87: 2–3
  personality disorders (1) 28: 2–3; (2) 87: 11–12.
      See also Personality, neurologic disease
      causing changes in
    in children (2) 34: 2–3
  physiologic precipitants (2) 87: 2–3
  prognosis (2) 87: 3
  psychological tests in (1) 7: 6–7; 72: 10–12; (2)
      87: 15
  psychoses in (1) **69: 1–14;** (2) 95: 1–3. *See also*
      Psychoses, symptomatic
  psychosocial and environmental factors in (2) 87:
      3–4
  reaction and compensation in (2) 87: 3
  signs and symptoms (2) 95: 2
  in spinal cord injury (2) 117: 6
  suicide in (1) 71: 3, 5
  after surgery (2) 121: 6
  terminology (1) 73: 1
    as distinguished from organic brain syndrome
        (1) 73: 2
  treatable causes (2) 95: 3
  treatment (2) 87: 15–17; 95: 6
    drugs (2) 87: 15, 16
    family services (2) 87: 16–17
    memory disturbance (2) 87: 16
    nutritional support (2) 87: 15
    perceptual dysfunction (2) 87: 15–16
    psychotherapy (2) 87: 17
Organic personality disorders (1) 28: 2–3. *See also*
    Personality, neurologic disease causing
    changes in

Orgasm
  clitoral versus vaginal (1) 45: 1, 2
  disorders (1) 47: 2–4
  female threshold (1) 47: 2
  inhibited female (1) 47: 2
  inhibited male (1) 47: 2–4
  premature ejaculation (1) 47: 3–4
  response of patient and partner to dysfunction (1)
      47: 2, 3
  retarded ejaculation (1) 47: 2–3
    partially (1) 47: 3
Orofacial disorders, speech in (2) 49: 3
Orthomolecular psychiatry (2) 160: 2–3
Osteoporosis, in menopause (2) 120: 7
Othello syndrome (1) 68: 7–8
Other disorders with physical manifestations (2) **43:
    1–9**
  DSM-III diagnostic criteria for (2) 43: 2
  encopresis (2) 43: 4–6
  enuresis (2) 43: 1–4
  night terrors (2) 43: 7–8
  sleepwalking (2) 43: 6–7
  stuttering (2) 43: 8–9
Outpatient care. *See* Ambulatory care
Overeating
  in bulimia (2) 102: 4–5; 103: 3. *See also* Bulimia
  night-eating syndrome (2) 103: 3
Overgeneralization, in stress-response syndrome (1)
    41: 4
Overprotectiveness, negative impact on social learn-
    ing (1) 2: 5

Pain (2) **104: 1–12**
  acute versus chronic (2) 104: 2
  biofeedback and relaxation therapy in (2) 109: 8–
      9
  in cancer (2) 104: 2–4
    behavioral and psychological factors in (2) 104:
        3
    clinical description (2) 104: 3
    control (2) 117: 4
    epidemiology (2) 104: 2–3
    mechanism of (2) 104: 3
    treatment (2) 104: 3–4
  central (2) 104: 5–6
  in childbirth
    determinants (2) 120: 4, 5
    endorphins role in (2) 120: 5
  chronic (2) **104: 1–12.** *See also* Pain disorder, ps-
      chogenic
    central biasing mechanism of (2) 104: 4
    of central origin (2) 104: 5–6
    classification (2) 104: 2
    decrease of peripheral inhibition causing (2)
        104: 4
    definition (2) 104: 2

denervation hypersensitivity causing (2) 104: 4
historical aspects (2) 104: 1
in low back (2) 104: 8–9
migraine headache (2) 104: 6–8. *See also* Migraine headache
of peripheral-central origin (2) 104: 4–5
of peripheral origin (2) 104: 2–4
prognosis (2) 104: 11
psychological mechanisms causing or modifying (2) 104: 6–11
    operant (2) 104: 8–9
    psychiatric (2) 104: 9–11
    psychophysiological (2) 104: 6–8
research in (2) 104: 11
vicious circle mechanism (2) 104: 4
control in cancer patient (2) 117: 4
definition (2) 104: 2
in depression (2) 104: 10–11
    clinical description (2) 104: 10
    epidemiology (2) 104: 10
differential diagnosis (1) 35: 8
on ejaculation (1) 47: 6
exclusion from conversion disorder (2) 100: 6
fear in surgical patient (2) 121: 3
hypnosis in (2) 112: 4
insufficient use of analgesics for (2) 121: 7
low back (2) 104: 8–9
paraplegic (2) 104: 5–6
    behavioral and psychological factors in (2) 104: 5–6
    clinical description (2) 104: 5
    epidemiology (2) 104: 5
    treatment (2) 104: 6
patient prone to (2) 104:
phantom limb (2) 104: 5
psychogenic (1) **35: 8–10;** (2) 104: 9–10
    clinical description (1) 35: 8–9; (2) 104: 9
    definition (1) 35: 8
    diagnosis (1) 35: 10
    differential diagnosis (1) 35: 10
    DSM-III criteria for (1) 35: 8
    epidemiology (1) 35: 8
    etiology (1) 35: 9–10
    pain description in (1) 35: 8–9
    personality characteristics in (1) 35: 9
    psychodynamics (1) 35: 9–10
    treatment and prevention (1) 35: 10; (2) 104: 10
in surgery (2) 121: 7
vaginismus (1) 47: 6
pancreatic carcinoma, psychiatric manifestations (2) 88: 13
pancreatic disorders
islet cell tumor (2) 88: 12
psychiatric manifestations (2) 88: 12–13
    hyperglycemia (2) 88: 13
    hypoglycemia (2) 88: 12–13
    pancreatic carcinoma (2) 88: 13

pancreatitis (2) 88: 13
Pancreatitis (2) 88: 13
Panic disorder (1) **32: 1–12;** (2) 95: 11–12. *See also* Anxiety disorders
agoraphobia caused by (1) 33: 4
agoraphobia with (1) 32: 3–4; 33: 2. *See also* Agoraphobia
    DSM-III criteria for (1) 33: 2
    psychotherapy in (1) 33: 12
    treatment (1) 33: 11–12
alcohol abuse in (1) 32: 11
anxiety distinguished from (1) 32: 1
beta-adrenergic nervous system in (1) 32: 6–7
biological model (1) 3: 6–8; 32: 6–9
cardiovascular disease associated with (1) 32: 4
in children, antidepressants for (2) 59: 15
clinical description (1) 32: 2–4
definition (1) 32: 1–2
depression in (1) 32: 10–11; 33: 6
diagnosis (1) 32: 10–11
differential diagnosis (1) 32: 9–11
in drug abuse (2) 90: 9
drug therapy (1) 10: 6–7
DSM-III on (1) 32: 1, 2; (3) 14: 5–6
epidemiology (1) 32: 2
etiology (1) 32: 4–9
familial nature (1) 32: 9; (3) 14: 10
first attack in (1) 32: 3
genetic factors in (1) 3: 7
hyperventilation role in (1) 32: 7–8
lactate provocation of (1) 32: 8
learning theory of (1) 32: 5–6
locus ceruleus role in (1) 32: 7–8
mitral valve prolapse associated with (1) 32: 4, 10; (2) 118: 6
overactivity of noradrenergic system in (3) 14: 11
physical symptoms in (1) 32: 3
psychoanalytic theories of (1) 32: 5
separation anxiety as basis of (1) 32: 6
suicide in (1) 32: 4
symptoms (1) 32: 1–3
treatment (1) 32: 4, 11–12; 33: 11–12
    behavioral (1) 32: 12
    in drug abuse (2) 90: 9
    drugs (1) 32: 11–12
    in emergency department (2) 95: 12
    psychotherapy (1) 32: 12
Paradigms
behavioral (1) 52: 11
descriptive phenomenology (1) 52: 11–14
interpersonal (1) 52: 10–11
in psychiatry (1) 52: 1–3, 6–14
Paralysis agitans, psychosis in (1) 69: 6
Paranoia (1) 68: 7–10. *See also* Paranoid disorder
conjugal (1) 68: 7–8
erotic (1) 68: 8–9
hypochondriac (1) 68: 9–10
inventor (1) 68: 10

Paranoia *(continued)*
  jealousy (1) 68: 7–8
  litigious (1) 68: 7
Paranoic delusions (1) 68: 2
Paranoid disorder (1) **68: 1–17**
  acute (1) 68: 10–11
  amok (1) 68: 12
  as atypical psychoses (1) 68: 12
  Capgras' syndrome (1) 68: 12
  change in environment influence on (1) 68: 5–6
  childhood premorbid personality (1) 68: 4–5
  civil commitment in (1) 68: 15
  classification (1) 68: 6–7, 11–12
  clinical course of (1) 68: 16–17
  clinical grouping (1) 68: 6–13
  definition (1) 68: 1–2
  diagnosis (1) 68: 13–14
  differential diagnosis (1) 68: 13–14
  DSM-III criteria for (1) 68: 1–2, 11
  in elderly (1) 68: 13
  epidemiology (1) 68: 3–4
  etiology (1) 68: 4–5
  grandiose paranoid reaction (1) 68: 10
  historical aspects (1) 68: 2–3
  hospitalization for (1) 68: 14–16
  inteviewing patient with (2) 95: 4–5
  marital disorder in (1) 68: 5
  narcissistic personality disorder distinguished from
       (1) 18: 9
  organic (1) 68: 13
  paranoia (1) 68: 7–10. *See also* Paranoia
  paranoid personality disorder distinguished from
       (1) 16: 10
  paranoid personality disorder in relatives (1) 16: 9–
       10
  paraphrenia (1) 68: 13
  precipitating factors (1) 68: 5–6
  prognosis (1) 68: 16–17
  in psychoses (1) 68: 12–13
  schizophrenia related to (1) 53: 19
  sexual disorders in (1) 68: 5
  shared (1) 68: 10
  situational alliance in (3) 36: 8
  social isolation effect on (1) 68: 5–6
  somatic illnesses in (1) 68: 6
  treatment (1) 68: 14–16
    drugs (1) 68: 15
    psychotherapy (1) 68: 15–16
Paranoid ideation
  in compulsive personality disorder (1) 22: 4
  in conduct disorder in adolescent (2) 37: 6, 8
  in elderly (2) 119: 5
    clinical features (2) 119: 5
    management (2) 119: 5
    prevalence (2) 119: 5
  in Huntington's disease (1) 28: 11–12
  psychological theories for (1) 16: 10
Paranoid personality
  antisocial personality distinguished from (1) 23: 3

impact of medical illness on (2) 82: 10
in medical setting (2) 82: 9–10
psychodynamics (2) 82: 10
Paranoid personality disorder (1) **16: 8–10;** 68: 13
  avoidance of social situations in (1) 33: 7
  clinical description (1) 16: 9
  definition (1) 16: 8
  diagnosis (1) 16: 10
  differential diagnosis (1) 16: 10
  drug therapy (1) 10: 4
  DSM-III criteria for (1) 16: 8
  epidemiology (1) 16: 8–9
  etiology (1) 16: 9–10
  genetics (1) 16: 9–10
  historical background (1) 16: 8
  narcissistic personality disorder distinguished from
       (1) 18: 9
  paranoid disorder distinguished from (1) 16: 10
  paranoid psychosis in relatives (1) 16: 9–10
  psychological theories for (1) 16: 10
  schizoid personality disorder distinguished from (1)
       16: 3
  schizophrenia in relatives (1) 16: 9–10
  shame-humiliation model for (1) 16: 10
  treatment (1) 16: 10
Paranoid position (1) 1: 10
Paranoid psychosis. *See* Paranoid disorder
Paranoid spectrum (1) 68: 13
Paraphilias (1) **46: 2–10;** (2) 41: 4–7
  associated features (1) 46: 7–8
  atypical (1) 46: 6–7
  aversion therapy in (1) 46: 10
  changing concepts in (1) 46: 3
  classification (1) 46: 3–4
  clinical description (1) 46: 4–8
  definition (1) 46: 1–3; (2) 41: 4
  diagnosis and differential diagnosis (1) 46: 9
  epidemiology (1) 46: 4
  essential characteristics (1) 46: 7
  etiology (1) 46: 8–9
  exhibitionism (1) 46: 6
  fetishism (1) 46: 5; (2) 41: 4–6
  gender identity disorders distinguished from (1)
       46: 9
  homosexuality distinguished from (1) 46: 9
  pedophilia (1) 46: 6
  perversion distinguished from (1) 46: 3
  predisposing factors (1) 46: 4
  prevalence (1) 46: 4
  psychodynamics in (1) 46: 8–9
  rationale for current classification (1) 46: 3–4
  sex ratio in (1) 46: 4
  sexually dangerous person (3) 28: 22–23
  sexual masochism (2) 41: (1) 46: 5–6
  sexual sadism (1) 46: 5–6; (2) 41: 6–7
  transvestism (1) 46: 5
  treatment (1) 46: 9–10
  voyeurism (1) 46: 6
  zoophilia (1) 46: 6

raphrenia (1) 53: 19; 68: 13
raplegic pain (2) 104: 5–6
rasitosis, delusions of (2) 100: 5
rasomnias (2) 105: 14–16; (3) 61: 13–14
  characteristics (2) 105: 14
  classification (2) 105: 2
  nightmares (2) 105: 15–16
  night terrors (2) 105: 15
  in preschool and school-age children (2) 52: 5–7
  sleepwalking (2) 105: 14–15
rasuicide. *See* Suicide, attempted
rasympathetic nervous system. *See also* Autonomic
        nervous system
rathyroid disorders (2) 88: 11–12
  hyperparathyroidism (2) 88: 11
  hypoparathyroidism (2) 88: 11–12
rens patriae (2) 71: 2; (3) 32: 4–5, 9
rent-child relationship
  with adolescents (2) 4: 10–11
  child disorders related to parenting disorders (2)
        50: 4–5
  child-elicited disorders (2) 50: 5
  child impact on parenting behavior (2) 50: 1
  definition (2) 50: 1–2
  developmental aspects (2) 50: 2–3
  disorders in (2) **50: 1–6**
    diagnosis (2) 50: 5–6
    prevention (2) 50: 6
    treatment (2) 50: 6
  misfit in (2) 50: 2
  oedipal-sexual differentiation and (2) 50: 3
  parenting disorders and (2) 50: 3–5
  phase-specific, interactional conflicts in nonpatho-
        logic family (2) 50: 2–3
    in infants (2) 50: 2
    in latency-aged child (2) 50: 3
    in preschool child (2) 50: 3
    in toddlers (2) 50: 3
  psychiatric disorder related to (3) 12: 23
rent management training (2) 61: 3–5
  background and underlying rationale (2) 61: 3–4
  characteristics of treatment (2) 61: 4
  efficacy (2) 61: 4–5
  limitations in (2) 61: 6–7
rents. *See also* Family; Fathers; Mothers
  adolescents relationship with (2) 4: 10–11
  behavioral assessment by (2) 11: 8
  and behavior therapy outcome (2) 61: 7
  in borderline personality disorder (2) 42: 7
  in child abuse (2) 50: 4
  in conduct disorder (2) 37: 4
    management training in (2) 61: 3–5
  consultation-liaison psychiatry for (2) 72: 7
  contingent reward methods used by (1) 2: 4–5
  cultural aspects of mothering (2) 120: 5
  depression in child related to depression in (2) 30:
        6
  factors inhibiting involvement in psychiatric treat-
        ment (2) 56: 7

and family development (2) 5: 3–4
  inconsistent (1) 2: 5
  indulgent (1) 2: 5
  instinct to mother (2) 120: 5
  interviews to assess children (2) 23: 7–8
  of learning disabled child
    information for (2) 48: 6–7
    role in management (2) 48: 7
  legal rights as advocate for child (2) 71: 1–2
  management training in child conduct disorders
        (2) 61: 3–5
  mental illness impact on child (2) 50: 4–5
  mid-life crisis in (2) 4: 11
  overprotective (1) 2: 5
  punitive methods by (1) 2: 4
  rating scales on children (2) 23: 4–6
  reaction to birth of mentally retarded child (2) 58:
        2–3
  reaction to death of (1) 41: 9–10
  rejection by
    avoidant personality due to (1) 24: 6–7
    effect on social learning in child (1) 2: 4
  relationship with child. *See* Parent-child relation-
        ship
  rooming-in with infant during hospitalization (2)
        72: 5
  of schizophrenic offspring (3) 7: 2–3
  and social learning of child (1) 2: 3–5
  in treatment planning of child (2) 56: 7
  vulnerability of (2) 18: 6
Pargyline, interactions with other drugs (2) 111: 8.
        See also Monoamine oxidase inhibitors
Parietal lobe
  anosognosia due to lesions (1) 28: 9
  denial of illness in (1) 28: 9
  psychosis related to tumors of (1) 69: 4
Parkinson's disease
  basal ganglia lesion in (1) 28: 7
  clinical features (1) 28: 11
  dementia distinguished from (1) 28: 11
  dopamine receptors role in (3) 50: 13–14
  dopaminergic transmission in (3) 42: 10
  drug interactions worsening (2) 111: 3–4
  locus ceruleus neurons in (3) 44: 6
  movement-related potentials in (3) 62: 4
  and neostriatum (3) 42: 10
  neuroleptics causing
    pathogenesis (1) 55: 22–23
    treatment (1) 55: 23, 24
  neurotransmitters in (1) 52: 15
  personality changes in (1) 28: 11
  psychosis related to (1) 28: 11; 69: 6
Parole
  legal considerations in treatment (3) 28: 8
  treatment considerations (3) 28: 7, 22
Parsimoniousness, in compulsive personality disorder
        (1) 22: 2
Passive-aggressive personality, antisocial personality
        distinguished from (1) 23: 3

Passive-aggressive personality disorder (1) **26: 4–6**
  definition (1) 26: 5
  diagnosis (1) 26: 6
  differential diagnosis (1) 26: 6
  epidemiology (1) 26: 5
  etiology (1) 26: 5–6
  historical aspects (1) 26: 4
  masochistic personality distinguished from (1) 27: 7
  prevention (1) 26: 6
  psychodynamics (1) 26: 4–5
  treatment (1) 26: 6
Passivity phenomena, in schizophrenia (1) 53: 8
Path analysis, in genetics (1) 62: 3–4
Patient
  perspective of problem (1) **6:**
    chief complaint (1) 6: 2
    classification (1) 6: 2
    clinical value of eliciting (1) 6: 3–4
    conditions of treatment (1) 6: 2
    desired relationship with therapist (1) 6: 2
    expression of patient requests (1) 6: 4–5
    goals of treatment (1) 6: 2
    methods or requests for treatment (1) 6: 2–3
    recording in clinical record (1) 6: 12
  request for treatment (1) 6: 2–5
    diagnostic value (1) 6: 3–4
    expression of (1) 6: 4–5
    process issues in eliciting (1) 6: 3–4
    resistance to expression (1) 6: 5
    types (1) 6: 2–3
Patient Evaluation Grid (2) 81: 8–9
Patients' rights (3) **35: 1–15.** *See also* Civil commitment; Mentally disordered offenders
  to aftercare (3) 35: 10–13
  historical background (3) 35: 1–2
  during institutionalization (3) 35: 7–10
  to mental health advocacy (3) 35: 13–15
  to refuse treatment (3) 35: 4–7
  to treatment (3) 35: 2–4
    in least restrictive setting (3) 35: 3
    in work therapy program (3) 35: 8–9
    Wyatt v. Stickney case (3) 35: 2–4, 7
    Youngberg v. Romero case (3) 35: 2–4, 7
Patterning (2) 160: 3
Patuxent prison treatment program (3) 28: 15
Pavlov, I. P.
  experimental neurosis studies (1) 2: 13
  and learning theory (1) 2: 10–11
Pavor nocturnus. *See* Night terrors
PCP. *See* Phencyclidine
Peabody Picture Vocabulary test (2) 21: 5–6
Pediatric consultation (2) **72: 1–7**
  child development perspective in (2) 72: 4–5
  common problems in (2) 72: 2–4
  direct consultation (2) 72: 5–6
  factors influencing child's reaction to medical illness (2) 72: 4

historical background (2) 72: 1
in hospital pediatric ward matters (2) 72: 3
importance of knowledge about medical illnesses in (2) 72: 3
for interconnection of physical and psychiatric disorders (2) 72: 5
for patients admitted for mainly social reasons (2) 72: 5–6
for patients whose illness causes debilitating psychologic stress (2) 72: 6–7
for primary psychiatric disorders (2) 72: 5
rationale for (2) 72: 1–2
  psychosocial influences (2) 72: 1–2
  somatopsychic influences (2) 72: 2
setting for (2) 72: 5
successful work in (2) 72: 4–7
Pediatrics
  behavioral (2) 72: 4
  impact on child psychiatry (2) 1: 4–5
  psychiatric consultation in (2) **72: 1–7.** *See also* Pediatric consultation
Pedigree analysis (2) 10: 6–7
Pedophilia (1) 46: 6
  psychiatric disorders in (3) 28: 23
Peer relationships
  in adolescence
    in early stage (2) 4: 7
    in middle stage (2) 4: 8
  alienation (1) 24: 7
  in attention deficit disorder (3) 66: 8
  in epidemic hysteria (3) 12: 17
  in group therapy (2) 63: 5
  substance abuse related to (2) 35: 2
Peer review, confidentiality issues in (3) 31: 11
Pemoline (Cylert)
  in antisocial personality disorder (1) 10: 3
  in attention deficit disorder (2) 36: 11; 59: 6; (3) 66: 15
    comparison with other drugs (3) 66: 18
    side effects (3) 66: 18–19
  in narcolepsy (2) 105: 13–14
  pharmacokinetics in children (2) 59: 4
  structure (2) 59: 6
Penetrance (1) 62: 2
Pentazocine (Talwin), psychiatric side effects (2) 91: 6
Pentobarbital challenge test (2) 90: 11
Pepsinogen, as marker for susceptibility to peptic ulcer (2) 78: 2
Peptic ulcer disease
  biofeedback and relaxation therapy in (2) 109: 9
  pepsinogen as marker for (2) 78: 2
Peptides, biopsy of gastrointestinal tissue in study of (2) 12: 3. *See also* Neuropeptides
Perception
  auditory (3) 67: 6–10
  basic components of (3) 67: 6
  in delirium (1) 73: 14

delusional (1) 53: 8
distortion as self-perpetuation of abnormal social
      learning (1) 2: 8
   in dyslexia (2) 48: 4
   event-related potentials in (3) 62: 2
   in hypochondriasis (1) 35: 12
   in language disorders (2) 49: 7; (3) 67: 6–10
   in major psychiatric syndromes (2) 95: 2
   in organic brain syndromes, treatment (2) 87: 15–
      16
   in pervasive developmental disorders (2) 27: 4–5
   repetition method of study (3) 67: 7–8
   in right hemisphere syndrome (1) 28: 9–10
   tests for (2) 20: 14
erceptual motor abilities, tests of (3) 52: 10–12
   auditory functions (3) 52: 10–11
   complex (3) 52: 11–12
   sensory functions (3) 52: 10
   visual functions (3) 52: 11
erfectionism, in compulsive personality disorder (1)
      22: 2, 3
erinatal period
   attention deficit disorder related to insult in (2)
      36: 2–3
   schizophrenia related to (1) 54: 13–14; (3) 15: 7–
      8
ermitil. See Fluphenazine
erphenazine
   in Alzheimer's disease (2) 119: 3
   in schizophrenia
      dosage (1) 55: 12
      preparations (1) 55: 13
ersonality
   affective disorders related to (1) 61: 5
   antisocial. See Antisocial personality
   borderline. See Borderline personality
   cancer related to (2) 128: 6
   circumplex model of (1) 15: 8–10
   definition (2) 42: 1
   depression causing changes in (1) 3: 4
   depression related to (1) 40: 4–5; (3) 55: 8
      nonbipolar disorder (1) 60: 6–7; (3) 13: 7–8
   development (2) 42: 2–4
      biological origins (2) 42: 2
      psychological origins (2) 42: 3–4
      psychosocial factors (2) 42: 4
   in drug addict (2) 90: 5
   genetic factors in (2) 42: 2
   histrionic. See Histrionic personality
   hypnosis benefit related to (2) 112: 6
   impact of medical setting on (2) **82: 1–11.** See also
      under in medical setting below
   impulsive. See Impulse disorders
   inadequate (1) 23: 3
   as instrumental learning (1) 2: 22
   in Korsakoff's syndrome (1) 73: 19
   medical illness related to specific types (2) 78: 2–3
   in medical setting (2) **82: 1–11**

   borderline person (2) 82: 6–8
   compulsive personality (2) 82: 2–3
   depressive-masochistic person (2) 82: 5–6
   histrionic personality (2) 82: 3–5
   narcissistic person (2) 82: 8–9
   paranoid person (2) 82: 9–10
   multiple. (1) **39: 8–10.** See also Dissociative dis-
      orders
      amnesia distinguished from (1) 39: 9
      clinical description (1) 39: 8–9
      definition (1) 39: 8
      differential diagnosis (1) 39: 9
      epidemiology (1) 39: 8
      etiology (1) 39: 9
      fugue distinguished from (1) 39: 7, 9
      malingering distinguished from (1) 39: 9
      schizophrenia distinguished from (1) 39: 9
      treatment (1) 39: 9–10
   in Munchausen syndrome (1) 35: 18
   narcissistic. See Narcissistic personality
   neurologic disease causing changes in (1) **28: 1–
      12**
      Alzheimer's disease (1) 28: 4
      anatomic correlations (1) 28: 4–7
      basal ganglia (1) 28: 6–7, 11–12
      bromocriptine therapy and (1) 28: 11
      cerebrovascular accident (1) 28: 4
      definition (1) 28: 2–3
      dementia (1) 28: 4
      etiology (1) 28: 3–4
      frontal lobe injury (1) 28: 1
      frontal lobe syndromes (1) 28: 10–11
      head trauma (1) 28: 3–4
      historical aspects (1) 28: 1–2
      Huntington's disease (1) 28: 11–12
      hypothalamic disease
         clinical presentation of lesions (1) 28: 7
         physiology (1) 28: 5–6
      importance to psychiatrist (1) 28: 2
      interaction of organic and functional factors in
         (1) 28: 3
      Jakob-Creutzfeldt disease (1) 28: 4
      limbic system (1) 28: 6
      neoplasms (1) 28: 4
      Parkinson's disease (1) 28: 11
      prevalence (1) 28: 3
      right hemisphere syndromes (1) 28: 9–10
      temporal lobe epilepsy (1) 28: 4
      temporal lobe syndrome (1) 28: 7–8
   in pain-prone patient (1) 35: 9
   paranoid. See Paranoid personality
   in paraphilias (1) 46: 7–8
   passive-aggressive. See Passive-aggressive personal-
      ity disorder
   and psychodynamics (1) 6: 9
   schizophrenia associated with (1) 53: 7
   and substance abuse (3) 12: 18
   substance abuse related to (2) 35: 2

Personality *(continued)*
  temperament. *See also* Temperament
  tests of (1) 7: 8–9; (2) 20: 14
    in children (2) 23: 6
  traits distinguished from disorder (1) 14: 2–3
Personality disorders (1) **14: 1–5**
  in alcoholism (2) 89: 3, 5
  antisocial personality (1) **23: 1–10.** *See also* Antiso-
    cial personality
  avoidant (1) **24: 1–11.** *See also* Avoidant personal-
    ity; Avoidant personality disorder
  biological model for (1) **3: 1–10**
    in affective disorders (1) 3: 2–5
    in borderline personality disorders (1) 3: 5–6
    in disorders with neuroanatomical determinants
      (1) 3: 9–10
    in lithium-responsive labile or explosive person-
      ality (1) 3: 8–9
    in panic anxiety and agoraphobia (1) 3: 6–7
  borderline (1) **17: 1–13.** *See also* Borderline per-
    sonality disorder
  brief reactive psychosis distinguished from (1) 70:
    13
  in children
    borderline (2) 42: 5–7. *See also* Borderline per-
      sonality disorder
    classification (2) 42: 1–2
    developmental considerations (2) 42: 2–4
    diagnosis (2) 42: 2
    etiology, modern concepts and theories (2) 42:
      4
    future directions in (2) 42: 7
    organic (2) 34: 2–3
  circumplex model for integrating DSM-III Axis II
    diagnosis (1) 15: 8–11
  classification (1) 14: 4–5; (2) 42: 1–2
    in children (2) 42: 1–2
  clinical analysis questionnaire in (1) 15: 5–6
  clinical syndromes associated with (1) 14: 3–4
  compulsive personality (1) **22: 1–8.** *See also* Com-
    pulsive personality disorder
  confused terminology in (1) 19: 1–2
  in conversion disorders (2) 47: 5
  definition (1) 14: 2–3; 28: 2–3; (2) 42: 1; 82: 2
  dependent personality (1) **26: 1–4.** *See also* De-
    pendent personality disorder
  diagnosis
    in children (2) 42: 2
    psychological tests in (1) **15: 1–12.** *See also* Psy-
      chological tests
  dimensional categorization (1) 14: 4–5
  dissociative disorders (1) **39: 1–11.** *See also* Disso-
    ciative disorders
  drug therapy (1) **10: 1–8**
  DSM-III on (2) 42: 1
    limitations of (1) 14: 1, 2
  episodic dyscontrol syndrome (2) 87: 12
  fluid model for (1) 3: 1–2

frontal lobe syndrome (2) 87: 11–12
histrionic (1) **19: 1–10.** *See also* Histrionic personality disorder
in hyperthyroidism (2) 88: 7–8
hysterical (1) **19: 1–10.** *See also* Hysterical personality disorder
impulsive personality disorder (1) 25: 6–7. *See also*
  Impulsive personality disorder
intermittent explosive disorder (2) 87: 12
masochistic personality (1) **27: 1–9.** *See also* Masochistic personality
Millon clinical multiaxial inventory in (1) 15: 7–8
MMPI in (1) 15: 5
multidimensional system for (1) 24: 3
narcissistic personality disorder (1) **18: 1–11.** *See
  also* Narcissistic personality disorder
with neuroanatomical determinants (1) 3: 9–10
neurologic disorders causing (1) **28: 1–12.** *See also*
  Personality, neurological disease causing
  changes in
neurosis related to (1) 31: 5–6
obsessive-compulsive disorder (1) **34: 1–10.** *See
  also* Obsessive-compulsive disorder
odd cluster (1) 16: 1
organic (2) 87: 11–12
  definition (2) 87: 1
paranoid (1) **16: 8–10;** 68: 13. *See also* Paranoid
  personality disorder
passive-aggressive (1) **26: 4–6**
personality research form in (1) 15: 6–7
personality trait distinguished from (1) 14: 2–3
psychological tests in (1) **15: 1–12.** *See also* Psychological tests
  for anxiety (1) 7: 8
  dimensional approach (1) 7: 5–9
  Minnesota Multiphasic Personality Inventory (1)
    7: 5
  multidimensional (1) 7: 5
  projective tests, limitations (1) 15: 2
  self-report (1) 7: 4
  structured interviews (1) 7: 4
  for symptoms (1) 7: 4
relationship with Axis I syndrome (1) 14: 3
schizoid (1) **16: 1–4.** *See also* Schizoid personality
  disorder
schizophrenia boundary with (1) 53: 19
schizotypal (1) **16: 4–8.** *See also* Schizotypal personality disorder
sex ratios in Axis II diagnoses (1) 24: 5
in sexually dangerous offender (3) 28: 23
social learning theory as basis of (1) 2: 22
spectrum disorders (1) 14: 3–4
Structural Analysis of Social Behavior in (1) 15: 7
suicide attempt in (1) 71: 14
in temporal lobe epilepsy (1) 3: 9–10
temporal lobe syndrome (2) 87: 12
terminology in (1) 19: 1–2
treatment, drugs (1) **10: 1–8**

Personality Disorders Questionnaire (1) 7: 4
16-Personality Factor Inventory (1) 7: 8–9
Personality Inventory for Children (2) 23: 6
Personality research form (1) 15: 6–7
Personality tests (1) 7: 8–9; (2) 20: 14
  in early childhood (2) 21: 6; 23: 6
    Children's Apperception Test (2) 21: 6
    Rorschach Inkblot Test (2) 21: 6
  in middle childhood and adolescence (2) 21: 10
Personality trait, definition (2) 42: 1. *See also* Personality
Perspective
  categorical versus individualistic (1) 6: 6
  clinician's (1) 6: 5–11
  multidimensional (1) 6: 6–7
  patient's (1) 6: 1–5. *See also* Patient, perspective of problem
Pervasive developmental disorders (2) **27: 1–9.** *See also* Developmental disorders, pervasive
Perversion. *See also* Paraphilias
  definition (1) 46: 3
  masochistic (1) 27: 1. *See also* Masochistic personality
  paraphilia distinguished from (1) 46: 3
  sexual, masochistic personality distinguished from (1) 27: 1, 7
Phantom limb pain (2) 104: 5
  behavioral and psychological factors in (2) 104: 5
  clinical description (2) 104: 5
  epidemiology (2) 104: 5
  treatment (2) 104: 5
Pharmacokinetics
  developmental aspects (2) 59: 2–4
  of neuroleptics (1) 55: 7–11
Pharmacology. *See* Drugs; Pharmacotherapy; Psychopharmacology
Pharmacotherapy. *See also* Drugs; Psychopharmacology
  in agoraphobia, with panic attacks (1) 10: 6, 7
  in Alzheimer's disease (2) 119: 3–4
  in antisocial personality disorder (1) 10: 3–4
  in anxiety disorder (1) 10: 5–6; 32: 12; (2) 39: 8
  in attention deficit disorder (3) 66: 15–21
  attention influenced by (3) 65: 9–10
  bioavailability in (1) 55: 9
  in bipolar disorder (1) 61: 18–21
  blood levels in
    interindividual variations (1) 55: 8
    route of administration versus (1) 55: 8–9
    therapeutic response versus (1) 55: 10
    toxic effects versus (1) 55: 10–11
  in borderline personality disorder (1) 10: 2–3; 17: 12
  in child psychiatry, in inpatient programs (2) 64: 15–16
  in chronic mental patients (3) 6: 7
  circadian rhythms in (3) 59: 3, 13
  controversy on benefit versus liability of (3) 72: 1

  in conversion disorder (1) 10: 8
  in dementia in elderly (2) 119: 3–4
  in depression (1) 61: 7–12
    chronic disorder (1) 61: 17–18
    as diagnostic tool (1) 3: 3
    heterocyclic antidepressants (1) 61: 8–11
    maintenance therapy (1) 61: 12–13
    monoamine oxidase inhibitors (1) 61: 11–12
    treatment-resistant cases (1) 61: 17–18
  in depressive neurosis (1) 40: 12–13
  in depressive personality (1) 10: 4–5
  drug interactions in (1) 55: 11; (2) **111: 1–11.** *See also* Drugs, interactions
  in elderly (3) 21: 10
  general principles (1) 10: 1
  in hallucinations of organic origin (2) 87: 13
  historical perspective (1) 55: 1–2
  issues in use of stimulants (3) 66: 21
  malpractice related to injuries in (3) 29: 10
  in migraine headache (2) 104: 7
  in obesity (2) 103: 9
  in obsessive-compulsive disorders (1) 10: 7
  in organic brain syndromes (2) 87: 15
  in panic disorder (1) 10: 6; 32: 11–12
  in paranoid disorder (1) 68: 15
  in paranoid personality disorder (1) 16: 10
  in personality disorders (1) **10: 1–8**
  in pervasive developmental disorders (2) 27: 9
  pharmacokinetics of neuroleptics (1) 55: 7–11
  in posttraumatic stress disorder (1) 10: 7
  psychiatric side effects (2) **91: 1–8.** *See also* Drugs, psychiatric side effects
  psychoanalysis combined with (1) 8: 12
  in schizophrenia (1) **55: 1–26.** *See also* Schizophrenia, treatment, drugs
    classes of drugs used (1) 55: 3–5
    preparation and dosages of neuroleptics (1) 55: 11–13
    side effects (1) 55: 20–26
    sites and actions (1) 55: 14–20
  in schizotypal and paranoid personality disorders (1) 10: 4
  in social phobia (1) 10: 7; 33: 13–14
  in stress response systems (1) 41: 15
  timing of medication administration based on biological rhythms (3) 59: 13
  of Tourette's disorder (2) 38: 6
  for violent patient (2) 95: 5, 9
Phase, definition (3) 59: 14
Phencyclidine (PCP)
  binding to opiate receptor and psychotomimetic action (3) 50: 13
  comparative rates of abuse with other drugs (3) 17: 14
  demographic trends in use (3) 17: 14–15
  epidemiology of abuse (3) 17: 14–15
  symptoms of ingestion (2) 35: 5
    physical symptoms (2) 90: 8

Phencyclidine (PCP) *(continued)*
  temporal trends in abuse (3) 17: 14
  toxic hallucinatory state due to (2) 90: 8
  treatment (2) 35: 5; 90: 8
Phenelzine. *See also* Monoamine oxidase inhibitors
  in depression (1) 61: 11
  in panic disorder (1) 32: 11
Phenomenology, in social learning theory (1) 2: 15–
      18
Phenothiazines
  cardiac arrhythmias related to (2) 111: 4
  controversy on benefit versus liability of (3) 72: 1
  drugs comprising (1) 55: 4–6
  efficacy related to affinity for dopamine receptors
      (3) 50: 3
  eye effects (1) 55: 26
  historical perspective (1) 55: 2
  interactions with other drugs (2) 111: 2–5
  lithium interaction with (2) 111: 11
  monoamine oxidase inhibitors interacting with (2)
      111: 3, 8
  receptor actions and extrapyramidal side effects
      with (3) 50: 13–14
  in schizophrenia
    dosage (1) 55: 12
    evidence for efficacy (1) 55: 5
    preparations (1) 55: 13
  skin effects (1) 55: 26
  structure (1) 55: 6
  tardive dyskinesia due to (1) 53: 14
  timing of drug administration based on biological
      rhythms (3) 59: 13
Phenotype (1) 62: 2; (2) 10: 1
Phenylketonuria, prevention of mental retardation in
      (2) 58: 4
Phenytoin (Dilantin)
  in antisocial personality disorder (1) 10: 3
  interactions with other drugs (2) 111: 2
  organic mental disorders precipitated by (2) 34: 6
Pheochromocytoma
  anxiety disorders distinguished from (1) 32: 9–10
  physical and psychiatric manifestations (2) 88: 10
Phobia (1) **33: 1–14.** *See also* Anxiety disorders
  of animals, age of onset (1) 33: 5
  in avoidant personality (1) 24: 9
  classification (1) 33: 1, 2
  clinical presentation (1) 33: 4–6
  definition (1) 33: 2–3
  differential diagnosis (1) 33: 6–7
  DSM-III on (3) 14: 5
  epidemiology (1) 33: 3–4
  etiology (1) 33: 7–9
  genetics of (1) 33: 9
  historical aspects (1) 33: 1
  incidence rate by age (1) 33: 3
  learning theory for (1) 33: 7–8
  mixed (1) 33: 7
  most common types (1) 33: 5

phobic features distinguished from (1) 33: 3
prevalence (1) 33: 3–4
psychoanalytic theory of (1) 33: 8–9
school (2) 39: 4
  behavior therapy (2) 39: 7
  biophysiologic mechanism for (1) 3: 7–8
  drug therapy in (2) 39: 8
    antidepressants (2) 59: 15
sexual (1) 47: 6–7
  definition (1) 47: 7
  differential diagnosis (1) 47: 7
  partner's reaction (1) 47: 7
simple
  anxiety in (1) 33: 5
  clinical presentation (1) 33: 5
  definition (1) 33: 3
  differential diagnosis (1) 33: 7
  drug therapy (1) 10: 7
  DSM-III on (1) 33: 2; (3) 14: 5
  fear in (1) 33: 5
  treatment (1) 33: 10–11
    exposure (1) 33: 10
    imaginal flooding (1) 33: 10
    outcome (1) 33: 11
    participant modeling and reinforced practice
        (1) 33: 10–11
    prolonged in vivo exposure (1) 33: 10
    systematic desensitization (1) 33: 10
social
  age of onset (1) 33: 6
  agoraphobia distinguished from (1) 33: 7
  in avoidant personality (1) 24: 9
  avoidant personality disorder distinguished from
      (1) 33: 7
  clinical presentation (1) 33: 5–6
  definition (1) 33: 2
  differential diagnosis (1) 33: 6–7
  drug and alcohol abuse in (1) 33: 6
  drug therapy (1) 10: 7
  DSM-III on (1) 33: 2; (3) 14: 5
  fears in (1) 33: 5
  paranoid personality disorder distinguished from
      (1) 33: 7
  treatment (1) 33: 13–14
    behavioral programs (1) 33: 13; (2) 39: 7
    drugs (1) 33: 13–14
  stressful life events in (1) 41: 8
  treatment (1) 33: 9–14
  systematic desensitization (2) 109: 1
Phobic character (1) 24: 3. *See also* Avoidant person-
      ality
Phobic features (1) 33: 3
Phonic behaviors (2) 38: 1, 2, 7
Phonology
  definition (2) 49: 2; (3) 67: 5. *See also* Language
  in expressive language disorder (2) 49: 4
  language disorders related to (3) 67: 2
Photoperiodism (3) 59: 7–8

definition (3) 59: 14
neuroanatomy of circadian oscillators and (3) 59: 8–10
Physical activity. *See* Exercise
Physical appearance, in mental status examination (2) 20: 4–5
Physical dependence, definition (2) 90: 2
Physical examination, in attention deficit disorder (2) 36: 7; (3) 66: 13. *See also* Mental status examination; Neurological examination
Physical illness. *See* Medical illness
Physician. *See also* Psychiatrist
confidentiality of patient records during investigation of (3) 31: 6–8
in depression treatment (1) 61: 5–6
impaired, confidentiality of treatment records of (3) 31: 7–8
insufficient use of analgesics by (2) 121: 7
knowledge of psychiatric disorder (2) 115: 5
missed diagnosis of suicide (1) 71: 8
primary care (2) 116: 2
level of psychiatric knowledge (2) 116: 3–4
resistance to diagnosing and treating psychiatric conditions (2) 116: 4–5
psychiatric disorders in practice of (3) 22: 7–8
responsibility for recognition of risk and prevention of suicide (1) 71: 1
role in suicide (1) 71: 8–9
teaching psychosomatic medicine to (2) 78: 8
undertreatment of depression by (1) 61: 5–6
Physician-patient relationship (2) **81: 1–10**
abandonment by physician (3) 29: 7–8
abuses in (3) 29: 11–12
alliances in (3) 36: 5–8
awareness of psychological nature of (2) 81: 7
breach of contract in (3) 29: 2–3
confidentiality as duty of (3) 31: 2
cross-cultural aspects (2) 81: 2–3
definition (2) 81: 1
dysfunction of
prevention (2) 81: 8–9
situations contributing to (2) 81: 8
element in (2) 81: 4
emphasis on (2) 116: 1–2
ethical considerations in (2) 81: 6–7
existential alliance (3) 36: 6
expectations in (2) 81: 1
feelings of physician and patient in (2) 81: 4–5, 7
goals of (2) 81: 4–7
historical context (2) 81: 1–3
hypnosis induction dependent on (2) 112: 4–5
ideal model of (2) 81: 6–9
implications (2) 81: 9–10
implied duty of physician in (3) 29: 3
in involuntary commitment (3) 36: 12
irrational alliance (3) 36: 7
medical alliance (3) 36: 6–7
in medical model (2) 81: 6

models of (2) 81: 3–6
modern trends in (2) 81: 3
patient's rights in (2) 81: 6
personality types influencing (2) **82: 1–11**
borderline personality (2) 82: 7–8
compulsive personality (2) 82: 2–3
depressive-masochistic personality (2) 82: 5–6
histrionic personality (2) 82: 3–5
narcissistic personality (2) 82: 8–9
paranoid person (2) 82: 9–10
placebo effect in (2) 81: 7
rational alliance (3) 36: 6–7
situational alliance (3) 36: 8
as social system (2) 81: 5
stresses on (2) 116: 2
support systems in (2) 81: 6–7
teaching of (2) 81: 9
time course and variability in (2) 81: 5, 7
transference in. *See* Transference
Physostigmine, depression due to (3) 55: 3–5
Piaget, Jean, contributions to cognitive development (2) 17: 1–4
Pica (2) 40: 2–3
clinical description (2) 40: 2
differential diagnosis (2) 40: 2
etiology (2) 40: 2
treatment and prevention (2) 40: 2–3
Pick's disease
Alzheimer's disease distinguished from (1) 28: 4
personality change in (1) 28: 4, 8
Pickwickian syndrome (2) 105: 10. *See also* Sleep apnea
Pimozide
as antipsychotic agent (1) 55: 3, 5
in monosymptomatic hypochondriasis (2) 100: 5
in Tourette's disorder (2) 38: 6
Pineal gland, as circadian rhythm oscillator (3) 59: 9
Piracetam, in Alzheimer's disease (2) 119: 3
Pituitary gland
in electroconvulsive therapy (3) 68: 5
psychiatric manifestations of disorders (2) 88: 13–14
acromegaly (2) 88: 13–14
Simmond's disease (2) 88: 14
tumor, organic mental disorders in children due to (2) 34: 8
Pituitary tumors, psychosis related to (1) 69: 4
Pixels (3) 51: 2
Placebo effect
and drug-related behavioral effects (3) 45: 8–9
historical context (2) 81: 1–2
in psychotherapy (1) 11: 8–9
Placidyl. *See* Ethchlorvynol
Plasticity
neuronal, in learning (2) 13: 4–5
synaptic (2) 13: 5
Platelets, monoamine oxidase levels as marker in affective disorders (3) 53: 7–8

Play, in child development (2) 2: 2–3
Poisoning, in attempted suicide (1) 71: 14–15
Policy. *See* Government; Public policy
Politics. *See also* Government; Public policy
  in deinstitutionalization (3) 5: 6–7; 6: 13. *See also* Deinstitutionalization
  in funding care for chronic mental patients (3) 5: 6; 6: 12–13
  of mental health services
    accountability to community (3) 5: 6
    chronic mental patients (3) 5: 6–7
    deinstitutionalization (3) 5: 6–7
    focus on treatment organization rather than practitioner (3) 5: 5
    funding of systems rather than clinical episodes (3) 5: 6
    historical background (3) 5: 1–5
    increasing numbers of professionals (3) 5: 5
Polle syndrome (2) 101: 5
Pollution, costs of disease related to (2) 79: 2
Porphyria, organic mental disorders in children due to (2) 34: 8–9
Positron emission tomography (3) 50: 14
  basic principles (3) 51: 3–4
  cautions and methodologic standards (3) 51: 7
  in schizophrenia (3) 51: 6
Postencephalitic syndrome (2) 34: 3–4
Postimperative negative variation (3) 62: 5–6
Postpartum period
  depression in (1) 60: 7; (2) 120: 6; (3) 13: 6
  psychiatric disturbances in (2) 88: 14–15; 120: 6
  psychosis in (2) 120: 6
  schizophrenia in (1) 54: 10–11
Post-traumatic disorders (1) **41: 1–15.** *See also* Post-traumatic stress disorder; Stress-response syndromes
Post-traumatic stress disorder (1) 41: 6–7; (2) 95: 12
  acute (1) 41: 7
  adjustment disorder distinguished from (2) 51: 2, 3
  brief reactive psychosis distinguished from (1) 41: 7
  delayed (1) 41: 7
  differential diagnosis (1) 41: 7
  drug therapy (1) 10: 7
  DSM-III on (3) 14: 6
  prevalence (3) 14: 10
  stresses causing (1) 41: 6
  symptoms (1) 41: 6–7
Potassium, lithium pharmacokinetics related to (2) 111: 10
Pragmatics
  definition (2) 49: 1
  in expressive language disorder (2) 49: 3–4
  of language (3) 67: 5
Preadmission certification (2) 79: 6
Preadolescence (2) 4: 5

Precipitating event (1) 6: 9
Predictive validity, in classification (2) 19: 9
Predictive value, of screening test (2) 11: 5–6
Preferred provider organizations, in cost containment (3) 5: 12
Pregnancy
  in adolescents, biological and social risks (2) 4: 13
  biopsychological interactions in (2) 120: 3–4
  change in relationship with woman's mother during (2) 120: 5–6
  depression in postpartum period (1) 60: 7; (2) 120: 6; (3) 13: 6
  and family development (2) 5: 5
  influence of heavy use of medication on subsequent feelings of mother (2) 120: 4–5
  instinct to mother (2) 120: 5
  pain determinants in (2) 120: 4, 5
  physical symptoms related to ambivalence and conflict in (2) 120: 3
  postpartum reactions (2) 120: 6. *See also* Postpartum period
  psychological reaction to physical symptoms in (2) 120: 4
  reactions to labor and delivery (2) 120: 4
Premenstrual syndrome (2) 120: 2
  borderline clinical state in (1) 17: 8
  sex hormone changes related to (2) 88: 14
  treatment (1) 17: 12; (2) 120: 3
Premorbid personality, of paranoid disorder (1) 68: 4–5
Prepuberty (2) 4: 5
President's Commission on Mental Health (3) 4: 12–13; 5: 4
Prevalence. *See also* Epidemiology
  of alcohol abuse (3) 18: 3–9
    community survey approach (3) 18: 7–9
    by mortality from cirrhosis (3) 18: 3–5
    by per capita consumption (3) 18: 5–6
  of antisocial personality (3) 19: 2–3
  of anxiety states (3) 14: 2, 3, 6–10
  of attention deficit disorder (2) 36: 2
  of bipolar disorder (3) 13: 8, 9
  of childhood psychiatric disorders (2) 11: 9–10; 29: 3; (3) 12: 4
  definition (1) 54: 2; 60: 2; 69: 1–2; (3) 11: 2; 22: 2–3
  of depression
    in children (2) 30: 5
    nonbipolar disorder (1) 60: 3, 4; (3) 13: 2–3
  lifetime (1) 54: 3; (3) 11: 2
  of mental retardation (2) 28: 3
  overall indices of psychiatric disorders at different ages (3) 12: 19–21
  period (3) 11: 2
  of phobias (1) 33: 3–4
  of psychoses in organic brain disease (1) 69: 13
  of schizophrenia (1) 54: 4; (3) 15: 1
    in children (2) 29: 3

treated (3) **22: 1–11**
  in ambulatory medical setting (3) 22: 6–8
  in ambulatory psychiatric setting (3) 22: 5–6
  cross-cultural variations in (3) 2: 7
  definition (3) 22: 1–2
  ecologic factors in (3) 22: 9
  factors influencing seeking care (3) 22: 8–11
  in general hospital (3) 22: 6
  illness behavior and (3) 22: 9–11
  in nursing home (3) 22: 6
  by physicians (3) 22: 7–8
  psychiatric case registry in study of (3) 22: 2
  in psychiatric hospitals (3) 22: 4–5
  public policy and (3) 22: 8–9
  for schizophrenia (3) 15: 4
  social class and (3) 22: 9
  true prevalence compared with (3) 22: 2–3
Prevention
  of affective disorders (1) 61: 24–26; (3) 13: 13
  of alcoholism (2) 89: 12
  of anxiety disorders (2) 39: 8–9
  of bipolar disorder (1) 61: 24–25
  in child psychiatry (2) 69: 3
  in children at risk for mental illness (3) 7: 11–12
  community mental health services role (3) 5: 10
  of conduct disorder (3) 12: 24–25
  of coronary artery disease by behavior therapy (2) 126: 7–8
  of dependent personality disorder (1) 26: 4
  epidemiology in (3) 11: 12–13; 12: 2, 23–25
  family planning role in (3) 7: 11
  health education role in (2) 79: 5–6
  mass media role in (2) 79: 4–5
  of mental retardation (2) 58: 3–5
  of parent-child relationship disorder (2) 50: 6
  of passive-aggressive personality disorder (1) 26: 6
  primary, secondary and tertiary (2) 69: 3
  risk factors and (3) 13: 13
  school consultation in (2) 70: 3–6
  in Tourette's disorder (2) 38: 7
  in treatment plan (2) 56: 8
Primary care medicine
  emphasis on physician-patient relationship in (2) 116: 1–2
  psychiatry in (2) **116: 1–8**
    advantages (2) 116: 3
    biomedical versus biopsychosocial models in (2) 116: 1
    education in (2) 116: 5–7
      effectiveness (2) 116: 7
      formats for (2) 116: 6–7
      objectives (2) 116: 5
    historical aspects (2) 116: 1
    problems in (2) 116: 2–3
      frequency and types (2) 116: 3
      underrecognition by physician (2) 116: 3–4
    risks and benefits (2) 116: 7–8
    resistance to diagnosing, treating or referring psychiatric problems (2) 116: 4–5
    undertreatment of depression in (1) 61: 5–6
Prison
  antisocial personality prevalence in (3) 19: 2–3
  Herstedvester treatment program in (3) 28: 15
  initial emotional reactions of mentally disordered offenders in (3) 28: 15
  Patuxent treatment program (3) 28: 15
  psychiatric treatment of mentally disordered offenders in (3) 28: 15
Probation, treatment considerations (3) 28: 7, 22
  legal considerations (3) 28: 8
Probationed Offenders Rehabilitation and Treatment program (1) 23: 8
Procainamide, psychiatric side effects (2) 91: 6
Prochlorperazine (Compazine), in schizophrenia
  dosage (1) 55: 12
  preparations (1) 55: 13
Progesterone. *See* Progestins
Progestins
  effects of (2) 9: 4
  prenatal treatment
    and gender identity (2) 9: 7
    and gender-role behavior (2) 9: 7
    and sexual orientation (2) 9: 8
Progressive muscle relaxation training (2) 109: 1–2. *See also* Relaxation therapy
Projective identification, in family therapy (3) 7: 9
Projective tests
  in children (2) 21: 6
  in middle childhood and adolescence (2) 21: 10
  of personality (1) 7: 9
    limitations in personality disorders (1) 15: 2
  in thought disorders (1) 7: 7
Prolactin
  in affective disorders (1) 64: 11–12
  drug effects on (2) 9: 12
  function (2) 9: 4
  neuroleptics effect on (1) 55: 14–15
  regulatory system for (1) 55: 14
  in sleep (3) 60: 5
Prolixin. *See* Fluphenazine
Pronestyl. *See* Procainamide
Propoxyphene, use in suicide (1) 71: 9
Propranolol. *See also* Beta-adrenergic blockers
  in anxiety disorders (2) 59: 18
  in generalized anxiety disorder (1) 10: 5
  psychiatric side effects (2) 91: 5
  in social phobia (1) 10: 7
Prospective reimbursement
  in cost containment (3) 5: 12
  for mental health care (3) 3: 10; 4: 14
  in psychiatry (3) 5: 13
Prospective studies (2) 11: 2. *See also* Cohort studies
Protective behavior control. *See* Overprotectiveness
Protein, involvement in long-term memory mechanism (2) 13: 5–6

Protein-sparing-modified fast (2) 103: 9
Pseudobulbar laughing (1) 73: 9
Pseudodementia (1) 59: 12; (2) 87: 7; 99: 4
  dementia distinguished from (2) 87: 7–8
Pseudohermaphroditism, male, sexuality in (1) 45: 3
Psychedelics. *See* Hallucinogens
Psychiatric assessment. *See* Diagnosis; Mental status
    examination; Psychological tests
Psychiatric case register, utilization of mental health
    services studied by (3) 22: 2
Psychiatric consultation. *See* Consultation psychiatry;
    Consultation-liaison psychiatry
Psychiatric disorders. *See also* Mental illness; Psycho-
    pathology
  anxiety as symptom of (3) 14: 1
  attention, habituation and information processing
      in (3) **65: 1–11.** *See also* Schizophrenia,
      cognitive function in
  brain function and dysfunction in (3) 42: 9–18
    dopaminergic neural system (3) 42: 9–10
    neostriatal organization and (3) 42: 17
  in cancer (2) 104: 3
  in children (2) 11: 9–10. *See also* Child psychiatry;
      Children
    epidemiologic studies (2) 11: 10–12
    overall prevalence (3) 12: 19–21
  in chronic mental patient (3) 6: 3. *See also* Chronic
      mental patients
    mental health care for (3) **6: 1–14.** *See also*
        Mental health services
  civil commitment for (3) **32: 1–16.** *See also* Civil
      commitment
  in conduct disorder (2) 37: 6–7
  in dementia (1) 73: 4
  depression in (1) 59: 10
  discounting of (1) 51: 4–5
  disease concept (1) 73: 1–2
  in drug abuse (2) 90: 5
  drug-induced (2) **91: 1–8.** *See also* Drugs, side ef-
      fects, psychiatric
  in elderly
    decreased incidence (3) 21: 4–5
    epidemiology (3) **21: 1–11.** *See also* Elderly
  epidemiology (3) **11: 1–13.** *See also* Epidemiology
  etiology
    categories of (2) 20: 2
    epidemiologic studies of (3) 12: 1–2, 4. *See also*
        Epidemiology
      in children (2) 11: 10–12
    psychosocial factors (1) **63: 1–17**
    stress (1) 63: 2–13
  expressed emotion related to (1) 63: 14–17
  functional. *See* Functional psychiatric disorders
  genetic studies of (2) **10: 1–9.** *See also* Genetics
  homosexuality in (1) 45: 5–6
  hypersomnia associated with (2) 105: 9
  in hypertensive patients (2) 118: 8–9
  and immune system (2) 128: 12–14

    autism (2) 128: 14
    depression (2) 128: 12–13
    schizophrenia (2) 128: 13–14
  incidence and prevalence (2) 116: 3
  in insomnia (2) 105: 4
  intelligence tests in (1) 7: 6
  labeling theory of (1) 51: 4–5
  language disorder as risk factor for (3) 67: 13
  in medical illness (2) **88: 1–15.** *See also* Consulta-
      tion-liaison psychiatry; Medical illness
  medical model for (1) **51: 1–7.** *See also* Medical
      model
    in diagnosis (1) 51: 2–4
  in night terrors (2) 43: 7
  organic (1) **73: 1–20.** *See also* Organic mental dis-
      orders
  pain due to (2) 104: 9–11
    in depression (2) 104: 10–11
    psychogenic pain (2) 104: 9–10
  prevalence. *See* Epidemiology; Prevalence
  in primary care medicine (2) **116: 1–8.** *See also*
      Primary care medicine
  psychological tests in (1) 7: 3
  psychosocial factors in (1) **63: 1–17.** *See also*
      Stressful life events
    stress (1) 63: 2–13
  resistance of primary care physicians to deal with
      (2) 116: 4–5
  resistance to application (1) 51: 4
  in sexually dangerous offender (3) 28: 23
  social support and (1) 63: 13–14
  stressful life events in (1) 41: 8; 63: 2–13. *See also*
      Stressful life events
  stress role in (1) 63: 2–13
  suicide in (1) 71: 2–3; (3) 20: 11–14
  treated prevalence of (3) **22: 1–11.** *See also* Preva-
      lence, treated
Psychiatric emergencies (2) **95: 1–14.** *See also* Emer-
    gencies, psychiatric
  in children and adolescents (2) 62: 9–11
Psychiatric examination. *See* Mental status examina-
    tion
Psychiatrist. *See also* Physician; Psychotherapist
  abandonment of patient by (3) 29: 7–8
  abuses in relationship with patient (3) 29: 11–12
  as agent of various masters (3) 36: 2–3
  allegiance conflict in forensic psychiatry (3) 36: 3
  in child placement conflicts (2) 71: 3–4
  in chronic mental patient care (3) 6: 14
  in consultation-liaison
    functions (2) 117: 1–2
    in patient evaluation (2) 117: 3–4
    requirements (2) 117: 2–3
  in criminal justice system (3) 27: 1–3. *See also*
      Forensic psychiatry
  economic issues for (3) 3: 1–2
  in forensic psychiatry (3) 27: 1–3; 36: 1
  in language disorder of childhood (2) 49: 9–10

in public policy formulation (3) 4: 16
relationship with patient. *See* Physician-patient re-
    lationship
in schools (2) **70: 1–9.** *See also* School
sexual relations with patients (3) 29: 11–12
Psychiatry
    changes in assumptions, perspectives and practice
        (1) 51: 1
    consultation in (2) **115: 1–8.** *See also* Consultation
        psychiatry; Consultation-liaison psychiatry
    consultation-liaison (2) **117: 1–8.** *See also* Consul-
        tation-liaison psychiatry
        in primary care medicine (2) **116: 1–8.** *See also*
            Primary care medicine
    cross-cultural (3) **2: 1–14.** *See also* Cross-cultural
        psychiatry; Culture
    disease theories in (1) 63: 1–2
    diversity of viewpoints in (1) 2: 1
    DRGs in (3) 5: 13
    economic aspects of manpower in (3) 3: 11–12
    emergencies in (2) **95: 1–14.** *See also* Emergencies,
        psychiatric
    epidemiology in (1) 54: 1–2; 60: 1; (3) **11: 1–13.**
        See also Epidemiology
    event-related potentials in (3) 62: 12–13
    family (3) **7: 1–15.** *See also* Family; Family ther-
        apy
    family planning role in (3) 7: 12
    forensic (3) **36: 1–13.** *See also* Forensic psychiatry
    genetic studies in (2) **10: 1–9.** *See also* Genetics
    geriatric (2) **119: 1–9.** *See also* Elderly
    government role in (3) **4: 1–16.** *See also* Govern-
        ment
    historical background (1) **52: 1–21.** *See also* His-
        torical background
    informed consent issues in (3) **30: 1–14.** *See also*
        Consent, informed
    international (3) 11:
    JCAH review for accreditation (3) 5: 11
    of law (3) **36: 1–13.** *See also* Forensic psychiatry;
        Legal issues; Malpractice
    malpractice in (3) **29: 1–13.** *See also* Malpractice
    medical model in (1) 6: 6; **51: 1–7;** 63: 1–2. *See
        also* Medical model
    memory importance in (3) 71: 1. *See also* Memory
    from molecular biological simplification to more
        realistic central nervous system dynamics
        (3) 72: 1–6
    nature-nurture problem in (2) 51: 1
    need for change in neurobiological approaches (3)
        72: 5–6
    orthomolecular (2) 160: 2–3
    paradigms in (1) 52: 1–3, 6–14
        behavioral (1) 52: 11
        biological (1) 52: 6–7
        descriptive phenomenology (1) 52: 11–14
        interpersonal (1) 52: 10–11
        psychoanalytic (1) 52: 7–8

    social (1) 52: 9–10
    in primary care medicine (2) **116: 1–8.** *See also*
        Primary care medicine
    research in. *See* Research
    role in chronic mental patient care (3) 6: 14
    school collaboration with (2) 70: 2–4. *See also*
        School
    social control function. *See* Civil commitment
Psychic determinism (1) 1: 1
Psychoanalysis (1) **1: 1–15; 8: 1–12.** *See also* Psy-
    choanalytic concepts; Psychodynamics
    activities involved in (1) 1: 1
    analysis of grandiose self (1) 18: 10
    attitude and responsibility of doctor in (1) 8: 3–5
        abstinence (1) 8: 4
        anonymity (1) 8: 4
        interpretation (1) 8: 4–5
        neutrality (1) 8: 4
    basic hypotheses of (1) 1: 1–2
        dream theory (1) 1: 5–6
        dynamic unconscious (1) 1: 1
        genetic point of view (1) 1: 2
        libido theory (1) 1: 7
        motivational point of view (1) 1: 1–2
        multiple function principle (1) 1: 2
        Oedipus complex (1) 1: 6
        psychic conflict (1) 1: 2, 7–8
        psychic determinism (1) 1: 1
        sexual stages (1) 1: 6–7
        social and adaptive point of view (1) 1: 2
    in borderline personality disorders (1) 17: 12–13
    in child psychiatry (2) **57: 1–6**
        indications for (2) 57: 6
        therapeutic situation (2) 57: 2–3
        transference (2) 57: 3
    choice among other orientations (1) 8: 10–12; 9:
        6–7
        diagnostic considerations in (1) 8: 10–11
        financial considerations (1) 8: 11–12
        goals of patient and (1) 8: 11
        motivation and capacities and (1) 8: 11
    combined with other therapy (1) 8: 12
    of compulsive personality disorder (1) 22: 7
    in consultation (1) 8: 9
    contemporary models (1) 1: 8–14
        ego psychological (1) 1: 8–10
        interpersonal system (1) 1: 12–13
        object relations theory (1) 1: 10–11
        self-theory (1) 1: 11–12
    contraindications for (1) 8: 11
    definition (2) 56: 2
    in depressive neurosis (1) 40: 12
    in determining etiology and mechanism of psychi-
        atric illness (1) 51: 5–6
    diagnostic considerations in choice of (1) 8: 10–11
    difficulties in testing theories of (1) 1: 14
    dream theory in (1) 1: 5–6
    duration of treatment (1) 8: 7–8

Psychoanalysis *(continued)*
  ego psychological model (1) 1: 8–10
  ethology influence on (1) 1: 13
  in family therapy format (1) 9: 8
  free association method in (1) 8: 2–3
  Freud's contributions to (1) 1: 3–8
  goals (1) 9: 3
    of patient (1) 8: 11
  in group therapy of children and adolescents (2)
        63: 4
  historical background (1) 1: 2–5; 9: 2; 52: 7–8, 19–
        20
  for hysterical personality disorder (1) 19: 9–10
  impact on affective disorders (1) 52: 19–20
  informed consent in (3) 30: 14
  interpersonal (1) 1: 12–13
  learning theories based on (1) 2: 13–15
  life cycle of stages (1) 1: 9–10
  medical model contrasted with (1) 51: 5–6
  memory systems impact on theory in (3) 71: 10
  motivation for (1) 8: 11
  in narcissistic personality disorder (1) 18: 9–10
  in obesity (2) 103: 12
  object relations theory (1) 1: 10–11
  in obsessive-compulsive disorder (1) 34: 8–9
  in phobias 8–9
  position of therapist in (1) 8: 8
  problematic aspects (1) 8: 12
  qualitative differences in (1) 8: 8–10
  rationale (1) 9: 3
  self theory (1) 1: 11–12
  session length, frequency and regularity (1) 8: 7–8
    once-weekly (1) 8: 9–10
    short-term therapy with limited number of ses-
        sions (1) 8: 9
    twice and three times weekly (1) 8: 10
  setting for (1) 9: 3
  spectrum of therapies in (1) 8: 7–10
  speech and silence by therapist in (1) 8: 8
  structural theory (1) 1: 5–8; (2) 57: 1–2
    psychic conflict (1) 1: 7–8
  technique (1) 9: 3
  termination (1) 8: 7
  theories of cure in (1) 8: 3
  therapeutic alliance in (1) 8: 5
  therapeutic process
    completion of interrupted mourning (1) 8: 6
    delineation and tolerance of affects (1) 8: 6
    expansion of condensation and development of
        meaning (1) 8: 5–6
    learning and identification (1) 8: 7
    recognizing inner conflict (1) 8: 6
    recognizing unconscious determinants (1) 8: 5
    transference (1) 8: 6–7
  topographical model of psychic conflict (1) 1: 7
  validation (1) 1: 14–15
  variable features in (1) 8: 7–8
  ways of studying (1) 8: 1

Psychoanalytic concepts. *See also* Psychoanalysis; Psy-
        chodynamics
  of adolescence (2) 4: 3, 5
  of anxiety (2) 39: 1–2, 4–5
  of borderline disorders (1) 17: 1–3
    personality disorder (2) 42: 5
  in child psychiatry development (2) 1: 4
  of conduct disorder (2) 37: 1–2
  of conversion disorder (2) 47: 4
  of depressive-masochistic personality (2) 82: 5
  of depressive neurosis (1) 40: 1, 4
  of dreams (3) 60: 11
  of family development (2) 5: 2–4
  of histrionic personality (1) 19: 6–7; (2) 82: 4
  in hysterical personality disorder (1) 19: 6–7
  of narcissism (1) 18: 1, 2
  of narcissistic personality disorder (1) 18: 6–7
  in obsessive-compulsive disorder (1) 34: 6–7
  in paraphilias (1) 46: 8–9
  of personality development (2) 42: 3
  of personality disorders (2) 42: 4
  of psychosexual disorders (2) 41: 1
  of psychosomatic disorders (2) 76: 3
  of sexual development, research on (1) 1: 14–15
Psychodynamic life narrative
  for medically ill (2) 108: 4–7
  transference gratification in (2) 108: 7
Psychodynamic psychotherapy
  in anxiety disorders (2) 39: 8
  in child psychiatry (2) **57: 1–6**
  choice among other orientations (1) 9: 6–7
  in family therapy format (1) 9: 8
  goals (1) 9: 3
  group therapy format (1) 9: 9
  historical aspects (1) 9: 2
  rationale (1) 9: 2–3
  setting for (1) 9: 3
  technique (1) 9: 3
Psychodynamics. *See also* Psychoanalysis; Psychoana-
        lytic concepts
  of amnesia (1) 39: 5
  in anorexia nervosa (2) 102: 4, 5
  of antisocial personality (1) 23: 5
  of anxiety (1) 32: 5
  of avoidant personality (1) 24: 2–3, 6
  of borderline personality disorder (1) 17: 5–6
  in child psychiatry (2) **18: 1–8; 57: 1–6**
    behavior modification (2) 57: 5. *See also* Behav-
        ior therapy
    choice of therapy (2) 57: 6
    developmental considerations (2) 18: 4–5
    developmental disorders (2) 57: 4
    infants and preschool children (2) 57: 4–5
    intervention on side of ego (2) 57: 5
    motivation in (2) 57: 2
    range of therapies (2) 57: 4–6
    self-observation in (2) 57: 3–4
    theoretic assumptions (2) 18: 2–4

therapeutic situation (2) 57: 2–3
transference (2) 57: 3
vulnerability and risk (2) 18: 5–8
of compulsive personality disorder (1) 22: 5–6
of conversion disorder (1) 35: 7; (2) 100: 7
of dependent personality (1) 26: 1
of depersonalization (1) 39: 10
of depressive-masochistic personality (2) 82: 5
of depressive neurosis (1) 40: 8–11
and development (2) 18: 4–5, 8
of enuresis (2) 43: 3
of factitious illness (1) 35: 18–19
of gambling (1) 25: 3
of histrionic personality (2) 82: 4
of homosexuality (1) 45: 7
of hypochondriasis (1) 35: 12–13
hypotheses on (1) 6: 8–9
    developmental crisis (1) 6: 9
    object relational model (1) 6: 9
    personality style (1) 6: 9
    precipitating event (1) 6: 9
    self-psychology model (1) 6: 9
    structural model (1) 6: 9
of masochistic personality (1) 27: 1–2, 5–7
of menopause symptoms (2) 120: 7
mental status examination of (1) 6: 10–11
of multiple personality (1) 39: 9
of narcissistic personality (2) 82: 9
of passive-aggressive personality disorder (1) 26: 4–
    5
patient desire to gain insight in (1) 6: 3
of phobias (1) 33: 8–9
of psychogenic pain disorder (1) 35: 9–10
of pyromaniacs (1) 25: 5
of schizoid character (1) 24: 2–3
of schizophrenia, in children (2) 29: 5
of sexual disorders (1) 47: 8–9
of somatoform disorders (1) 35: 2
in stress-response systems (1) 41: 13
of stuttering (2) 43: 8–9
of substance abuse in adolescents (2) 35: 2
of suicide (1) 71: 2
of traumatic neurosis (2) 18: 7–8
sychoendocrinology (2) 9: 1. *See also* Neuroendocri-
        nology
sychogenic pain disorder (1) 35:
sycholinguistics, of language disorders (3) 67:
        3, 5
sychological assessment. *See* Psychological tests
sychological autopsy (3) 20: 1
sychological tests (1) **7: 1–10;** (3) **52: 1–25.** *See
        also* Behavioral assessment
of abstraction (3) 52: 8–10
    nonverbal tasks (3) 52: 9–10
    verbal tasks (3) 52: 8–9
of adaptive behavior
    in early childhood (2) 21: 6
    in infants (2) 21: 3

in middle childhood and adolescents (2) 21: 9–
    10
as adjunct in neuropsychiatric diagnosis (3) 52: 15–
    17
in adolescents (2) 21: 6–10
in anxiety (1) 7: 8
aphasia batteries (3) 52: 8
applications in biological psychiatry (3) 52: 15–21
    as adjunct in neuropsychiatric diagnosis (3) 52:
        15–17
    confirming treatment effects (3) 52: 21
    determination of deficits in conditions of interest
        (3) 52: 15
    elucidating natural history of cognitive change
        in disease (3) 52: 19–21
    mapping patterns of deficit (3) 52: 17–19
attention (3) 52: 4–5
in attention deficit disorder (2) 36: 7–8; (3) 66: 14–
    15
Benton-Iowa battery (3) 52: 15
in borderline personality disorder (1) 17: 11–12
Boston Process Approach (3) 52: 14
categorical versus dimensional systems of (1) 7: 3–
    4
in children (2) **21: 1–10**
    in early childhood (2) 21: 3–6
        adaptive behavior (2) 21: 6
        Children's Apperception Test (2) 21: 6
        cognitive assessment (2) 21: 3–6
        Kaufman assessment battery for children (2)
            21: 5
        Leiter test (2) 21: 5
        McCarthy scales of children's abilities (2) 21:
            5
        Peabody Picture Vocabulary test (2) 21: 5–6
        personality (2) 21: 6
        Rorschach Inkblot Test (2) 21: 6
        Stanford-Binet test (2) 21: 4
        Wechsler preschool and primary scale of intel-
            ligence (2) 21: 4–5
    in epidemiologic studies (2) 11: 6–8; (3) 12: 6–
        8
        Child Behavior Checklist (2) 11: 6–7
        child's version of Schedule for Affective Dis-
            orders (2) 11: 7
        Diagnostic Interview for Children and Adoles-
            cents (2) 11: 7–8
        Diagnostic Interview Schedule for Children (2)
            11: 8
    in infancy (2) 21: 2–3
        Bayley Scales of infant development (2) 21: 2
        Brazelton's neonatal assessment scale (2) 21:
            2
        Cattell infant intelligence scale (2) 21: 2–3
        Sequenced Inventory of Communication De-
            velopment (2) 21: 3
        Vineland Adaptive Behavior Scales (2) 21: 3
        Yale developmental schedules (2) 21: 3

Psychological tests, in children *(continued)*
  instrument issues in (2) 21: 1
  in middle childhood and adolescents (2) 21: 6–
      10
    academic achievement (2) 21: 10
    adaptive behavior (2) 21: 9–10
    cognitive assessment (2) 21: 6–7
    Halstead-Reitan Neuropsychological Battery
        (2) 21: 8
    Luria-Nebraska Neuropsychological Battery (2)
        21: 8–9
    neuropsychological assessment (2) 21: 7–9
    personality (2) 21: 10
    Thematic Apperception Test (2) 21: 10
    Wechsler Adult Intelligence Scales-Revised (2)
        21: 6–7
  variety of available instruments (2) 21: 1–2
  for classic-prototypic classification (1) 7: 4
  clinical analysis questionnaire (1) 15: 5–6
  computers in (1) 7: 5
  concepts in (1) 15: 3–5; (3) 52: 2
  in confirming treatment effects (3) 52: 21
  decline in usage (1) 7: 10
  definition (1) 7: 1
  in dependent personality disorder (1) 26: 4
  in depression (1) 7: 8
  in determination of deficits in conditions of inter-
      est (3) 52: 15
  in development evaluation (2) 20: 14
  in diagnosis of psychopathology (1) 7: 3
  dimensional scores (1) 7: 5–9
  in elucidating natural history of cognitive change
      in disease (3) 52: 19–21
  empirical versus theoretical design of (1) 15: 4–5
  in epidemiologic studies in child psychiatry (2) 11:
      6–8; (3) 12: 6–8
  in forensic evaluation (3) 27: 13–14
  in frontal lobe syndrome (2) 87: 12
  goals (1) 7: 2
  Halstead-Reitan Neuropsychological Battery (2) 21:
      8; (3) 52: 14
  historical background (1) 7: 2; 15: 1–3
  indications for (1) 7: 3
  in infancy (2) 21: 2–3
  intelligence (1) 7: 5–6; (2) 20: 14. *See also* Intelli-
      gence tests
  interpersonal and environmental (1) 7: 9
  of interpersonal behavior (1) 7: 9
  item characteristics in (3) 52: 2
  in language disorders (2) 49: 8; (3) 52: 6–8
    comprehension (3) 52: 7
    fluency (3) 52: 7–8
    naming (3) 52: 7
    reading (3) 52: 6
    repeating (3) 52: 8
    writing (3) 52: 6–7
  Luria-Nebraska Neuropsychological Battery (2) 21:
      8–9; (3) 52: 14–15

in mapping patterns of deficit (3) 52: 17–19
as marker
  in affective disorders (3) 53: 9
  in schizophrenia (3) 53: 14
of memory (3) 52: 12–14; 71: 10–14
methodologic considerations in (3) 52: 21–25
  age and education factors (3) 52: 21–22
  data reduction (3) 52: 23–25
  repeated measures and practice effects (3) 52:
      22–23
  selection of test (3) 52: 23
Millon clinical multiaxial inventory (1) 15: 7–8
Minnesota Multiphasic Personality Inventory (1) ?
    5; 15: 5
multidimensional instruments (1) 7: 5
in neurologic disorders (1) 7: 6–7
neuropsychological assessment (1) **72: 1–15;** (2)
    21: 7–9. *See also* Neuropsychological as-
    sessment
  diagnostic prescriptive approach (2) 21: 9
  functional approach (2) 21: 9
in organic brain syndromes (2) 87: 15
Peabody Picture Vocabulary test (2) 21: 5–6
for perception (2) 20: 14
of perceptual motor abilities (3) 52: 10–12
  auditory functions (3) 52: 10–11
  complex (3) 52: 11–12
  sensory functions (3) 52: 10
  visual functions (3) 52: 11
personality (1) 7: 8–9; (2) 20: 14
  in children (2) 23: 6
in personality disorders (1) **15: 1–12**
  clinical analysis questionnaire (1) 15: 5–6
  limitations (1) 15: 2
  Millon clinical multiaxial inventory (1) 15: 7–8
  MMPI (1) 15: 5
  personality research form (1) 15: 6–7
  projective tests (1) 15: 2
  rating scales (1) 15: 2–3
  self-report scales (1) 15: 3
  structural analysis of social behavior (1) 15: 7
personality research form (1) 15: 6–7
projective (1) 7: 7, 9; 15: 2
in psychiatric assessment (2) 20: 14, 15
rating scales (1) 15: 2–3. *See also* Rating scales
reaction time (3) 52: 3–4
reliability (1) 7: 1; 15: 3; (3) 52: 2
  alternate form (1) 7: 1
  split-half (1) 7: 1
  test-retest (1) 7: 1
Schedule for Affective Disorders and Schizophreni
    (SADS) (1) 7: 4
selection of (3) 52: 23
self-report (1) 7: 4; 15: 3. *See also* Self-report tests
standard battery (1) 7: 2
standardization (2) 21: 1; (3) 52: 2
Stanford-Binet test (2) 21: 4
of stress (1) 7: 9

Structural Analysis of Social Behavior (1) 15: 7
test-retest reliability (2) 21: 1
Thematic Apperception Test (2) 21: 10
in thought disorders (1) 7: 7–8
validity (1) 7: 1–2; 15: 3–4; (2) 21: 1; (3) 52: 2
   concurrent (1) 7: 2
   construct (1) 7: 2
   content (1) 7: 1–2
   criterion-related (1) 7: 2
   faking good or bad (1) 7: 5
   predictive (1) 7: 2
Wechsler Adult Intelligence Scales-Revised (2) 21:
   6–7
Wechsler preschool and primary scale of intelligence (2) 21: 4–5
sychometrics. *See* Psychological tests
sychomotor epilepsy (1) 28: 8. *See also* Epilepsy,
   temporal lobe
sychomotor retardation, in children with depression
   (2) 30: 3
sychopathic behavior. *See* Antisocial personality;
   Conduct disorders; Juvenile delinquency
sychopathology. *See also* Psychiatric disorders
  animal models for (3) **46: 1–18.** *See also* Animal
    models
  in anorexia nervosa (2) 102: 4
  in bulimia (2) 102: 5
  categories (2) 20: 2
  classification (1) 14: 4
  definition (1) 2: 9
  learning models for (1) 2: 1–25. *See also* Social
    learning
  as medical disorder (1) 6: 8
  uncertainties in (1) 2: 1
sychopharmacologic bridge strategy, in neurotransmitter study (3) 55: 2
sychopharmacology (3) **45: 1–13.** *See also* Drugs;
   Pharmacotherapy
  behavioral measures in (3) 45: 2, 11
  in children and adolescents (2) **59: 1–22**
   alcohol used with (2) 59: 20
   antianxiety agents (2) 59: 16–18
   anticonvulsants (2) 59: 18
   antidepressants (2) 59: 8, 10–11, 14–16
   antihistaminic-antimuscarinic sedatives (2) 59:
    18
   clonidine (2) 59: 18
   dosage regimens (2) 59: 19
   drug combinations (2) 59: 19–20
   ethical considerations (2) 59: 20–21
   ethical management of innovative therapy (2)
    59: 20–21
   future prospects (2) 59: 22
   interaction with other treatment modalities (2)
    59: 21–22
   lithium (2) 59: 8, 10–11, 16
   medical management with (2) 59: 18–20
   neuroleptics (2) 59: 7, 10–14

   propranolol (2) 59: 18
   stimulants (2) 59: 4–6, 8–12
  clinical contributions (2) 59: 1–4
   developmental pharmacokinetics (2) 59: 2–4
   developmental toxicology (2) 59: 1
  epidemiologic studies producing advances in (3)
    11: 7
  experimental approaches in (3) 45: 1–2
  factors influencing behavioral effects of drugs (3)
    45: 2–10
   constitutional and trait-state factors (3) 45: 5–8
    age differences (3) 45: 6–7
    cyclical variations (3) 45: 7
    genetically related (3) 45: 5
    individual differences (3) 45: 5–6
    physiologic abnormality (3) 45: 8
    sex differences (3) 45: 6
    state of health (3) 45: 7–8
    strains of species (3) 45: 5
   experimental factors (3) 45: 8–10
    manipulations (3) 45: 8
    placebo effect (3) 45: 8–9
    situational factors (3) 45: 9–10
    state dependency or conditioning studies in
     animals (3) 45: 9
   procedural factors (3) 45: 2–5
    chronicity (3) 45: 4
    dose-response analyses (3) 45: 3
    drug-drug interactions (3) 45: 4–5
    route of administration (3) 45: 4
    time-response analyses (3) 45: 3–4
    training variables (3) 45: 5
  goals of (3) 45: 1
  interpretation of drug-induced behavioral altera-
    tions (3) 45: 10–13
   assessing extent of behavioral change (3) 45: 11–
    13
   behavioral inventory (3) 45: 10–11
   selection of behavioral measures (3) 45: 11
   subject selection (3) 45: 13
  from molecular biological simplification to more
    realistic central nervous system dynamics
    (3) 72: 1–6
  need for change in research orientation (3) 72: 5–6
  receptors and (3) **50: 1–14**
   antidepressants (3) 50: 10–11
   benzodiazepines (3) 50: 9–10
   future directions (3) 50: 14
   interactions (3) 50: 11–13
   neuroleptics site of action (3) 50: 3–6
   and psychotomimetic actions of opiates (3) 50:
    13
   and subtypes (3) 50: 8–9
   and tardive dyskinesia (3) 50: 6–7
Psychophysiologic insomnia (3) 61: 5–6
Psychophysiologic mechanisms
  in migraine headache (2) 104: 6–8
  in pain (2) 104: 6–9

Psychoses (2) **95: 1–7.** *See also* Schizophrenia
  in Addison's disease (2) 88: 10
  in adolescents, epidemiology (3) 12: 18
  agoraphobia distinguished from (1) 33: 6
  amphetamine (1) 64: 4; (2) 90: 8–9
  atypical (1) **70: 1, 14–16**
    brief reactive psychosis distinguished from (1)
        70: 15
    case description (1) 70: 15–16
    clinical features (1) 70: 14
    differential diagnosis (1) 70: 15–16
    DSM-III definition (1) 70: 14
    treatment (1) 70: 14–15
  in avoidant personality (1) 24: 9–10
  in basal ganglia disorders (1) 69: 5–6
  in borderline personality disorder (1) 3: 6
  borderline personality disorder distinguished from
        (1) 17: 10–11
  in brain infections (1) 69: 4–5
  in brain injury (1) 69: 2–3
  in brain tumor (1) 69: 3–4
  brief reactive (1) 41: 7; **70: 11–14.** *See also under*
        reactive *below*
  in cerebrovascular disease (1) 69: 9
  in children
    classification (2) 29: 2–3
    schizophrenia distinguished from (2) 29: 2
  chronic. *See* Chronic mental patients
  classification (1) 69: 13–14
    in childhood (2) 29: 2–3
    problems in (1) 70: 1
  conversion disorder distinguished from (2) 47: 6
  corticosteroids causing (2) 88: 9
  cross-cultural definitions (3) 2: 3–4
  cultural relativism of (3) 2: 2–3
  in Cushing's syndrome (2) 88: 8–9
  cycloid (1) 70: 3–4
  in degenerative disorders (1) 69: 5–8
  in dementia (1) 69: 7
  in demyelinating diseases (1) 69: 8
  differential diagnosis
    for atypical psychosis (1) 70: 15–16
    for brief reactive psychoses (1) 70: 13
    for schizoaffective disorder (1) 70: 6–7
    for schizophreniform disorder (1) 70: 10
  drug abuse causing (2) 90: 8, 9
  drug reactions in (2) 95: 6–7
    akathisia (2) 95: 7
    dystonia (2) 95: 7
    neuroleptic malignant syndrome (2) 95: 7
  as emergency (2) 95: 1–7
  in epilepsy (1) 69: 2
  event-related potentials in (3) 62: 12–13
  in Friedreich's ataxia (1) 69: 7
  functional disorders (2) 95: 3
  hospitalization for (2) 95: 6
  in Huntington's disease (1) 28: 11–12; 69: 6
  in hyperthyroidism (2) 88: 7
  in hypochondriasis (2) 100: 4–5

  in interictal period of complex seizure disorder (2
        87: 14
  in metabolic and toxic disorders (1) 69: 9
  in motor neuron disease (1) 69: 7
  movement-related potentials in (3) 62: 4
  in multiple sclerosis (1) 69: 8
  in muscular disorders (1) 69: 7–8
  in myxedema (2) 88: 5–7
  in narcolepsy (1) 69: 8–9
  not elsewhere classified (1) **70: 1–16**
    atypical psychosis (1) **70: 14–16.** *See also under*
        atypical *above*
    brief reactive psychosis (1) **70: 11–14.** *See also
        under* reactive *below*
    schizoaffective disorder (1) **70: 1–8.** *See also*
        Schizoaffective disorder
    schizophreniform disorder (1) **70: 8–11.** *See als*
        Schizophreniform disorder
  organic. *See also under* symptomatic *below*
  organic mental disease distinguished from func-
        tional illness (2) 95: 1–3
  paranoid disorders (1) **68: 1–17.** *See also* Paranoi
        Paranoid disorders
  paranoid symptoms as most prominent feature (1
        68: 12–13. *See also* Paranoia; Paranoid
        disorders
  in Parkinson's disease (1) 28: 11; 69: 6
  in postpartum period (2) 120: 6
  prognosis (1) 68: 16–17
  psychological tests in (1) 7: 7–8
  reactive (1) 68: 12–13; **70: 11–14**
    atypical psychosis distinguished from (1) 70:
        15
    case description (1) 70: 13–14
    classification problems (1) 70: 1
    clinical features (1) 70: 12
    definition (1) 70: 1, 11–12
    diagnostic criteria (1) 70: 12
    differential diagnosis (1) 70: 13
    follow-up and family studies (1) 70: 12
    historical aspects (1) 70: 11–12
    predisposing conditions (1) 70: 12
    prognosis (1) 68: 17
    treatment (1) 70: 13
  schizoaffective disorder (1) **70: 1–8.** *See also*
        Schizoaffective disorder
  schizophrenia (1) **53: 1–19.** *See also* Schizophreni
  schizophrenia-like. *See under* symptomatic *below*
  schizophreniform (1) 68: 12. *See also* Schizophren
        form disorder
  skin picking in (2) 101: 3
  social phobia distinguished from (1) 33: 7
  steroid-induced (2) 88: 9
  stimulant-induced (1) 64: 4; (2) 90: 8–9
    animal models for (3) 46: 5–12. *See also* Stimu
        lants, psychosis induced by
  as stress response (1) 41: 7
  in Sydenham's chorea (1) 69: 5
  symptomatic (1) **69: 1–14**

in brain infections (1) 69: 4–5
in brain trauma (1) 69: 2–3
in brain tumor (1) 69: 3–4
in cerebrovascular disease (1) 69: 9
comparison with true schizophrenia (1) 69: 10–
    12
    clinical features (1) 69: 10–11
    genetic comparisons (1) 69: 11–12
    relationship between psychosis and brain dis-
        order (1) 69: 12
    treatment and prognosis (1) 69: 11
criteria for (1) 69: 1
in degenerative disorders (1) 69: 5–8
in demyelinating diseases (1) 69: 8
in epilepsy (1) 69: 2
implications for schizophrenia concept (1) 69:
    13–14
localization in brain (1) 69: 9–10
in metabolic and toxic disorders (1) 69: 9
in narcolepsy (1) 69: 8–9
pathogenesis (1) 69: 12–13
prevalence (1) 69: 13
symptoms related to brain lesion (1) 69:
    10
in toxic disorders (1) 69: 9
treatment (2) 95: 3–6
   in emergency (2) 95: 3–6
   hospitalization (2) 95: 6
   interview (2) 95: 3–5
   rapid tranquilization (2) 95: 5–6
in Wilson's disease (1) 69: 6–7
Psychosexual disorders (1) **46: 1–18.** *See also* Gender
    identity disorders; Paraphilias; Psychosex-
    ual dysfunction; Sexual disorders
classification (2) 41: 2
definition (2) 41: 1–2
DSM-III on (2) 41: 1–2
fetishism (2) 41: 4–6
gender identity disorders (1) **46: 10–18;** (2) 41: 4.
    See also Gender identity
historical background (2) 41: 1
paraphilias (1) **46: 2–10;** (2) 41: 4–7. *See also*
    Paraphilias
sexual masochism (2) 41: 6–7
sexual sadism (2) 41: 6–7
split between pediatrics and child psychiatry on
    (2) 41: 1–2
Psychosexual dysfunction (1) **47: 1–12.** *See also* Psy-
    chosexual disorders; Sexual disorders
analysis of psychological causes (1) 47: 8–9
behavioral analysis (1) 47: 8
couples' interaction in (1) 47: 9
definition (1) 47: 1
desire phase disorders (1) 47: 5
diagnostic techniques in (1) 47: 8
etiology and evaluation (1) 47: 7–9
excitement phase disorders (1) 47: 4–5. *See also*
    Impotence
frigidity (1) 47: 5

impaired sexual desire (1) 47: 5
   partner reaction to (1) 47: 5
   sexual phobia distinguished from (1) 47: 5
impotence (1) 47: 4. *See also* Impotence
inhibited female orgasm (1) 47: 2
inhibited male orgasm (1) 47: 2–4
inhibited sexual desire, definition (1) 47: 1
orgasm phase disorders (1) 47: 2–4
premature ejaculation (1) 47: 3–4
prognosis (1) 47: 12
psychiatric disorders causing (1) 47: 8
psychodynamics (1) 47: 8–9
response of patient and partner to (1) 47: 2, 3
retarded ejaculation (1) 47: 2–3
   partially (1) 47: 3
treatment (1) 47: 9–12. *See also* Sex therapy
   highly individualized nature (1) 47: 8
   results of (1) 47: 12
unconscious conflicts in (1) 47: 11–12
Psychosis. *See* Psychoses
Psychosocial adaptation (2) 58: 1, 2. *See also* Adapta-
    tion
Psychosocial deprivation
   failure to thrive due to (2) 40: 5–6
   mental retardation in (2) 58: 5
Psychosocial dwarfism (2) 40: 4
   clinical description (2) 40: 4
   differential diagnosis (2) 40: 4
   endocrine correlates (2) 9: 10
   etiology (2) 40: 4
   prognosis (2) 40: 4
   treatment (2) 40: 4
Psychosocial dysfunction, alcohol abuse associated
    with (3) 18: 15–16
Psychosocial factors
   in bulimia (2) 102: 6–7
   in child psychiatric disorders (3) 12: 22–23
Psychosocial skill training, for chronic mental pa-
    tients (3) 6: 8
Psychosocial stress (1) **63: 2–13.** *See also* Stress;
    Stressful life events
Psychosocial treatment (1) **9: 1–11.** *See also* Psycho-
    therapy; Social work
   choosing among formats (1) 9: 10–11
   choosing among orientations (1) 9: 6–7
   classification (1) 9: 1, 2
   cognitive-behavioral (1) 9: 3–4. *See also* Behavior
      therapy
   experiential (1) 9: 5–6
   formats for (1) 9: 7–11
   orientations (1) 9: 1–7
   psychodynamic (1) 9: 2–3. *See also* Psychoanalysis
   strategic-systems approach (1) 9: 4–5
Psychosomatic disorders (2) **100: 1–10.** *See also* Hy-
    pochondriasis; Psychosomatic medicine;
    Somatization; Somatoform disorders
   in agoraphobia (1) 33: 4–5
   anxiety disorders distinguished from (1) 32: 11
   biomedical hypothesis for (1) 6: 8

Psychosomatic disorders *(continued)*
  in children
    family dynamics (2) 110: 4
    with physical manifestations (2) **43: 1–9**
      encopresis (2) 43: 4–6
      enuresis (2) 43: 1–4
      night terrors (2) 43: 7–8
      sleepwalking (2) 43: 6–7
      stuttering (2) 43: 8–9
  cognitive development related to (2) 78: 5
  conversion disorder distinguished from (1) 35: 3–4
  definition (2) 76: 1–2
  in dependent personality disorder (1) 26: 2
  enmeshment in (2) 110: 4–5
  family therapy in (2) 110: 4–5
  grief reaction in (2) 78: 6–7
  historical aspects (2) 76: 3–4; 126: 2
  hypochondriac paranoia (1) 68: 9–10
  hypochondriasis (1) **35: 10–14.** *See also* Hypo-
    chondriasis
  in panic disorder (1) 32: 3
  psychoanalytic concepts (1) 35: 2; (2) 76: 3
  psychotherapy in (2) 108: 1
  spirals of (2) 110: 4–5
Psychosomatic medicine (2) **76: 1–7; 78: 1–9.** *See*
    also Behavioral medicine; Consultation-
    liaison psychiatry; Psychosomatic dis-
    orders
  abuse of terminology by physicians (2) 76: 2
  behavioral medicine differences from (2) 76: 5
  behavioral medicine overlap with (2) 76: 5–6
  behavior pattern associated with medical disorders
    (2) 78: 2–3
  biological markers in (2) 78: 2
  biopsychosocial model in (2) 78: 3–4
  circumstances and place of illness in specific situa-
    tion role (2) 78: 3–4
  consequential theory of (2) 78: 7–8
  consultation-liaison psychiatry differences from (2)
    76: 5
  consultation-liaison psychiatry overlap with (2)
    76: 5–6
  debate over source of training in (2) 76: 6
  definition (2) 76: 1–2; 78: 1
  historical background (2) 76: 3–4; 78: 1–3
  implementation (2) 78: 7
  intellectual tradition in (2) 76: 5–6
  neurobiological models (2) 78: 1–2
  role in medical center (2) 78: 8–9
  somatopsychic emphases in (2) 78: 6
  specialized hospital units for (2) 78: 8–9
  stress role (2) 78: 4–5. *See also* Stress; Stressful life
    events
  teaching in (2) 78: 8, 9
  two-person conflict theory in (2) 78: 3–4, 7
Psychostimulants. *See* Stimulants
Psychosurgery (2) 160: 4–5
  for antisocial personality (1) 23: 9
  neurosurgery distinguished from (2) 160: 4

  in obsessive-compulsive disorder (1) 34: 9–10
  in schizophrenia (1) 55: 2
  in temporal lobe epilepsy (2) 160: 4–5
Psychotherapist. *See also* Psychiatrist
  abstinence of (1) 8: 4
  anonymity of (1) 8: 4
  attitude and responsibilities in psychoanalysis (1)
    8: 3–5
  interpretation by (1) 8: 4–5
  neutrality in psychoanalysis (1) 8: 4
  position in psychoanalysis (1) 8: 8
  speech and silence in psychoanalysis (1) 8: 8
Psychotherapist-patient relationship, in group therapy
    (2) 63: 4–5. *See also* Physician-patient re-
    lationship
Psychotherapy (2) 56: 2
  abreaction (2) 108: 2
  in adjustment disorders (2) 51: 6
  advances in (1) 11: 1
  in agoraphobia with panic attacks (1) 33: 11–12
  alleviating guilt (2) 108: 9
  in amnesia (1) 39: 6
  in anorexia nervosa (2) 40: 8; 102: 8
  of antisocial personality (1) 23: 7
  in anxiety disorders (1) 32: 12; (2) 39: 7–8
  approaches in medical illness (2) **108: 1–12.** *See*
    also under in medically ill *below*
  in attention deficit disorder (3) 66: 21–22
  of avoidant personality (1) 24: 10–11
  in borderline personality disorders (1) 17: 12–13
    in children (2) 42: 5–6
  brief
    in depressive neurosis (1) 40: 12
    in stress-response syndromes (1) 41: 15
  in Briquet's syndrome (1) 35: 16
  in bulimia (2) 102: 9
  in child psychiatry (2) **57: 1–6**
    in inpatient programs (2) 64: 17
  choice of technique
    among formats (1) 9: 10–11
    intelligence tests in (1) 7: 6
    among orientations (1) 9: 6–7
    psychoanalysis (1) 8: 10–12
  clarification (2) 108: 2
  classification (1) 9: 1, 2; 11: 12
  client-centered (1) 9: 6
  cognitive and experiential learning opportunities
    (1) 11: 10
  cognitive-behavioral (1) 9: 3–4. *See also* Behavior
    therapy
  combination of psychoanalysis with other therapy
    (1) 8: 12
  of compulsive personality disorder (1) 22: 7
  conflicts between researchers and practitioners (1)
    11: 1–2
  confrontation (2) 108: 8–9
  connecting affect with underlying content (2) 108:
    9
  of conversion disorder (1) 35: 7–8

cost-effectiveness (1) 11: 6−7
  for medical care related to (2) 79: 6−8
credibility of (1) 11: 1
in dependent personality disorder (1) 26: 4
in depersonalization disorder (1) 39: 11
in depression
  in children and adolescents (2) 30: 7−8
  in medically ill (2) 99: 5
effectiveness (1) 11: 2−4
  specific method for particular types of problems
    (1) 9: 1
of enuresis (2) 43: 4
experiential (1) 9: 5−6
family format (1) 9: 7−8. See also Family therapy
focal therapy (1) 9: 2−3. See also Focal therapy
formats for (1) 9: 7−11
forms most effective for various patients (1) 11: 4−
    5
in fugue (1) 39: 7
of gamblers (1) 25: 3
goals, in medically ill (2) 108: 3−4
group (1) 9: 8−10; (2) **63: 1−7.** See also Group
    therapy
in histrionic personality disorder (1) 19: 9−10
of hypochondriasis (1) 35: 13−14
in hysterical personality disorder (1) 19: 9
individual format (1) 9:
informed consent in (3) 30: 14
interpretation (2) 108: 2
without knowledge of etiology of psychiatric dis-
    order (1) 51: 6
in language disorders of childhood (2) 49: 9
long-term effect of (1) 11: 8
long-term exploratory (1) 9: 2, 3. See also Long-
    term exploratory therapy
malpractice related to (3) 29: 12−13
manipulation (2) 108: 2
marital format (1) 9: 7−8. See also Marital therapy
in masochistic personality (1) 27: 8−9
medical facilities use related to (1) 11: 7
in medically ill (2) **108: 1−12**
  alleviating guilt (2) 108: 9
  confrontation (2) 108: 8−9
    with unexpressed affect (2) 108: 8−9
  connecting affect with underlying content (2)
    108: 9
  drug addict (2) 108: 10−11
  eliciting fears and personal meanings (2) 108:
    4
  engagement of nonmotivated patient (2) 108:
    11−12
  goals (2) 108: 3−4
  modalities used in (2) 108: 2
  psychodynamic life narrative (2) 108: 4−7
  psychodynamic perspective on supportive inter-
    ventions (2) 108: 7−8
  special problems in (2) 108: 9−12
  support of self-esteem in narcissistic character
    (2) 108: 10

suspicious and distrustful patient (2) 108: 10−11
  therapeutic stance in (2) 108: 11−12
  transference in (2) 108: 2
in mental retardation (2) 58: 5−6
modalities of (2) 108: 2
in multiple personality (1) 39: 9
mutual storytelling (2) 39: 8
in narcissistic personality disorder (1) 18: 10−11
nonspecific effects in (1) 11: 9−11
nontraditional, definition (2) 56: 2
in obesity (2) 103: 12
in obsessive-compulsive disorder (1) 34: 8−9
in organic brain syndromes (2) 87: 17
orientations in (1) 9: 1−7
outcome research on (1) **11: 1−15**
  box score method (1) 11: 3
  clarifying goals in (1) 11: 14
  and conflicts with practitioners (1) 11: 1−2
  cost-effectiveness (1) 11: 6−7
  difficulty in comparing behavioral and verbal
    therapies (1) 11: 4
  durability of treatment effects (1) 11: 8
  effectiveness of therapy (1) 11: 2−4
  forms of psychotherapy most effective for vari-
    ous patients (1) 11: 4−5
  future prospects (1) 11: 14−15
  inadequate evidence to support sweeping gener-
    alizations (1) 11: 11−13
  length of treatment (1) 11: 7
  limited generalization of efficacy findings (1) 11:
    13−14
  limited scale of (1) 11: 14
  meta-analysis (1) 11: 3−4
  nonspecific effects (1) 11: 9−11
  placebo effect (1) 11: 8−9
  positive effects as artifacts (1) 11: 8−11
  premature notion of (1) 11: 11−12
  representativeness of psychotherapy practice (1)
    11: 12−13
  safety (1) 11: 5−6
  special problems in (1) 11: 13−14
  standardizing interventions in (1) 11: 14
  technical considerations (1) 11: 11−12
  therapist experience related to outcome (1) 11:
    7−8
in panic disorder (1) 32: 12
in paranoid disorders (1) 68: 15−16
in paranoid personality disorder (1) 16: 10
in passive-aggressive personality disorder (1) 26:
    6
of phobias (1) 33: 10−11
placebo effect (1) 11: 8−9
promotion of development of self-esteem in (1)
    11: 10
psychoanalysis (1) **8: 1−12.** See also Psychoanalysis
psychodynamic (1) 9: 2−3. See also Psychoanalysis
  definition (2) 56: 2
psychodynamic life narrative (2) 108: 4−7
of psychogenic pain disorder (1) 35: 10

Psychotherapy *(continued)*
  psychosocial (1) **9: 1–11.** *See also* Psychosocial
      treatment
  in psychosomatic disorders (2) 108: 1
  of pyromaniacs (1) 25: 5
  Rashomon effect in (1) 11: 12
  reality-testing strategies in (1) 11: 10
  research on. *See under* outcome research on *above*
  safety of (1) 11: 5–6
  of schizotypal personality disorder (1) 16: 8
  sex therapy distinguished from (1) 47: 9
  in sexual disorders (1) 47: 9–12
  of sexually dangerous offender (3) 28: 22–23
  short-term, in cancer pain (2) 104: 4
  in somatoform disorders (2) 100: 10
  strategic-systems approach (1) 9: 4–5. *See also*
      Strategic therapy model
  in stress response systems (1) 41: 15
  suggestion (2) 108: 2
  supportive
    in borderline personality disorders (1) 17: 13
    definition (2) 56: 2
    in medically ill (2) 99: 5; 108: 8–9
    psychodynamic perspective on (2) 108: 7–8
  therapeutic stance (2) 108: 11–12
  in Tourette's disorder (2) 38: 6–7
  transference in (2) 108: 2, 7
  variety of theories and methods for (1) 11: 2
Psychoticism (1) 2: 19
Psychotic proneness (1) 7: 7
Psychotropic drugs, adverse reactions (2) 95: 6–7.
              See also Drugs; Pharmacotherapy; Psycho-
              pharmacology
Puberty
  basal metabolic rate in (2) 9: 5
  blindness effect on (2) 9: 5
  definition (2) 4: 5
  neurotransmitter interactions influence on (2) 12:
      10–11
  onset of (2) 9: 4–5
  secular trends in (2) 9: 5
Public health programs, health promotion (2) **129: 1–
      6.** *See also* Health promotion
Public policy. *See also* Government; Politics
  critical issues for research in mental health (3) 4: 4–
      6
  financing mental health care (3) 3: 10; 4: 13–14
  on hospital and residential treatment of children
      (2) 64: 5–6
  in mental retardation treatment (2) 58: 1
  priorities in research (3) 4: 4–5
  psychiatrist role in (3) 4: 16
  in research (3) 4: 5
  utilization of mental health services related to (3)
      22: 8–9
Pulmonary edema, in narcotic overdose (2) 90: 7
Punitive methods, negative impact on social learning
      (1) 2: 4

Pupillography, after stimulant therapy in attention
      deficit disorder (3) 66: 16
Pyromania (1) 25: 4–5
  in adolescents (1) 25: 5
  DSM-III definition (1) 25: 4
  other forms of arson distinguished from (1) 25: 4–
      5
  psychodynamics (1) 25: 5
  sexual tension in (1) 25: 5
  treatment (1) 25: 5

Quality assurance, confidentiality issues in (3) 31: 5
Questionnaires. *See also* Rating scales
  in child psychiatric epidemiology (3) 12: 6–8
  clinical analysis questionnaire (1) 15: 5–6
  Diagnostic Interview Scale (1) 15: 2–3
  in epidemiologic studies in child psychiatry (2) 12:
      6–7
  interview instruments (2) 20: 13, 15
  MMPI (1) 15: 5
  in psychiatric assessment (2) 20: 13, 15
  rating scales (2) **23: 3–7.** *See also* Rating scales
  self-report. *See* Self-report tests
  Structural Analysis of Social Behavior (1) 15: 7
Quinacrine, psychiatric side effects (2) 91: 6–7

Race
  alcohol abuse related to (3) 18: 9
  antisocial personality related to (3) 19: 4–5
  as bipolar disorder risk factor (1) 60: 10; (3) 13:
      11
  as depression risk factor, nonbipolar disorder (1)
      60: 6; (3) 13: 7
  as schizophrenia risk factor (1) 54: 13; (3) 15: 8
  suicide rates by (3) 20: 4–6
Radioligand binding (3) 50: 1–3. *See also* Receptors
Rape
  emergency management (2) 95: 13–14
  offenders (3) 28: 22–23
  as paraphilia (1) 46: 9
Rapid eye movement sleep. *See* REM sleep
Rapid tranquilization (2) 95: 5–6
Rashomon effect (1) 11: 12
Rating scales (1) 15: 2–3; (2) **23: 3–7.** *See also*
              Questionnaires
  advantages and limitations (2) 23: 4
  in attention deficit disorder (3) 66: 14–15
  in children (2) 20: 13, 15
  in depression in childhood (2) 20: 13
  in diagnosis of childhood psychiatric disorders (2)
      19: 5
  interview instruments (2) 20: 13
  observer scales (2) 23: 6–7
  parent scales (2) 23: 4–6

for behavior problems (2) 23: 5
for competencies (2) 23: 5
personality inventory for children (2) 23: 6
psychopathology (2) 20: 13
self-ratings (2) 23: 7
for specific syndromes (2) 20: 13
teacher scales (2) 23: 6
ational-emotive therapy (1) 9: 4
aynaud's disease, biofeedback control of skin temperature in (2) 109: 7
eaction formation, in dependent personality disorder (1) 26: 3
eaction time
and brain function (3) 52: 3
determination (3) 52: 3–4
in schizophrenia (3) 65: 4
eactive attachment disorder (3) 12: 12–13
eactive disorders (2) 51: 1. *See also* Adjustment disorders
eadiness potential (3) 62: 3–4
eading. *See also* Dyslexia
alexia distinguished from dyslexia (3) 52: 6
conduct disorder associated with retardation in (3) 12: 15
epidemiology of disorders (3) 12: 15
evaluation in mental status examination (2) 20: 7, 8
eality-testing, in psychotherapy (1) 11: 10
ebelliousness, in adolescents (2) 4: 10–11
eceptive aphasia (2) 49: 5–6
eceptors (3) **50: 1–14**
acetylcholine
and neuroleptic side effects (1) 55: 25
neuroleptics interaction with (1) 55: 19
alpha-adrenergic
and neuroleptic side effects (1) 55: 25
neuroleptics interaction with (1) 55: 20
altered function in affective disorders (1) 64: 9–10
antidepressants effect on (1) 64: 9–10
and mechanisms of action (3) 50: 10–11
benzodiazepine (1) 32: 8–9
subtypes (3) 50: 9–10
blockade causing interaction of neuroleptics with other drugs (1) 55: 26
dopamine (1) 64: 5. *See also* Dopamine, receptors for
in assay of neuroleptics (1) 55: 9–10
neuroleptic efficacy related to affinity for (3) 50: 3–6
neuroleptics interaction with (1) 55: 16–18
subtypes (3) 50: 9
supersensitivity and tardive dyskinesia (3) 50: 6–7
up-regulation (3) 50: 6
down-regulation hypothesis for affective disorders (3) 55: 3, 6
and drug actions (3) **50: 1–14**
in electroconvulsive therapy (3) 68: 4

future directions in studying role in psychiatry (3) 50: 14
histamine
and neuroleptic side effects (1) 55: 25
neuroleptics interaction with (1) 55: 19–20
lithium and carbamazepine stabilization effect on (1) 64: 10
on lymphocytes (2) 128: 11
muscarinic cholinergic, as marker in affective disorders (3) 53: 8
neuroleptics interaction with (1) 55: 16–20
side effects due to (1) 55: 20–25
of neurotransmitters, circadian rhythms of (3) 59: 3
for norepinephrine (3) 50: 11
opiate
psychotomimetic actions of opiates related to (3) 50: 13
subtypes (3) 50: 13
radioligand binding assay (3) 50: 1–3
selection for research (2) 12: 4–5
side effects of drugs related to (3) 50: 11–14
blockage by multitransmitter interactions (3) 50: 13–14
multitransmitter interactions (3) 50: 11–12
psychotomimetic actions of opiates (3) 50: 13
tricyclic antidepressants
muscarinic-cholinergic interactions (3) 50: 12
noradrenergic alpha-receptor interactions (3) 50: 12–13
subtyping related to drug responses (3) 50: 8–9
supersensitivity
lithium effect on (3) 50: 7
and tardive dyskinesia (3) 50: 6–7
Reciprocal inhibition (1) 2: 12; (2) 77: 3–4
Reciprocal reinforcement (1) 2: 7
Reconstruction, Freud's concept (1) 1: 4
Records
case formulation in (1) 6: 12
chief complaint in (1) 6: 12
in child psychiatric epidemiology (3) 12: 11
confidentiality of (3) 31: 5
consultation notes (2) 115: 4–5
mental status examination in (1) 6: 12
negotiated treatment plan in (1) 6: 13
patient access to (3) 31: 11–13
patient's perspective in (1) 6: 12
Recreational therapy (2) 56: 3
Red blood cells
lithium ion ratio related to bipolar disorder (1) 62: 18
Xg locus related to bipolar disorder (1) 62: 17
Redefinition, in family therapy (2) 62: 8–9
Reflex, conditioned (1) 2: 10–11
Regression (2) 82: 1
in amnesia (1) 39: 5
in medical setting (2) 82: 1
in psychoanalytic theory (1) 1: 7

Regurgitation, in infants (2) 40:
Rehabilitation, biofeedback and relaxation therapy in
    (2) 109: 7–9
Rehearsal, and modeling in behavior therapy (2) 77:
    8–9
Reich, W., on compulsive personality disorder (1)
    22: 3
Reimbursement
    prospective (3) 4: 14
    restrictions for mental health care (3) 4: 13–14
Reinforced practice (1) 33: 10–11
Reinforcement (2) 13: 2
    expectancy as (1) 2: 16
    locus of control of (1) 2: 16
    self (1) 2: 16–17
    of social learning (1) 2: 7–8
Rejection
    influence on child (1) 2: 4
    parental, avoidant personality due to (1) 24: 6–7
Relationship therapy, definition (2) 56: 2
Relativity of form (3) 2: 3
Relativity of process (3) 2: 3
Relaxation therapy (2) **109: 1–11.** *See also* Biofeed-
        back
    in asthma (2) 109: 9–10
    audiotapes used in (2) 109: 2
    basic elements in (2) 109: 2
    basic methods (2) 109: 2–3
    in cancer (2) 109: 10–11
    clinical applications (2) 109: 5–11
    cognitive mediation in (2) 77: 9–10
    in diabetes management (2) 109: 10
    EEG feedback in (2) 109: 5
        in panic and anxiety disorders (1) 32: 12
    in gastrointestinal disorders (2) 109: 9
    in headache (2) 109: 5–6
    historical aspects (2) 109: 1
    in hypertension (2) 109: 6–7
    hypnosis. *See* Hypnosis
    in insomnia (2) 109: 10; (3) 61: 5–6
    in irritable bowel syndrome (2) 109: 9
    meditation (2) 109: 2–3
    in migraine headache (2) 104: 7–8
    negative side-effects (2) 109: 11
    in neuromuscular rehabilitation (2) 109: 7–9
    in pain disorders (2) 109: 8–9
    in peptic ulcer disease (2) 109: 9
    in phobia (2) 109: 1
    practice requirement in (2) 109: 2
    progressive muscle relaxation training (2) 109: 1–
        2
    rationale for (2) 77: 9
    in Raynaud's disease (2) 109: 7
    in single session (2) 109: 2
    systematic desensitization (2) 109: 1–2
    in temporomandibular joint syndrome (2) 109: 8–
        9
    types (2) 77: 9
    at worksite (2) 129: 3–4

yoga (2) 109: 3
Relaxation training (2) 77: 9–10. *See also* Relaxation
        therapy
Reliability
    of DSM-III classification system (2) 19: 10
    of psychological tests (1) 7: 1; 15: 3; (3) 52: 2
Religion
    as bipolar disorder risk factor (3) 13: 11
    suicide rates by (3) 20: 6–7
REM sleep (3) 60: 2. *See also* Dreaming
    in animals (3) 60: 8
    cholinergic neurons role in (3) 60: 7–8, 11–12
    in depression (3) 53: 5
        cholinergic stimulation test (3) 53: 7
    deprivation effects (3) 60: 12–13
        and propensity for REM sleep (3) 60: 8–9
    developmental considerations (2) 52: 1–2
    and dreaming (3) 60: 11–12
    hormonal changes in (3) 60: 5
    latency (3) 60: 2
        in affective disorders (3) 55: 4
        in borderline personality disorder (1) 17: 11
        circadian rhythm related to (3) 59: 5
    locus ceruleus neuron silence in (3) 44: 5
    in narcolepsy (2) 52: 8; 105: 13; (3) 61: 12
    neurochemistry of (3) 60: 7–8
    psychological and physiological characteristics of
        (3) 60: 3–4
    respiratory function in (3) 60: 4
    rhythmicity of (3) 59: 6–7
    at sleep onset in narcolepsy (2) 105: 13
    temperature control in (3) 60: 4
Renal disease. *See* Kidney
Repetition
    as reinforcer of social learning (1) 2: 7
    test for (3) 52: 8
Reportable situations (3) 31: 13–16
    child abuse (3) 31: 15–16
    drug abuse (3) 31: 15
    safeguarding the patient or a third party (3) 31: 1
        15
Repression
    Freud's concept (1) 1: 5; 39: 1
    as solution learning (1) 2: 14–15
Research
    animal models (3) **46: 1–18.** *See also* Animal mod
        els
    in anxiety disorders (3) 14: 11
    in attention and information processing (3) 65: 3
        8
    in child psychiatry (2) 1: 1
        epidemiologic studies (2) 11: 9–14
    in cognitive function (3) 65: 3–8
    conduct of (3) 4: 5
    confidentiality issues in (3) 31: 11
    consultation-liaison psychiatry role in (2) 117: 8
    crossover design in (3) 45: 8–9
    dissemination and assessment of (3) 4: 5–6
    in electroconvulsive therapy (3) 68: 1–2

in epidemiology (2) **11: 1–9**
  assessment instruments (2) 11: 6–8
  in child psychiatry (2) 11: 9–14
  choosing sample (2) 11: 3–4
  defining case in (2) 11: 4
  one versus two stage assessment procedure (2)
    11: 4–6
  selecting informants for assessment of child's
    behavior (2) 11: 8–9
  selection of strategy (2) 11: 2
on event-related potentials (3) 62: 12–13
genetic studies (2) **10: 1–9.** *See also* Genetics,
government role (3) 4: 3–6
  state role (3) 4: 4
historical background in mental health (3) 4: 3–6
informed consent for human experimentation in
    (3) 30: 11–12
on language disorders (3) 67: 3–10
  on hemispheric specialization (3) 67: 10–13
  neuropsychologic approach (3) 67: 6–13
  psycholinguistic approach (3) 67: 3, 5
on learning disabilities (2) 48: 4–5
in mental retardation (2) 28: 2
from molecular biological simplification to more
    realistic central nervous system dynamics
    (3) 72: 1–6
National Institute of Mental Health role (3) 4: 3–6
need for change in neuropsychiatry (3) 72: 5–6
in neurochemistry
  in affective disorders (3) **55: 1–8**
  brain function assessment (2) 12: 1–5
  clinical considerations (2) 12: 5–9
    additional clinical sources of variance (2) 12:
      8
    cerebrospinal fluid samples (2) 12: 9
    diagnostic group mean values (2) 12: 5
    medication effects (2) 12: 8–9
    neurochemical and behavior measures (2) 12:
      9
    neuroendocrine and neurochemical challenge
      tests (2) 12: 6–8
    relationships among measures (2) 12: 8
    sample collection and effects of stress on chil-
      dren (2) 12: 5–6
    stability of variables over time (2) 12: 6
  developmental considerations (2) 12: 9–11
  laboratory considerations (2) 12: 12
  methodologic considerations (2) 12: 1, 5–12
neurotransmitter strategies (3) 43: 1–2
in pain disorders (2) 104: 11–12
placebo effect (3) 45: 8–9
priorities in (3) 4: 4–5
on psychoanalysis (1) 1: 14–15
in psychopharmacology (3) **45: 1–13**
in psychosocial problems of biological illness (2)
    117: 8
social (3) 4: 4
social reactions to sexuality findings (1) 45: 7–8
strategies for study in psychiatry

support of (3) 4: 5
on therapeutic outcome (2) 63: 6–7
training in (3) 4: 4
Reserpine
  catecholamine depletion by (3) 55: 2
  depression due to (2) 91: 5; (3) 55: 3–4
  in schizophrenia
    dosage (1) 55: 13
    preparations (1) 55: 13
  structure (1) 55: 4
Residential treatment
  in child psychiatry (2) **64: 1–19**
    in assessment process (2) 64: 11–12
    behavior therapy in (2) 64: 14
    clinical administration in (2) 64: 8–11, 15
    design of activities program in (2) 64: 13
    design of daily schedule in (2) 64: 13
    design of living unit in (2) 64: 13
    dismantling apparatus of illness during treatment
      in (2) 64: 12
    education in (2) 64: 16
    evaluation and follow-up (2) 64: 18
    exploitation of live events in (2) 64: 13–14
    family treatment in (2) 64: 16–17
    future needs in (2) 64: 18–19
    group therapy in (2) 64: 15
    historical background (2) 64: 1–3
    individual therapy in (2) 64: 17
    isolation versus community orientation (2) 64:
      14–15
    long-term placement (2) 64: 17
    milieu therapy (2) 64: 12–15
    outcome (2) 64: 17–18
    pharamacotherapy (2) 64: 15–16
    planning in (2) 64: 6–8
    public policy on (2) 64: 5–6
      certificate of need determination for (2) 64: 5
      rate setting in (2) 64: 5–6
    regressive or progressive emphasis in (2) 64: 14
    seclusion and restraint in (2) 64: 15
    security considerations (2) 64: 13
    termination (2) 64: 12
    treatment components in (2) 64: 12–18
  comparison with hospital and group home (2) 64:
    2, 3
  spectrum of services for children (2) 64: 4
  types (2) 64: 1
Resistance, Freud's concept (1) 1: 3
Respiration
  in REM sleep (3) 60: 4
  in sleep apnea (3) 61: 8–10
Restless legs syndrome (2) 105: 7–8; (3) 61: 11
Restraints
  alliance-based application (3) 36: 13
  for children (2) 64: 15
  procedure for (2) 95: 9
  for violent patient (2) 95: 9
Restriction fragment length polymorphisms (2) 10: 3–
    4

Reticular activating system
  in arousal (3) 66: 6
  in delirium (1) 73: 16
  neuroleptics action on (1) 55: 14
Retrospective studies (2) 11: 2
Reye's syndrome
  attention deficit disorder linked to (2) 36: 3
  organic mental disorders in (2) 34: 5
Rheumatoid arthritis, biofeedback in (2) 109: 7
Rhythm Test (3) 52: 4–5
Right hemisphere syndromes (1) 28: 9–10
Risk factors. *See also* Epidemiology
  of anxiety disorders (3) 14: 4–5, 10–11
  for bipolar disorder (1) 60: 10–11; (3) 13: 10–
      12
  consequences of disorders distinguished from (3)
      13: 12–13
  in coronary heart disease (2) 126: 1–2
    psychological (2) 126: 2–5
  definition (1) 60: 2; (3) 11: 1
  for depression (1) 40: 2; (3) 55: 8
    nonbipolar disorder (1) 60: 5–7; (3) 13: 5–8
  for drug abuse, change over time (3) 17: 2
  parameters related to variations in estimate in epi-
      demiologic studies (1) 60: 1
  and prevention (3) 13: 13
  relative risk (3) 13: 12
  for schizophrenia (1) 54: 5–14; (3) 15: 6–12
    age (1) 54: 13; (3) 15: 8
    family environment (1) 54: 8–9; (3) 15: 8–9
    genetic (1) 54: 6–8; 62: 4–12; (3) 15: 7–8
    perinatal (1) 54: 13–14; (3) 15: 7–8
    race (1) 54: 13; (3) 15: 8
    sex (1) 54: 13; (3) 15: 8
    social causation versus social selection (1) 54: 9–
        10; (3) 15: 10–11
    social class (3) 15: 10–11
    society complexity (1) 54: 11–13; (3) 15: 11–
        12
    stressful life events (1) 54: 10–11; (3) 15: 9–
        10
  for suicide (1) 59: 11; (2) 95: 11; (3) 32: 14
  for surgery patient (2) 121: 3–5
  for violent behavior (3) 32: 14
Ritalin. *See* Methylphenidate
Ritualistic behavior, in children (1) 34: 8. *See also*
      Obsessive-compulsive disorder
Rogers Criminal Responsibility Assessment Scales (3)
      27: 13–14
Rorschach Inkblot Test (1) 7: 7; (2) 21: 6
  limitations in personality disorders (1) 15: 2
Rotter, J.B., contribution to social learning theory
      (1) 2: 15–16
Rubella syndrome, organic mental disorders after (2)
      34: 4
Rumination (2) 40: 4–5
  clinical description (2) 40: 4–5
  treatment (2) 40: 5

Sadism, sexual (1) 46: 5–6
  development in children (2) 41: 6–7
SADS (1) 7: 4
Safety, of psychotherapy (1) 11: 5–6
Salivary glands, in neurochemistry studies on chil-
      dren (2) 12: 2–3
Saltatory conduction (3) 42: 6
Salzman, L., on compulsive personality disorder (1)
      22: 3
Sampling, in epidemiologic studies (2) 11: 3–4
  geographic (2) 11: 3
  school (2) 11: 3
  select groups (2) 11: 3–4
Schedule for Affective Disorders, child's version in
      epidemiologic studies (2) 11: 7
Schedule for Affective Disorders and Schizophrenia
      (SADS) (1) 7: 4
Schilder's disease, psychosis in (1) 69: 8
Schizoaffective disorder (1) 53: 18 19; **70: 1–8**
  biological and psychosocial aspects (1) 70: 5–
      6
  case description (1) 70: 8
  classification (1) 70: 2–4
    genetic considerations (1) 62: 19–20
    problems in (1) 70: 1
  clinical features (1) 70: 4–5
  definition (1) 70: 1–2
  diagnosis (1) 70: 6–7
    criteria for (1) 70: 4, 5
  different concepts of (1) 70: 2–4
  differential diagnosis (1) 70: 6–7
  as distinct category (1) 70: 3–4
  DSM-III on (1) 59: 5
  as form of affective disorder (1) 70: 3
  as form of schizophrenia (1) 70: 2–3
  future research in (1) 70: 7–8
  genetics (1) 62: 19–20
  historical aspects (1) 70: 1–2
  schizophrenia distinguished from (1) 70: 6
  treatment (1) 70: 7
    antidepressants (1) 70: 7
    antipsychotics (1) 70: 7
    electroconvulsive therapy (1) 70: 7
    lithium (1) 70: 7
Schizoid character
  avoidant personality (1) **24: 1–11.** *See also*
      Avoidant personality
  constitutional theories on (1) 24: 1–2
  psychoanalytic conceptions (1) 24: 2
  schizoid personality (1) 24: 1–2, 7–8. *See also*
      Schizoid personality disorder
  schizotypal personality (1) 24: 8. *See also*
      Schizotypal personality disorder
Schizoid personality
  avoidant personality distinguished from (1) 24: 2
      7–8
  historical background (1) 24: 1–2
Schizoid personality disorder (1) **16: 1–4**

avoidant disorder distinguished from (2) 39: 6
clinical description (1) 16: 2–3
definition (1) 16: 1–2
dependent personality disorder distinguished from (1) 26: 4
depressive neurosis distingished from (1) 40: 7
diagnosis (1) 16: 3
differential diagnosis (1) 16: 3
epidemiology (1) 16: 2
etiology (1) 16: 3
historical aspects (1) 16: 1
narcissistic personality disorder distinguished from (1) 18: 9
as premorbid personality in schizophrenia (1) 16: 2–3
schizotypal personality disorder distinguished from (1) 16: 7
treatment (1) 16: 3–4
chizophrenia (1) **53: 1–19.** See also Psychoses
acute illness (1) 53: 7–13
   affective changes in (1) 53: 9
   delusions in (1) 53: 8
   hallucinations in (1) 53: 8–9
   mode of onset (1) 53: 7–8
   passivity phenomena in (1) 53: 8
   residual defect after (1) 53: 13, 16
   thought disorder in (1) 53: 9–11
in adolescents, epidemiology (3) 12: 18
adoption studies on (1) 62: 8–10
adversity role in (1) 63: 9–10
affective psychoses distinguished from (1) 53: 18–19
affective symptoms in (1) 53: 9; 70: 2. See also Schizoaffective disorder
age as risk factor in (1) 54: 13; (3) 15: 8
age of onset (1) 53: 7
anorexia nervosa distinguished from (2) 40: 7
antibodies in (2) 128: 13–14
antisocial personality related to (3) 19: 6–7
atypical (1) 70: 3. See also Schizoaffective disorder
autism distinguished from (2) 29: 2
   EEG features (2) 29: 5
   epidemiologic features (2) 29: 3
as autoimmune disorder (2) 128: 13–14
in avoidant personality (1) 24: 9–10
benzodiazepine effects in (3) 61: 15
beta-adrenergic blockers causing improved cognition in (3) 72: 2–3
biologically oriented social learning theory of (1) 2: 20–21
biological markers in (1) 62: 11–12
in blacks (3) 15: 8
Bleuler's concept (1) 53: 1–2
borderline (1) 17: 6–7. See also Borderline; Borderline personality disorder; Schizotypal personality disorder
borderline personality disorder distinguished from (1) 17: 10–11
boundaries of (1) 53: 18–19

in brain tumor (1) 69: 3–4
catatonia in (1) 53: 12–13, 15
cerebral blood flow in (1) 64: 6–7
changes in clinical presentation since early 20th century (1) 53: 18
in children (2) **29: 1–8**
   autism confused with (2) 27: 1–2. See also Autism; Developmental disorders, pervasive
   classification (2) 29: 2–3
   clinical description (2) 29: 3–4
   definition (2) 29: 1–3
   epidemiology (2) 29: 3
   etiology (2) 29: 4–6
   future prospects in (2) 29: 7–8
   hallucinations in (2) 20: 11
   historical aspects (2) 29: 1
   infantile psychosis distinguished from (2) 29: 2
   neurological soft signs in (2) 29: 5
   organic factors (2) 29: 5
   prognosis (2) 29: 7
   psychodynamics (2) 29: 5
   treatment (2) 29: 7
chronic (1) 53: 13–15. See also Chronic mental patients
   brain dysfunction distinguished by neuropsychological assessment (1) **72: 1–15.** See also Neuropsychological assessment
   cognitive functions in (1) 53: 14
   delusions and hallucinations in (1) 53: 13
   depression in (1) 53: 13–14
   drug therapy in (3) 6: 7
   emotional defects in (1) 53: 13
   family impact of (3) 6: 9
   neuropsychological assessment in (1) 72: 13–15
   positive and negative symptoms in (1) 53: 15
   tardive dyskinesia in (1) 53: 14
   thought disorder in (1) 53: 11–13
classification (1) 53: 15–16; 54: 3–4; 69: 13–14
   based on response to neuroleptics (3) 50: 8
   in children (2) 29: 2–3
clinical course (1) 53: 16–18
clinical features (1) 68: 12
   in children (2) 29: 3–4
cognitive function in (3) **65: 1–11**
   conceptual issues and novel applications in (3) 65: 8–11
   continuous performance tasks (3) 65: 5–6
   creativity and adaptive traits (3) 65: 8–9
   distractibility and dichotic listening (3) 65: 5
   electrodermal activity and habituation (3) 65: 6
   evoked cortical responses (3) 65: 7–8
   generalized versus specific deficits (3) 65: 9
   habituation of blink reflex (3) 65: 6
   high-risk studies of patient's children (3) 65: 10–11
   medications and neurophysiology of (3) 65: 9–10
   new models in (3) 65: 11

Schizophrenia, cognitive function in *(continued)*
    reaction time (3) 65: 4
    recovery during treatment (3) 52: 20–21
    research on (3) 65: 3–8
    residual performance deficits in remission as
        marker (3) 65: 10
    secondary factors causing dysfunction (3) 65: 8
    signal detection methodology (3) 65: 9
    significance of processing dysfunction versus epi-
        phenomenon (3) 65: 8
    smooth pursuit eye movements (3) 65: 6–7
    visual integration (3) 65: 5
    visual masking (3) 65: 4–5
  computed tomography in (1) 62: 11–12; 64: 6;
    (3) 51: 6
  creativity in (3) 65: 8–9
  culture and (1) 54: 11–12; (3) 15: 2–3, 11–12
    definitions (3) 2: 3–5; 15: 2–3
    epidemiologic studies (3) 2: 7–8
    outcome studies (3) 2: 10–12
  definition (1) 53: 4–7, 15; 54: 3–4; (3) 15: 1–3
    in children (2) 29: 1–3
    clinical (3) 15: 2–3
    culture determining (3) 2: 3–5; 15: 2–3
  delirium distinguished from (1) 73: 15; (2) 87: 5
  delusions in (1) 53: 8
  depression associated with (1) 53: 13–14; 59: 10
  differences in patients exhibiting positive versus
    negative
  differential diagnosis (1) 53: 18–19
    neuropsychological assessment in (1) 72: 14
  dissociative disorders confused with (1) 39: 2
  dopamine hypothesis in (1) 64: 4–5; (3) 53: 14
  dopamine receptor changes in (3) 50: 7–8
  drift hypothesis explaining low social class associa-
    tion with (1) 54: 9–10
  DSM-III definition (1) 53: 6, 15
  EEG in (2) 29: 5
  endorphins role in (1) 64: 5–6
  epidemiology (1) **54: 1–15**
    in adulthood (3) **15: 1–12**
    case-definition problems in (1) 54: 3–4; (3) 15:
        1–3
    in childhood (2) 29: 3
    community survey studies (3) 15: 4–6
    cross-cultural studies (3) 2: 7–8
    detection problems in (3) 15: 4–6
    DSM-III influence on (1) 54: 15
    future prospects (1) 54: 14–15
    problems in determining incidence and preva-
        lence rates (1) 54: 2–3
    rates (1) 54: 4–5; (3) 15: 1
    treated prevalence versus true prevalence (3) 15:
        4
  etiology
    in children (2) 29: 4–6
    stressful life events (1) 63: 9–10

event-related potentials in (3) 62: 7–8, 11–13
evoked potentials in (3) 53: 13
expressed emotion related to (1) 63: 14–17
eye blinking rate (3) 53: 13
family in (1) 54: 8–9; (3) 7: 2–5; 15: 8–9. *See
    also* Family, with schizophrenic offspring
  differentiation in (3) 7: 3
  double bind in (3) 7: 3–4
  family thinking in (3) 7: 3
  pseudomutual relationships in (3) 7: 3, 7
  role allocation in (3) 7: 2–3
  therapist sensations in working with (3) 7: 3
  therapy for (3) 7: 4–5
family therapy in (3) 7: 4–5
four A's for (1) 53: 3
genetics of (1) 54: 6–8; **62: 1, 4–12;** (3) 15: 6–7
    12; 53: 12
  adoption studies (1) 62: 8–10; (3) 53: 12
  affective disorders and (1) 62: 19–20
  biological markers and linkage study (1) 62: 11
    12
  heterogeneity (1) 62: 10
  mode of inheritance (1) 62: 10
  polygenic-multifactorial models (1) 62: 11
  population and family studies (1) 62: 4–6
  single gene models (1) 62: 10–11
  twin studies (1) 62: 6–8; (3) 53: 12
global behavior in (1) 53: 12–13
glucose utilization in brain in (3) 51: 6
hallucinations in (1) 53: 8–9
after head injury (1) 69: 3
hebephrenic (1) 53: 15
high-risk patient for, attention and information
    processing deficit in (3) 65: 10–11
historical background (1) 52: 16–18; 53: 1–4; (2)
    29: 1
HLA antigens in (1) 62: 12; (3) 53: 13
hypochondriasis distinguished from (1) 35: 13
hypofrontality in (1) 64: 7
immunity in (2) 128: 13–14
inability to reason abstractly in (1) 53: 10
incidence rates (1) 54: 4–5
infantile psychosis distinguished from adult dis-
    order (2) 29: 2
information processing in (3) 53: 14; 65: 1–2. *See
    also under* cognitive function in *above*
integrative neural defect role in (1) 2: 20
intellectual function in (1) 53: 14
Kraepelin's concept (1) 53: 1
latent (1) 17: 6–7; 53: 16. *See also* Borderline;
    Borderline personality disorder;
    Schizotypal personality disorder
learning role in (1) 2: 12
lifetime risk (1) 62: 4–6
LSD effects distinguished from symptoms of (3)
    46: 12–13
lymphocytes in (2) 128: 13

markers in (3) 53: 12–15
  dopamine beta-hydroxylase (3) 53: 14
  evoked potentials (3) 53: 13
  eye blinking rate (3) 53: 13
  histocompatibility antigens (3) 53: 13
  monoamine oxidase (3) 53: 14
  psychological tests (3) 53: 14
  smooth-pursuit eye tracking (1) 62: 11; (3) 53:
    14–15; 65: 6–7
migration related to (1) 54: 11; (3) 15: 9
military service related to (1) 54: 11
monoamine oxidase in platelets in (1) 62: 11; (3)
  53: 14
morbid risk (1) 54: 5
multiple personality distinguished from (1) 39:
  9
neurobiology (1) **64: 1–2, 4–7, 13–15**
  brain abnormalities (1) 64: 6
  cerebral blood flow (1) 64: 6–7
  dopamine hypothesis (1) 64: 4–5
  neuropeptides role (1) 64: 5–6
  viral mechanisms (1) 64: 6
neurochemistry (1) 64: 4–6
neuropathology (1) 64: 6–7
neuropeptides in (1) 64: 5–6
neuropsychological assessment in (1) 72: 10
obsessive-compulsive disorder distinguished from
  (1) 34: 8
occupation related to (1) 54: 10; (3) 15: 10–11
organic (1) **69: 1–14;** (2) 29: 5. *See also* Psychoses, symptomatic
organic psychoses compared with (1) 69: 10–12
paranoid disorder distinguished from (1) 68: 14
paranoid disorder related to (1) 53: 19
paranoid personality disorder in relatives (1) 16: 9–
  10
perinatal factors in (1) 54: 13–14; (3) 15: 7–
  8
personality associated with (1) 53: 7
personality disorders associated with (1) 14: 3
personality disorders boundary with (1) 53: 19
phenothiazines effect on outcome (1) 53: 17
physique associated with (1) 53: 7
positive emission tomography in (3) 51: 6
postpartum (1) 54: 10–11
prevalence rates (1) 54: 4; (3) 15: 1
  in children (2) 29: 3
prognosis (1) 53: 16–18
  in children (2) 29: 7
  culture related to (3) 15: 11–12
  family environment related to (3) 15: 9
  prognostic indicators (1) 53: 16, 17
psychodynamics, in children (2) 29: 5
psychological tests in (3) 53: 14
psychotherapy benefit in (1) 11: 5
race as risk factor in (1) 54: 13; (3) 15: 8
reaction time in (3) 65: 4

relationship between diagnostic criteria in different
  hospitals (1) 53: 4, 5
in remission, residual performance deficits as
  marker in (3) 65: 10
remitting (1) 70: 8–9. *See also* Schizophreniform
  disorder
Research Diagnostic Criteria of Spitzer, Endicott
  and Robins for (1) 53: 5
risk factors for (1) 54: 5–14; (3) 15: 6–12
schizoaffective disorder as form of (1) 70: 2–3. *See
  also* Schizoaffective disorder
schizoaffective disorder distinguished from (1) 70:
  6
schizoid personality disorder as premorbid personality in (1) 16: 2–3
schizophreniform disorder distinguished from (1)
  70: 8–9
schizophrenogenic mother role in (1) 2: 20
schizotypal personality disorder in relatives (1) 16:
  4–7
season of birth related to (1) 54: 14; (3) 15: 7–8
sex as risk factor in (1) 54: 13; (3) 15: 8
signs and symptoms (2) 95: 2
smooth pursuit eye tracking in (1) 62: 11; (3) 53:
  14–15; 65: 6–7
social causation versus social selection in (1) 54: 9–
  10; (3) 15: 10–11
social class and (1) 54: 9–10; (3) 15: 10–11
societal factors in (1) 54: 11–13; (3) 15: 11–12
speech in (1) 53: 10
stimulants causing improved cognition in (3) 72: 2–
  3
stressful life events predisposing to (1) 54: 10–11;
  (3) 15: 9–10
suicide in (1) 71: 3, 4–5, 10
symptomatic psychoses compared with (1) 69: 10–
  12
  clinical features (1) 69: 10–11
  genetic comparisons (1) 69: 11–12
  relationship between psychosis and brain dis-
    order (1) 69: 12
  treatment and prognosis (1) 69: 11
symptoms (1) 64: 4
symptoms of first rank (1) 53: 2–3
tardive dyskinesia in (1) 53: 14
theories of, implications of organic psychoses on
  (1) 69: 13–14
thought disorder in (1) 53: 9–12
treated prevalence for (3) 15: 4
treatment (1) **55: 1–26**
  in children (2) 29: 7
  compliance in (1) 55: 2
  drugs (1) **55: 1–26**
    chemical classes used in (1) 55: 3–5
    dopamine receptor interaction (1) 55: 17
    evidence for efficacy and specificity (1) 55: 5–
      7

Schizophrenia, treatment, drugs *(continued)*
  interactions with other agents (1) 55: 11
  interindividual variations in blood levels (1)
    55: 8
  pharmacokinetics (1) 55: 7–11
  preparations and dosages (1) 55: 11–13
  route of administration versus (1) 55: 8–9
  side effects (1) 55: 20–26
  sites and actions (1) 55: 14–20
  therapeutic response versus (1) 55: 10
  toxic effects versus (1) 55: 10–11
  electroconvulsive therapy (1) 55: 2; (2) 160: 4
  family therapy (3) 7: 4–5
  hemodialysis (1) 55: 2–3
  historical perspective (1) 55: 1–2
  nonpharmacologic (1) 55: 2–3
  psychosurgery (1) 55: 2
  stimulants (3) 72: 2–3
  twin studies on (1) 62: 6–8
  type I and type II syndromes (1) 53: 15
  in underdeveloped countries (1) 53: 17–18
  varieties of (1) 53: 15–16
  viral mechanisms (1) 64: 6
  Washington University of St. Louis definition (1)
    53: 5
Schizophrenic spectrum disorders (1) 53: 19
  genetic relationship with schizophrenia (1) 62: 9
Schizophreniform disorder (1) 68: 12; **70: 8–11**
  case description (1) 70: 10–11
  classification (1) 70: 9
    problems in (1) 70: 1
  clinical features (1) 70: 9–10
  definition (1) 68: 12
  diagnostic criteria (1) 70: 9
  differential diagnosis (1) 70: 10
  DSM-III definition (1) 68: 12; 70: 8–9
  prognosis (1) 68: 17
  schizophrenia distinguished from (1) 70: 8–9
  treatment (1) 70: 10
Schizotaxia (1) 2: 20–21
Schizotypal personality, avoidant personality distin-
    guished from (1) 24: 8
Schizotypal personality disorder (1) **16: 4–8**
  clinical description (1) 16: 5–6
  definition (1) 16: 4–5
  depression in (1) 16: 7
  depressive neurosis distinguished from (1) 40: 7
  diagnosis (1) 16: 7
  differential diagnosis (1) 16: 7–8
  drug therapy (1) 10: 4
  DSM-III criteria (1) 16: 4–5
  epidemiology (1) 16: 5
  etiology (1) 16: 6–7
  genetics (1) 16: 6–7
  historical background (1) 16: 4
  paranoid personality disorder distinguished from
    (1) 16: 10

as premorbid personality in schizophrenia (1) 16:
    6
  prevention (1) 16: 8
  psychobiological markers (1) 16: 6–7
  schizoid personality disorder distinguished from (1)
    16: 3
  schizophrenia in relatives of (1) 16: 4–7
  symptoms (1) 16: 4, 6
  treatment (1) 16: 8
  types of clinical presentation (1) 16: 6
Schizotype (1) 2: 20
Schneider, K., on schizophrenia (1) 53: 2–3
School. *See also* Learning disability
  ambivalence and uncertainty toward mental health
    programs in (2) 70: 1–2
  burn-out in (2) 70: 4
  consultation in (2) **70: 1–9**
    ambivalence and uncertainty in (2) 70: 1–2
    closing trust gap between teachers and psychia-
      trist (2) 70: 8
    continual assessment of (2) 70: 7
    determination of role of mental health profes-
      sional (2) 70: 6–7
    implications of collaboration (2) 70: 6–7
    indirect method in (2) 70: 2–3
    in-service programs for teachers (2) 70: 7
    method of beginning (2) 70: 7
    obstacles to collaboration (2) 70: 7–8
    in primary prevention (2) 69: 6; 70: 4–6
    psychiatry-school collaboration (2) 70: 2–4
    reducing psychosocial dynamics interfering with
      learning (2) 70: 2–3
    in secondary prevention (2) 70: 3–4
    skills required in (2) 70: 8–9
    training in (2) 70: 9
    Yale Child Study Center program in New Haven
      School System (2) 70: 4–6
  drug abuse in (3) 17: 9
  educational programs in attention deficit disorder
    (2) 36: 8–9
  health promotion in (3) 129: 3
  important role in child socialization (2) 70: 1
  in inpatient setting (2) 64: 16
  interactional conflict and stress in (2) 70: 4
  in learning disabilities (2) 48: 5–6
  mission of (2) 70: 2
  poor performance in depression (2) 30: 3
  preventive mental health services in (2) 69: 6; 70:
    4–6
  psychiatry collaboration with (2) 70: 2–4
  samples in epidemiologic studies (2) 11: 3
  as social system (2) 70: 4
School age development (2) **3: 1–6.** *See also* Latency
School avoidance, differential diagnosis (2) 39: 6
School failure, significance (2) 70: 2. *See also* Learn-
    ing disabilities
School phobia. *See* Phobia, school

reening
　for developmental disorder (2) 2: 4–5, 7
　predictive value in (2) 11: 5–6
　sensitivity and specificity in (2) 11: 5–6
ripts, in social cognition (2) 17: 7–8
arch warrant, as discovery procedure (3) 31: 9
asonal variations
　in affective disorders (1) 61: 3–4
　as biological rhythms (3) 59: 7–11
　in bipolar disorder (3) 59: 11
　birth season related to schizophrenia (1) 54: 14;
　　　(3) 15: 7–8
　in depression (3) 59: 11
　neuropharmacology of (3) 59: 10–11
　suicide and (3) 20: 10
　time of birth related to bipolar disorder (3) 13: 12
clusion
　alliance-based application (3) 36: 13
　of children (2) 64: 15
curity personnel, for violent patient (2) 95: 9
dation, as side effect of tricyclic antidepressants (2)
　　　91: 2
dative/hypnotics
　abuse
　　by adolescents (2) 35: 3–4
　　comparative rates with other drugs (3) 17: 8,
　　　10
　　demographic trends (3) 17: 10
　　epidemiology (3) 17: 7–8, 10
　　temporal trends (3) 17: 10
　adverse effects (2) 111: 1
　　psychiatric (2) 91: 3–4
　antihistamines used as (3) 61: 15
　benefits (3) 61: 15
　CNS depression due to (2) 111: 1
　comparison of different agents (3) 61: 16
　danger in sleep disorder (3) 61: 5
　　in sleep apnea (2) 105: 12; (3) 61: 10, 15
　daytime hangover due to (3) 61: 15
　drugs comprising (2) 111: 1
　hazards in elderly (2) 119: 8
　in insomnia, beneficial use in transient form (2)
　　　105: 6
　insomnia due to (2) 105: 6–7; (3) 61: 7
　interactions with other drugs (2) 111: 1–2
　in jet lag (3) 59: 13
　mortality associated with (3) 61: 14–15
　nightmares as rebound symptom after chronic use
　　　(2) 105: 6–7, 16
　overdose
　　assessment (2) 90: 6
　　emergency management (2) 90: 6–7
　　symptoms (2) 90: 3, 6
　prevalence of use (3) 61: 14
　psychiatric side effects (2) 91: 3–4
　reasons for use (3) 61: 14
　risks of prescribing (3) 61: 14–15

　withdrawal syndrome (2) 35: 4; 90: 10–11; 111:
　　　1; (3) 61: 7
　　cumulative dose response testing procedure for
　　　(2) 90: 11
　　pentobarbital challenge test for (2) 90: 11
　　symptoms (2) 90: 3, 10–11
　　treatment (2) 90: 11
Segregation analysis (2) 10: 6–7
Seizures. See Convulsions; Epilepsy
Self-centeredness, in narcissistic personality disorder
　　　(1) 18: 3–4
Self-dynamism (1) 1: 13
Self-esteem
　depression related to loss (1) 40: 9
　evaluation in mental status examination in chil-
　　　dren (2) 20: 12
　in learning disability (2) 48: 7–8
　narcissism and (1) 18: 2
　pathologic regulation (1) 18: 2–3
　psychotherapy influence on development of (1)
　　　11: 10
　regulation determinants (1) 18: 2
　support in narcissistic character (2) 108: 10
Self-evaluation, dysfunctional (1) 2: 17
Self-image, early versus late maturation in adoles-
　　　cence and (2) 4: 6
Self-mutilation
　in Lesch-Nyhan disorder (1) 27: 5
　in masochistic personality (1) 27: 1
Self-reinforcement (1) 2: 16–17
Self-report tests
　of anxiety (1) 7: 8
　for children's behavior disorders (2) 23: 7
　of depression (1) 7: 8
　　in childhood (2) 20: 13
　in epidemiologic studies in child psychiatry (2) 11:
　　　6–7; (3) 12: 8
　of interpersonal behavior (1) 7: 9
　of memory (3) 71: 13
　of suicidal potential (1) 7: 8
　of symptoms of psychiatric disease (1) 7: 4
　uses (1) 15: 3
Self theory (1) 1: 11–12
Self-verbalizations (1) 2: 18
Selye, Hans
　on biological stress response systems (1) 41: 12–
　　　13
　on stress (2) 78: 4–5
Semantics
　definition (2) 49: 1; (3) 67: 5. See also Language
　in expressive language disorder (2) 49: 3
Senile squalor (2) 119: 7
Sensitivity
　definition (2) 11: 5
　in screening tests (2) 11: 5–6
Sensitization (2) 13: 1–2
　definition (3) 65: 2–3

Sensitization *(continued)*
  in memory (3) 71: 2–3
  molecular basis (2) 13: 4–5
Sensorimotor autonomy (1) 2: 21–22
Sensory attachment (1) 2: 21–22
Sensory function
  disorders in conversion (1) 35: 6
  evoked potentials in assessment (3) 62: 3
Separation
  animal models (3) 55: 7
  in borderline personality development (1) 17: 6;
      (2) 82: 7
  in depression in childhood (2) 30: 6
  depressive neurosis in adult related to childhood
      experiences (1) 40: 11
  development of (2) 2: 6
  evaluation in mental status examination (2) 20: 5
  in family development (2) 5: 2
  and immune system (2) 128: 6–7
  parent-child relationship disorders related to (2)
      50: 3
Separation anxiety. *See* Anxiety, separation
Separation-individuation process, in dependent per-
      sonality disorder (1) 26: 3
Separation studies. *See* Adoption studies
Sequenced Inventory of Communication Develop-
      ment (2) 21: 3
Serotonergic neural systems (3) 44: 6–12. *See also*
      Monoamine neural systems; Serotonin
  anatomy and physiology in brain (3) 44: 8–12
  in diencephalon and thalamus (3) 44: 8
  in dorsal raphe (3) 44: 8–12
  electrophysiologic studies (3) 44: 9–12
  localization in brain (3) 44: 8–9
  in septohippocampal complex (3) 44: 8–9
Serotonin. *See also* Monoamine neural systems
  in affective disorders (1) 64: 8–9
  in attention deficit disorder (3) 66: 11
  in depression (3) 55: 5–6
    norepinephrine dichotomy with (3) 55: 6
  in electroconvulsive therapy (3) 68: 4
  and limbic-hypothalamic-pituitary axis dysregula-
      tion in melancholia (3) 54: 5–6
  in pain of depression (2) 104: 10–11
  in pervasive developmental disorders (2) 27: 7–8
  in sleep (3) 60: 7
Serpasil. *See* Reserpine
Sex. *See also* Men; Women
  alcohol abuse related to (3) 18: 7, 9
  as antisocial personality risk factor (3) 19: 3
  as bipolar disorder risk factor (1) 60: 10; (3) 13:
      10
  as borderline personality disorder risk factor (1)
      17: 7–8
  and childhood psychiatric disorders (2) 11: 10
  definition (1) 46: 1
  as depression risk factor (1) 60: 5–6; (3) 13: 5, 6

differences in Axis II personality disorders (1) 24:
    5
differences in sexual response (1) 45: 1
and drug-related behavioral effects (3) 45: 6
identity disorders (2) 41: 2–4. *See also* Gender
    identity disorders
and illness behavior (3) 22: 10
and paraphilias (1) 46: 4
reassignment of normal male after penile trauma
    (2) 9: 6
as schizophrenia risk factor (1) 54: 13; (3) 15:
    8
  in children (2) 29: 3
suicide method by (3) 20: 3–4
suicide rates by (3) 20: 2–4
Sex conversion surgery, in male transsexualism (1)
    46: 14
Sex hormones (2) 9: 2
  and behavior (2) 9: 5–9
    gender identity (2) 9: 6–7
    gender-role behavior (2) 9: 7
    intelligence level and sexually differentiated cog
        nitive abilities (2) 9: 8–9
    sexual orientation (2) 9: 7–8
  in fetus (2) 9: 2–3
  and gender identity (2) 9: 6–7
    in male pseudohermaphroditism (2) 9: 6
    in prenatal virilization of female fetus (2) 9: 6–
      in congenital adrenal hyperplasia (2) 9: 6–7
      after prenatal treatment with progestins (2) 9:
          7
  sex reassignment of normal male (2) 9: 6
  and gender-role behavior (2) 9: 7
  and homosexuality (2) 9: 8
  in infants (2) 9: 3
  and intelligence (2) 9: 8–9
  in prepubescent children and adolescents (2) 9: 3–
      4
  psychiatric manifestations of disorders (2) 88: 14–
      15
    androgen (2) 88: 15
    estrogen (2) 88: 14–15
  and sexual orientation (2) 9: 7–8
Sex print
  definition (1) 46: 1–2
  in homosexuality (1) 45: 5, 6
  immutability versus plasticity of (1) 45: 7
Sex therapy (1) **47: 9–12**
  behavioral aspect (1) 47: 10–11
  current concepts (1) 47: 9–10
  effect on nonsexual marital problems (1) 47: 10
  integrated treatment (1) 47: 10
  outcome (1) 47: 12
  psychotherapeutic aspect (1) 47: 11–12
  psychotherapy distinguished from (1) 47: 9
  training in (1) 47: 12
Sexual abuse. *See* Rape

xual assault, offenders (3) 28: 22–23. *See also* Rape

xual behavior. *See also* Sexuality
in adolescents, trend toward younger age of initiation (2) 4: 12–13
endocrine influences on (2) 9: 5–9
  gender identity (2) 9: 6–7
  gender-role behavior (2) 9: 7
  intelligence level and sexually differentiated cognitive abilities (2) 9: 8–9
  sexual orientation (2) 9: 7–8
variability in (1) 45: 2

xual development
neurotransmitter interactions influence on (2) 12: 10–11
Tanner stages of (2) 4: 4

xual differentiation
estrogens role in (2) 9: 4
in fetus (2) 9: 2–3
in postnatal period (2) 9: 3
puberty onset (2) 9: 4–5
testosterone role in (2) 9: 2–4

exual disorders
androgen levels related to (2) 88: 15
antihypertensive drugs causing (2) 118: 8
classification (1) 46: 2
developmental (2) **41: 1–7**
distinguishing between organic and psychological causes (1) 47: 7–8
dyspareunia (1) 47: 6
ejaculatory pain (1) 47: 6
epidemiology (1) 47: 1
gender disorders distinguished from (1) 46: 2
gender identity (2) 41: 2–4
genital muscle spasm causing (1) 47: 6
in histrionic personality disorder (1) 19: 5
in hysterical personality disorder (1) 19: 3, 4
pain (1) 47: 6. *See also* Dyspareunia
in paranoid disorder (1) 68: 5
phobia (1) 47: 6–7
pleasure facilitators (1) 46: 2–10. *See also* Paraphilias
psychosexual dysfunction (1) **47: 1–12.** *See also* Psychosexual disorders; Psychosexual dysfunction
theories of, frames of reference (1) 45: 8
vaginismus (1) 47: 6

exual dysfunction. *See* Psychosexual disorders; Psychosexual dysfunction; Sexual disorders

exual function. *See* Sexual behavior; Sexual response cycle; Sexuality

exual identity, definition (1) 46: 2

exuality (1) **45: 1–8.** *See also* Sexual behavior
androgens role (1) 45: 2, 3
  prenatal influence (1) 45: 3–4
definition (1) 46: 1–2
developmental aspects (1) 46: 2

disorders of (1) **45: 1–18.** *See also* Gender identity disorders; Paraphilias
frames of reference for normalcy (1) 45: 7, 8
Freud's theories on (1) 1: 6–7
homosexuality (1) **45: 4–7.** *See also* Homosexuality
in latency (2) 3: 2
in menopause (2) 120: 7
menstrual cycle effect on (1) 45: 2–3
normal human response (1) 45: 1–2. *See also* Sexual response cycle
psychoneuroendocrine associations
  in adult (1) 45: 2–3
  prenatal (1) 45: 3–4
research on, social reactions to (1) 45: 7–8
in transsexualism (1) 46: 11–12

Sexually dangerous offender (3) 28: 22–23
antiandrogens in (3) 28: 23–25
behavior therapy for (3) 28: 23
personality disorder in (3) 28: 23

Sexual masochism (1) 46: 5–6

Sexual orientation, sex hormones effect on (2) 9: 7–8
in congenital adrenal hyperplasia (2) 9: 7–8
after prenatal treatment with progestins (2) 9: 8

Sexual phobia (1) 47: 6–7

Sexual promiscuity
differential diagnosis (1) 18: 8; 19: 8–9
in narcissistic personality disorder (1) 18: 8

Sexual response cycle (1) 45: 1–2; 47: 1. *See also* Sexuality
brain role in (1) 45: 2
impairment (1) 47: 1. *See also* Psychosexual dysfunction
sex differences in (1) 45: 1

Sexual sadism (1) 46: 5–6

Shamanism (3) 2: 12–13

Shame, paranoid personality disorder related to (1) 16: 10

Shapiro, D., on compulsive personality disorder (1) 22: 3–4

Sheltered living, for chronic mental patients (3) 6: 10

Shock therapy. *See* Electroconvulsive therapy

Shoplifters (1) 25: 4

Short stature, psychiatric significance (2) 20: 4

Sick role behavior
physician-patient relationship determining (2) 81: 5
requirements for coping (2) 108: 3
and somatization reactions (1) 35: 2

Signal detection methodology (3) 65: 9

Sign learning (1) 2: 14–15

Simmond's disease, psychiatric manifestations (2) 88: 14

Sinequan. *See* Doxepin

Single-major-locus model (2) 10: 5–7
in affective disorders (1) 62: 17
in schizophrenia (1) 62: 10–11

Skin
  artifacts put on or through (2) 101: 3–4
  conductance-electrodermal activity as marker in depression (3) 53: 8
  differential diagnosis of psychiatric disorders involving (2) 101: 3–4
  in factitious disease (2) 101: 3–4
  fibroblast cultures in neurochemistry studies on children (2) 12: 3
  galvanic skin response in biofeedback (2) 109: 5
  neuroleptic toxicity to (1) 55: 26
  thermal feedback of temperature in biofeedback (2) 109: 5, 7
Skinner, B.F.
  contributions to behavior therapy (1) 9: 3–4
  contribution to learning theory (1) 2: 11–12
Sleep (3) **60: 1–13**
  age effects on timing, duration and character (3) 60: 9
  in animals (3) 60: 8
  cholinergic neurons role in (3) 60: 7–8, 11–12
  definitions in (3) 60: 3
  deprivation (3) 61: 1–2
    cell-mediated immunity after (2) 128: 4
    effects of (3) 60: 12–13
    as therapy in bipolar disorder (1) 61: 22
  developmental considerations (2) 52: 1–2
  disorders in. See Sleep disorders
  duration related to longevity (3) 60: 9
  in dysthymic disorder (1) 61: 14
  in elderly (2) 105: 4–5
  epidemiologic studies of (3) 61: 2
  evaluation in all-night recording (2) 105: 1
  evolution and phylogeny of (3) 60: 8
  functions of (3) 60: 12–13
  health risks of decreased or increased duration (3) 61: 2
  hemolysis during (2) 105: 16
  hormonal changes in (3) 60: 5
  hygiene related to (2) 105: 16
  individual patterns of duration (3) 60: 9
  influence of previous history on (3) 60: 8–9
  latency, multiple sleep latency test of (2) 105: 3
  locus ceruleus neuron activity in (3) 44: 5
  major phases of (3) 60: 2
  measurements of (3) 60: 2, 3
  neurochemistry of (3) 60: 7–8
  neuroendocrinology of (3) 60: 5–6
  neuropeptides role in (3) 60: 7
  periodic movements in (3) 61: 10–11
  recall of dreaming in (3) 60: 9–10
  regulation by brain clocks (3) 60: 1–2
  REM. See REM sleep
  requirements for
    influence of deprivation (3) 61: 1–2
    variation in (3) 61: 1
    at various ages (3) 61: 1
  search for center in brain (3) 60: 7

  serotonin role in (3) 60: 7
  stages of (3) 60: 2
  theories of function (3) 60: 13
Sleep apnea (2) 105: 9–12; (3) **61: 8–10**
  in adolescents (2) 52: 9–10
  all-night EEG recordings in (2) 105: 10–11
  alveolar hypoventilation syndrome (2) 105: 10
  in children and adolescents (2) 105: 11
  clinical features (2) 52: 9; 105: 10; (3) 61: 8–9
  danger of hypnotics in (2) 61: 10, 15; 105: 12
  diagnosis (2) 105: 12
  evaluation (3) 61: 9–10
  multiple sleep latency test in (2) 105: 11
  narcolepsy distinguished from (2) 105: 12
  obstructive versus central (2) 105: 10
  pathophysiology (2) 105: 11; (3) 61: 8
  physical findings in (2) 105: 10
  prevalence (3) 61: 9
  snoring in (3) 61: 9
  treatment (2) 52: 10; (3) 61: 10
    tracheostomy (2) 105: 12
Sleep disorders (2) **105: 1–16**
  in adolescents (2) 52: 8–11
  alpha-delta sleep (2) 105: 8–9
  in attention deficit disorder (3) 66: 7
  atypical polysomnographic features (2) 105: 8–9
  bed-wetting. See under enuresis below
  in children (2) **52: 1–11**
    adolescents (2) 52: 8–11
    with depression (2) 30: 3, 7
    infants and toddlers (2) 52: 2–5
    preschool and school-age (2) 52: 5–8
    prevalence (2) 52: 2
    unique challenges for clinician (2) 52: 1
  classification (2) 52: 2; 105: 1–3; 109: 10; (3) 61: 4
  conditions causing difficulty in initiating and maintaining
  danger of hypnotics in (2) 61: 10, 15; 105: 12; (3) 61: 5
  daytime experience importance in evaluating (3) 61: 3
  definition (2) 105: 9
  delayed sleep phase syndrome (2) 52: 10–11; (3) 59: 11–12
  in delirium (1) 73: 13–14
  in dementia (2) 119: 8
  in depressive neurosis (1) 40: 5–6
  diagnostic procedures for (2) 119: 8
  drugs causing (2) 119: 8
  DSM-III classification (2) 109: 10
  dysfunctions in sleep (2) 105: 2. See also Parasomnias
  in elderly (2) 105: 4–5; 119: 7–8; (3) 21: 3
  enuresis (2) 43: 1–4; 52: 7; (3) 61: 13–14. See also Enuresis
    related to other disorders (2) 43: 3
  epidemiology (2) 105: 3–5

excessive somnolence (2) 105: 2, 9–14; (3) 61: 12–
13. *See also* Hypersomnia
familiar sleep setting and bedtime ritual in (3) 61:
6
historical background (2) 105: 1
history-taking in (2) 105: 3; 119: 8; (3) 61: 2–4
hypersomnia (2) 105: 2, 9–14. *See also* Hypersomnia
in infants and toddlers (2) 52: 2–5
enuresis (2) 52: 7
insomnia (2) 52: 7–8
nightmares (2) 52: 6
night terrors (2) 52: 5–6
nightwaking (2) 52: 3–4
rhythmic motor behaviors (2) 52: 4–5
sleepwalking and sleeptalking (2) 52: 6
initiating and maintaining sleep (2) 105: 5–9; (3)
61: 5–8. *See also* Insomnia
affective disorders associated with (3) 61: 5
classification (2) 105: 2, 5
drug and alcohol use associated with (3) 61: 6–
7
psychophysiologic (3) 61: 5–6
sleep-wake schedule disorders (3) 61: 7–8
insomnia. *See* Insomnia
Kleine-Levin syndrome (2) 105: 14
menstrual cycle related to (2) 105: 14
most common disorders seen in sleep centers (3)
61: 5
multiple sleep latency test in (2) 105: 3
myoclonus (2) 105: 7–8
differential diagnosis (2) 105: 7–8
treatment (2) 105: 8
narcolepsy (2) 105: 12–14; (3) 61: 12–13. *See also*
Narcolepsy
nightmares (2) 52: 6; 105: 15–16
night terrors (2) 43: 7–8; 52: 5–6; 105: 15; (3)
61: 14. *See also* Night terrors
parasomnias (2) 105: 14–16; (3) 61: 13–14
periodic movements in sleep (3) 61: 10–11
prevalence (2) 105: 4
referral to sleep disorders center in (2) 105: 16
relaxation therapy and biofeedback in (2) 109: 10
restless legs syndrome (2) 105: 7–8
in shift workers (3) 59: 12
sleep and excessive daytime sleepiness (3) 61: 8–
11
sleep apnea (3) 61: 8–10. *See also* Sleep apnea
sleep disorder centers for (3) 61: 4–5
sleep logs in (3) 61: 3–4
of sleep-wake cycle (2) 105: 2; (3) 61: 7–8. *See
also* Sleep-wake cycle
in delirium (1) 73: 13–14
sleepwalking (2) 43: 6–7; 52: 6; 105: 14–15; (3)
61: 14. *See also* Sleepwalking
snoring, in sleep apnea (3) 61: 9
stimulants causing (3) 66: 18–19
treatment (2) 119: 8

Sleep disorders centers (3) 61: 4–5
referral to (2) 105: 16
Sleeping pills (3) 61: 14–16. *See also* Sedative/hyp-
notics
hazards in elderly (2) 119: 8
insomnia due to (3) 61: 7
Sleep paralysis
in narcolepsy (2) 52: 8; (3) 61: 12
normal occurrence during sleep (3) 61: 12
Sleeptalking, in preschool and school-age children
(2) 52: 6
Sleep terrors. *See* Night terrors
Sleep-wake cycle
classification of disorders in (2) 105: 2
cortisol role in (3) 60: 5
delayed sleep phase syndrome (2) 52: 10–11; (3)
59: 11–12
developmental considerations (2) 52: 1–2
in newborn (3) 59: 3
ontogenic aspects (3) 59: 3
regulation by brain clock (3) 60: 1–2
REM latency related to (3) 59: 5
REM sleep rhythmicity in (3) 59: 6–7
temperature rhythm related to (3) 59: 4–5
theoretical models for (3) 60: 6–7
variability of oscillator controlling (3) 59: 4
Sleepwalking (2) 43: 6–7; 105: 14–15; (3) 61: 14
clinical description (2) 43: 6; 105: 14
diagnosis (2) 43: 2, 6
differential diagnosis (2) 105: 14–15
DSM-III diagnostic criteria (2) 43: 2, 6
etiology (2) 43: 6; 105: 15
night terrors similarities to (2) 43: 7
in preschool and school-age children (2) 52: 6
prevalence (2) 43: 6
psychological problems in (2) 43: 6
treatment (2) 43: 6–7; 105: 15
antianxiety drugs in (2) 59: 17
Smoking
advertising influence on use (2) 129: 5
alcohol use related to (2) 129: 5
costs of disease related to (2) 79: 2
health education on (2) 129: 3, 5–6
interactions with antipsychotic drugs (2) 111: 4
mass media influence on (2) 129: 4
sanctions influence on control (2) 129: 5–6
Smooth pursuit eye tracking, as marker in schizophrenia (1) 62: 11; (3) 53: 14–15; 65: 6–
7
Snoring, in sleep apnea (2) 105: 10; (3) 61: 9
Social breakdown syndrome (2) 119: 7
Social class
alcohol abuse related to (3) 18: 9
and anorexia nervosa (2) 102: 6
antisocial personality related to (3) 19: 3–4
as bipolar disorder risk factor (1) 60: 10; (3) 13: 10–
11
and bulimia (2) 102: 6

Social class *(continued)*
  as depression risk factor
    in children (2) 30: 6
    nonbipolar disorder (1) 60: 6; (3) 13: 6–7
  and illness behavior (3) 22: 10–11
  and impulse control (1) 25: 2
  in mental illness (1) 52: 9
  obesity related to (2) 103: 2
  and puberty onset (2) 9: 4
  schizophrenia related to (1) 54: 9–10; (3) 15: 10–11
  suicide rates by (3) 20: 7
  and utilization of mental health services (3) 22: 9, 10
Social cognition (2) **17: 1–8.** *See also* Cognitive development; Cognitive function
Social control. *See also* Civil commitment
  in drug abuse prevention (3) 17: 1–2
  patient's rights (3) **35: 1–15.** *See also* Patients' rights
Social development. *See* Cognitive development; Social learning
Social isolation
  in avoidant personality (1) 24: 4–5. *See also* Avoidant personality
  differential diagnosis (1) 16: 3, 7
  etiology
    in schizoid personality disorder (1) 16: 3
    in schizotypal personality disorder (1) 16: 7
  of medically ill (2) 108: 4
  in paranoid disorder (1) 68: 5–6
  in schizoid personality disorder (1) 16: 1, 2
  in schizotypal personality disorder (1) 16: 4–7
Socialization (2) **17: 1–8.** *See also* Cognitive development, social perspective on; Social learning
Social learning (1) **2: 1–25.** *See also* Behavior therapy
  by adopting social belief systems (1) 2: 3
  in avoidant personality (1) 24: 3
  in child behavior therapy (2) 61: 2
  cognitive (2) 77: 4–8
  in hypochondriasis (1) 35: 12
  neuropsychological development of (1) 2: 21–22
  parental attitudes and behavior effect on (1) 2: 3–5
  persistence of early experiences (1) 2: 6–7
  in pervasive developmental disorders (2) 27: 5
  principles of (1) 2: 2–3
  in psychotherapy (1) 11: 10
  reinforcement (1) 2: 7–8
    reciprocal (1) 2: 7
    repetitive experiences in (1) 2: 7
    social stereotypes in (1) 2: 7–8
  self-perpetuation of (1) 2: 8–9
    behavior generalization and (1) 2: 8–9
    perceptual and cognitive distortion in (1) 2: 8
  sources of abnormalities (1) 2: 3–5

behavior control methods (1) 2: 4–5
contingent reward methods (1) 2: 4–5
family communication styles (1) 2: 5
inconsistency (1) 2: 5
indulgent methods (1) 2: 5
overprotectiveness (1) 2: 5
parental feelings and attitudes (1) 2: 3–4
parental rejection (1) 2: 4
punitive methods (1) 2: 4
random early childhood experiences (1) 2: 6
theories of (1) 2: 9–23
  Bandura (1) 2: 16–17
  behaviorally oriented (1) 2: 10–12
  biologically oriented (1) 2: 18–22
  cognitively oriented (1) 2: 15–18
  Dollard and Miller (1) 2: 14
  Ellis (1) 2: 17–18
  Eysenck (1) 2: 19–20
  Meehl (1) 2: 20–21
  Millon (1) 2: 21–22
  Mowrer (1) 2: 14–15
  Pavlov (1) 2: 10–11
  psychodynamically oriented (1) 2: 13–15
  Rotter (1) 2: 15–16
  Skinner (1) 2: 11–12
  varieties of perspectives (1) 2: 9–10
  Watson (1) 2: 11
  Wolpe (1) 2: 12
Social phobia. *See* Phobia, social
Social psychiatry
  historical background (1) 52: 9–10
  psychosocial stress (1) 52: 9. *See also* Stress; Stressful life events
  social class studies (1) 52: 9. *See also* Social class
  social structure of mental institutions (1) 52: 10
  urbanization role in mental illness (1) 52: 9–10
Social skills training
  for chronic mental patients (3) 6: 8
  in social phobia (1) 33: 13
Social stressors. *See* Stressful life events
Social support
  and depression (3) 13: 8
    in elderly (3) 21: 8–9
  for family in alcoholism (2) 89: 10
  functions (1) 63: 13
  in prevention of affective disorders (3) 13: 13
  and psychiatric disorders (1) 63: 13–14
  in self-help groups (2) 89: 9
  and vulnerability to depression (1) 63: 8
Social withdrawal. *See* Withdrawal
Social work. *See also* Psychosocial treatment
  family services for chronic mental patients (3) 6: 9
  historical origins (3) 7: 1–2
  housing assistance for chronic mental patients (3) 6: 10
  income assistance for chronic mental patients (3) 6: 9–10

psychosocial skill training for chronic mental patients (3) 6: 8
Society
 mental illness related to. *See also* Cross-cultural psychiatry; Culture
 schizophrenia related to complexity of (1) 54: 11–13; (3) 15: 11–12
 stress-response syndromes related to (1) 41: 14
Sociocultural hypotheses (1) 6: 9–10
Socioeconomic status. *See* Social class
Sociopathy. *See also* Antisocial personality
 conduct disorder (2) **37: 1–9.** *See also* Conduct disorder
 mentally disordered offenders (3) **28: 1–26.** *See also* Mentally disordered offenders
Sodium, lithium pharmacokinetics related to (2) 111: 10, 11
Sodium amytal
 in conversion disorder (1) 10: 8
 in fugue (1) 39: 7
Sodium lactate, panic attack provoked by (1) 32: 8
Soiling. *See* Encopresis
Solution learning (1) 2: 14–15
Solvents, toxic effects (2) 90: 4
Somatization disorder (1) **35: 14–16;** (2) 100: 7–9. *See also* Briquet's syndrome; Psychosomatic disorders; Somatoform disorders
 antisocial personality related to (3) 19: 7
 clinical forms (2) 100: 1–2
 confused terminology of (2) 100: 7–8
 definition (2) 47: 1; 100: 1
 depression associated with (1) 59: 10
 diagnostic criteria (2) 100: 7–8
 motivations for (2) 100: 1
 personal and sociocultural factors (2) 100: 1
Somatoform disorders (1) **35: 1–19;** (2) **100: 1–10.** *See also* Hypochondriasis; Psychosomatic disorders
 Briquet's syndrome (1) **35: 14–16;** (2) 100: 7–9. *See also* Briquet's syndrome
 causes of symptoms in (1) 35: 1–2
 in children and adolescents (2) **47: 1–7.** *See also* Conversion disorders, in children and adolescents
 classification (2) 47: 1
 conversion disorders (1) **35: 3–8;** (2) 100: 5–7. *See also* Conversion disorders
 cultural and social factors in (1) 35: 2
 definition (2) 47: 1
 depression as underlying cause (2) 100: 2
 factitious illness (1) **35: 16–19;** (2) 101: 1. *See also* Factitious illness
 health and sickness behavior in (1) 35: 2; (2) 100: 9–10
 historical aspects (1) 35: 1–2
 hypochondriasis (1) 35: 10–14; (2) **100: 2–5.** *See also* Hypochondriasis
 psychoanalytic concept (1) 35: 2

psychogenic pain disorder (1) 35: 8–10; (2) 104: 11. *See also* Pain, psychogenic disorder
 psychotherapy in (2) 100: 10
 somatization disorder (2) 100: 7–9. *See also* Briquet's syndrome
 types (2) 100: 1–2
Somatoparaphrenia (1) 69: 4
Somnambulism. *See* Sleepwalking
Somniloquy. *See* Sleeptalking
Spatial ability, androgens related to (2) 9: 8–9
Specificity
 definition (2) 11: 5
 in screening tests (2) 11: 5–6
Specificity theory, of psychosomatic disorders (2) 76: 3
Speech
 discrimination between consonants and vowels in language disorders (3) 67: 8–10
 evaluation in mental status examination (2) 20: 8–9
 hemispheric specialization in perception (3) 67: 10–13
 language development relation to (3) 67: 2
 in major psychiatric syndromes (2) 95: 2
 motor control tests (2) 49: 9
 in schizophrenia (1) 53: 10
Speech disorders (2) 49: 2–3. *See also* Language disorders
 articulation (2) 49: 2
 causes (2) 20: 8–9
 developmental, language disorder distinguished from (3) 67: 2
 diagnostic evaluation (2) 49: 7–9
 orofacial (2) 49: 3
 perceptual dysfunction in language disorders (3) 67: 6–10
 stuttering (2) 43: 8–9; 49: 2–3
 treatment (2) 49: 9
Speech therapy
 in articulation disorder (2) 49: 2
 in stuttering (2) 49: 2–3
Spinal cord injury
 behavioral responses in (2) 117: 5
 consultation-liaison psychiatry in (2) 117: 5–6
 course of disease disability in (2) 117: 1–3
 depression in (2) 117: 5–6
 organic mental syndrome in (2) 117: 6
 pre-illness psychopathology in (2) 117: 3
 stress in (2) 117: 5
Spiroperidol
 as antipsychotic agent (1) 55: 3, 5
 efficacy related to affinity, for dopamine receptors (3) 50: 3–4
Splitting, in object relations theory (1) 1: 11
S-R Inventory of Anxiousness (1) 7: 8
Stanford-Binet test (1) 7: 5–6; (2) 21: 4
Startle reaction, in stress-response syndrome (1) 41: 2–3

Starvation, effects in anorexia nervosa (2) 102: 3
State asylums for insane, historical background (3)
6: 2
State government. *See also* Government
in research on mental health (3) 4: 4
role in mental health, historical background (3) 4:
1–2
State Trait Anxiety Inventory (STAI) (1) 7: 8
Stelazine. *See* Trifluoperazine
Stereotypies (2) 38: 1
in developmental disorders (2) 38: 7
evaluation (2) 38: 7
stimulant-induced (3) 46: 10–11
Stereotyping, as reinforcer of social learning (1) 2: 7–
8
Steroid psychosis (2) 88: 9
Stimulants. *See also* Amphetamines
abuse (3) 17: 13–14
comparative rates with other drugs (3) 17: 13
demographic trends (3) 17: 13–14
temporal trends (3) 17: 13
animal model for psychosis induced by (3) 46: 5–
12
anorexia due to (3) 66: 19–20
in antisocial personality disorder (1) 10: 3
in attention deficit disorder (1) 10: 3; (2) 36: 9–
11; 59: 4, 6; (3) 66: 15–21
in adults (3) 66: 18
behavior therapy with (3) 66: 21
distinguishing good from poor responders (3)
66: 16
electronic pupillography after (3) 66: 16
evoked cortical response to (3) 66: 16
indications (3) 66: 15–16
mechanism of action (3) 66: 6, 11–12
methylphenidate compared with amphetamine
(3) 66: 17–18
noradrenergic neural system and beneficial
action in (2) 36: 4–5
as paradoxic response (3) 66: 16–17
pemoline compared with other agents (3) 66:
18
side effects (3) 66: 18–20
in children and adolescents (2) 59: 4–6, 8–12
choice of agent (2) 59: 9
follow-up in (2) 59: 11
interactions with other drugs (2) 59: 11
medical workup prior to use (2) 59: 10
paradoxical response, neurotransmitters role in
(2) 12: 11
in pervasive developmental disorders (2) 27: 9
side effects (2) 59: 9, 10–11
clinical assessment of effects (2) 59: 8–9
deficit disorder (2) 36: 4–5
delirium due to (2) 90: 8–9
dose optimization (2) 59: 5
endocrine side effects (2) 9: 12
growth effects (3) 66: 19–20

noradrenergic neural system and beneficial action
in attention
organic mental disorders precipitated by (2) 34: 5–
6
overdose symptoms (2) 90: 3, 8–9
in pervasive developmental disorders (2) 27: 9
pharmacokinetics (2) 59: 4
psychiatric side effects (2) 91: 4
psychosis induced by (1) 64: 4; (2) 90: 8–9
animal model for (3) 46: 5–12
behavioral dimensions related to stimulants
(3) 46: 10–12
dose requirements for (3) 46: 5–6
generality of psychostimulant effects (3) 46: 9–
10
residual effects of repeated administration (3)
46: 9
sequential effects of long-term administration
(3) 46: 6–9
clinical description (3) 46: 5
in schizophrenia, improved cognition in (3) 72: 2–
3
side effects (2) 36: 10–11; 59: 9; (3) 66: 18–20
endocrine (2) 9: 12
psychiatric (2) 91: 4
stereotypies due to (3) 46: 10–11
structure of (2) 59: 6
Tourette's disorder precipitated by (2) 36: 11; 38:
4; (3) 66: 19
withdrawal symptoms (2) 90: 3
Stimulus, conditioned (1) 2: 10–11
Stimulus arrangements (2) 77: 5
Stimulus barrier (2) 18: 7
Stimulus control, in behavior therapy (2) 77: 10–11
Stimulus enrichment (1) 2: 21–22
Stimulus generalization (1) 2: 8, 11
in anxiety disorders (2) 39: 5
Stimulus impoverishment (1) 2: 21
Stimulus nutriment (1) 2: 21
Stimulus set (3) 62: 6–8
Stomach, bypass surgery in obesity
emotional response to (2) 103: 6, 7
positive effects (2) 103: 6, 8
Stranger anxiety, development (2) 39: 5
Strategic therapy model (1) 9: 4–5
choice among other orientations (1) 9: 7
in family or marital therapy format (1) 9: 8; (2)
110: 8
goals (1) 9: 5
historical aspects (1) 9: 4–5
rationale for (1) 9: 5
setting for (1) 9: 5
techniques (1) 9: 5
Streamlining communications, in family therapy (2)
110: 8
Stress. *See also* Anxiety
adversity (1) 63: 3–12
arrhythmias related to (2) 118: 5

asthma linked to (2) 128: 3
autoimmune disorders related to (2) 128: 3–4
biological response systems (1) 41: 12–13
bodily responses to (2) 72: 2
in cancer (2) 117: 4
in children's medical illness (2) 72: 2
classification of stressors (2) 121: 1
conversion disorder as reaction to (2) 100: 6
coping mechanisms related to biological response
    to (2) 121: 1–2
corticosteroids and response to (2) 9: 9
definition (1) 63: 2; (2) 121: 1
in depression etiology (3) 21: 8–9
endocrine correlates in children (2) 9: 9–10
in end-stage renal disease (2) 117: 5
family as mediator response to (2) 121: 2
hallucinations in children due to (2) 20: 10–11
health promotion at worksite related to (2) 129: 3–
    4
of hospitalization (2) 121: 2
hypertension related to (2) 118: 7–8
and immune system (2) **128: 2–6.** *See also* Im-
    mune system, stress effects on
  cell-mediated processes (2) 128: 4–6
  humoral processes (2) 128: 2–4
  mediation of (2) 128: 10–12
insomnia due to (2) 105: 6
life events causing (1) 41: 4–5. *See also* Stressful
    life events
of medical staff in high-stress medical settings (2)
    117: 7
in mental illness (1) 52: 9
in migraine headache (2) 104: 7
pain due to (2) 104: 6–8
physiologic response to (2) 78: 5
in psychiatric disorders (1) 41: 8; **63: 2–13**
psychological responses to (1) **41: 1–15.** *See also*
    Stress-response syndromes
psychological tests of (1) 7: 9
psychosocial (1) **63: 2–13**
  life events (1) 63: 3–12. *See also* Stressful life
    events
  psychiatric disorders related to (1) 63: 2–3
in psychosomatic disorders (2) 78: 4–5
responses to (1) **41: 1–15.** *See also* Stress-response
    syndromes
social class related to (3) 15: 10
in spinal cord injury (2) 117: 5
stressors distinguished from psychological state (2)
    121: 1
of surgery (2) 121: 2–3
and susceptibility to streptococcal infections (2)
    128: 3
temperature of skin as index of (2) 109: 5
ressful life events (1) **41: 1–15.** *See also* Stress;
    Stress-response syndromes
in adjustment disorders (2) 51: 1–3
adversity (1) 63: 3–12

in bipolar disorder (1) 59: 8
definition (1) 63: 3
in depression (1) 63: 5–9
  in elderly (3) 21: 8–9
  mode of action (1) 63: 11–12
  as risk factor (1) 60: 7; (3) 13: 8
early parent death and later depression (1) 63:
    11
formative versus triggering role in psychiatric dis-
    orders (1) 63: 10
methodologic problems in determining causation
    (1) 63: 3–5
normal and abnormal responses to (1) 41: 2–6
and relative risk of psychiatric disorder (1) 63: 10
in schizophrenia (1) 54: 10–11; 63: 9–10; (3) 15:
    9–10
and suicidal behavior (1) 63: 11
types of causal effect due to (1) 63: 10
validity of concept (2) 51: 3
Stressors
  classification (2) 121: 1
  DSM-III on (2) 19: 11, 13
  duration of (2) 121: 1
Stress-response syndromes (1) **41: 1–15.** *See also*
    Anxiety disorders; Stress; Stressful life
    events
  adjustment disorders (1) 41: 7. *See also* Post-trau-
    matic stress disorder (1) 41: 6–7
  in childhood and adolescence (2) **51: 1–6**
  biological systems (1) 41: 12–13
  brief reactive psychoses (1) 41: 7
  clinical description (1) 41: 10–12
  after death of loved one (1) 41: 9–10
  denial states (1) 41: 2–6
  diagnosis (1) 41: 6–8
  after divorce (1) 41: 10
  drug therapy in (1) 41: 15
  effects of stressful events on thinking and feeling
    (1) 41: 4
  emergency management (2) 95: 12
  epidemiology (1) 41: 8–10
  etiology (1) 41: 12–14
  fear of repitition in (1) 41: 10
  fear of sharing fate with victim (1) 41: 11–12
  grief (1) 41: 5–6, 8. *See also* Grief reaction
  hallucinations in children (2) 20: 10–11
  historical background (1) 41: 1–2
  hypersomnia (2) 105: 9
  influence of preexisting neurotic conflicts or func-
    tional deficits on (1) 41: 12
  insomnia (2) 105: 6; (3) 61: 2–3
  intrusive states (1) 41: 2–6
  in latency-aged child (2) 3: 5
  memory processing and storage in (1) 41: 14
  overgeneralization in (1) 41: 4
  perception and attention during (1) 41: 2–4
  phases of (1) 41: 2
  physical disorders (1) 41: 8–9

Stress-response syndromes *(continued)*
  post-traumatic stress disorder (1) 41: 6–7. *See also*
        Post-traumatic stress disorder
  psychiatric disorders (1) 41: 8
  psychological systems (1) 41: 13–14
  rage at perceived source and ensuing guilt (1) 41:
        11
  recovery from chronic illness or handicap (1) 41:
        6
  severity of life events as potential stressors in (1)
        41: 4–5. *See also* Stressful life events
  sex differences in (1) 41: 10
  shame over helplessness in (1) 41: 10–11
  shocking perceptions in (1) 41: 12
  signs and symptoms (1) 41: 2–6
  social response systems in (1) 41: 14
  suppression of unwanted memories in (1) 41: 12
  survivor guilt in (1) 41: 11
  symptoms (1) 41: 10–12
  transient hypochondriasis (2) 100: 4
  treatment (1) 41: 15
     emergency management (2) 95: 12
  unbidden perceptual experiences in (1) 41: 3–4
  uncomplicated bereavement (1) 41: 8
Stroke. *See* Cerebrovascular disease
Structural Analysis of Social Behavior test (1) 15: 7
Structural model of psychic conflict (1) 1: 7–8
Structural rearrangement, in family therapy (2) 110:
        8
Stuttering (2) 43: 8–9
  in childhood (2) 49: 2–3
     prognosis (2) 49: 2
     speech therapy for (2) 49: 2–3
     types (2) 43: 8
  definition (2) 43: 8; 49: 2
  development of (2) 43: 8
  diagnosis (2) 43: 2, 9
  DSM-III diagnostic criteria (2) 43: 2, 9
  etiology (2) 43: 8–9
  genetic factors in (2) 43: 8
  historical aspects (2) 43: 8
  neurogenic (2) 43: 8
  psychodynamics of (2) 43: 8–9
  treatment (2) 43: 9
Subacute necrotizing encephalomyopathy, organic
        mental disorders in children due to (2)
        34: 8
Subacute sclerosing panencephalitis, organic mental
        disorders in (2) 34: 4–5
Subcortical dementia (1) 73: 10–11
Submission
  animal studies of (1) 27: 5
  culture influence on (1) 27: 4–5
  in masochistic personality (1) 27: 2–3
Subpoena
  as discovery procedure (3) 31: 9–10
  procedure after receipt (3) 31: 9, 10
  validity of request for release of information (3)
        31: 3

Substance abuse (2) **90: 1–12**
  abuse involvement in (2) 90: 1–2
  abuse liability in (2) 90: 1, 2
  addiction. *See also* Addiction
     definition (2) 90: 1
     personality characteristics (2) 90: 5
  in adolescents. *See under* in children and adoles-
        cents *below*
  adverse effects (2) 90: 1
  in agoraphobia (1) 33: 5
  alcohol (2) **89: 1–12;** (3) **18: 1–16.** *See also* Alco
        hol abuse; Alcoholism
  amnesia distinguished from memory effects of (1)
        39: 6
  antisocial personality associated with (2) 90: 5; (3
        19: 6
  anxiety disorder in (2) 90: 9
  in attention deficit disorder (3) 66: 20
  behavioral and psychiatric problems associated
        with (2) 90: 4–5
  in children and adolescents (2) **35: 1–6**
     alcohol (2) 35: 2–3
     amphetamine and sympathomimetic agents (2)
        35: 4–5
     antisocial personality disorder related to (2) 35:
        2
     arylcyclohexylamine derivatives (2) 35: 5
     barbiturates and sedative-hypnotics (2) 35: 3–4
     cocaine (2) 35: 4
     contributing factors (2) 35: 2
     depression distinguished from (1) 59: 11–12
     developmental issues in (2) 4: 13–14
     epidemiologic studies (3) 12: 17–18
     hallucinogens (2) 35: 5
     marijuana (2) 35: 5
     opioids (2) 35: 4
     peer group related to (2) 35: 2
     personality factors and (2) 35: 2
     phencyclidine (2) 35: 5
     prevalence (2) 35: 1–2
  classification (3) 17: 1
  clinical picture (2) 90: 2, 3
  comparison of heroin use in U.S. soldiers in Viet-
        nam and those on U.S. mainland (3) 17
        2–3
  costs to society (3) 3: 3–5
  definition (2) 90: 1
  delirium due to (2) 90: 8–9
  depression in (2) 90: 5
  DSM-III on (2) 35: 1
  epidemiology (3) **17: 1–16**
     in adults (3) **17: 1–16**
     amphetamines and other stimulants (3) 17: 13–
        14
     cocaine (3) 17: 11–13
     Epidemiologic Catchment Areas data (3) 17: 6–
        7
     hallucinogens (3) 17: 15
     high-school survey (3) 17: 4, 9

household survey (3) 17: 4, 8
marijuana (3) 17: 15−16
narcotics (3) 17: 10−11
phencyclidine (3) 17: 14−15
sedatives/hypnotics/tranquilizers (3) 17: 7−8, 10
surveys on use (3) 17: 4−6
forensic evaluation for (3) 27: 13
hallucinations in (2) 87: 13; 90: 8, 9
individual reaction patterns to psychotomimetics
       (2) 90: 9−10
infections in (2) 90: 3
insomnia related to (3) 61: 6−7
medical and psychiatric complications (2) 90: 2−4
natural history of (3) 17: 2−4
panic disorder in (2) 90: 9
physical dependence in (2) 90: 2
psychiatric complications (2) 90: 5, 7−9
psychosis due to (2) 90: 9
psychotherapy benefit in (1) 11: 5
psychotropic drugs (2) 90: 7−10
    approach to patient in medical setting (2) 90: 4
    narcotic overdose (2) 90: 7
    narcotic withdrawal (2) 90: 12
    sedative overdose (2) 90: 6−7
    sedative withdrawal (2) 90: 10−11
reporting statutes on (3) 31: 15
risk factors for, change over time (3) 17: 2
signs and symptoms of overdose and withdrawal
       (2) 90: 3
sleep disorders related to (3) 61: 6−7
social control influence on (3) 17: 1−3
in social phobia (1) 33: 6
stages of initiation (3) 17: 3−4
substance dependence distinguished from (2) 35: 1
supportive intervention with hospitalized addict
       (2) 108: 10−11
surgery in (2) 121: 4
surveys on use (3) 17: 4−6
temporal patterns in (3) 17: 2
tolerance in (2) 90: 2
treatment, adverse reactions, psychosis and toxic
       delirium due to
types of drugs involved in (2) 90: 2
withdrawal symptoms in (2) 90: 2, 3. *See also*
       Withdrawal syndrome
ubstance dependence, substance abuse distinguished
       from (2) 35: 1
ubstantia nigra, dopaminergic system in (3) 44: 7
uccess
ambition and (2) 17: 5
attributions related to (2) 17: 5−6
development of feelings related to (2) 17: 5
udden death, psychiatric aspects in heart disease (2)
       118: 5
uggestion, in psychotherapy (2) 108: 2
uicidal behavior. *See also* Suicide; Suicide attempt
in adjustment disorders (1) 41: 7
and competency to stand trial (3) 27: 6
diagnosis (1) 71: 11−12

emergency management (2) 95: 10−11
history-taking on (1) 61: 6
hospitalization for (1) 71: 11
inability of primary care physician to diagnose (2)
       116: 4
in post-traumatic stress disorder (1) 41: 7
self-report tests of (1) 7: 8
Suicide (1) **71: 1−16**
administrative strategies to reduce (1) 71: 13
in adolescents (1) 71: 5−6
    developmental aspects (2) 11: 13−14
    prevalence (2) 4: 12
age of (3) 20: 4, 5, 10−11
in alcoholism (1) 71: 3, 4, 10
    recent loss related to (1) 71: 4
altruistic (1) 71: 1−2
anomic (1) 71: 2
antidepressants in, toxicity (1) 71: 9
attempted suicide different from (1) 71: 13−14;
       (3) 20: 14. *See also* Suicide attempt
attempted suicide prior to (1) 71: 7
biological correlates (1) 71: 12−13
in bipolar disorder (1) 59: 8
borderline personality disorder related to (1) 17: 9−
       10
in children (2) 30: 3−4
clinical recognition of patient at risk (1) 71: 11−12
cohort effect (3) 20: 10−11
communication of intent (1) 71: 7−8, 11
in conduct disorder (2) 37: 6
corticosteroids related to (1) 71: 12
in depression (1) 59: 9−11; 71: 2−4, 10
developmental aspects (2) 11: 13−14
after discharge from psychiatric hospital (1) 71: 12
drugs taken in attempts (1) 71: 9
egoistic (1) 71: 1
in elderly, rates for (3) 21: 3, 4
emergency management (2) 95: 10−11
epidemiology (3) 12: 18; **20: 1−14**
    age (3) 20: 4, 5, 10−11
    cohort effect (3) 20: 10−11
    demographic factors (3) 20: 2, 3
    geographic variations (3) 20: 6, 8−9
    immigration influence (3) 20: 9−10
    marital status (3) 20: 5−6
    occupation (3) 20: 10
    psychiatric factors (3) 20: 11−14
    racial differences (3) 20: 4−6
    religion (3) 20: 6, 8
    seasonal factors (3) 20: 10
    sex differences (3) 20: 2−4
    social class (3) 20: 7
    sociocultural factors (3) 20: 8−10
    sources of information (3) 20: 1
    unemployment (3) 20: 7−8
evaluation of thoughts of (1) 71: 7−8
factors associated with (1) 59: 11
family history as risk factor (1) 71: 6−7
family therapy in (2) 62: 10−11

Suicide *(continued)*
  genetics of (1) 71: 6
  geographic variations (3) 20: 6, 8–9
    international (3) 20: 6, 8
    regional within U.S. (3) 20: 8–9
  historical background (1) 71: 1–2
  hopelessness correlation with (1) 71: 4
  hospitalization for (2) 95: 11
  immigration and (3) 20: 9–10
  incidence rates (3) **20: 1–14.** *See also under* epide-
        miology *above*
  lethality of intent (2) 95: 11
  malpractice related to (3) 29: 8–9
  marital status and (3) 20: 5–6
    during bereavement for spouse (3) 20: 6
    influence of children (3) 20: 5–6
  in masochistic personality (1) 27: 6–7
  methodological problems in study of (1) 71: 9–10
  methods of, sex differences (3) 20: 3–4
  missed diagnosis (1) 71: 8
  occupation and (3) 20: 10
  in organic brain syndrome (1) 71: 3, 5
  in panic disorder (1) 32: 4
  physician responsibility for recognition of risk and
        prevention (1) 71: 1, 8–9
  prediction of (3) 32: 14
  presence of concrete plan (1) 71: 11
  prevention
    early diagnosis and treatment of affective dis-
        orders in (1) 61: 25–26
    suicide prevention centers in (1) 71: 13
  progression to (1) 71: 10–11
  psychiatric illness role in (1) 71: 2–3; (3) 20: 11–
        14
  psychoanalytic explanation (1) 71: 2
  racial differences (3) 20: 4–6
  reducing opportunity for (1) 71: 11
  risk factors for (1) 71: 9–12
    assessment of (1) 71: 12; (2) 95: 10–11
    family history (1) 71: 6–7
    during treatment of depression (1) 61: 6–7
  in schizophrenia (1) 71: 3, 4–5, 10
  seasonal variation (3) 20: 10
  sex differences (3) 20: 2–4
  social class and (3) 20: 7
  sociocultural factors in (3) 20: 8–10
  statistics on (1) 71: 1, 5–6; (3) **20: 1–14.** *See also*
        under epidemiology *above*
  stressful life events in (1) 63: 11; 71: 4
  suicide prevention centers for (1) 71: 13
  systematic clinical studies of (1) 71: 2–3
  telephone management (2) 95: 14
  in terminal medical illness (1) 71: 3, 5
  treatment
    emergency management (2) 95: 10–11
    inadequacies in (1) 71: 9
    telephone management (2) 95: 14
  unemployment and (3) 20: 7–8
  in younger age population (3) 20: 10–11
Suicide attempt (1) **71: 13–16**
  act of (1) 71: 14–15
  in antisocial personality and hysteria (1) 71: 3
  assessment of risk in (1) 71: 15–16
  in children (1) 71: 15
  clinical characteristics (1) 71: 13–14
  costs of care (2) 79: 1
  as cry for help (1) 71: 14
  by cutting (1) 71: 15
  diagnosis (1) 71: 15–16
  differences from completed suicide (1) 71: 13–14;
        (3) 20: 14
  disposition from emergency room (2) 95: 11
  emergency management (2) 95: 10–11
  epidemiology (3) 12: 18
  frequency compared to suicide (1) 71: 7
  hospitalization for (1) 71: 16
  in personality disorders (1) 71: 14
  by poisoning (1) 71: 14–15
  prior to committing suicide (1) 71: 7
  prognosis (1) 71: 14, 16
  progression to completed suicide (1) 71: 14
  reasons for (1) 71: 14
  repeat potential (1) 71: 14
  similarities to completed suicide (1) 71: 6–7; (3)
        20: 14
  as symptom (1) 71: 13
  treatment (1) 71: 16
Suicide prevention centers (1) 71: 13
Sundowning (2) 119: 6
Superego
  in adolescents (2) 4: 12
  in conduct disorder (2) 37: 1–2
  in ego psychological model (1) 1: 9
  in narcissistic personality disorder (1) 18: 4, 7–8
  psychoanalytic concept (1) 1: 8; (2) 57: 2
Supportive psychotherapy. *See* Psychotherapy, sup-
        portive
Suprachiasmatic nucleus, in circadian rhythm regula·
        tion (3) 59: 9; 60: 1–2
Surgery (2) **121: 1–9**
  anxiety levels and outcome of (2) 121: 4–5
  in Briquet's syndrome (2) 121: 4
  consultation-liaison psychiatry in (2) **121: 1–9**
  cost-benefit studies of psychiatric intervention (2)
        121: 9
  fears associated with (2) 121: 2–3
  heart, psychiatric aspects (2) 118: 3–5
  hysterectomy (2) 120: 8–9
  ICU syndrome in (2) 121: 7–8
  informed consent in (2) 121: 8–9
  insufficient use of analgesics in (2) 121: 7
  in malingering patient (2) 121: 4
  neurosurgery distinguished from psychosurgery (2·
        160: 4
  for obesity (2) 103: 6–8
  pain in (2) 121: 7

postoperative reactions (2) 121: 6–7
  anxiety reactions (2) 121: 6
  behavioral management (2) 121: 6–7
  depression (2) 121: 6
  organic mental syndromes (2) 121: 6
preoperative evaluation to identify psychological
      risks in (2) 121: 3–5
preoperative preparation for (2) 121: 5
psychological adaptation to (2) 121: 8
psychosurgery (2) 160: 4–5. See also Psychosurgery
refusing (2) 121: 3
risk factors for psychiatric disorders in (2) 121: 3–
      5
in sleep apnea (3) 61: 10
stress of (2) 121: 2–3
  reduction in (2) 121: 5
in substance abuse (2) 121: 4
unrealistic or magical expectations concerning (2)
      121: 4
Suspiciousness. See also Paranoid disorder; Paranoid
      personality disorder
in elderly (3) 21: 3
Sydenham's chorea, psychosis related to (1) 69: 5
Sympathetic nervous system. See also Autonomic
      nervous system
  beta-adrenergic system in panic disorder (1) 32: 6–
      7
  in biological stress response systems (1) 41: 13
Sympathomimetic agents, psychiatric side effects (2)
      91: 4
Synapse
  anatomic features (3) 42: 2–4
  asymmetric and symmetric (3) 42: 3
  excitatory (3) 42: 3
  in habituation and sensitization (2) 13: 4–5
  heterogeneity in structure (3) 42: 3
  inhibitory (3) 42: 3
  location on postsynaptic neuron (3) 42: 3–4
  memory and (3) 71: 1–3
  of neostriatal afferents (3) 42: 11–15
  in neurotransmitter action (3) 43: 4–5
  neurotransmitter storage at (3) 42: 3
  transmission across (3) 42: 4
    and behavioral plasticity (3) 42: 7–8
  type I and type II (3) 42: 2–3
Synaptic plasticity (2) 13: 5
Syntax
  definition (2) 49: 1; (3) 67: 5. See also Language
  in expressive language disorder (2) 49: 3
Syphilis, cerebral (1) 69: 5
Systematic desensitization. See Desensitization, sys-
      tematic
Systems analysis
  in biofeedback (2) 109: 4–5
  and biopsychosocial model (2) 110: 1–2
  in family therapy (2) 62: 1; (3) 7: 5
  in hospital administration (2) 64: 9
  in psychiatric consultation (2) 115: 3–4

Tactual Performance Test (3) 52: 11–12
Tagamet. See Cimetidine
Taiwan, outcome of neurotic disorders in (3) 2: 12–
      13
Tangentiality, in schizophrenia (1) 53: 10
Tanner stages (2) 4: 3, 4
Taractan. See Chlorprothixene
Tarasoff case (2) 95: 10; (3) 29: 9–10; 31: 14–15
Tardive dyskinesia. See Dyskinesia, tardive
Taxes, smoking and alcohol use related to (2) 129: 5–
      6
Taxonomy, classification distinguished from (3) 12:
      5. See also Classification
T cells
  in cell-mediated immunity (2) 128: 2
  suppression linked to stress (2) 128: 4–5
Tea and toast syndrome (2) 119: 7
Teachers
  behavioral assessment by (2) 11: 8
  rating scales on children (2) 23: 6
Tegretol. See Carbamazepine
Telephone emergencies (2) 95: 14
  suicide (2) 95: 14
Television, as source of health information (2) 79: 4–
      5
Temazepam. See Benzodiazepines
Temperament
  anxiety disorders related to (2) 39: 5
  importance in child development (2) 2: 2
  match between child and parent (2) 50: 2
  passive-aggressive personality disorder related to
      (1) 26: 5
  role in social learning (1) 2: 19
Temperature
  and biofeedback (2) 109: 5
    in migraine (2) 109: 6
    in Raynaud's disease (2) 109: 7
  circadian rhythm of (3) 59: 1–2
  in REM sleep (3) 60: 4
  sleep-wake cycle related to rhythm in (3) 59: 4–5
Temporal lobe, in memory (2) 13: 4; (3) 71: 7
Temporal lobe disorders (1) 28: 1, 2, 4; (2) 87: 12.
      See also Epilepsy, temporal lobe; Limbic
      system
  clinical presentation (1) 28: 7–8
  differential diagnosis (1) 28: 8
  Korsakoff's syndrome associated with (1) 73: 20
  neurophysiologic correlates (1) 28: 6
  psychoses related to (1) 69: 9
Temporal lobe epilepsy. See Epilepsy, temporal lobe
Temporomandibular joint syndrome, biofeedback and
      relaxation therapy in (2) 109: 8–9
Testamentary capacity, testimonial privilege related to
      (3) 31: 5–6
Testimonial privilege (3) **31: 1–10**. See also Confiden-
      tiality
  in civil commitment (3) 31: 4
  in competency proceedings (3) 31: 5

Testimonial privilege *(continued)*
 with condition an element of claim or defense (3)
  31: 2–3
 in criminal cases (3) 31: 8–9
 discovery procedures (3) 31: 9–10
 in examinations on behalf of third party (3) 31: 4
 in fee collection (3) 31: 8
 of group therapy (3) 31: 5
 of hospital records (3) 31: 5
 for identity of patient (3) 31: 6
 of impaired physician's treatment records (3) 31: 7–
  8
 in investigation of physician (3) 31: 6–8
 for life and accident insurance claims (3) 31: 3
 in malpractice case of other patient treated by defendant
 physician (3) 31: 7
 for testamentary capacity (3) 31: 5–6
Testosterone. *See also* Androgens; Sex hormones
 delinquency related to (2) 9: 10–11
 and sexual differentiation
  in fetus (2) 9: 2
  in prepubescent child and adolescent (2) 9: 3–4
 in type A behavior (2) 126: 6
Tests. *See* Behavioral assessment; Neuropsychological
  assessment; Psychological tests
Tetracycline, lithium interaction with (2) 111: 10, 11
Thematic Apperception Test (2) 21: 10
 limitations in personality disorders (1) 15: 2
Therapeutic alliance. *See also* Alliance
 in forensic psychiatry (3) 36: 4–8
 in psychoanalysis (1) 8: 5
Therapeutic contract. *See* Contract, therapeutic
Therapeutic privilege, to withhold informed consent
  (3) 30: 7
Therapeutic stance (2) 108: 11–12
Therapist. *See* Psychotherapist
Thiamine
 deficiency in Wernicke's encephalopathy (2) 87:
  10
 in Wernicke-Korsakoff syndrome (1) 73: 20
Thinking. *See also* Cognitive function
 development in adolescence (2) 4: 7, 8; 17: 3–4
 disorders. *See also* Cognitive dysfunction
  causes (2) 20: 10
  content (2) 20: 9
  hallucinations (2) 20: 10–11. *See also* Hallucinations
  in major psychiatric syndromes (2) 95: 2
  in mania (1) 53: 12
  in psychiatric disorders (1) 53: 11
  in schizophrenia
   acute illness (1) 53: 9–11
   chronic illness (1) 53: 11–13
  speed or flow (2) 20: 9–10
 evaluation in children (2) 20: 9–12
 false beliefs as basis for faulty reasoning (1) 2: 18
 in family with schizophrenic offspring (3) 7: 3
 psychological tests in disorders (1) 7: 7–8

role in social learning (1) 2: 3
 stressful events effect in stress-response syndrome
  (1) 41: 4
Thioridazine (Mellaril)
 in Alzheimer's disease (2) 119: 3
 in antisocial personality disorder (1) 10: 3
 interactions with other drugs (2) 111: 5
 receptor actions and minimal extrapyramidal side
  effects with (3) 50: 13–14
Thiothixene (Navane)
 half-life (1) 55: 8
 in rapid tranquilization (2) 95: 5
 in schizophrenia
  dosage (1) 55: 12
  preparations (1) 55: 13
Thioxanthenes, in schizophrenia
 dosage (1) 55: 12
 preparations (1) 55: 13
Thorazine. *See* Chlorpromazine
Thorndike, E. L., contribution to learning theory (1)
  2: 10
Thought disorder. *See* Thinking, disorders
Thyroid disease
 depression in (1) 59: 12
 factitious (2) 101: 5
 organic mental disorders in children due to (2) 34:
  7
 psychiatric manifestations (2) 88: 5–8
  hyperthyroidism (2) 88: 7–8
  hypothyroidism (2) 88: 5–7
Thyroid hormones
 in affective disorders (1) 64: 11
 in anorexia nervosa (2) 102: 4
 lithium interaction with (2) 111: 10
Thyroid stimulating hormone
 blunted response to TRH in depression (3) 53: 6
 in sleep (3) 60: 5
Thyrotropin-releasing hormone, in affective disorders
  (1) 64: 11
Tics
 chronic (2) 38: 2
 definition (2) 38: 1
 differential diagnosis (2) 38: 2, 5
 phonic (2) 38: 1, 2, 7
 in Tourette's disorder (2) 38: 2–3
 transient (2) 38: 1–2
Tobacco. *See* Smoking
Toddlers, sleep disorders in (2) 52: 2–5
Tofranil. *See* Imipramine
Toilet training, encopresis related to (2) 43: 5
Tolerance
 definition (2) 35: 1
 in drug abuse (2) 90: 2
 types (2) 90: 2
Tomography
 computed
  abnormality as marker in schizophrenia (1) 62:
   11–12
  in Alzheimer's disease (3) 51: 6

basic principles (3) 51: 3
cautions and methodologic standards (3) 51: 7
data collection process for (3) 51: 1
in dementia (2) 119: 2
in organic brain syndromes (2) 87: 14–15
in schizophrenia (1) 64: 6; (3) 51: 6
technical factors influencing studies on (3) 51: 7
positron emission (3) 50: 14
basic principles (3) 51: 3–4
in schizophrenia (3) 51: 6
Tonsillar enlargement, sleep apnea due to (2) 105: 11
Topographical model of psychic conflict (1) 1: 7
TOPS (2) 103: 11
Torticollis, biofeedback in (2) 109: 8
Tourette's disease, precipitation by stimulants (2) 36: 11
Tourette's disorder (2) **38: 2–7**
attention deficit disorder related to (2) 38: 3
chronic tic disorder distinguished from (2) 38: 2, 5
clinical description (2) 38: 2–3
diagnosis (2) 38: 5
criteria for (2) 38: 2
differential diagnosis (2) 38: 5
EEG in (2) 38: 3, 5
epidemiology (2) 38: 3
epilepsy distinguished from (2) 38: 5
etiology (2) 38: 3–5
genetic factors in (2) 38: 3–4
involuntary nature of tics in (2) 38: 3
neurochemistry of (2) 38: 4–5
obsessive-compulsive behaviors in (2) 38: 3
prevention (2) 38: 7
stimulants precipitating (2) 38: 4; (3) 66: 19
tics in (2) 38: 2–3
treatment (2) 38: 5–7
behavior therapy (2) 38: 6
clonidine (2) 38: 6; 59: 18
haloperidol (2) 38: 6
neuroleptics (2) 59: 7, 12
pimozide (2) 38: 6
psychotherapy (2) 38: 6–7
Toxic disease, psychosis in (1) 69: 9
Toxic hallucinatory state (2) 90: 8
Toxins, in attention deficit disorder (3) 66: 12–13
Toxoplasmosis, organic mental disorders after (2) 34: 4
Trace elements, organic mental disorders in children due to (2) 34: 10
Tracheostomy, in sleep apnea (2) 105: 12; (3) 61: 10
Training. See also Education
attainment of clinical personal goals (3) 4: 8–9
for community child psychiatry (2) 69: 7–8
critical issues in 1980s (3) 4: 8–9
determination of clinical needs (3) 4: 8
early programs in child psychiatry (2) 1: 4–5
government role in (3) 4: 6–9
historical background (2) 1: 4–5; (3) 4: 6

limitation in resources for (3) 4: 9
in mental health research (3) 4: 4
National Institute of Mental Health in (3) 4: 6–8
in psychosomatic medicine (2) 76: 6; 78: 8, 9
in school consultation (2) 70: 9
in sex therapy (1) 47: 12
Trance states. See Fugue
Tranquilizers. See also Sedative/hypnotics
abuse, epidemiology (3) 17: 7–8, 10
for rapid action (2) 95: 5–6
Tranquilization, rapid (2) 95: 5–6
contraindications (2) 95: 6
drugs used in (2) 95: 5–6
Transactional analysis
in family therapy (2) 110: 8
in group therapy of children and adolescents (2) 63: 4
Transcendental Meditation (2) 109: 2–3
Transcultural psychiatry (3) **2: 1–14.** See also Cross-cultural psychiatry; Culture
Transference. See also Countertransference
in borderline personality disorder (2) 101: 7
Freud's concept (1) 1: 4–5
idealizing, in narcissistic personality disorder (1) 18: 6–7
irrational alliance (3) 36: 7
in medically ill (2) 108: 2, 6, 7
mirror, in narcissistic personality disorder (1) 18: 6–7
in physician-patient relationship. See Physician-patient relationship
in psychoanalytic process (1) 8: 6–7
in psychodynamic life narrative (2) 108: 7
in psychodynamic therapy of child (2) 57: 3
use in gratification (2) 108: 7
Transient ischemic attacks, dementia in (2) 87: 9
Transplantation
cardiac, psychiatric aspects (2) 118: 5
renal. See Kidney, end-stage disease
Transsexualism
definition (1) 46: 10
female (1) 46: 15–16
clinical course (1) 46: 15
etiology (1) 46: 15
treatment (1) 46: 15–16
male (1) **46: 10–15**
classification (1) 46: 10–11
clinical description (1) 46: 11–12
core-gender identity in (1) 46: 11
cross-dressing in (1) 46: 11
diagnosis and differential diagnosis (1) 46: 14
epidemiology (1) 46: 11
erotic pleasure in penis in (1) 46: 12
etiology (1) 46: 12–14
gender-role behavior in (1) 46: 11
psychodynamic concept (1) 46: 13–14
sexuality, object choice and sexual identity in (1) 46: 11–12
treatment (1) 46: 14–15

Transsexualism, male, treatment *(continued)*
   sex conversion surgery (1) 46: 14
   underlying diagnosis in (1) 46: 12
   wish for castration in (1) 46: 12
Transvestism (1) 46: 5
   transient transsexual feelings in (1) 46:
      11
Trauma
   head. *See* Head trauma
   neuroses related to (1) 31: 7
   organic mental disorders due to (2) 34: 7
   psychological responses to (1) **41: 1–15.** *See also*
      Stress-response syndromes
Trazodone, safety in heart disease (2) 99: 6
Treated prevalence (3) **22: 1–11.** *See also* Prevalence,
      treated
Treatment
   adjunctive therapy (2) 56: 3
   behavior therapy (2) 56: 2; **61: 1–9; 77: 1–12.**
      See also Behavior therapy
   biofeedback (2) **109: 4–11.** *See also* Biofeedback
   biological therapy (2) 56: 2–3. *See also* Pharmaco-
      therapy
   of chronic mental patients (3) 6: 5–12. *See also*
      Chronic mental patients
   cognitive therapy (2) 56: 2. *See also* Cognitive
      therapy
   community care (3) 6: 2–3. *See also* Community
      mental health services
   conditions of (1) 6: 2
   conflict in, classification of (1) 6: 11
   day hospital (3) 6: 8
   in dependent personality disorder (1) 26: 4
   diagnosis based on response to (2) 19: 6
   drugs. *See* Drugs; Pharmacotherapy; Psychophar-
      macology
   electroconvulsive therapy (2) 56: 3; (3) **68: 1–9.**
      See also Electroconvulsive therapy
   family therapy (2) 56: 2; (3) **7: 4–10.** *See also*
      Family therapy
   group therapy (2) 56: 2. *See also* Group therapy
   hospitalization, in child psychiatry (2) **64: 1–19.**
      See also Hospitalization; Hospitals
   informed consent for (3) **30: 1–14.** *See also* Con-
      sent, informed
   intelligence tests in planning (1) 7: 6
   legal considerations for mentally disordered of-
      fenders (3) **28: 2–9**
   malpractice related to
      adverse outcomes (3) 29: 10
      inappropriate treatment (3) 29: 11
   mental health care. *See* Mental health services
   for mentally retarded (2) **58: 1–7.** *See also* Mental
      retardation, treatment approaches
   milieu therapy (2) 56: 3
   from molecular biological simplification to more
      realistic central nervous system dynamics
      in applications (3) 72: 1–6

   motivation versus apathy toward (3) 28: 10, 17–
      18
   negotiation of (1) 6: 12
   organic therapies (2) **160: 1–5**
      drugs. *See* Drugs; Pharmacotherapy; Psychophar-
         macology
      electroconvulsive therapy (2) 160: 4. *See also*
         Electroconvulsive therapy
      nutritional (2) 160: 1–3
         diet (2) 160: 1–2
         megavitamins (2) 160: 2–3
         minerals (2) 160: 3
      optometric training (2) 160: 3–4
      patterning (2) 160: 3
      psychosurgery (2) 160: 4–5. *See also* Psychosur-
         gery
   in passive-aggressive personality disorder (1) 26: 6
   patient goals of (1) 6: 2
   patients (3) 5: 8–9
   patients' right to (3) 35: 2–4
   planning for. *See* Treatment planning
   psychoanalysis (1) **8: 1–12.** *See also* Psychoanalysi
   psychological tests as aid in role-inducing patient
      in (1) 7: 3
   psychosocial (1) **9: 1–11.** *See also* Psychosocial
      treatment; Psychotherapy
   psychotherapy (2) 56: 2. *See also* Psychotherapy
      outcome research (1) **11: 1–15.** *See also* Psycho-
         therapy, outcome research on
   relationship therapy (2) 56: 2
   relaxation therapy (2) **109: 1–11.** *See also* Relaxa-
      tion therapy
   requests or methods desired by patient for (1) 6: 2
      3
      administrative (1) 6: 2
      advice (1) 6: 2
      clarification (1) 6: 2
      confession (1) 6: 2
      control (1) 6: 2
      medical (1) 6: 2–3
      nothing (1) 6: 3
      psychodynamic insight (1) 6: 3
      psychological expertise (1) 6: 3
      reality contact (1) 6: 3
      set limits (1) 6: 3
      social intervention (1) 6: 3
      succorance (1) 6: 3
      ventilation (1) 6: 3
   right to aftercare in deinstitutionalized patient (3)
      35: 10–13
   right to refuse (3) 32: 10
   of sexual disorders (1) **47: 9–12.** *See also* Sex ther-
      apy
   social learning as crucial element in (1) 2: 2
   social therapy (2) 56: 3
   supportive therapy (2) 56: 2
   therapeutic alliance in forensic psychiatry (3) 36: 4
      8

utilization of various mental health services by psychiatric
treatment planning (2) **56: 1–9**
  advocacy in (2) 56: 9
  availability of resources and (2) 56: 8–9
  classification system importance for (2) 19: 2–3
  conceptual models of (2) 56: 3–4
  continuity of care in (2) 56: 8
  definition (2) 56: 1
  developmental model for (2) 56: 4
  diagnostic evaluation role in (2) 56: 1–2
  integrative model for (2) 56: 3
  multiaxial model for (2) 56: 4, 5
  periodic reviews in (2) 56: 8
  process of (2) 56: 4–6
  public health model for (2) 56: 3–4
  special considerations in (2) 56: 6–8
    for children not living in stable environment (2) 56: 7–8
    clinical service programs and their sites (2) 56: 6–7
    persons involved in plan (2) 56: 7
    prevention services (2) 56: 8
  Winnicott model for (2) 56: 3
Triangulation, in anorexia nervosa (2) 110: 5
Triazolam. *See* Benzodiazepines
Trifluoperazine (Stelazine)
  half-life (1) 55: 8
  in rapid tranquilization (2) 95: 5
  in schizophrenia
    dosage (1) 55: 12
    preparations (1) 55: 13
Triflupromazine, in schizophrenia
  dosage (1) 55: 12
  preparations (1) 55: 13
Trilafon. *See* Perphenazine
Trust, failure as antecedent to paranoid disorder (1) 68: 4–5
Tryptophan, in treatment-resistant chronic depression (1) 61: 17–18
Tuberculin reaction, conditioning influence on (2) 128: 10
Twin studies
  abnormally high rate of psychopathology due to specific
  in affective disorders (1) 62: 14–15; (3) 53: 4
  in agoraphobia (3) 14: 10
  in alcoholism (3) 53: 9
  in anxiety disorders (1) 32: 9; (3) 14: 4, 10
  application in genetics of psychiatric disorders (2) 10: 2
  in attention deficit disorder (3) 66: 10
  in bipolar disorder (3) 13: 11–12
  in depression (3) 13: 7
  in phobias (1) 33: 9
  psychodynamics (1) 62: 7–8
  of puberty onset (2) 9: 5

in schizophrenia (1) 54: 6–7; 62: 6–8; (3) 15: 6; 53: 12
  birth trauma explaining concordance of psychopathology (1) 62: 8
  environmentally caused phenocopy (1) 62: 8
  equal environments assumption in (1) 62: 7
  pairwise versus probandwise concordance rates (1) 62: 6
  sources of bias in (1) 62: 6–7
  in stuttering (2) 43: 8
  in symptomatic psychoses (1) 69: 12
  in Tourette's disorder (2) 38: 4
Type A behavior
  behavior therapy of (2) 126: 6–7
  coronary artery disease related to (2) 78: 3; 126: 2–5
    atherogenesis (2) 126: 5–6
    hostility and suppressed anger (2) 126: 4–5
    implications for treatment (2) 126: 6–8
    initial studies showing relationship (2) 126: 3
    studies not showing relationship (2) 126: 3–4
  and coronary bypass surgery (2) 118: 4
  cortisol related to (2) 126: 6
  in hypertension (2) 118: 7
  muscle vasodilatation related to (2) 126: 6
  testosterone levels and (2) 126: 6
Tyramine, urinary levels as marker in depression (3) 53: 9

Uganda, neurotic disorders in (3) 2: 8–9
Ultradian rhythms (3) 59: 6–7. *See also* Biological rhythms
Unbalancing, in family therapy (2) 62: 8
Unconscious, dynamic (1) 1: 1, 7
Unconscious determinants, free association in recognition of (1) 8: 5–6
Unemployment, suicide and (3) 20: 7–8
Unsigned contract (3) 36: 9
Urbanization. *See also* Culture; Society
  antisocial personality related to (3) 19: 4
  and mental illness (1) 52: 9–10
Urine, in neurochemistry studies on children (2) 12: 2
Utilization of services. *See* Mental health services, utilization

Vaginismus (1) 47: 6
  DSM-III criteria for (1) 47: 6
Validity
  of animal models (3) 46: 2–3
  in classification systems (2) 19: 8–9
  concurrent (1) 15: 3–4
  construct (1) 15: 4; (2) 19: 8
  content (1) 15: 3; 19: 8

Validity *(continued)*
  discriminative (1) 15: 4
  of DSM-III (2) 19: 10
  predictive (1) 15: 3–4; (2) 19: 9
  of psychological tests (1) 7: 1–2; 15: 3–4; (3) 52: 2
Valium. *See* Diazepam
Vasopressin
  in affective disorders (1) 64: 12
  and limbic-hypothalamic-pituitary axis dysregulation in
  melancholia (3) 54: 8
Ventricular fibrillation, stress related to (2) 118: 5
Verbal abstraction tests (3) 52: 8–9
Vesprin. *See* Triflupromazine
Vestibular nerve disorder, anxiety disorders distinguished from (1) 32: 10
Vicarious conditioning (1) 2: 16, 17
Vicarious learning (1) 2: 3
Vicarious reinforcement (2) 77: 5
Vineland adaptive behavior scales (2) 21: 3
Violent behavior
  predictors of (3) 32: 13–14
  risk factors for (3) 32: 14
Violent patient (2) **95: 7–10.** *See also* Dangerousness
  emergency management (2) 95: 8–10
    drugs (2) 95: 5, 9
    psychiatrist's reaction influencing (2) 95: 8
    restraints (2) 95: 9
    security personnel in (2) 95: 9
    use of significant others (2) 95: 9
    verbal intervention (2) 95: 8
    weapons (2) 95: 9–10
  epilepsy in adolescents (2) 37: 5
  interviewing of (2) 95: 8–9
  prediction of (2) 95: 7–8, 10.
  signs of imminence (2) 95: 8
  with weapons (2) 95: 9–10
Viruses, in schizophrenia (1) 64: 6
Viscosity (1) 28: 7–8
Vision
  event-related potentials in selective attention (3) 62: 6–7
  information processing by brain (3) 71: 4–6
Vistaril. *See* Hydroxyzine
Visual evoked response
  in selective attention (3) 62: 6–7
  to stimulants in attention deficit disorder (3) 66: 16
Visual masking, as measure of information processing (3) 65: 4–5
Visual perception, tests of (3) 52: 11
Vitamins
  in depressed debilitated persons (1) 61: 2–3
  therapeutic use in psychiatry (2) 160: 2–3
    toxicity (2) 160: 3
Vocational training, for chronic mental patients (3) 6: 10

Vomiting
  in bulimia (2) 102: 5
  complications in bulimia (2) 40: 6
  desensitization treatment in cancer patient (2) 11⁷ 4
  relaxation therapy and biofeedback in (2) 109: 1 11
  self-inducing in bulimia (2) 40: 6
Voxels (3) 51: 1–2
Voyeurism (1) 46: 6
Vulnerability
  to depression (1) 63: 6–8
  loss in childhood related to (1) 63: 11
  markers for (3) 53: 1. *See also* Markers
    possible use (3) 53: 2
  methodologic considerations in determination (1) 63: 7
  psychodynamics in children (2) 18: 5–6

Waiver, informed consent withheld in (3) 30: 7
War
  schizophrenia related to (1) 54: 11
  stress-response syndrome after (1) 41: 10
Watson, J. B.
  and behaviorism (2) 1: 4
  contribution to learning theory (1) 2: 11
Weapons, approach to patient with (2) 95: 9–10
Wechsler Adult Intelligence Scale (2) 21: 6–7
  Block Design perceptual motor test (3) 52: 11, 22
Wechsler intelligence tests (1) 7: 6
Wechsler Memory Scale (3) 52: 12
Wechsler preschool and primary scale of intelligence (2) 21: 4–5
Weight, regulation mechanisms (2) 103: 4
Weight gain, in infancy and childhood (2) 40: 3. *Se also* Obesity
Weight loss (2) **103: 6–12.** *See also* Obesity
  in anorexia nervosa (2) 102: 3
  psychiatric side effects of drugs used for (2) 91: 4
Weight Watchers (2) 103: 11
Welfare services, for chronic mental patients (3) 6: ᵉ 10
Wernicke-Korsakoff's syndrome. *See* Korsakoff's syndrome
Wernicke's encephalopathy, amnesic syndrome due to (2) 87: 10
Wide Range Achievement Test, in Halstead-Reitan Neuropsychological Test Battery (1) 72: ᵉ 6
Wilderness programs, for antisocial personality (1) 23: 8–9
Wilson's disease
  organic mental disorders in children due to (2) 34 7–9
  psychosis in (1) 69: 6–7

ithdrawal. *See also* Avoidant personality
  in children (2) 30: 2–3
  definition (2) 35: 1
  depression in children related to (2) 30: 2–3
  in schizophrenia (1) 53: 12
ithdrawal syndrome
  to alcohol (2) 35: 3
    treatment (2) 89: 8
  anxiolytics (1) 32: 12; (2) 90: 10–11; 91: 3
  barbiturates (2) 35: 4
  benzodiazepines (1) 32: 12; (2) 91: 3
  narcotics (2) 90: 3, 12
  opioids (2) 35: 4
  sedative/hypnotics (2) 35: 3–4; 90: 3, 10–11;
    111: 1
  sleep disorders in (3) 61: 7
  of stimulants (2) 90: 3
  symptoms (2) 90: 2
olpe, J.
  contributions to behavior therapy (1) 9: 3
  contributions to learning theory (1) 2: 12
omen. *See also* Obstetrics-gynecology; Sex
  Briquet's syndrome in (1) 35: 15
  dependent personality disorders in (1) 26: 2
  histrionic personality disorder in (1) 19: 5
  hysterical personality disorder in (1) 19: 3–4
  Tanner stages in (2) 4: 3, 4
  transsexualism in (1) 46: 15–16
ork
  biological rhythms and shift work (3) 59: 12

  and depression risk (1) 63: 12–13
  difficulties in alcoholism (2) 89: 6
Worksite, health promotion at (2) 129: 3–4
Work therapy, patients' rights regarding (3) 35: 8–9
World Health Organization
  on alcoholism (2) 89: 6
  outcome study of schizophrenia (3) 2: 10–12
  in psychiatric epidemiology (3) 11: 10, 11
World War II, mental health services during (3) 4: 9
Worthlessness, low self-esteem in children equivalent
  to (2) 30: 3
Writing disorders (3) 52: 6–7
Wyatt v. Stickney (3) 35: 2–4, 7

Xanax. *See* Alprazolam
XYY genotype, and criminal behavior (1) 23: 6

Yale Children's Inventory (2) 36: 7
Yale developmental schedules (2) 21: 3
Yoga (2) 109: 3
Youngberg v. Romero (3) 35: 2–4, 7

Zeitgeiber (3) 19: 14
Zoophilia (1) 46: 6